The French Language Today
A linguistic introduction

Second edition

Adrian Battye, Marie-Anne Hintze and Paul Rowlett

London and New York

First published 1992
by Routledge
11 New Fetter Lane, London EC4P 4EE

Simultaneously published in the USA and Canada
by Routledge
29 West 35th Street, New York, NY 10001

Second edition 2000

Routledge is an imprint of the Taylor & Francis Group

© 1992 Adrian Battye and Marie-Anne Hintze; 2000 Adrian
Battye, Marie-Anne Hintze and Paul Rowlett

Typeset in 10/12 Goudy by Florence Production Ltd, Stoodleigh, Devon
Printed and bound in Great Britain by St Edmundsbury Press,
Bury St Edmunds, Suffolk

British Library Cataloguing in Publication Data
A catalogue record for this book is available from the British
Library

Library of Congress Cataloguing in Publication Data
Battye, Adrian.
  The French language today : a linguistic introduction /
Adrian Battye, Marie-Anne Hintze, and Paul Rowlett.—2nd ed.
    p. cm.
  Includes bibliographical references and index.
    1. French language–Grammar.   2. French language—Variation.
I. Hintze, Marie-Anne.   II. Rowlett, Paul.   III. Title.

PC2105.B37 2000
440–dc21   99–087392

ISBN 0–415–19837–2 (hbk)
ISBN 0–415–19838–0 (pbk)

For Simona, Earl and Marc

The French Language Today

Reviews of the first edition:

'. . . the best basic introduction to French linguistics available.'
The Modern Language Journal

'. . . a welcome contribution to the specialist literature. It is full of useful and detailed material, and the approach adopted by the authors is original.'
Journal of French Language Studies

'. . . an informative and well written text . . . for those interested in making the study of the French language more appealing and more contemporary, FLT is a welcome addition to the literature.'
Canadian Journal of Linguistics

This book provides a comprehensive introduction to the French language from the perspective of modern linguistics. Placing French within its social and historical context, the authors illuminate the complex and diverse aspects of the language in a lively and accessible way. A variety of topics is covered, including the historical development of Standard French, the sound system of French, its word-formation and sentence patterns and its stylistic and geographical varieties.

Fully updated and revised, the book has been made more user-friendly by the inclusion of the following new features:

- a further reading guide at the end of each chapter
- a glossary of linguistic terms
- an expanded bibliography and index.

The late **Adrian Battye** was Lecturer in Romance Linguistics at the University of York until 1993. **Marie-Anne Hintze** is Senior Lecturer in French at the University of Leeds. **Paul Rowlett** is Head of French at the University of Salford.

Contents

Preface to the second edition

The second edition has been written with very much the same goals as the first. Further, while there are a number of changes, at times significant, in the presentation of the material, the book is essentially unaltered in its structure. It seems to us that *The French Language Today* is still unique in the market in providing undergraduate students with a comprehensive description of the linguistic structure of the modern language, and in placing this description within both a historical and a social context. Consequently, we were keen that the book should not be allowed to fall by the wayside simply because it was deemed to be out of date.

However, this is more than a timely update. In response to comments from readers of the first edition, we have also endeavoured to make the book more user-friendly. In doing so, we have seen the book as a text on the linguistics of French, rather than a potted grammar or an introduction to linguistics with exemplification from French. Our aim has been to highlight patterns, generalisations and explanations in a more marked way than was the case in the first edition, rather than presenting a catalogue of facts in the style of a reference or teaching grammar. In particular, we have tried to clarify confusing passages, highlight interrelations between topics and, not insignificantly, make the style lighter and more engaging. In addition, we have included Further reading guides at the end of each chapter, as well as a Glossary of terms. It is hoped that the Further reading guides will allow curious readers to pursue their interests in suitable sources in the primary and more advanced secondary literature, and that the Glossary of terms will make it easier for readers dipping into the odd section to cope with what may well be unfamiliar terminology. (Terms in bold in the text appear in the Glossary.) Finally, we have updated the statistical information, especially in Chapter 1.

While the names of three authors appear on the front cover, the second edition has been prepared by just two people. Adrian Battye died in spring 1993, barely a year after the first edition was published. He was therefore deprived of the satisfaction of knowing how successful it was. Given how much this book owes to him, we never doubted that it would be appropriate to retain his name on the second edition, as well as his decision to dedicate the book to his wife. This is our modest memorial to a sadly missed colleague, teacher and friend.

Marie-Anne Hintze and Paul Rowlett
Leeds/Salford, October 1999

Preface to the first edition

The original idea for this book grew out of a shared perception of the needs of our own undergraduates. For aspiring specialists in the French language there has long existed a gap in the technical literature as there is no work which attempts to bridge the gap between highly technical research work on the French language in all domains of linguistic study and the needs of students who have already acquired a sound knowledge of French, but still require an introduction to the basic concepts and techniques of linguistics, the scientific study of language.

The French Language Today is our attempt to fill this gap. In assembling the following chapters we have sought to present the various sub-domains of linguistics (i.e. phonetics, morphology, syntax, sociolinguistics and stylistics) using, as our illustrative material, data drawn exclusively from the French language. In the body of the text technical linguistic terms are printed in bold type face (for instance, **syntax**) when used for the first time and where an explanation of their meaning will be found. We have assumed throughout that our potential readers will already have a good written and oral competence in French, and, for this reason, we have provided glosses and translations for the examples given only when the words and phrases involved are archaic, regional or stylistically marked usages which students of French embarking on a course in higher education may not be reasonably expected to know. Cross-referencing throughout the book is signalled in the following manner (1: 5.3) which means Chapter 1, section 5, subsection 3.

The discipline of linguistics seeks to study language (i.e. the faculty shared by all normal human beings to communicate by means of a shared set of rules) in all its manifestations. The basic assumption of linguistics is that language is a system: in words often attributed to the father of modern linguistics, Ferdinand de Saussure (1857–1913): 'La langue est un système où tout se tient.' This view of language as a system implies that it can be studied systematically, precisely and objectively. In the context of the present volume, we are assuming throughout that the French language represents just one such highly complex linguistic system.

In this way, uncovering the structures of the French language will enable us to understand better the underlying system of that language. This is because to be Francophone implies the mastery of a series of rules which, to a greater or lesser degree, allow one to produce and understand linguistic structures which are recognisably French. The linguistic structures referred to here may be of different types; they may be concatenations of sounds which tell us that *bonjour* is a French word while *namaskar* is not; they may be units of words combined according to strictly ordered principles which dictate that while *utilité* is a French word *téutile* is not; they may also be rules of sentence structure which allow us to recognise 'le train s'est mis en marche' as a well-formed sentence of French, while 'train le s'est en marche mis' is not.

This idea of system and the attendant notion of structure in language can also be applied to the different usages or functions to which the French language can be put. Although the French spoken in Canada, in Marseilles and in New Caledonia may present certain particularities, it is none the less the same language. Similarly a political address and a conversation about a football match will exhibit differences in choice of words, sentence structure and even pronunciation. Yet, despite these differences, they will still be conducted in a language which is recognisably French.

The following chapters address questions such as: How is it that one of the many dialects spoken in the territory now described as northern France and related to a single parent language (Latin) should have developed today to be the national language of France as well as being spoken in other parts of the world? This question is addressed in Chapter 1.

Chapter 2 will consider issues such as: What are the sounds of the French language? How are they correctly formed? Why is it necessary to use methods other than the French writing system to accurately represent these sounds?

In Chapter 3 we move on to consider the internal structure of the word in French. Why is it desirable to talk in terms of rules of word formation? What sort of abstract information is encoded into word forms in French? Is there as much irregularity in French verb forms as there appears to be in traditional presentations of this topic?

After considering word structure, we turn, in Chapter 4, to an examination of sentence structure in French. Can the great variety of sentence structures found in French be reconciled with a few word order patterns? What are the rules which govern these orders? What is a proform? And why is it that such a term is to be preferred in dealing with French instead of the more traditional term of pronoun? What are the tenses of French? Do they provide information about time only or are there other meanings to be associated with these forms?

Chapter 5 considers selected aspects of variation in French. How can one identify which geographical region of France a speaker comes from simply by listening to his or her pronunciation? What differences in vocabulary are there between the French spoken in France and that in Canada? Can the notion of system, alluded to earlier, and variation within a language such as French be reconciled?

Clearly the coverage of these aspects of the French language cannot be exhaustive and certain aspects of our presentation may be considered incomplete by more specialist readers. However, we hope that this book will serve to illustrate what a stimulating field of study the French language is *per se* and that views which claim that it is somehow a monolithic or immutable representation of the human language faculty should be discarded. We hope also that the following pages will present an introduction to how aspects of the French language may be treated in a rigorous linguistic perspective and that the bibliography will provide the interested reader with suggestions for further reading.

Adrian Battye and Marie-Anne Hintze
York/Aix-en-Provence, December 1990

Acknowledgements

We would, first of all, like to repeat our thanks to those students and colleagues (Jacques Durand, Tony Lodge, Rebecca Posner, Ruth King, Jim Coleman, Annie Rouxeville, Jean-Philippe Watbled, Wendy Ayres-Bennett and, especially, John Green and Aidan Coveney) whose support was so important in the preparation of the first edition. For pointing out both its strengths and weaknesses, we are also grateful to those who took the time and trouble to write reviews, namely Barbara E. Bullock, John Gallagher, Douglas E. Kibbee, Juta Langenbacher-Liebgott, Jean-Pierre Montreuil, Paul Rastal, Raymond Sindou and Udo Thelen. For the second edition, we would, in addition, like to thank Marc Bastoul, Odile Cyrille, Rebecca Posner and Mark Snowden for their comments on various parts of the manuscript or their data about French. Of course, the usual disclaimers apply.

In addition to Claire L'Enfant, Sarah Dann and Sue Bilton, who saw the first edition through commission to publication, we would like to thank Louisa Semlyen for her continued support for the idea of a second edition, as well as Miranda Filbee and Katharine Jacobson for always being at the end of an e-mail when we needed them.

We would also like to thank the following for their permission to use copyright material: Editions Leméac and Editions Bernard Grasset for granting us permission to reproduce an extract from *La Sagouine* (1974) by A. Maillet; Oxford University Press for material from their edition of Molière's *Œuvres complètes* (1959); Slatkine Reprints for permission to quote from Streicher's edition of Vaugelas's *Remarques sur la langue française* (1970); *Le Figaro*, *Le Monde*, *L'Express* and *Le Nouvel Observateur* for permission to reproduce their copyright material.

1 The external history of the French language

The standardisation of French and its distribution in the world today

In Chapters 2–4 we analyse the linguistic structure of the French language today. Before that, we focus on the external, or sociolinguistic, history of French, that is, the developing relationship between the French language and its users. In 1: 3–7 we outline the key historical and socio-cultural factors which have played a part in the evolution and diffusion of French. But first, we consider the status of French around the world: Where, and by whom, is it spoken?

1 *La francophonie*: How many French speakers are there in the world?

The term *francophonie* was originally coined in 1880 by the geographer Onésime Reclus to refer to countries where French is used, and this is one of the meanings the term retains today (1: 7.1). Now, although it may be relatively easy to pinpoint 'Francophone' countries on a map, that is, countries where French has a particular status and officially recognised functions, determining the exact size of the world's Francophone population is no easy task, not least because few countries include questions on language use in their censuses. Furthermore, we can't assume that Francophone countries are monolingual, or that all, or even the majority, of their population are French speakers. As we'll see when we examine matters more closely, French is frequently used in multilingual societies, and in many cases it's the language (but not necessarily the only language) of a minority of the population.

When considering language use it helps to distinguish between societies and individuals. For instance, in many countries, and in France itself, French isn't the only language spoken by many individuals. Nevertheless, in society, it enjoys a privileged position by virtue of its status as **official language**, that is, a language used in government, administration and education, at national, regional or local level. Elsewhere, French may be a **vehicular language**, used as a means of communication by speakers of different languages. Yet again, as in North Africa for instance, French may be a language with special status, widely used by intellectuals or educated elites for academic or cultural purposes. As for individuals, they may be mother-tongue speakers, having acquired the language in childhood, and French may be their usual or **vernacular language**. Others may speak French as a second language, having acquired it through education generally, and/or having been taught, wholly or in part, through the medium of French. Finally, there may be foreign language learners, for whom French is only a school subject and whose level of proficiency may be fairly limited.

It's on the basis of individual bilingualism that the 1999 French government report *Etat de la francophonie dans le monde* provides the following figures for numbers of French speakers, classified either as *francophones réels* (112,660,000), that is, first- or second-language speakers who use the language daily, or *francophones occasionnels* (60,612,000), often living in developing countries or in bilingual societies, using French occasionally, while normally using another language. To these are added the 100–110 million learners of French as a foreign language. Given these figures, a league table ranking the languages of the world according to numbers of speakers would place French in tenth or eleventh position behind Chinese, English, Hindi, Spanish, Russian, Arabic, Bengali, Portuguese, Malay and possibly Japanese. The perception that French fulfils a special role as a world language, second only to English, therefore rests not on the absolute number of speakers, but, rather, on its presence throughout the world and its cultural prestige.

2 The geographical distribution of French

The map in Appendix II shows that French is spoken on every continent. However, this isn't a recent development; French spread across Europe and further afield well before it came to dominate in France (1: 5.1). For instance, the Norman dialect of Northern France extended to England after the Conquest (1066), and not only had a profound influence on the subsequent development of English, but is also the source of the surviving varieties of French spoken in the Channel Islands (5: 2.2). Similarly, the Crusades brought the first contacts between France and the Middle East (notably Syria and Lebanon). The development of overseas trading-posts and colonisation from the seventeenth century onwards led to the diffusion of French in parts of North America and the Indian Ocean; in the eighteenth century, to Oceania; and in the nineteenth and early twentieth centuries, to Asia and large portions of Africa. Further, by the end of the seventeenth century, French had become the major international language of culture in the courts of Europe, and of diplomacy, a status it retained until 1919, when, at the insistence of US President Wilson and British Prime Minister Lloyd George, the Treaty of Versailles was drafted in English as well as French. Let's now see, continent by continent, and country by country, where and by whom French is spoken today.

2.1   Europe

French is the historic language of several countries and regions of Europe. France, with its population of 58.5 million (1999 census), accounts for nearly half the world total of mother-tongue French speakers. In Monaco (population 30,000), as in France, French is the only official language and the vernacular language of virtually the whole population.

In the Aosta Valley in Italy, French was recognised as an official language, together with Italian, in 1948, and the use of French has progressively increased in the education system where, since 1993, both languages are used as a medium of instruction. It's estimated that about 20,000 people, mostly concentrated in the more rural areas, of the total population of 116,000 speak French or a local variety of Franco-Provençal (5: 2.2). In the Vallées vaudoises, west of Turin, an estimated 20,000 speakers also use a local variety of Franco-Provençal, together with Italian and Piedmontese.

In Switzerland, French shares with Italian and German the status of national official language, a fourth, Romansch, having regional official status. According to Rossillon (1995: 61), 19.2 per cent of the population, that is some 1.3 million people, are mother-tongue French speakers. These people live in the west of the country (in the cantons of Vaud, Geneva, Neuchâtel and Jura, where French is the sole official language for administration and education). In the canton of the Valais (officially bilingual German/French since 1844), the population now predominantly speak French. The Swiss dialects of Franco-Provençal have, apart from a handful of lexical items, disappeared in favour of French in all but a few mountain valleys and in Valais.

The Grand Duchy of Luxembourg has a population of approximately 395,000. Its national language is a Germanic dialect, Luxembourgish, with Standard German as the written medium of communication. French is the mother tongue of a minority of the population only, but all three languages have official status. In reality, French is used throughout the Duchy and, especially in urban areas, a trilingual situation prevails, thanks to the status and prestige accorded to French since 1946, as the language of education and administration.

The peaceful coexistence of French with other languages in Europe doesn't extend to Belgium where a situation of linguistic conflict has existed between French and Flemish speakers for much of the country's history. We shouldn't forget that the border between France and Belgium is a mere 160 years old, and takes no account of a 1,000-year-old language boundary separating Flemish-speaking Flanders in the north from the four French-speaking provinces (Hainault, Namur, Liège and Luxembourg) of Wallonia in the south. Traditionally, the French-speaking areas were dominant economically and politically, while they represented a minority of the population. French was the sole official language until 1932, when Dutch was given official status in Flanders. Nowadays, the Flemish, who represent about 52 per cent of a total population of ten million, have the stronger economy. This situation of social, economic and political imbalance lies behind numerous political conflicts, and is exacerbated by the fact that the officially bilingual capital, Brussels, lies north of the linguistic boundary, yet is in reality 85 per cent Francophone. Indeed, confrontation between the two linguistic communities and the resulting perceived threat posed to the unity of the Belgian state led, in 1993, to an amendment to the constitution allowing the virtual separation, on linguistic lines, of the French-speaking and Flemish-speaking communities within a federal state.

Within Great Britain, finally, on the Channel Islands of Jersey, Guernsey and Sark, French may be used for some official purposes, but it's only on Jersey that French is officially recognised as an administrative language together with English.

2.2   The Americas

The largest French-speaking community on the American continent is in Canada where, in the 1996 population census, 24 per cent of the total population of 30,286,600 reported French to be their mother tongue. However, two-thirds of Canada's French speakers are concentrated in the province of Quebec, where they form some 80 per cent of the population of 7,419,900. The remainder are concentrated in New Brunswick, Ontario, Manitoba, Nova Scotia and Saskatchewan (Canada Yearbook 1999). Although census figures from 1971 to 1996 indicate that the numbers of people who use French in most contexts and those who only use it in the home in Quebec have increased slightly, they also make it clear that, outside Quebec and New Brunswick, French is significantly losing ground to English.

The presence of French in Canada goes back to the early seventeenth century and the establishment of fur trading-posts along the lower Saint Lawrence river and settlements in the bay of Fundy (Acadia) and along the Gulf of Saint Lawrence. Acadia was surrendered to Britain in 1713, and in 1755 two-thirds of its inhabitants were forcibly driven out in what is called *le grand dérangement*. Some found their way to other settlements on the eastern seaboard of North America, a few travelling down by sea as far as Louisiana, which had been claimed by France as a colony in 1682. As a result, with the exception of New Brunswick (approximately 245,000 speakers), only a small minority of French speakers remain in Acadia today. Fifty years after Acadia, the Saint Lawrence lowlands, officially named Quebec, were ceded to Britain in 1763. The British North America Act of 1887, which established the Confederation of Canada, recognised French and English as the official languages, but the late nineteenth and early twentieth centuries witnessed the progressive erosion of the rights of French speakers in courts, legislatures and schools outside Quebec. As in Belgium, conflict surrounding the language issue isn't recent, and is closely bound up with economic and political issues. In 1967 the report of the Royal

Commission on Bilingualism and Biculturalism recognised that Franco-phones suffered discrimination in terms of social advancement in industry and commerce. This led in 1969 to the Official Languages Act, establishing French and English as the official languages of Canada with equal status in federal government and administration. French and English also have equal status at the provincial level in New Brunswick, whereas since the adoption of Bill 101 in 1977, after the separatist *Parti québécois* came to power, French has been the sole official language of the province of Quebec. Bill 101 is also known as the *Charte de la langue française* and requires French to be the normal language of the workplace, communications and business. In addition, the provincial government of Quebec maintains the Office de la langue française, which offers a legal mechanism to protect the rights of French speakers and plays a role in developing new terminology. While the future of French in Quebec seems to have been consolidated by the efforts of the federal government and its commitment to the preservation of both English and French language and culture within a multicultural society, the future of French beyond the provincial limits of Quebec (diluted by anglicisation in response to social and economic pressures) is much more debatable.

French is also the official language of Saint-Pierre et Miquelon (population 6,100), an island group situated in the Gulf of Saint Lawrence which administratively forms part of France as a *collectivité territoriale*.

Within the United States there are two major concentrations of French speakers. First, in the New England states of Maine, Massachusetts, Rhode Island, Connecticut, Vermont and New Hampshire, approximately 200,000 descendants of the 2–3 million immigrants from Quebec (particularly in the nineteenth century) still claim French as their mother tongue (Rossillon 1995: 32). However, the maintenance of French is steadily being eroded by the shift from bilingualism to English monolingualism. The second concentration is in Louisiana (a French colony from 1682 to 1803), where the ranks of the initial colonists from France were swelled by immigrants from Acadia – the Cajuns (or *(a)cadiens*). In the 1990 US census, over a million inhabitants of Louisiana claimed French ancestry, with 261,678 stating that they spoke French, Cajun or Louisiana Creole at home. The most widely spoken variety is called *français (a)cadien*, similar to the variety spoken in Canada. However, a small number of descendants of the earliest colonists use a more or less standard variety of French, and there are also some speakers of a French-lexicon creole, similar to Haitian Creole (on creoles see 5: 5). In 1968 a state agency, the Conseil pour le développement du français en Louisiane (CODOFIL), was founded to promote and preserve the French language in Louisiana through education and the promotion of Cajun culture. (On the linguistic situation of Francophone Louisiana, see Valdman 1997.)

In the Caribbean and South America, three territories which are legally and administratively part of France as *départements d'outre-mer* – the islands of Martinique and Guadeloupe, as well as French Guyana – have French as their official language, that is, the language of administration, education and of the urban professional elites. However, the majority of the population (950,000 overall according to the 1999 French census) also use a French-lexicon creole for private and unofficial purposes. Indeed, according to Chaudenson (1989: 156), 20 per cent of the population in Martinique, 40 per cent in Guadeloupe and 70 per cent in Guyana are monolingual in creole. French, and Haitian Creole since 1987, are the official languages of the Republic of Haiti, where French is spoken by less than 10 per cent of the population of 7 million, the rest being predominantly monolingual in creole. These cases illustrate a situation which is common in other areas of the Francophone world. The use of French isn't regional (as it is in Belgium or Canada, for instance); rather, it's determined by function. French coexists with other languages, each having distinct and complementary roles. This is a situation which linguists call **diglossia**: one language is used for official or formal functions (the H or high language), while the other (the L or low language) is used in more personal or informal discourse.

2.3   Asia

In India there are small communities of approximately 10,000 French speakers in the former trading-posts of Pondicherry, Mahé, Karikal, Chandernagor and Yanaon. French still retains a certain prestige among the educated elites in Laos, Cambodia and Vietnam (formerly French Indo-China), although since independence it has lost its status as official language, and the use of French has greatly declined to the benefit of English and, more recently, vernacular languages.

In the Middle East, notably in Syria and Lebanon (both French protectorates after the First World War), Arabic is the official language, French having been relegated since independence to the position of second language in competition with English. Syria, in particular, has pursued a policy of arabisation in every aspect of life, to the detriment of French in education. However, in Lebanon, where bilingualism or even trilingualism is common, and despite the lack of official status, there remains a substantial Francophone population (800,000) and a strong attachment to French as a vehicle for literary and scientific works (Rossillon 1995: 93). Small proportions of the population in Syria (12,000), Turkey (10,000) and Israel (500,000) have also maintained a French-speaking tradition.

2.4   Oceania

In the Pacific French is present on a number of islands and archipelagos, in particular in the now independent state of Vanuatu (the Anglo-French Condominium of New Hebrides until 1980), where both French and English are official languages alongside Bichlama, the national vehicular language. Perhaps unsurprisingly, given that there are 105 indigenous languages, French and English are the languages of education. Of a total population of 159,800 in 1993, the number of Francophones was estimated at 45,000 (Rossillon 1995: 96).

French is also the official language of three *territoires d'outre-mer*: Wallis and Futuna (population 13,000), French Polynesia (an archipelago which includes Tahiti, the Society Islands and the Marquesas) and New Caledonia. In Polynesia (population 212,000) Tahitian has been an official language alongside French since 1980 and tends to be used as the *lingua franca*, French being reserved for official and administrative purposes. In contrast, in New Caledonia (population 180,000) French is both the official and the main vehicular language and appears to be securely established.

2.5 Africa and the Indian Ocean

There is a further group of French-speaking islands in the Indian Ocean. After independence from France in 1960, Madagascar, the world's fourth largest island (population 13.3 million), pursued a vigorous policy in favour of Malgache, the local Indonesian language, promoting it as the official language and the language of education. However, French is still taught as a second language and is widely used among the intellectual elite in administration and in international contacts; but this group represents only 15–20 per cent of the population.

North of Madagascar lies a group of islands consisting of four main islands (population 500,000), which acceded to independence in 1975 to form the Islamic Republic of the Comoros. The island of Mayotte (40,000 French speakers), however, voted to remain French as a *collectivité territoriale*. Here, French and Arabic are official languages, but French is principally used in international relations and in education, and is little spoken by the population.

East of Madagascar lie the Mascarenes: Réunion, Mauritius and Rodrigues. A French colony since 1665, Réunion (population 705,000) is today a *département d'outre-mer*. Standard French is therefore the official language used for formal or official purposes, whereas a regional variety of French and/or a French-lexicon creole are used for other situations, and the two stand in a diglossic relation to one another (Chaudenson 1979b). Approximately 75 per cent of the population are thought to be French-speaking.

In the Republic of Mauritius (population c. one million), an independent member of the Commonwealth since 1968, having been a French colony up to 1814 when it became a British possession, English has been retained as the official language, although its use is confined to education, parliament and the judiciary. In the 1990 census 0.2 per cent of the population declared English to be the language used at home, compared with 3.3 per cent for French and 60.4 per cent for Mauritian Creole. Nevertheless,

French has a semi-official status, is acceptable in parliamentary debates and widely used in the media and education. It's also a *lingua franca* between the different ethnic groups that make up the population. In the Seychelles (population 73,782 in 1990), where creole, French and English are the official languages, and on the island of Rodrigues (population *c.* 38,000), where the official language is English, the population consists for the most part of native French-lexicon creole speakers.

The largest French-speaking areas outside Europe, and the largest potential Francophone populations, are concentrated in Africa. With regard to the status of French in the countries where it's used, two different situations prevail. In the countries of the Maghreb (Algeria, Tunisia and Morocco, total population 53.6 million in 1993), independence from France (achieved between 1956 and 1962) was followed by a period of more or less militant arabisation, with Arabic replacing French as the official language and as the medium of instruction in schools. However, partly for practical reasons, French appears to have held its own in these countries, despite the lack of official status. Rossillon (1995) estimates that the proportion of Francophones varies from one-third (of the population aged over 15) in Morocco to one-half in Algeria and Tunisia, proportions which have risen since independence due to the spread of education, which is largely bilingual in practice, and to the influence of the media. Positive attitudes towards French and/or Arabic–French bilingualism, especially in Morocco and Tunisia, rest upon the belief that a knowledge of French offers access to social advancement and the modern world.

South of the Sahara, seventeen countries, for the most part former French and Belgian colonies, together with the small enclave of Djibouti on the east coast, have adopted French as their official language, either alone or in conjunction with one or more other languages. These states – which cut a great swathe across the west and centre of the continent – are Benin, Burkina Faso, Burundi, Cameroon, the Central African Republic, Chad, Congo, Gabon, Guinea, Ivory Coast, Mali, Mauritania, Niger, Rwanda, Senegal, Togo and Zaire. Note that French is very much a minority language in the African context, since most countries have very complex multilingual situations in which the various languages spoken often have clearly defined and separate functions and uses. Therefore, French is nowhere the first language, although it's the (or one of the) official language(s), and used in education. Consequently, French is usually the language spoken and used by well-educated urban professional elites, for whom it's seen as an instrument of economic progress and social advancement. Furthermore, French is used to varying degrees from one country to another, and the proportion of the 140 or so million inhabitants of these Francophone states using French as a habitual working language will, on average, not exceed 5–10 per cent. But although the presence of French in these countries is linked to a colonial past, it can be viewed by some of their leaders as a 'supra-ethnic' language, offering both an alternative to internal language issues and ethnic conflict and ready-made links to the outside world.

Given that 74 per cent of the world's Francophone population (Rossillon 1995: 126) live in Africa, it has been suggested that the future of French as an international language, aided by demographic expansion and improved schooling, lies here. Indeed, for Rossillon, the challenge to France and *la francophonie* (1: 7) lies in fostering *la francisation de l'Afrique Noire* through investment in education programmes and the media, a point echoed by Ager (1996: 180), who stresses that the opportunities for the maintenance of French are inextricably linked with France's willingness to bear the costs of supporting it.

We have seen that French is no longer a uniquely European language, but one that finds currency in the Americas, Asia, Oceania and Africa, and is spoken by some 2.5 per cent of the world's population. Furthermore, in most countries where it's present, French owes its position, not to the absolute number of speakers, but to state intervention and government language-planning policies which give it status and prestige by determining its role in official domains. Such status-planning policies, in turn, imply a view of the language as a fairly homogeneous and invariant entity, possessing a set of common linguistic norms acceptable to all Francophones. In other words, they rest on the concept of a universal Standard French. In reality, of course, like all languages with a significant degree of diffusion, French is subject to considerable variation. Aspects of this variation will be dealt with in Chapter 5, but first we examine the historical emergence of French and the attitudes that not only shaped its past, but may well condition its future.

3   A brief survey of the external history of French

In the rest of this chapter, we sketch the external history of French, tracing, first, the linguistic and social processes up to the seventeenth century (1: 3) which contributed to the emergence of the national standard in France, and, then, examining in some detail (1: 4–7) the complex developments which have taken place over the last 300 years.

As a prelude, consider first the term 'standard language'. As Hudson (1996: 32) points out, 'standard languages are the result of a direct and deliberate intervention by society'. In countries such as Britain and France for example, speakers are aware of the existence of established norms prescribing correct usage in grammar, vocabulary, spelling and even pronunciation (even if they may not always respect these norms). In the case of French and English, these norms were established over a number of centuries in response to both objective and subjective pressures. On an objective level, in modern societies, a standard language serves a functional purpose, since it provides the means to communicate, govern and educate effectively by resisting change and suppressing variation. It also acquires a symbolic value as a marker of group identity. On a subjective level, as a consequence of the promotion of one (form of the) language over others, attitudes frequently emerge towards the standard, particularly in its written form, as being more elegant, clearer, 'better' than other varieties.

Sociolinguists generally agree that standard languages are typically shaped by four major processes. First, social processes involve selection of one particular variety in preference to others, and acceptance of this variety by the community at large. Second, linguistic processes of codification and elaboration determine the rules of correct usage and provide the language with the resources necessary to fulfil a wide range of functions (for instance, a writing system or new terminology). (See Haugen 1966, Milroy and Milroy 1991 and, for a detailed application of this sociolinguistic framework to the history of French, Lodge 1993.)

3.1   The emergence of French and Romance varieties spoken in France

Like Spanish, Italian, Portuguese and Romanian, French is a Romance language. Similarities between these languages are due to their common ancestry: Latin (originally the ancient dialect of the central Italian region of Latium, whose capital was Rome).

The prehistory of French begins with the colonisation of Gaul (an area which included all of present-day France, as well as modern Belgium and parts of Germany and Switzerland) by the Romans in the first two centuries BC, and the introduction of Latin in what were predominantly Celtic-speaking areas. Over the course of the next five centuries, Gaulish gradually died out in favour of Latin, the language of writing, politics, administration, the law and education. Traces of the original Gaulish still survive, however, in French vocabulary in words relating to rural activities, features of the landscape and domestic pursuits, such as *glaner, bruyère, chêne, alouette, cervoise* (see Wise 1997: 33 for further examples).

By the fifth century AD, at least in the west of Europe, the political unity represented by the central power of Rome had disintegrated, and in the territories once ruled over by the now fragmented Roman Empire the local varieties of Latin began to diverge from their common ancestor in a development which gave rise to the Romance varieties and languages we know today.

In Gaul, Germanic hordes had begun to sweep across the territory from AD 400. The Visigoths established their sway in the south-west, setting up their capital in what was to become Toulouse. The Burgundians settled along the Rhône valley and established their capital in Lyons. In the north and north-east the Franks dominated. By the end of the fifth century they occupied an area stretching from the Rhine to the Loire, and, by the end of the sixth, had extended their control over most of Gaul.

One strange characteristic of these so-called barbaric hordes was their willingness to give up their own languages and, after a period of bilingualism, adopt the Romance, that is Latin-based, varieties they encountered in their new territories. This is a puzzling fact (conquerors usually impose their language on the conquered!), but it may be explained, at least in part, by the facts that the Germanic tribes would have found in Gaul a culture far more sophisticated than their own and that they soon converted to Christianity, whose teaching was either in Latin or the local Romance variety. However, in speaking Latin, the Germanic invaders retained some of their speech habits, causing the language to change rapidly, especially in the areas the Franks occupied first and which witnessed the greatest social disruption. In the south (more strongly romanised than the north, since Roman civilisation had been established there very early), Roman law and municipal administration persisted despite the collapse of the empire. North of the Loire, Roman civilisation was less well rooted and was replaced by the feudal, less centralised organisation of the Franks. While the language used in written documents, Latin, remained relatively stable, the spoken form of Latin, used by the uneducated in day-to-day communication and activities, increasingly began to diverge from the written form. Germanic influence affected not only **phonology** and **syntax** (Rickard 1989: 8–17), but also vocabulary. The Franks contributed many terms relating either to their way of life and activities as farmers or soldiers, *jardin, haie, renard, faucon, guerre, garder, blesser*, or to new social structures, for example *baron* and *fief* (Wise 1997: 36–8). Two centuries of disruption due to the Germanic invasions led to the gradual fragmentation of Latin and the emergence of a number of regional dialects forming a more linguistically innovative group in the north, known collectively as the Langue d'Oïl, and a more conservative group in the south, the Langue d'Oc, where Germanic influence was less strong. The words used to designate these related varieties are the words for 'yes', *oc* in the south and *oïl* (giving us *oui* today) in the north.

The dialectal divisions that had emerged by the end of the tenth century AD have largely persisted into modern times, and the dialect map in Appendix I reflects the two major groups. The Franco-Provençal varieties are a transitional group in that they present some characteristics typical of the northern Langue d'Oïl group and some typical of the southern Langue d'Oc group. In view of our interest in the growth of the modern standard language, we'll concentrate exclusively on the Langue d'Oïl, for it's one of these varieties (spoken in the Ile-de-France, the region around Paris) which ultimately became the standard language.

3.2 The development of Langue d'Oïl varieties up to 1600

Although, in linguistic terms, French today is 'Modern Latin' as spoken in France, and while it's possible with surviving written documents to trace the development from Latin to the linguistic system described in Chapters

2–4, we might wonder whether there's a point at which it's appropriate to talk of the beginnings of French, that is, when it was deemed no longer to make sense to think of the varieties spoken in Gaul as Latin. Although a precise date can't be given, there is a general consensus (see Wright 1982, 1991, Lodge 1993) that an awareness of a vernacular, distinct from Latin, emerged at the end of the eighth century. The Carolingian reforms set in motion by Charlemagne to restore the classical purity of the Latin of the Church and administration, and impose a standard pronunciation of Latin throughout his empire, highlighted the differences between the various spoken forms of Latin and the written variety. Official recognition of the fact that the newly reformed Latin of the Church could no longer be understood by the congregations came in 813 when, at the Council of Tours, French bishops enjoined priests to deliver their sermons in the *rustica romana lingua* (the Romance speech of the countryside) or the *theotisca lingua* (the Germanic tongue), so that everyone might understand. By the ninth century, a diglossic situation had emerged (1: 2.2), in which Latin retained the prestige associated with its use as the language of the Church, government, learning and serious writing, while the numerous local, uncodified and variable vernaculars essentially fulfilled the purposes of everyday communication. Gradually, as we'll see, this diglossic situation (which persisted until the sixteenth century) was steadily eroded as the emerging standard took over the functions of Latin.

Further evidence in dating the emergence of the concept of French as a separate language in the middle of the ninth century is provided by the earliest extant vernacular prose text, the *Serments de Strasbourg* (842), which records in a Latin chronicle the text of oaths sworn to seal an alliance between two of Charlemagne's grandsons, Louis the German and Charles the Bald, against the threat posed to them by their brother Lothair. Louis took the oath in *romana lingua* and Charles repeated the same oath in *theotisca lingua*. The Latin chronicle also includes the text of the different oaths taken by Louis's and Charles's troops, and records them in a form which clearly seeks to approximate the spoken language, and to develop new spelling conventions. However, to suggest that a concept such as the French language miraculously came into existence in 842, and to identify the labels *romana lingua* and *theotisca lingua* with French and German respectively, would be, at best, a gross oversimplification and, at worst, a distortion of reality. Such a conclusion would prejudge entirely the whole issue of the linguistic reality which existed at the dawn of the Middle Ages in the territory now recognised politically as France. In fact, we'll suggest later that what is commonly thought of as the French language stems, largely, from cultural and linguistic stereotypes created in the seventeenth century.

To return briefly to the *Serments de Strasbourg*, here is a short extract with a word-for-word and an idiomatic translation (based on Ewert 1954: 352; see also Ayres-Bennett 1996: 16, 18):

Pro Deo   amur et   pro christian poblo et   nostro commun
for of-God love   and for Christian people and our   common
   salvament
   salvation
For the love of God and the salvation of the Christian people and our
own salvation

d'   ist di in avant, in quant   Deus savir   et   podir
from this day forward, in how-much God   knowledge and power
   me   dunat,
   to-me gives,
from this day onward, in so far as God grants me knowledge and power,

si salvarai eo cist meon fradre Karlo in ajudha et   in cadhuna
so will-save I   this my   brother Karl   in help   and in every
   cosa,
   thing,
so will I assist this brother of mine Charles with help and with every-
thing

si cum om per dreit son   fradra salvar dift
so as   one by right one's brother to-save ought
as by rights one should assist one's brother

Significantly, the text has many features which are atypical of Latin. Latin
had a complex system of endings for nouns (case morphology) which gave
information about the function the noun plays in the sentence; yet the
case morphology here has been radically pruned down. The *-s* ending on
Deus (line 2) indicates the singular masculine subject of a sentence. Compare
this with *Deo* in line 1, where the *-s* is absent and, rather than being the
subject of the sentence, the word is interpreted as having the sort of relation to the noun *amur* that can be expressed in English using 'of' (*pro Deo
amur* is therefore glossed as 'for the love of God'). Turning to the verbs,
note the future tense form *salvarai* (line 3). This survives as *sauverai*, and
is based on the pattern still used to form the synthetic future, that is, the
infinitive plus a subject agreement ending (3: 3). Crucially, this is morphologically different from the Latin.

Traditionally, histories of French take the *Serments de Strasbourg* as their
starting point and delineate three major periods in the evolution of French:
Old French (up to the mid-fourteenth century), Middle French (up to 1600)
and Modern French (from 1600 to the present day). The Old French period
saw the first attempts to use the vernacular as a literary medium, and the
first stages in the long process of standardisation whereby, from the complex
linguistic reality which emerged through the dialectalisation of Latin, one
dialect came to be selected as the norm. The Middle French period sees

Table 1.1

Date	Illustrative text	Period
842	*Serments de Strasbourg*	Old French
12th century	Garnier de Pont-Sainte-Maxence	
	Conon de Béthune	
c. 1350		Middle French
1420(?)	*Les XV joyes de mariage*	
1530	Palsgrave's *Esclarcissement de la langue françoyse*	
1539	*Edit de Villers-Cotterêts*	
1600–present		Modern French
1647	Vaugelas's *Remarques sur la langue française*	

French expanding its functions to the detriment of Latin in official domains, with parallel developments in its linguistic resources and greater stability in its written form. Modern French, as we'll see in more detail later, was first identified with a socio-cultural elite. It's highly codified and has come to be recognised and accepted as the standard spoken and written language in France. (See Table 1.1 for a summary and reference to the illustrative texts we'll be quoting within each period.)

A final word of caution: the labels Old French and Middle French don't correspond to national standard languages spoken by the majority of the population, in the way that Modern French does. For instance, to think of Old French as a standard language on a par with Modern French is to impose a conception of political, linguistic and national unity onto an earlier social structure which was feudal in organisation. Old French is better conceived of as a reflection of the variety written for the ruling elite of Northern France during the period *c.* 1100–1350. For an interesting exposition of the greater sense of linguistic pluralism which underlies the Old French period, and of attitudes at the time towards 'correct written forms' of French, see Rudder (1986: 65–164).

3.3   *Francien: a standard language in the making*

Francien is the modern name given to the medieval Oïl dialect spoken in the Ile-de-France (i.e. Parisian) region of Northern France. In the twelfth and thirteenth centuries, just as the term France was ambiguous (referring either to the Parisian region or to the kingdom in general), so the term *françois* referred either to the dialect of the Ile-de-France or to the Langue d'Oïl in general.

It's clear from the map in Appendix I that there was a great deal of variation in the Langue d'Oïl area. Why, then, was Francien perceived or 'selected' as the variety to be spoken by those who 'wanted to get on' or 'had made it', to the detriment of other varieties spoken in Northern France? It's certainly not because of any inherent linguistic superiority, nor because of a rich literary tradition (in fact, quite the opposite, since Francien is barely represented in the surviving literary texts of the Old French period). The variety's importance was established only slowly, and thanks largely to the historical role of the Ile-de-France in the political development of Northern France and the subsequent unification of both northern and southern territories to form France as we know it today.

Demographic and economic factors also played a part; there was an important concentration of population within the Ile-de-France, which then, as now, was a highly prosperous area. Political power was established in Paris only late in the Old French period (from the twelfth century onwards), when the kings began to hold court in various monastic houses around Paris (notably the Abbey of Saint-Denis, the spiritual centre of the kingdom). The prosperity of Paris and, later, the setting up of the royal court with its bureaucracy and the law courts there could only enhance the prestige of the area and confirm its importance in the new evolving administrative structure. Added to these demographic, economic and political factors, there were intellectual and cultural factors which further confirmed Paris's linguistic importance. Many schools were founded there, which, in 1252, constituted themselves as the University of the Sorbonne. All these institutions gave Paris a prestige which far outweighed that of other northern cities. The court became a source of literary patronage; hence, poets began to abandon their native variety in favour of the more acceptable language of the court. See how bitterly the poet Conon de Béthune expressed his dismay at having his language criticised by the queen (Wagner 1964: 61):

> Mon langaigë ont blasmé li Francois.
> *my   language have criticized the French*
> The French have criticized my way of speaking.

Conon de Béthune was born in Artois (a region which now straddles the French–Belgian border). Nevertheless, he was clearly a speaker of an Oïl dialect (Picard). *Li François* he refers to aren't the French as we would understand the term today, but, rather, the inhabitants of the Ile-de-France. Similarly, in the next passage from his *Chansons* (Rickard 1989: 41–2), *françois* refers to the Ile-de-France variety, the prestige variety used by the court.

> encore   ne soit   ma parole françoise
> *although not may-be my speech French*
> Although my way of speaking isn't French,
>
> si   la puet on   entendre   en françois,
> *yet it can   one understand in   French*
> still it be understood in France.

ne cil ne sont bien apris   ne cortois
they   are not well-educated nor polite
They are ill-educated and rude

s'il m' ont repris,   se   j' ai dit mos   d'   Artois
who me have corrected, because I said   a word from Artois
who correct me for using Artois words

car je ne fui pas nouriz   a Pontoise.
since I   was not brought up in Pontoise
because I wasn't brought up in Pontoise.

Conversely, native Francien-speaking poets often displayed a degree of linguistic smugness and superiority. A clear example of this is Garnier de Pont-Sainte-Maxence (Price 1984: 12), who, in 1174, in concluding his poem on Saint Thomas the Martyr, writes:

Mis langages est boens, car en France fui   nez.
my language is   good, since in France (I)-was born
My way of speaking is good, because I was born in France.

The final important factor in establishing Francien's predominant sway was the geographical one. It's clear from the map of the Langue d'Oïl-speaking area that Francien occupies a central position as a transitional variety among the others. Assuming the peripheral varieties weren't mutually comprehensible, this means that Francien was a sort of *lingua franca* over the whole of the Langue d'Oïl domain, that is, a variety which was comprehensible to all.

By the end of the thirteenth century, Francien had become a dialect with a special status, the desirable norm for speech. In writing, Latin was losing some ground as the vernaculars acquired new functions, being increasingly used for literary works and in administrative documents.

3.4 Middle French: the growing sense of nationhood

Middle French refers to a written variety associated with the period from the mid-fourteenth to the beginning of the seventeenth century. This was a turbulent period in French history, but one during which the Valois dynasty (1328–1589) began to establish firm control by the monarchy over most of the territory recognised today as France. By 1453, at the end of the Hundred Years War, Normandy, Guyenne and Gascony had come under the control of the French crown, Provence and Anjou in 1481 and Brittany in 1491. Unrest caused by wars with Italy in the early part of the sixteenth century and outbreaks of civil war due to the Wars of Religion (1562–93) to some extent weakened the growing sense of French nationhood which was embodied in the person of the monarch, but the events of the sixteenth century form a backdrop against which the consolidation of royal power and centralisation of authority could take place in the seventeenth century under Louis XIV.

This new sense of nationhood, arising out of political unification, had important linguistic repercussions. French, the accepted norm of Paris, acquired new functions, gradually displacing other vernaculars and Latin as the language of government and the law, and encroaching on Latin as the language of learning.

Royal recognition of the importance of French as a unifying influence in the territory over which the king ruled culminated in François I's promulgation in 1539 of the *Edit de Villers-Cotterêts*. The edict talks in terms of Latin being replaced by *langaige maternel françois*, which is traditionally interpreted as meaning that the only variety of French acceptable for legal and official documents was to be that of the ruling elite and, ultimately, the king. Some specialists in the history of the French language cite this edict as an example of the high-handed imposition of the variety of a language spoken by a political elite upon native speakers of other related varieties, but this is probably an exaggeration. François I's main aim was to establish a single administrative language; he probably had no interest in imposing this variety outside the courtroom (that is, as the spoken language of everyday life). Here is the relevant part of the edict, which is also an example of the Middle French standard which prefigures the Standard French of the modern period:

> Et pour ce que de telles choses sont souuent aduenues sur l'intelligence des mots latins contenus esdits arrests, nous voulons d'ores en auant que tous arrests, ensemble toutes autres procedures . . . soient prononcez, enregistrez et délivrez aux parties en langaige maternel françois et non autrement.
>
> (Brunot 1966: 30)

By the end of the fifteenth century, French was already in widespread literary use, but Latin remained pre-eminent for works of serious scholarship, in education and religious matters. The advent of printing, the Reformation and the Renaissance revival of the study of classical Greek and Latin stimulated the development of French as a suitable medium for scholarly purposes. Indeed, as a consequence of the efforts of the Humanists to restore Latin to its classical purity, Latin was seen to be unsuited to the expression of contemporary needs. Thus, in the course of the sixteenth century, French became increasingly used in domains such as history, geography, mathematics and surgery.

Much debate at this time focused on the role of French and the relative merits of French and Latin. But for authors such as Joachim du Bellay who, in 1549, published his *Deffense et Illustration de la langue francoyse*, there was no doubt that French had the potential to compete with Latin, although to attain similar prestige and scope it would have to be both elaborated (through expansion of vocabulary and stylistic innovation) and codified in order to give it stability and permanence (Lodge 1993: chs 3 and 4, Wise 1997: 49–56). It was also in the Middle French period that the first systematic descriptions of what was termed the French language were produced. Such documents show an increasing concern for codification of the language, and a perception of the need for a set of established norms that those who wished to master French could follow. An important insight into the criteria used for establishing these norms was given by John Palsgrave who published his *Esclarcissement de la langue françoyse* in 1530:

> in all this worke I moost folowe the Parisyens and the countrys that be conteygned betwene the ryver Seyne and the River Loyrre … for within that space is contayned the herte of Fraunce, where the tonge is at this day moost parfyte, and hath of moost auncyente so contynued … there is no man, of what parte of Fraunce se ever he be borne, if he desyre that his writynges shulde be had in any estymacion, but he writeth in suche language as they speke within the boundes that I have before rehersed.
>
> (cited in Pope 1952: 37)

Here we see the growing feeling that the best French (careful how this is interpreted!) is that spoken in and around the seat of power, that is, in Paris and the Loire valley where the ruling aristocracy had their country homes. In fact, the geographical area alluded to in Palsgrave's quotation corresponds very closely to the area in which the Francien variety of the Old French period was spoken. While Palsgrave's grammar was written for non-native speakers of French who wished to learn the language, his comments nevertheless reflect the prevailing linguistic attitude of the time, an attitude which he was willing to accept and to follow in writing his grammar (and, incidentally, an attitude which holds sway in certain quarters even today!).

Returning to the extract from the *Edit de Villers-Cotterêts*, and considering the next, written a century earlier, from *Les XV joyes de mariage* (a collection of tales telling of the perils of marriage), note how, despite some unfamiliar features, this variety of written French is quite easily recognisable to those who read Modern French:

> Et encore je tiens a plus beste veil homme qui cuide faire le jolis et se marie avec jeune femme. Quant je voy faire telles chouses, je m'en ry en considerant la fin qu'il en avendra, car sachez si l'omme veil prent jeune femme, ce sera grant aventure si elle se atent a lui de ses besongnes. … Or considerez si c'est bien fait, mectre deux choses contraires

ensemble! C'est a comparer ad ce que l'en met en ung sac ung chat et ung chien: ils avront tousjours guerre liens jusque a la fin.

(Rychner 1967: 101–2)

There are several interesting features in these two extracts from the Middle French period, but for reasons of space we'll be rather selective. The orthography is somewhat different from that of Old French because, in the Middle French period, orthography wasn't conceived of as a mere vehicle for recording pronunciation. Indeed, there are a number of non-phonetic (unpronounced) features, whose presence is motivated mainly by etymological considerations. For example, consider consonant doubling, due to Latin influence, in the spelling of *teLLes*, *aRRests*, *(h)oMMe* and *eLLe*. Certain letters are included because they are present in etymologically related Latin forms, for instance *meCtre* (related to MECTUM). Other letters reflect pronunciations which were modified in the Old French period, for example *auLtrement*. Equally interesting is the use of orthographic *s*, which, by this stage, would no longer have been pronounced before another consonant, but which probably signals lengthening of the preceding vowel, for example *beSte*, *doreSnavant*. A handful of words haven't survived into Modern French, such as *cuide* 'think' (replaced by *pense*) and *liens* 'inside', 'within'. Morphologically we find the form *esdits*, a contraction of *en les* giving *es* 'in the'. There are also certain spelling conventions to note, such as the attachment of *g* to the end of *ung* and the spelling of final [i] as *y* (e.g. *ry*, *voy*).

The Middle French period can, then, be seen as a time when the French language was having to adapt itself to new uses in legal, administrative and technical documents, as well as literary texts. Essentially, it was taking over many of the prestige functions previously fulfilled by Latin. The passage from the Middle French to the Modern French period might be characterised (following Ewert 1954: 2) as a move from a period of experiment and tentative reform, with no precise focusing on linguistic norms, to one of prescriptivism, standardisation and codification.

4 The growth of Standard French

4.1 Preliminaries

While the late Middle Ages saw considerable elaboration in the functions of French, as well as in its linguistic resources, the seventeenth and eighteenth centuries were marked by intense activity directed towards codification of the language, slowing down (while not checking entirely) the spontaneous internal evolution of the language. Note that, within language standardisation, codification has the twin goals of suppressing variation and halting change. This is achieved, first, by the production of explicit rules laid down in prescriptive works, such as grammars and dictionaries, which set out correct usage in pronunciation, spelling, syntax and vocabulary, and, second, the identification of the group(s) in society whose usage is to be held up as the desirable norm.

In the seventeenth century a political and social structure was identified, whose variety of French, and whose hegemony, still dominate in France today. The consolidation of the political power of a ruling elite around the court of Louis XIV brought with it the desire for a set of canons, or norms, which would codify the language behaviour of this group. Those willing to adopt the linguistic usage of this elite could thereby gain access to it. In sociolinguistic terms, in the seventeenth century, the usage of the ruling elite, held up as the model to be followed, was both a vehicle of social promotion (those who spoke it could hope to get on in life) and, at the same time, a vehicle of social exclusion (for those who didn't master this usage, the road to social promotion was barred).

4.2 The dawn of the seventeenth century

As the Valois dynasty finally came to an end with the reign of the depraved Henri III (1551–89), the last of the *rois maudits*, a new dynasty was ushered in by the elevation to the French throne of the first Bourbon king, Henri IV (1589–1610), the king of Navarre in Béarn (a region in southern France near the Spanish border).

In the early part of the seventeenth century, the Bourbon kings were served by a triumvirate of outstanding but, at least in the case of the last two, ruthless ministers. The first of these was Sully (1559–1641), who is generally credited with having established the tax system and the centralised financial system at the heart of the modern French economy. The second 'great' minister of this period was Cardinal Richelieu (1585–1642), who built on Sully's economic reforms and set about concentrating power in the hands of the monarch, setting in motion the development of the power structure in France, popularly considered to centralise all political authority in a few individuals in Paris. The third member of the trio was Richelieu's 'worthy' successor Cardinal Mazarin (1602–61), who continued his predecessor's programme of centralisation. In the last part of the seventeenth century, the king, Louis XIV (1643–1715, born 1638), *le roi soleil*, came to dominate the political arena as a direct result of the 'public relations' machinery which Richelieu, in particular, had put in place.

As mentioned already, the political and social evolution in the seventeenth century can be understood, in many ways, as a reaction to the turmoil of the late sixteenth century. Realising the potential for disorder which lay in unbridled individualism and a loose national power structure, the seventeenth-century political elite of France tried to present the necessity for a highly codified and regimented social structure which centred on the power of the king. This political structure would provide the stability which (in theory, at least) would lead to the economic prosperity of that elite. In practice, it isn't at all clear that this political unity actually existed beneath the surface. The seventeenth century in France was certainly not conflict-free, as shown by both the *Frondes* (1648–52) and the frequent food riots in Paris which finally forced the court to leave the city and move to Versailles. It's probably more realistic to view the craving for norms, both social and linguistic, in seventeenth-century France as a result of both linguistic and social insecurity. The ruling elite needed a badge of identity, and the grammarians and institutions who codified the standard variety of French helped them find one.

This new sense of the need for order and regimentation in society (often referred to as classical values) made itself felt not only in the political but also in the social sphere, where the concept of *honnêtes hommes* developed. The *honnêtes hommes* were individuals who in their conduct displayed the virtues, social graces and intelligence which were desirable attributes of those who were to be counted as members of the ruling elite. Part and parcel of being one of these *honnêtes hommes* was being suitably refined to frequent the *salons* (polite meeting places for conversation and literary and artistic pursuits), organised by women. The role of women in creating a cultured and refined social life for the political elite of seventeenth-century France can-not be overestimated. Ayres-Bennett (1990) points out that 'in this age of anti-pedantry the relative ignorance of women became a positive virtue', as if women were considered to possess a natural tendency to favour refinement and good manners, which allowed them to give valid judgements on questions of linguistic usage without getting lost in arid and futile pedantic debate. It's in the context of this view of the refining and unpretentious qualities of women that comments such as those by Vaugelas in his *Remarques sur la langue française* (1647) should be interpreted: 'Pour l'ordinaire les gens de lettres, s'ils ne hantent pas la Cour ou les Courtisans, ne parlent pas si bien ny si aisement que les femmes' (Vaugelas 1970: 505).

The cult of the *honnêtes hommes* had important repercussions on the linguistic plane, for one of the major tests of belonging to the *honnêtes hommes* was one's *Usage* (the word is now being used in the more tech-nical sense in which it was understood in the seventeenth century; this sense will be explained in some detail later; 1: 4.4). The greater discipline and codification that were accepted as necessary attributes of the social life of the ruling elite of France were transposed into their language. Anything which smacked of provincialism, pedantry or vulgarity was to be banished from *le bon Usage*, the language to be used in polite and courtly circles.

The *Usage* of the political elite was to be a reflection of the refined and cultured standards they were required to set themselves in order to be considered part of that elite. One early seventeenth-century grammarian of French, Du Perron (1556–1618), sums up this attitude very succinctly in the following statement: 'aux Etats Monarchiques, il faut s'étudier à parler le seul langage de la cour, en laquelle se trouve tout ce qu'il y a de politesse dans le Royaume' (Vaugelas 1970: xix).

One of the best-known and most influential commentators on language who began to influence the norms of this polite, refined French in the early seventeenth century was the court poet Malherbe (1555–1628), whose particular task was to 'degasconise' the language of the court and define a new literary style. Henri IV (Henri de Navarre), it will be remembered, was from Béarn. His influence, and that of his retinue, on courtly language and manners had, apparently, made them seem rather provincial and uncouth; hence the need for Malherbe's work, whose main concern was to achieve such goals as *clarté*, *pureté* and *précision*. He therefore prohibited the use of archaisms, neologisms (newly coined words) and borrowings from French dialects or from other languages, all of which were potential sources of ambiguity or misunderstanding. As an example of the dictates Malherbe laid down, consider his attitude towards the word *autrefois* (Wartburg 1967: 171), which in the sixteenth century referred both to future and past time, as in (i) and (ii):

(i)   Il fut autrefois.
(ii) Il sera autrefois. (i.e. Il sera un jour.)

However, such apparent temporal ambiguity was deemed intolerable by Malherbe, and he laid down that only past time reference was permitted, and that sentences such as (ii) were to be banished from the *Usage* of the *honnêtes hommes*.

4.3   *L'Académie française*

Cardinal Richelieu's subtle political sense left him in no doubt concerning the value of language as an arm in his campaign to give France a durable political structure. And it's he who founded the Académie française (1635), an embodiment of the official recognition of the importance of language as a means of giving a sense of identity to a group of individuals. The Académie française represented for Richelieu an efficient means of maintaining a controlling influence on norms of sociolinguistic behaviour. It was a useful vehicle for dispensing praise or criticism to writers who supported or failed to support the ruling political regime, and for controlling what they wrote. While the *Edit de Villers-Cotterêts* (1: 3.4) started a long tradition of linguistic legislation concerned with policies of status planning (giving official instructions as to the status of a language in a particular society), the founding of the Académie française represents a major aspect of corpus planning, that is, planning with a view to defining the nature of the language and its quality.

The programme of the Académie hasn't, even now, been completed. The idea of works on French rhetoric and poetics was soon dropped, a grammar was eventually published in 1932 but wasn't well received and has had little influence. There have been eight editions of the Académie's dictionary

(1694, 1718, 1740, 1760, 1798, 1835, 1878, 1935), but, in truth, though influential, none was ever considered a definitive lexicographic study of the French language at the time of its publication.

Paradoxically, the Académie's modest success in language planning isn't really surprising since this is a notoriously fraught endeavour, and the fact that the Académie has never really 'shown its hand' (by completing its initial programme) means that it can still go on working. In fact, it could be argued that the official programme of the Académie is far less important than its symbolic function, as an officially recognised body under the patronage of the monarch (or, in today's republican France, the President), one of whose major concerns is to monitor and record Standard French. The following extract from article 24 of the statutes of the Académie clearly states one of its major aims, namely 'donner des règles certaines à notre langue . . . et la rendre pure, éloquente et capable de traiter des arts et des sciences' (Caput 1986: 11).

In practice, the Académie has tended to follow the evolution of Standard French rather than drive it. The lasting influence it has had has been in two areas. First, in orthography, where its conservative approach, favouring the existing tendency towards etymological spellings (best exemplified in its 1835 edition), has been accepted. After all, the *honnête homme* would be familiar with Latin, and making the written language accessible to a wider public wasn't a preoccupation of the times. Second, where the Académie's influence on standard literary French has been very strong, at least until recently, is in its officially sanctioned dictionary. In fact, the lexical items included in early editions were selected according to very strict criteria. The following types of words, in particular, were excluded: first, archaic and so-called 'low' words (familiar, vulgar or slang terms); second, neologisms; and, finally, technical terms from most spheres of activity (with the notable exception of certain noble arts, such as fencing, horse riding and hunting). Exclusions such as these meant that the number of lexical items in the officially sanctioned variety of French was rather low. Future generations of writers in particular (Voltaire in the eighteenth century and Hugo in the nineteenth (1: 4–5)) were to react against this officially sanctioned 'impoverishment' of the vocabulary of French, seeing it as a weakening of the expressive powers of literary French.

Individual members of the Académie (the *académiciens*) have also had an important role to play in the growth and acceptance of Standard French. In fact, it was the twenty-second member called to join the Académie who, perhaps more than anyone else, came to be perceived as the ultimate arbitrator of what is called *le bon Usage* (correct Standard French). This was Claude Favre de Vaugelas (1585–1650), generally known as Vaugelas.

Vaugelas's particular brief was to work on preparing the dictionary, but his progress was apparently rather slow and, towards the end of his life, his friends prevailed upon him to publish some of the observations that he had been noting in his *cahiers* throughout his career. Thus were born the (in)famous

Remarques sur la langue française, published in 1647, which, rather than a comprehensive grammar treatise, takes the form of a miscellany of observations on points of debate in matters of pronunciation, syntax and vocabulary. For, unlike Malherbe, who was principally concerned with the literary language, Vaugelas was first and foremost an observer of linguistic usage in the court circles in which he moved, and his main purpose was to comment on the appropriate forms to be used in writing and speech in polite society.

Vaugelas's *Remarques* has been much misrepresented since its publication, and some have viewed it as part of an elitist conspiracy to create a totally artificial standard for French. In reality, Vaugelas's purpose in publishing his *Remarques* was to provide the *honnêtes hommes* with a reference work which would guide them in their attempts to conform to *le bon Usage*, that is, a guide for the upwardly mobile. Indeed, his purpose is expressed very clearly in the full title of his work, namely, *Remarques sur la langue française, utiles à ceux qui veulent bien parler et bien escrire.*

4.4   *Vaugelas and* le bon Usage

The most enduring concept to come down to us from Vaugelas's *Remarques* is that of *le bon Usage*, a phrase which the grammarian Maurice Grevisse picked up in the twentieth century for his contemporary equivalent of Vaugelas's book. But what exactly is *le bon Usage*? To fully understand this, we need to examine in some detail Vaugelas's preface. *Usage* is conceived of as something quite arbitrary which is beyond the control of the grammarian:

> Ce ne sont pas ici des Lois que je fais pour nostre langue de mon authorité privée; Je serois bien temeraire, pour ne pas dire insensé; car à quel titre et de quel front pretendre un pouvoir qui n'appartient qu'à l'usage, que chacun reconnoist pour le Maistre et le Souverain des langues vivantes?
>
> (Vaugelas 1970: ix)

L'Usage for Vaugelas thus remains a rather nebulous concept. In the same preface he goes on to present acceptance of the dictates of *l'Usage* very much as an act of faith, for, just as religious belief in the final analysis defies reason and logical argument, so, too, in the linguistic domain, *l'Usage* must be accepted on faith, and one shouldn't expect it to be based on reason. Vaugelas sees himself, then, as the servant of *l'Usage* in his *Remarques*. He isn't taking it upon himself to make authoritarian statements about what sort of language should be considered correct and socially acceptable; rather, he presents himself in his preface as simply observing and recording the norms of polite conversation (in the seventeenth-century French court): 'J'ai deu esloigner de moi tout soupçon de vouloir establir ce que je ne fais que rapporter' (Vaugelas 1970: i–ii).

In fact, the definition of *l'Usage* for Vaugelas is more difficult to understand than the above paragraph suggests, for Vaugelas distinguishes two types of *Usage*: *le bon* and *le mauvais Usage*. The implications of these labels are self-evident; *honnêtes hommes* are expected to model their linguistic behaviour on *le bon Usage*. But then, of course, the crucial question has to be faced of where *le bon Usage* is to be found. According to Vaugelas, the answer is as follows:

> Voici donc comme on definit le bon Usage: c'est la façon de parler de la plus saine partie de la cour, conformément à la façon d'escrire de la plus saine partie des Autheurs du temps. Quand je dis la Cour, j'y comprens les femmes comme les hommes, et plusieurs personnes de la ville où le prince reside, qui par la communication qu'elles ont avec les gens de la cour participent à sa politesse.
>
> (Vaugelas 1970: ii)

The elitist flavour of this pronouncement is self-evident and, to a certain extent, it's these sentiments which modern, democratically minded individuals find rather distasteful in Vaugelas's thinking. In fact, his attitude towards the language of the common folk (*le peuple*), let alone provincials, is particularly disparaging: 'Le peuple n'est le maistre que du mauvais Usage, et le bon Usage est le maistre de nostre langue.' One need only compare this with Palsgrave's statement the previous century concerning the source of the best French to understand the shift of emphasis that has taken place in the space of a hundred years, from a norm in which geographical considerations are given prominence, and whose social overtones are left implicit, to a social (more overtly elitist) norm where geographical considerations are absent.

Some credit must be paid, however, to Vaugelas's linguistic sensitivity. He paints a picture of the painstaking care needed to become accustomed to *le bon Usage*, a picture which is possibly one of the clearest statements ever of linguistic conformity:

> Ce n'est donc pas une acquisition si aisée à faire que celle de la pureté du langage, ... car il ne faut pas s'imaginer que de faire de temps en temps quelque voyage à la Cour, et quelque connoissance avec ceux qui sont consommez dans la langue, puisse suffire à ce dessein. Il faut estre assidu dans la Cour et dans la frequentation de ces sortes de personnes pour se prévaloir de l'un et de l'autre, et il ne faut pas insensiblement se laisser corrompre par la contagion des Provinces en y faisant un trop long sejour.
>
> (Vaugelas 1970: v)

Beneath this elitist statement of how one maintains correct French, there is a very perceptive sociolinguistic observation. Vaugelas isn't attempting to build artificially some standard which has never existed. He shows very clearly here that he is well aware of the flux and variation which is inherent in all linguistic communities; otherwise, why would he suggest that the acquisition of *le bon Usage* is such a long and laborious process? And why, more importantly, does he suggest that, once acquired, one's mastery of it has to be maintained by regular and sustained contact with the group on whom *le bon Usage* is based?

Although Vaugelas's *Remarques* offer somewhat patchy coverage of the French language, the work touches upon pronunciation, grammar and vocabulary, and offers two guiding principles, namely *pureté* in lexical matters, that is concern for *le mot juste*, and *netteté* in syntax, expressing the grammatical relationships between all the elements of a sentence to avoid ambiguity. Let's look in turn at examples of his observations on each of these levels. It's interesting to note that even Vaugelas sometimes 'got it wrong', as the following *remarque* on pronunciation shows (only the relevant part is quoted):

Le onziesme

Plusieurs parlent et escrivent ainsi, mais tres-mal. Il faut dire, l'onziesme; car surquoy fondé, que deux voyelles de cette nature en cette situation, ne facent pas ce qu'elles font par tout, qui est que la premiere se mange?

(Vaugelas 1970: 77)

In point of fact, Vaugelas's perception of the exceptional nature of this pronunciation is quite right, but in the final analysis the very elusive and illogical *bon Usage* got the better of him in this case, as it's the condemned pronunciation which is today officially sanctioned.

With respect to vocabulary, Vaugelas's observation on the correct form of the conjunction *parce que* is noteworthy, because in this *remarque* he shows himself to be at odds with his predecessor Malherbe and, in this case, his point of view is the one which has won through:

Parce que & pource que

Tous deux sont bons, mais *parce que* est plus doux, & plus usité à la Cour, & [presque] par tous les meilleurs Escrivains. *Pource que* est plus du Palais, quoy qu'à la Cour quelques-uns le dient aussi. ... M. de Malherbe ... met presque tousjours *pource que* jusques à avoir esté sur le point de condamner *parce que*, qui est dans la bouche & dans les escrits de la pluspart du monde. ... Sa raison estoit, que *pource que* a un rapport exprés ou tacite à l'interrogation pourquoi.

(Vaugelas 1970: 47)

The reference to *le Palais* in this *remarque* is to the law courts of Paris, which suggests that in the seventeenth century *pource que* was typical of the usage of the legal profession, rather than the aristocracy.

Even with respect to the grammar of French, it's interesting to note again how careful an observer of *le bon Usage* Vaugelas was. Consider the very reasonable tone adopted in his comments on the use of *c'est que* and *est-ce que*:

> Ce terme est quelquefois superflu & redondant, par exemple lors qu'il est employé de cette sorte *quand c'est que je suis malade*. Une infinité de gens le disent ainsi, & particulierement les Parisiens et leurs voisins. ... Il faut dire simplement *quand je suis malade*. Cela est hors de doute. Mais on n'est pas si asseuré, que cette autre façon de parler soit mauvaise *quand est-ce qu'il viendra?* car les uns la condamnent, & soutiennent qu'il faut dire *quand viendra-t-il?* & les autres disent qu'elle est fort bonne, & pour moi je suis de cet avis.
>
> (Vaugelas 1970: 457–8)

Without doubt, Vaugelas feels that the use of *est-ce que* in questions is quite acceptable, and doesn't condemn too harshly the use of *c'est que* in non-interrogative contexts. We will see later that in the eighteenth century this second usage was condemned much more roundly (as it would be today). Considering the acceptability of *est-ce que* in questions, Vaugelas's observation here is a pertinent and accurate reflection of what was to become Modern French usage.

4.5 Some literary reflections on seventeenth-century attitudes to language

The seventeenth-century author who gives modern readers a glimpse of the impact of the attitudes towards language embodied in the work of Vaugelas and his colleagues is Molière (1622–73). In the following extract from *Les Femmes savantes*, we see Molière satirising some of the excesses of the seventeenth century's concern with *le bon Usage*. The extract shows Molière's awareness, not only of the involvement of women in the linguistic debates of the times, but also of the excessive zeal of some refined ladies in bowing to the dictates of the grammarians. The extract also contains examples of lower-class Parisian usage (see Martine's stigmatised pronunciation of *étugué* and *cheux* and the grammatical lapses which are italicised in the text). These points are used by Molière for comic effect, a reflection of the low prestige accorded to varieties of French which didn't conform to *le bon Usage* at this time. Note also the reference to *un mot sauvage et bas*, presumably a word which hadn't been sanctioned by the Académie (1: 4.3) and which attracts censure as stylistically inappropriate. Philante and Bélise are representatives of exaggeratedly purist attitudes. Philante's husband, Chrysale, represents the voice of moderation. Martine, their servant, gives as good as she gets:

CHRYSALE: Quoi l'avez-vous prise à n'être pas fidèle?

PHILANTE: C'est pis que cela.

CHRYSALE: Pis que tout cela?

PHILANTE: Pis.

CHRYSALE: Comment diantre, friponne! Euh? A-t-elle commis . . .

PHILANTE: Elle a, d'une insolence à nulle autre pareille,
            Après trente leçons, insulté mon oreille
            Par l'impropriété d'un mot sauvage et bas,
            Qu'en termes décisifs condamne Vaugelas.
                . . .

CHRYSALE: Du plus grand des forfaits je la croyais coupable.

PHILANTE: Quoi? Vous ne trouvez pas ce crime impardonnable?

CHRYSALE: Si fait.

PHILANTE: Je voudrois bien que vous l'excusassiez.

CHRYSALE: Je n'ai garde.

BÉLISE: Il est vrai que ce sont des pitiés:
            Toute construction est par elle détruite,
            Et des lois du langage on l'a cent fois instruite.

MARTINE: Tout ce que vous prêchez est, je crois, bel et bon;
            Mais je ne saurois, moi, parler votre jargon.

PHILANTE: L'impudente! appeler un jargon le langage
            Fondé sur la raison et sur le bel usage!

MARTINE: Quand on se fait entendre, on parle toujours bien,
            Et tous vos biaux dictons *ne servent pas de rien.*

PHILANTE: Hé bien! ne voilà pas encore de son style?
            Ne servent pas de rien!

BÉLISE: ô cervelle indocile!
            Faut-il qu'avec les soins qu'on prend incessamment,
            On ne te puisse apprendre à parler congrûment?
            De *pas* mis avec *rien* tu fais la récidive
            Et c'est, comme on t'a dit, trop d'une négative.

MARTINE: Mon Dieu! je n'*avons* pas *étugué* comme vous
            Et *je parlons* tout droit comme on parle *cheux* nous.

PHILANTE: Ah! Peut-on y tenir?

BÉLISE: Quel solécisme horrible!

PHILANTE: En voilà pour tuer une oreille sensible.

BÉLISE: Ton esprit, je l'avoue, est bien matériel
            Je n'est qu'un singulier, *avons* est pluriel.
            Veux-tu toute ta vie offenser la grammaire?

                                      (Molière 1959: 583)

It's perhaps overzealous interpreters of Vaugelas of the kind represented here by Bélise and Philante who have given his *Remarques* such a bad name in some quarters today. A comic playwright such as Molière, who was such a subtle observer of the foibles of his time, wouldn't have included an exchange like this in *Les Femmes savantes* unless his audience recognised how topical the question was. And, despite the comic tone, we can assume that, because of the direct reference to Vaugelas, the audience would be well informed about the ongoing debate surrounding *le bon Usage*, and the growth of the standard which *le bon Usage* represented.

Molière's satirising of the linguistic debate which surrounded the French language in the seventeenth century shouldn't lead us to think that the debate wasn't taken seriously in literary circles. This would be quite the wrong impression. Vaugelas's work was immensely popular and influential, as shown by the following examples of 'corrections' which Pierre Corneille (1606–84) made to his own texts in order to make them conform to the canons of *le bon Usage*. The first two examples of 'corrections', taken from the play *Clitandre* (Lathuillère 1966: 493), show how Corneille was at pains to suppress words which were too *osé* or which seemed too popular (the emphasis is ours):

> ... l'ingrate Dorise,
> Qui le *caresse* autant comme elle vous méprise.
>
> > (*Clitandre*, I, v. 161–2)

> L'impétueux *bouillon* d'un courroux féminin.
>
> > (*Clitandre*, III, v. 1047)

In the first example the word *caresse* was perceived to be too overtly sensual, and in later editions Corneille replaced it by the more acceptable word *idolâtre*. In the second example the word *bouillon*, with its culinary over-tones, must have been considered to be lacking in refinement, and the verse was recast as: 'Le courroux d'une femme, impétueux d'abord' (*Clitandre*, III, v. 1047).

The above corrections clearly echo Vaugelas's and Malherbe's restrictive attitude towards the lexicon, but they went beyond vocabulary; Corneille also revised his grammar. Vaugelas himself expressed the opinion in one of his *Remarques* that both *N'ont-ils pas fait* and *Ont-ils pas fait* were accept-able, although later literary usage favoured the version with *ne*. For example, in the 1637 edition of *Le Cid*, Corneille wrote: 'Dois-je pas à mon père avant qu'à ma maîtresse?' (Nurse 1978: 82), but, in the 1682 edition of his works, Corneille provided the following 'correction': 'Je dois tout à mon père avant qu'à ma maîtresse' (Nurse 1978: 82).

4.6 Some theoretical reflections

Let's briefly consider some influential work on the development of stan-dard languages, to throw some light on the codification of Standard French in the seventeenth century, and to see what insight might be provided into the further growth of the standard up to the present day. Le Page and Tabouret-Keller (1985) propose the important hypothesis that human linguistic behaviour can be understood as a series of 'acts of identity', in which people reveal both their personal identity and their search for social roles. Le Page and Tabouret-Keller also stress that successful communication depends on speakers and hearers sharing linguistic rules and values. How could we communicate effectively if, for instance, we were unsure about what sort of vocabulary or level of grammatical complexity was appropriate in a given situation? Linguistic communities are groups of individuals who, over time, have developed a series of norms governing their linguistic behaviour. By respecting these shared norms, speakers are able to create and project their desired identity.

In the French context, work such as Vaugelas's represents the growth of a consensus about the prevailing linguistic norms for those who wished to be part of the growing social elite and to distinguish themselves from the Parisian *populace*. Someone who wished to be identified as a member of this elite in the seventeenth century would demonstrate this by adapting their linguistic behaviour to *le bon Usage* of Vaugelas.

We mentioned earlier (1: 3) how standard languages grow up when a group of speakers perceives the need for a shared set of linguistic norms. Groups with such shared linguistic norms are termed by Le Page and Tabouret-Keller highly focused communities. This means that the communities in question have a set of well-defined and generally accepted rules which govern individual interaction. Some of the factors pinpointed by the authors as promoting focusing are: (i) tight social networks implying close daily interaction in the community; (ii) an external threat which leads to a sense of common purpose; (iii) a powerful model, such as a leader or a prestige group.

We suggest that, to a greater or lesser degree, these three factors can be identified in seventeenth-century France, and therefore promoted the development of the standard. Vaugelas's own preface, quoted earlier, encouraged close daily interaction in the social network of the elite. Vaugelas talked of the necessity of being 'assidu dans la Cour et dans la frequentation de ces sortes de personnes [ceux qui sont consommez dans la langue] . . . et il ne faut pas insensiblement se laisser corrompre par la contagion des Provinces en y faisant un trop long sejour' (Vaugelas 1970: v).

The sense of an external threat might be identified in those varieties of French impregnated with *le mauvais Usage* seen earlier or those which weren't orientated towards the norm embodied in *le bon Usage* (that is, the language of the lower classes, both of Paris and the provinces, might represent *le mauvais Usage* in seventeenth-century France). Finally, a powerful model, in the shape of the king and his court, was undeniably available to promote this focusing of group identity in the power elite of the seventeenth century.

Given that a highly focused group existed in seventeenth-century France in the form of the social elite of the time, and in view of the way the group set about identifying the linguistic norms which were to govern linguistic interaction, both oral and written, we now come to the final part of the equation. Standard languages are perceived, by those with social aspirations, to be prestigious. By speaking a standard language, one can expect to achieve social promotion. Consequently, standard languages come to be identified by the groups who adopt their norms as intrinsically good and correct; anything which deviates from the standard is, by reaction, bad or incorrect. This positive feeling towards a standard language creates what might be termed the 'myth' of that standard language. This 'myth' leads to the common perception that the standard should be immutable and protected at all times from language change. What we are calling the standard language 'myth', Milroy and Milroy's (1991) 'ideology of the standard', seems to have taken shape in France in the seventeenth century, and its repercussions are still being felt today, when even the popular press evoke the seventeenth century as the high point of the French linguistic tradition:

> La langue française est si bien adaptée à l'expression des pensées les plus complexes, des nuances les plus subtiles que, depuis trois siècles – depuis Molière – rien n'a pu réellement l'entamer.
>
> (Zoe Oldenberg, *L'Express*, 24 August 1984: 21)

It's within this theoretical framework, we suggest, that the seventeenth century, and its importance in the development of the accepted standard of French, is to be interpreted. The seventeenth century can be conceptualised as the age in which the norms, which have come to be accepted as standard, were set in place, but, as Milroy and Milroy (1991) underline, this is only the first stage of a more lengthy development. The eighteenth, nineteenth and twentieth centuries built on the foundation laid in the seventeenth century.

5 The eighteenth century: a linguistic Garden of Eden or a hardening of attitudes?

In eighteenth-century France the ruling elite (at least until the Revolution in 1789) was intent on perpetuating the social and political structures inherited from the seventeenth century. In linguistic terms, this meant accepting the policies and the conception of the French language that had been set up by grammarians such as Vaugelas. Indeed, on the surface at least, it appears that the dominant linguistic ideology of the eighteenth century was of a kind of linguistic 'golden age' in seventeenth-century France, where a language of such purity and clarity had been defined that the cultural elite of eighteenth-century France could do little more than protect its integrity, but certainly couldn't seek to improve or modify it.

Seventeenth-century authors were revered as linguistic demi-gods, as seen here in the well-known statement by the eighteenth-century writer and moralist Vauvenargues (1715–47): 'Ne vous semble-t-il pas que Racine, Pascal, Bossuet et quelques autres ont créé la langue française?' (Wartburg 1967: 191). Indeed, a thinker as subtle and as influential as Voltaire saw himself very much as continuing the linguistic tradition of the previous century:

> C'est dans le siècle de Louis XIV que cette éloquence a eu son plus grand éclat et que la langue a été fixée. Quelques changements que le temps et le caprice lui préparent, les auteurs du XVIIe siècle et du XVIIIe siècle serviront toujours de modèle.
>
> (quoted in Séguin 1972: 63–4)

The legacy of these eighteenth-century attitudes can still be felt today, but one shouldn't be misled by them. While Voltaire and the others paint a picture of linguistic immobility and purity, we must bear in mind that this is at best only a literary conceit designed to support a cultural myth. Beneath the literary outpourings of the eighteenth century, which have been immortalised in the 'official anthologies', there can be little doubt that French, and particularly spoken French, was evolving and adapting to new social realities. However, few written examples of these aspects of the French language have come down to us from the eighteenth century (for consideration of non-standard varieties of French, see Chapter 5).

In the above quotation, and despite his adulation of the seventeenth century, Voltaire does entertain the possibility of the need for change in Standard French. He was in fact quite critical of the Académie's 1718, 1740 and 1762 dictionaries, finding them too short and lexically restricted (Caput 1986: 45–6). It had to be recognised, he admitted, that the lexicon needed to keep up with the times and with new scientific, philosophical and political ideas and discoveries.

Overall, however, the tone of the linguistic debate in the eighteenth century, especially regarding syntax, appears more dogmatic than in the seventeenth century. It was noted earlier that Vaugelas drew attention to the use of *c'est que* in contexts like *quand c'est que je suis malade*. He wasn't unduly dismissive of this usage and, despite suggesting that *quand je suis malade* was sufficient, he did admit that *une infinité de gens* in and around Paris favoured the longer form. Sixty years after the publication of Vaugelas's *Remarques*, the Académie was much more scathing about this usage, calling it 'une façon de parler basse et du petit peuple' (Foulet 1921: 284). So, at the very beginning of the eighteenth century we already witness a hardening of attitudes, reflected in a growing unwillingness to accept variation from the norms of Standard French.

One way of conceptualising what took place in the eighteenth century with regard to the French standard is to picture, following François (1959), the eighteenth century as the end point of a process set in motion in the sixteenth century, when one could argue that spoken French was still believed to be primary, and that its written form (although highly conventionalised) sought to reproduce phonetic reality. However, by the eighteenth century the relationship between written and spoken French is more or less the exact opposite. Standard French is based upon a written language, which its speakers believe to have been fixed by the writings of certain *bons auteurs* and by grammarians such as Vaugelas; it's therefore for the spoken language to conform to these fixed norms.

A tangible consequence of eighteenth-century attitudes towards the writers of the seventeenth century is the vogue for the production of commentaries and corrected editions of works by seventeenth-century authors. As the earlier quotations from Voltaire and Vauvenargues show, the eighteenth century came to view the writings of the previous century as being somehow 'special'. Voltaire was quite convinced, for instance, that one of the major functions of the Académie should be the production of definitive editions of the so-called 'classical' authors, although he paradoxically admitted that the need for these definitive editions was motivated by the *fautes* that had slipped in:

> Pour l'Académie française, quel service ne rendrait-elle pas aux lettres, à la langue et à la nation, si, au lieu de faire imprimer tous les ans des compliments, elle faisait imprimer les bons ouvrages du siècle de Louis XIV épurés de toutes les fautes de langage qui s'y sont glissées?
>
> (Wilson-Green 1937: 106)

It's quite striking to see, even in such a major work as *L'Encyclopédie* (which many would assume to be the quintessential product of the eighteenth-century French Enlightenment), how close linguistic thinking still was to the models set up in the seventeenth century. Here is how Beauzée (1717–89), the author of the entry on *l'Usage* in *L'Encyclopédie*, describes the concept: 'Le bon usage est la façon de parler de la plus nombreuse partie de la Cour, conformément à la façon d'écrire de la plus nombreuse partie des auteurs les plus estimés du temps' (Diderot and d'Alembert 1765: *Encyclopédie*, XVI, 517). The echoes here of Vaugelas's definition of *le bon Usage* are quite clear, even if there is a slightly more democratic tone. In the same way, prescriptive grammarians were still justifying the norms they advocated by reference to the usage of a privileged group.

Besides launching the still prevalent image of the seventeenth century as a kind of linguistic 'golden age', the eighteenth century also witnessed the clearest articulation of the notion of the prestige which surrounded the French language. In the seventeenth century the prestige of *le bon Usage* which underpinned the emergent standard was taken rather for granted, simply because this was the *Usage* of *les honnêtes hommes*. However, it should be remembered that France was also the most wealthy and powerful country in Europe, economically and politically. With the dawn of the eighteenth century and the increasingly prominent role played by French internationally as the language of diplomacy (where it replaced Latin from 1714 onwards), French came to be viewed as the language of culture, refinement and beauty, and was widely adopted by the aristocracies of most European states. For writers of the time, this situation could only be attributed to the superiority of the French language. To quote Voltaire again:

> La langue française est de toutes les langues celle qui exprime avec le plus de facilité, de netteté et de délicatesse, tous les objets de la conversation des honnêtes gens; et par là elle contribue dans toute l'Europe à un des plus grands agréments de la vie.
>
> (quoted in Séguin 1972: 14)

Consider, also, the following extract from Rivarol's essay *De l'universalité de la langue française* (1784) where the myth-making imagery of the eighteenth century couldn't be clearer:

> L'éclat du siècle de Louis XIV: les beaux jours de la France étaient arrivés. . . . Il y eut un admirable concours de circonstances. Les grandes découvertes qui s'étaient faites depuis cent cinquante ans dans le monde avaient donné à l'esprit humain une impulsion que rien ne pouvait plus arrêter, et cette impulsion tendait vers la France. Paris fixa les idées flottantes de l'Europe et devint le foyer des étincelles répandues chez tous les peuples. L'imagination de Descartes régna dans la philosophie, la raison de Boileau dans les vers; Bayle plaça le doute aux pieds de la vérité; Bossuet tonna sur la tête des rois. . . . Notre théâtre surtout achevait l'éducation de l'Europe: c'est là que le grand Condé pleurait aux vers du grand Corneille et que Racine corrigeait Louis XIV. Rome toute entière parut sur la scène française et les passions parlèrent leur langage.
>
> (Rivarol 1991)

This essay, whose very title is eloquent, also contains what is probably one of the clearest statements of this new international prestige of Standard French. In the following extract we see how the ideas of the eighteenth-century French ruling elite about the international prestige of its language were founded on a series of what one can only term 'self-justificatory' myths, with little logical foundation:

> Mais cette honorable universalité de la langue française, si bien reconnue et si hautement avouée dans notre Europe, offre pourtant un grand problème: elle tient à des causes si délicates et si puissantes à la fois que, pour les démêler, il s'agit de montrer jusqu'à quel point la position de la France, sa constitution politique, l'influence de son climat,

le génie de ses écrivains, le caractère de ses habitudes, et l'opinion qu'elle a su donner d'elle au reste du monde, jusqu'à quel point, dis-je, tant de causes diverses ont pu se combiner et s'unir pour faire à cette langue une fortune si prodigieuse.

(Rivarol 1991)

Rivarol also attempts to give his view of the universality of the French language a pseudo-philosophical basis by claiming that French was the only language of western Europe which had remained faithful to *l'ordre direct*, that is, the subject–verb–object order favoured in most types of French sentence. Rivarol's meaning here, then, is that the French language alone reflects directly the human thought process (linguistically a very dubious claim, incidentally!), and it's this fidelity to *l'ordre direct* which means that French possesses *cette admirable clarté*, which even today some commentators like to identify as a special quality of the French language (again, it must be stressed that this point of view is really more a subjective judgement than an empirical or objective fact). However, having established to his own satisfaction that Standard French was the language of logic and reason, and that it was unparalleled in its expressive clarity, Rivarol goes on to justify further its prestige, by claiming it to be structurally superior to the other major languages of Europe, both past and present: 'ce qui n'est pas clair n'est pas français: ce qui n'est pas clair est encore anglais, italien, grec ou latin' (Rivarol 1991). How could such an inherently superior language fail to gain acceptance?

5.1 A linguistic revolution?

It was with the 1789 Revolution, and the consequent transfer of political power in France to a rising industrial bourgeoisie, that Standard French truly became the national language of France, for it was only then that the French language begins to be viewed as a symbol of Frenchness and a necessary attribute of all the citizens of the new Republic.

Both practical and ideological motives were to inspire state intervention in linguistic matters and attempts to implement a policy of linguistic assimilation as a means of gaining effective control of the nation. Having abolished the federal, provincial structures of the *Ancien Régime*, it was clear to the revolutionary leaders that their goal of achieving the internal unification of France by granting equal status to all citizens and creating a single system of laws and administration within a highly centralised political structure would be served by the imposition of a single language. Moreover, internal unity was essential in the face of the external threat posed to the survival of the new regime by the risk of invasions on the nation's borders from opponents to the Revolution. Thus, the standard language became the symbol of a newly perceived national identity with, in its train, the crystallisation of a feeling that the dialects and the regional languages spoken in France constituted some kind of external threat. (Recall from 1: 4.6 that Le Page and Tabouret-Keller (1985) cite the perception of some kind of external threat as a factor favouring the focusing of a standard language.) Well known are the attacks during this period on varieties of French and other languages spoken in France, such as 'le fédéralisme et la superstition parlent bas-breton' and 'la contrerévolution parle italien, et le fanatisme parle basque'. Non-standard French came to be identified with the archaic, feudal social structure that had been overturned: 'cette foule de dialectes corrompus, dernier reste de la féodalité, sera contrainte de disparaître; la force des choses le commande' (Brunot 1967: 13–14). Thus, it was felt necessary from the Revolution onwards not just to encourage the spread of Standard French, but also to actively impose it in those areas (that is, rural France and the peripheral territories) where its penetration was weak.

While the notion that France should be unified linguistically was new, the Revolution was drawing upon ideas already present in the eighteenth century, when hostility to the dialects, non-standard varieties and, one assumes, minority languages was common. Furthermore, the notion that a firm grasp of the national language was an important attribute of citizenship seems already to be present in the article in the *Encyclopédie* entitled 'Le grammairien':

> Le grammairien contribuera à ce que les citoyens deviennent plus éclairés et plus instruits d'où il devra résulter qu'ils en penseront avec plus d'ordre et de profondeur; qu'ils s'exprimeront avec plus de justesse, de précision, et de clarté; qu'ils seront plus disposés à devenir utiles et vertueux.
>
> (Du Marsais, in Diderot and d'Alembert, 1765: *Encyclopédie*, VII, 847)

This article foreshadows the linguistic ideals of the Revolution, but it's nevertheless worth noting that those qualities so prized in seventeenth-century French, such as *clarté* and *précision*, are here still attributed to it, but are now identified with citizenship, and not with a social elite. Indeed, as Lodge (1993: 216) remarks, it's paradoxical that after 1789 the state should seek, in the name of democracy and equality, to impose on all its citizens the variety that had been elaborated as the badge of the dominant minority group. After the Revolution, the use of the French language becomes mandatory for anyone who wishes to be considered French.

The drive to achieve linguistic unity throughout France was made more pressing by the realisation that the language of reason and enlightenment was only accessible to a minority of the population. This was revealed by the results of a survey, conducted by the Abbé Grégoire at the behest of the revolutionary government, to ascertain how widespread the use of French was in the various regions of France. The original data were gathered using a questionnaire which contained questions like: 'L'usage de la langue française est-il universel dans votre région?' (Certeau *et al.* 1975: 12). The Grégoire report was presented to the Comité d'Instruction Publique in May 1794 with the self-explanatory title *Rapport sur la nécessité d'anéantir les patois et d'universaliser l'usage de la langue française.* Summing up his findings, Grégoire reported that, of the total population only three million could speak French fluently, six million had a smattering of French, while six million more knew no French at all. While stressing the practical benefits to be gained from a single language, Grégoire's report also pointed out the importance of a national standard in fostering a sense of nationhood:

> [O]n peut uniformer la langue d'une grande nation de manière que tous les citoyens qui la composent puissent sans obstacle se communiquer leurs pensées. Cette entreprise ... est digne du peuple français ... qui doit être jaloux de consacrer au plutôt, dans une République unie et indivisible, l'usage unique et invariable de la langue de la liberté.
>
> (Certeau *et al.* 1975: 302)

Two centuries later, the importance of Grégoire's work was given official recognition when, in December 1989, the celebrations of the bicentenary of the French Revolution concluded with a ceremony in which his mortal remains were transferred to the Panthéon to rest alongside those of other French national heroes. There can be no doubt that his conclusion that a shared language was a necessary condition for a national identity to emerge was important in shaping the linguistic and educational policies of post-revolutionary governments. Throughout the nineteenth and into the twentieth century, the French language was to remain a political issue.

6 The nineteenth century and the affirmation of national French

As we've just seen, before the Revolution, French couldn't have been considered the national language of France, that is, the language spoken by the majority. The nineteenth century saw a rapid diffusion of the national standard in France, which could be typified as less geographically and more socially orientated. ('Standard' French increasingly became the language of communication of the working classes, and was no longer the preserve of a privileged, mostly urban, elite.) In parallel with this extension of French came a significant decline in the use of dialects and regional languages. Both phenomena were underpinned by the beliefs elaborated at the time of the Revolution: the superiority of the standard variety over all other varieties and its embodiment of the values of democracy and nationhood.

While state language-planning policies played a part in the diffusion of French, notably through the development of state education (1: 6.1) and the persecution of local languages and dialects, it can be argued that social and economic changes were equally, if not more, influential in promoting acceptance of the national standard. The setting up of highly centralised political and administrative structures, compulsory military conscription (from 1792), universal male suffrage (1848), the development of postal services and the press, all contributed to breaking down the isolation of small, self-sufficient rural communities and to greater integration within a wider society. In addition, the nineteenth century witnessed the industrialisation of France and a shift from an aristocratic–peasant economy to a national–industrial market economy. A consequence of this was an increased mobility of population, as agricultural workers flowed from rural areas to the increasingly industrialised major cities. This growth in mobility of population was facilitated by the improvement of the road network. According to Balibar and Laporte (1974: 51), 40,000 kilometres of new roads had been constructed in France and an equal number of new roads were already under construction by the time of the Revolution. 'La langue circule le long des routes' is how Brunot (1966) envisages the influence of this new road system on the linguistic situation in nineteenth-century France. Later in the same century the growth of the railways was to have an even greater effect on the mobility of the population and, thereby, on its language.

The consequence of this population movement towards the industrial centres of France was an increase in linguistic diversity in urban communities. This diversity within the speech community aided the diffusion of Standard French in that, by adopting and sharing a common standard, communication was facilitated among workers of differing linguistic backgrounds, as well as between the workers and the industrial middle classes. The need for a national standard (at least in industrial centres) was, then, generally perceived and accepted at this time. Even within rural communities, mastery of the standard language was becoming an essential prerequisite to social and professional advancement.

The external history of French in the nineteenth century is, perhaps, more difficult to trace, simply because it's closer in time, and because much more documentation is available to us on what the linguistic situation in France was like. Indeed, it's tempting to think that it's only with the nineteenth century that a true picture of the stylistic diversity of French begins to emerge, after two centuries of concerted efforts by grammarians and *bons auteurs* to hide the linguistic variation inherent in the standard, and to propagate the belief of an immutable and codifiable norm. Yet it would be wrong, at the same time, to imagine that the nineteenth century marks some radical new departure in attitudes towards the French language.

A literary document which shows the interaction of different varieties of French in an urban community is in Balzac's *Le Cousin Pons* ([1846] 1974) where, among other interesting types of linguistic behaviour, the author attempts to record faithfully examples of regional French and popular Parisian French. Balzac's intent in recording the accents of his characters was to reflect reality as closely as possible, and not to create a comic effect as was the case with Molière (1: 4.5). Consider the following exchange between Mme Cibot (a Parisian concierge) and Rémonencq (a dealer from the Auvergne); Mme Cibot is discussing the illness of M. Pons:

> – Pauvre homme! Qui donc a pu le chagriner? C'est n'un brave homme qui n'a son pareil sur terre que dans son ami, monsieur Schmucke! . . . Je vais savoir de quoi n'il retourne! Et c'est moi qui me charge de savonner ceux qui m'ont sangé mon monsieur. . . .
> – Ch'est-i de mochieur Ponche que vouche parlez? demanda le marchand de ferraille qui fumait une pipe.
> – Oui papa Rémonencq, répondit madame Cibot à l'Auvergnat.
> – Eh bienne! il est plus richeu que moucheu Montichtrolle, et que les cheigneurs de la curiochité . . . cheu me connaîche assez dedans l'artique pour vous direu que le cher homme a deche trégeors!
>
> (Balzac 1974: 107–8)

A further important consequence of the industrialisation of the French economy and the increase in literacy was the growth of mass-circulation, popular works of literature, such as Eugène Sue's *Mystères de Paris* (1942/3). Clearly, the consumption of such mass-produced, written French depended on the consumers' acceptance and understanding of a national standard.

The affirmation of national Standard French, as traced in the previous paragraphs, had an important effect on the literary production of the time. However, the literary output of the nineteenth-century *bons auteurs* doesn't mark a profound reorientation of perceptions of the French language; certain important myths persist. The writers of the early nineteenth century were acutely aware of the need to renew certain aspects of the French literary tradition. In this context, Mme de Staël (1766–1817) published her study *De l'Allemagne*, which sought to convey to the French the positive aspects of German and English culture, and, in particular, the greater adaptability and variety of literary German and English in comparison with literary French. German and English appeared to Mme de Staël to have greater lexical resources, which allowed the more accurate reflection of feeling in writing, and more freedom of expression in works of imagination. (It must be emphasised that Mme de Staël's comments apply to the literary languages; it would be quite absurd to conclude that somehow at the dawn of the nineteenth century the Germans and the English were able to express their innermost feelings in a more sensitive manner than the French, or that they had more fertile imaginations than their French counterparts.)

Mme de Staël's comments are associated with the rise of the Romantic movement in French literature. The most noteworthy exponent of this literary and artistic movement was Victor Hugo (1802–85), who is probably best conceived of as embodying in his literary output a kind of uneasy compromise between the classical literary constraints of the previous two centuries and the pressure for change and innovation in language in the nineteenth century. In the preface to his play *Cromwell* Hugo appears to reject the normative tendencies set in place in the seventeenth century and closely followed in the eighteenth: 'Une langue ne se fixe pas. L'esprit humain est toujours en marche.' However, in reality, Hugo's output was less a break with tradition than he would have us believe. Consider the following extract from 'Réponse à un acte d'accusation', probably written in 1834, and published in *Les Contemplations* (1854), where he pictures himself as being put on trial by his critics:

> Je suis ce monstre énorme,
> Je suis le démagogue horrible et débordé,
> Et le dévastateur du vieil ABCD. . . .
> Quand je sortis du collège . . .
> La langue était l'état avant quatre-vingt-neuf;
> Les mots, bien ou mal nés, vivaient parqués en castes;
> Les uns, nobles, hantant les Phèdres, les Jocastes,
> Les Héropes, ayant le décorum pour loi, . . .
> Les autres, tas de gueux, drôles patibulaires
> Habitant les patois; quelques-uns aux galères
> Dans l'argot; dévoués à tous les genres bas,
> Déclinés en haillons dans les halles; sans bas,
> Populace du style au fond de l'ombre éparse;
> Vilains, rustres, croquants que Vaugelas leur chef
> Dans le bagne lexique avait marqués d'une F;
> N'exprimant que la vie abjecte et familière,
> Vils, dégradés, flétris, bourgeois, bons pour Molière. . . .
> Je fis souffler un vent révolutionnaire
> Je mis un bonnet rouge au vieux dictionnaire,
> Plus de mot sénateur! Plus de mot roturier!
> Je fis une tempête au fond de l'encrier,
> Et je mêlai, parmi les ombres débordées,
> Au peuple noir des mots l'essaim blanc des idées;
> Et je dis; Pas de mot où l'idée au vol pur
> Ne puisse se poser, tout humide d'azur.
>   (Hugo 1972: 22–3)

Hugo's claim to have set off *un vent révolutionnaire* is an exaggeration, and the form of the above extract (mainly classical alexandrines) shows how attached to the literary canons of the seventeenth century he remained. It's none the less true that in comparison to the highly selective literary vocabulary sanctioned by the Académie's successive dictionaries, Hugo's vocabulary is indeed much more rich and colourful.

It can be argued that many *bons auteurs* of this period remained obsessed by such considerations as *clarté* and *pureté* in their literary production, and thereby represent continuity in the French classical tradition. Perhaps the quintessential French novelist of the nineteenth century is Gustave Flaubert (1821–80). From the linguist's point of view, Flaubert's obsession with style appears to be the logical continuation of the literary attitudes of seventeenth-century France. His famous *affres du style* and his meticulous sentence-by-sentence search for *le mot juste*, reflected in the painstaking writing and rewriting which surrounded the maturation of his novels such as *Madame Bovary*, can be viewed as the artist actually entering into the living myth of the *clarté* of his mother tongue.

6.1   *L'instruction publique*

The strongest force which led to the affirmation and diffusion of national Standard French in the nineteenth century was the establishment of elementary education for all, although such *instruction publique* became compulsory and free only in the 1880s with the *lois Ferry*. The exponents of *instruction publique* were *les instituteurs*, whose principal task was the teaching of the French language, as the following revolutionary decree shows:

> Il fut décidé, sur la proposition du Comité de Salut Public, que des instituteurs de langue française seraient nommés dans un délai de 10 jours, dans tous les départements dont les habitants parlaient bas-breton, italien, basque et allemand.
>
> (quoted in Séguin 1972: 227)

Although the decrees of 1793–4, making the teaching of French compulsory in all primary schools, couldn't be implemented until well into the next century for lack of teachers and funds, the rhetoric linking language and national identity was to inspire educational policy throughout the century, particularly after 1870 and the shock of defeat in the war with Germany.

To pick up the terminology of Le Page and Tabouret-Keller (1985) again, the focusing effect of *les instituteurs* was of crucial importance in the development of national Standard French. In the *Dictionnaire de pédagogie* (1882), the reference work for all *instituteurs*, the role of the French language in producing model citizens is emphasised:

> On peut dire sans exagération de la langue maternelle qu'elle est le fond même de l'enseignement à l'école primaire. Elle domine et pénètre toutes les autres études. Par là [l'élève] devient, même s'il reste dans la sphère la plus humble, un élément de valeur pour la société, une forme utile mise par l'école au service du pays.
>
> (Désirat and Hordé 1988: 93)

Indeed, it's no accident that during the Third Republic (1872–1940) the minister of *l'instruction publique* had recognised legislating on orthography and grammar as one of his functions. Since then, the dictates of the minister on the French language are published in *Le Bulletin officiel*, issued regularly by the ministry to all teachers in France.

Les instituteurs were trained, then, to envisage themselves as producing good French citizens via the linguistic training they provided. This idea is taken a step further in the following quotation from *Le Bulletin officiel* (1921), where the notion of linguistic training fostering national unity is underscored: 'Nos instituteurs ... sentent bien que donner l'enseignement du français, ce n'est pas seulement travailler au maintien et à l'expansion d'une belle langue et d'une belle littérature, c'est fortifier l'unité nationale' (Désirat and Hordé 1988: 94).

In the same edition of *Le Bulletin officiel* we find yet another factor identified by Le Page and Tabouret-Keller (1985) as contributing to the focusing of a standard, namely, the identification of an external enemy which poses a threat to the standard. For *les instituteurs* of the late nineteenth and early twentieth centuries (just as for their revolutionary predecessors), this is identified with non-standard varieties of French, which are seen as 'poor' and debased and, by implication, as the vehicles of ignorance:

> Nul n'ignore les difficultés que rencontre l'instituteur dans l'enseigne-ment de la langue française. Lorsque les enfants lui sont confiés, leur vocabulaire est pauvre, et il appartient plus souvent à l'argot du quartier, au patois du village, au dialecte de la province, qu'à la langue de Racine ou de Voltaire. Le maître doit se proposer pour but d'amener ces enfants à exprimer leurs pensées et leurs sentiments de vive voix ou par écrit en langage correct.
>
> (Désirat and Hordé 1988: 97)

When we consider the firm implantation of the French language and the demise of regional languages and the dialects of French today (in contrast to the multiplicity of Romance dialects which are still widely spoken in Spain and, especially, Italy), we can only conclude that the *instituteurs* have very effectively carried out the precepts of their training. However, they have also clearly been helped by the willingness of their pupils to coop-erate in the diffusion of Standard French in the context of a new social and economic order, and in the light of the perceived advantages and opportunities to be gained in mastering the national tongue.

7   French in the twentieth century: protection from the Coca-Cola culture!

The present-day diffusion and status of French, both nationally and inter-nationally (1: 1–3), is impressive when compared with its modest beginnings as just one of the many medieval varieties of the Langue d'Oïl. Yet much of the discourse surrounding the French language in the twentieth century was marked by anxiety and the feeling that it was somehow under threat (and note once again the important focusing effect of such ideas). Just as in the seventeenth and eighteenth centuries concern over the contamination of French by provincial or popular usage led to moves to preserve the norms of the language, so, in the twentieth century, there was a preoccupation with the defence of French. On the one hand, an outside enemy is identified in the all-pervasive international presence of the English language and Anglo-American culture (disparagingly referred to as the 'Coca-Cola culture') and, on the other, partly as a consequence of this influential culture, an enemy within is identified in the growing laxity of French speakers, whose syntax and vocabulary deviate from the ideal codified written standard and are corrupted by the vagaries of spoken usage and borrowings from English. The following quote from the journal *Défense de la langue française* (published by the Académie-sponsored association of the same name) is a characteristic expression of these views: 'Notre langue est de plus en plus menacée, tant dans sa forme, par la prolifération des fautes de style, de grammaire, d'orthographe, que par l'invasion de la langue anglaise' (March 1991, quoted in Ball 1997: 206).

All these concerns seem to derive from what might almost be termed a loss of confidence in itself on the part of the French nation (see Flaitz 1988). In fact, the identification of Anglo-American as an external threat isn't really in tune with historical reality, since, from 1870 onwards, the most obvious external threat to France was from Germany. France's transformed status on the international scene has been at the heart of this loss of confidence (Gordon 1978: ch. 2). Following the economic crisis years of the 1930s, the French suffered a series of psychologically damaging blows to their prestige, starting with the German occupation (1940–4) and the lingering memory of France's collaboration. These psychological blows to the French nation's self-confidence continued with the loss of the Far-Eastern Empire (French Indo-China) in the early 1950s and culminated with the Algerian War of Independence. Throughout this period, France had a succession of weak and ineffectual governments and, by the end of the 1950s, was ripe for political reform. On the linguistic plane this loss of confidence translated itself into attitudes like the following:

Elle [la langue française] perd ses qualités, néglige ce qu'il y avait en elle d'inattaquable et de permanent. Baragouin, le français tel qu'on le parle parodie à peine ... les élégances classiques et les références littéraires. Décadences encore du style et du ton comme si, d'un même mouvement de ressac, la langue perdait son caractère universel et son talent d'éternité.

(Beaucé 1988: 13–14)

It was with the strongly patriotic figure of General de Gaulle that France began to renew its national identity. Having been the leader of France's government in exile during the Second World War occupation, de Gaulle was an important symbol of French pride and national identity. It isn't therefore surprising that during the presidency of de Gaulle the linguistic debate about the protection of the French language hotted up. The particular target of patriotic venom in the 1960s was Anglo-American vocabulary which had been borrowed into French. The best-known statement of this linguistic patriotism is René Etiemble's *Parlez-vous franglais?* where 'l'anglofolie' is painted as having created '[un] sabir atlantique, cette variété new look du franglais' (1964: 33). (*Un sabir* is a term for a language which is composed of words and structures borrowed from a variety of different, and unrelated, languages; the term is pejorative.) Etiemble's book, at a distance of nearly forty years, can be viewed as a massive overreaction at a time when France's political identity was being redefined. The attitudes which gave rise to the climate in which Etiemble wrote have more recently been described in the following terms: 'Ainsi, la condamnation des emprunts américains, loin d'etre fondée sur la réalité d'une menace, n'est que l'expression détournée d'un anti-américanisme nourri par la nostalgie du prestige d'autrefois' (Hagège 1987: 113).

The tangible result of the linguistic anti-Americanism of the 1960s (which *comme par hasard* coincides with France's withdrawal from NATO) was renewed direct state intervention in language policy concerning both corpus and status planning. Corpus planning came to the fore through the setting up of organisations to develop officially approved terminology, monitor the quality of French used in official documents and the media, and safeguard the position of the French language internationally. The first of these government bodies to be established was Le Haut Comité pour la défense et l'expansion de la langue française (1966), attached to the Prime Minister's office. Its principal objectives were threefold: (i) to study and recommend measures to ensure the defence and the expansion of the French language; (ii) to establish the necessary links with private and public organisations with competence in matters of cultural and technical cooperation; (iii) to promote and encourage all initiatives linked to the defence and expansion of the French language, and to evaluate the results achieved (for further details, see Bostock 1986: 64). The committee (renamed in 1973 Haut Comité de la langue française) has been responsible for setting up Commissions ministérielles de terminologie, whose task is to establish official terminology in specialised fields and suggest appropriate alternatives to borrowings. In the most recent reorganisation of these official institutions (1989) the Conseil supérieur de la langue française (whose members include the Prime Minister, the minister for education and the *secrétaire perpétuel* of the Académie française) is responsible for the promotion of French abroad, while the Délégation générale à la langue française formulates, implements and monitors governmental language policy, and coordinates the work of the ministerial commissions whose decisions are periodically brought together in a *Dictionnaire des termes officiels*. To quote a few examples, in 1985 *baladeur* was proposed to replace 'walkman', *logiciel* for 'software', *commercialisation* for 'marketing', while the 1990s saw the adoption of *ludiciel* 'games software', *didacticiel* 'educational software', *cédérom* 'CD-ROM' and *message électronique*, abbreviated to *mél*, 'e-mail'. However, despite these official efforts to ward off the inroads of English terms, and although linguists (such as Hagège) may reject the idea that French is under serious threat from English, media journalists in particular are frequently the target of condemnation by zealous observers of 'abuses of the language' in terms strikingly reminiscent of those of Etiemble: 'Parce qu'"occasion" se dit en anglais "opportunity", tout n'est plus qu'"opportunités". C'est d'un ridicule achevé, et cela constitue, surtout, une preuve supplémentaire de l'invasion du français par un patois planétaire à base de sabir américanoïde' (Jean Dutourd, member of the Académie française, 'Les choses de la vie', *Le Nouvel Observateur* 20–26 August 1998).

Besides vocabulary, the government continues to play an important role in controlling grammar. This legislative function, as already noted, devolved to the *ministre de l'instruction publique* during the Third Republic, and is now entrusted to *le ministre de l'éducation nationale*. Consider some of the following *tolérances* issued in 1977, as instructions to teachers and examiners, by the then minister René Haby in the *Journal officiel de la République française*:

11 Accord du participe passé conjugué avec *avoir* dans une forme verbale précédée de *en* complément de cette forme verbale:
J'ai laissé sur l'arbre plus de cerises que je n'en ai CUEILLI.
J'ai laissé sur l'arbre plus de cerises que je n'en ai CUEILLIES.
L'usage admet l'un et l'autre accord.

23 *Avoir l'air:*
Elle a l'air doux.
Elle a l'air douce.
L'usage admet que, selon l'intention, l'adjectif s'accorde avec le mot *air* ou avec le sujet du verbe *avoir*. On admettra l'un et l'autre dans tous les cas.

(Grevisse 1994: 1431, 1435)

The latter part of the twentieth century also saw a return to status planning, using direct linguistic legislation, to enforce the use of French and confirm its status. For example, in 1992, the French constitution was amended to stress that French is the official language of the Republic: *La langue de la République est le français*. However, the first venture into the domain of legislation in the post-war era was the *Loi Bas–Lauriol* (1975), which laid down three domains in which the use of French was to be compulsory, namely work contracts, advertising and consumer information. As a general principle it established that: '(L)e recours à tout terme étranger est prohibé lorsqu'il existe une expression ou un terme approuvés dans les conditions prévues par le décret de 1972 relatif à l'enrichissement de la langue' (*L'Express*, 23 November 1984: 73).

In order to oversee the application of this law, a sort of French language consumer watchdog committee was set up in 1976, L'Association générale des usagers de la langue française (AGULF). Its aim was to provide a forum for those French speakers who are 'soucieux de défendre leur commun patrimoine linguistique et culturel' and to initiate proceedings against those who breached the provisions of the law. However, despite a small number of successful prosecutions, the impact of the *Loi Bas–Lauriol* remained slight, as it was only poorly enforced (Judge 1993). In recognition of this fact, and to provide a more vigorous response to the continued perceived threat to the integrity of the French language, in 1994 the then *ministre de la culture et de la francophonie*, Jacques Toubon, introduced new legislation. The Toubon Law threatens much heavier penalties for failure to comply with its provisions, and requires French to be used in international conferences in France, employment contracts, commerce, teaching, advertising and the media. Whether or not the Toubon Law has greater success than its predecessor, its very existence underlines and recognises the importance of the language to its users as a symbol of national identity in a context of linguistic and economic insecurity.

So, despite some calls for caution, the French government still chooses to play a high-profile role in language planning in France, continuing a tradition, going back beyond the seventeenth century, of treating the language of the ruling elite as an important symbol of French national unity. But this continuing involvement in the attempt to plan the evolution of the standard provokes strong reactions. On the one hand, guardians of the standard strongly resist any change in the language or attempts to incorporate change in the written norm (whether from foreign influence or from the influence of the spoken language). When the government has proposed reform (however limited in scope) to bring the standard into line with contemporary usage, it has met with widespread reluctance, if not opposition. This applies no less to grammatical *tolérances* such as those above (which aren't implemented by teachers) than to the numerous abortive attempts over the course of the twentieth century to modify standard orthography or to proposals to combat sexism in language. Such reluctance to accept change clearly demonstrates the strength of the ideology of the standard and the prestige of the written norm among its users, even today. See, for instance, the reaction of Maurice Druon, a member of the Académie française, to the proposed introduction of feminine forms for the names of trades and professions:

> Ah! ma chère langue française, que l'on admirait tant pour ses vertus de clarté, de précision et d'élégance, ma bonne et loyale langue que toutes les nations avaient choisie pour rédiger leurs traités, régler leurs différends, conclure leurs accords, comment va-t-il falloir l'écrire maintenant? . . . Où sont-ils passés, tous les grands défenseurs du sacro-saint Usage? . . . Quelle terreur soudaine . . . les paralyse-t-elle, alors qu'il n'y

a ni droite ni gauche dans l'affaire, mais seulement respect ou irrespect du fondement de notre culture et du plus grand monument immatériel de notre civilisation, la langue?

(Druon, 'Lettre ouverte au premier ministre', *Le Figaro*, 29 September 1998)

On the other hand, linguists (see Rudder 1986, Hagège 1987, 1998) would agree that *la crise du français* is more a matter of social attitudes than of language, and that the fossilisation of written and formal French would carry the greater threat. See, for instance, the views of Rudder:

[L]a seule peur que j'éprouve pour le français, c'est ce qui se passait pour le latin ou l'arabe – c'est qu'il y a une langue de référence très éloignée de la réalité de la langue. Et plus il y a de surveillance de la langue de référence, de la langue orale qui ressemble à l'écrit, plus il y aura le risque, à force de surgrammaticalisation si je peux me permettre ..., de condamner la langue à devenir duelle. ... J'ai regardé un peu la langue, mais de plus loin. Je ne crois pas au français classique. Le français classique n'a jamais existé ... il y a un français de référence, celui de Vaugelas, qui n'a jamais existé ... qu'on nous montre comme modèle et je proteste un peu contre ça.

(Transcribed from *Apostrophes*, Antenne 2, March 1987)

Rudder's fear that Standard French may become a dead written standard like classical Arabic (the language of the Koran, not the everyday language used by Arabs, which can vary considerably from the Middle East to North Africa) or classical Latin is perhaps an overstatement, but it's certainly no exaggeration when he says that the model of Vaugelas and the attendant seventeenth-century mythology of the French language's *clarté* are still prevalent in certain circles today. As Lodge (1993) points out, there is a risk of creating an ever-increasing gap between the standard formal written variety and the ever-changing spoken and informal varieties, leading in turn to a situation of diglossia. This point may not have been reached yet, but there is concern that the defence and the promotion via the education system of a standard norm, which is increasingly divergent from the language of everyday discourse, disadvantages socially, economically and culturally those who fail to master it. These are issues not just for France but for the rest of the French-speaking world (see Ager 1996).

7.1 A new international role for French: la francophonie?

Political commentators may be heard to venture the claim that France has re-established a sense of self-confidence in itself in recent years. It has put behind it the trauma of the Algerian War of Independence, and the political stability which the institutions of the Fifth Republic (proclaimed in

January 1959) have given to it are of great importance in producing this new sense of purpose. Political stability at home has meant that increasingly attention has turned to the international role of French. The indication over the last few decades of this renewed interest in French as a world language is the linguistic community referred to as *la francophonie*, which we described in 1: 1.

We saw earlier that the word *francophonie* was actually coined in the nineteenth century to describe the French-speaking community. A second sense in which the word is used nowadays is to refer to the loose international grouping which has emerged in the post-colonial period of recent French history. *La francophonie* might be conceived of as the French equivalent to the British Commonwealth, but, while the symbolic centre of the Commonwealth is the British crown, no similar apolitical figure could be identified in France, and, therefore, the symbolic basis of *la francophonie* is none other than the single language which unites the fifty-two member-states, namely French.

The modern concept of *la francophonie* was launched in 1962 with a special edition of the journal *L'Esprit* with the title *Le français, langue vivante*. It contained a number of contributions on the French language by eminent non-French scholars, artists and political leaders, such as Prince Sihanouk of Cambodia and Léopold Senghor of Senegal. The idea of a loose international 'club' of francophone states was born (although one member, Quebec, is part of a larger political entity, namely Canada). The first formal meeting of this 'club' was in Paris in 1986; it was billed as bringing together '[les] chefs d'états et de gouvernements ayant en commun l'usage du français' (Beaucé 1988: 87). Since then, meetings held every two years have gradually defined its organisational structure and aims.

It would clearly be wrong to suggest that France's involvement in, and undoubted backing for, *la francophonie* is purely altruistic, for evidently it has much to gain from the existence of such an entity. Valéry Giscard d'Estaing, in a speech delivered in 1974, expressing his growing support for the founding of this 'club', set out some very important reasons for the maintenance of a French linguistic and cultural presence in as many parts of the globe as possible:

> There is an interdependence between the economic power of a nation and the radiation of its culture. I mean interdependence advisedly. This means not only that the material presence of a nation opens the way to its intellectual presence but also that this, in turn, thanks especially to the vehicle of language, contributes to economic dynamism on world markets. This is why the radiation of French culture in the world must be ceaselessly reinforced and extended. This is why this linguistic and intellectual community one calls Francophonia must be considered an essential element in our political policy.
>
> (Gordon 1978: 66)

While some commentators have maintained that, in the past, 'the economic and commercial side to the movement has never been blatantly exploited' (Bostock 1986: 109), others haven't failed to underline the economic advantages that could come to France from the success of the ideal of *la francophonie*: 'L'image d'une entreprise est liée à l'image globale de son pays. La préférence pour un partenaire économique ne peut négliger la préexistence de liens culturels, c'est-à-dire d'une attraction et – mieux encore – d'une compréhension linguistique' (Beaucé 1988: 16–17).

At the dawn of the twenty-first century, *la francophonie* is still an evolving concept. The 1993 summit marked a shift in the definition of this linguistic community from 'l'ensemble des pays ayant le français en commun' to 'l'ensemble des pays ayant le français en partage'. The idea of partnership is now presented as central to the objectives and actions of the movement, inspired by a common wish to cooperate in economic development, to defend linguistic and cultural diversity and promote the fundamental values and liberties contained in the Universal Declaration of Human Rights (see Ager 1996: 59).

So the success of *la francophonie* is perceived by speakers of French as a vehicle for maintaining the prestige of the French language on the international political stage, as a living symbol of the perpetuation of France's traditionally important role in international politics. Just as importantly, in view of the spread of English as a global language, it's seen as the symbol of cultural and linguistic independence from the English-speaking world and a means of maintaining diversity world-wide.

In that respect, it's crucial to the survival of French internationally that it should retain its position as an official or working language of major international institutions, be it as one of the official languages of the United Nations or as a working language within the World Health Organisation, the United Nations Educational, Scientific and Cultural Organisation, the Organisation for Economic Co-operation and Development or the North Atlantic Treaty Organisation. Within European institutions, French is anxious to retain its position as the most widely used language today, notably within the Council of Europe and the European Court of Justice, as well as in the institutions of the European Union.

8 Final remarks

Having arrived at the present day, this review of the external history of the French language draws to a close. What we hope to have emphasised here is that if French is seen by its users as ideally represented by a stable and rigidly codified standard, this is above all due to official attitudes towards the language, attitudes which have long sought to invest it with the symbolic power to represent ideals such as national unity and international prestige. The next three chapters seek to describe the sound system and the grammar of the standard language whose history we have briefly traced here. The fifth chapter will redress the balance somewhat, and show that, despite all the efforts of officialdom to fix the French language, it is, in reality, a linguistic system which is full of variation and subject to change, as are all natural human languages.

Further reading

For general information about the world's languages, see Crystal (1992). Walter (1988) gives a survey of the position of French around the world. Rossillon (1995) provides statistics about the use of French and information on Francophone institutions. See also Haut Conseil de la Francophonie (1999), which provides an update on a variety of topics, from numbers of Francophones across the world to reports on education, media, economics and science. Gordon (1978), Deniau (1992) and Ager (1996) examine the Francophone movement, its historical and ideological background and the linguistic, political and economic issues facing the Francophone countries.

See Hudson (1996) and Fasold (1984, 1990) for comprehensive introductions to key concepts and issues in sociolinguistics, and Ferguson (1959) on diglossia. Haugen (1966) is an influential study of the processes at work in language standardisation; see also Milroy and Milroy (1991). On the relationship between individual linguistic behaviour and society, see Le Page and Tabouret-Keller (1985).

Lodge (1993) provides a detailed application of Haugen's standardisation model to the history of the French language. For a historical overview of the evolution of French, see Rickard (1989) and Picoche and Marchello-Nizia (1989). See Wright (1982, 1991) for a discussion of the relationship between Latin and the emerging Romance varieties in the early Middle Ages. On Vaugelas's influence on the development of the French language see Ayres-Bennett (1987). Ayres-Bennett (1996) contains a collection of texts from early Old French to the modern period, exemplifying the major developments in the language. Ewert (1954) and Price (1984) offer comprehensive studies of the internal evolution of French. For a wide-ranging study of the vocabulary of French, see Wise (1997), and Walter (1997) for a survey of lexical borrowings in French.

See Désirat and Hordé (1988: ch. 3) for an overview of attitudes to the standard in modern times, and of the official institutions concerned with language. Etiemble (1964) and de Broglie (1986) exemplify the attitudes towards the modern decline of the language; for contrary views see de Rudder (1986) and Hagège (1987, 1998). Judge (1993) gives a historical overview of state language planning in France.

2 The sound system of French

In Chapters 1 and 5 we examine the relationship between the French language, its speakers and society. In this chapter, as in Chapters 3 and 4, we take a different perspective, viewing French as a linguistic system of patterns and structures. First, we describe in a structured and systematic way, drawing on the insights and tools of **phonetics**, the inventory of speech sounds used in French, how they are produced, and how they differ from one another. Second, and more abstractly, we look at how speech sounds are used to convey meaning; that is, we'll be looking at aspects of the **phonology** of French.

1 The point of reference

The very concept of 'the sound system of French' implies that it is possible to define the sounds and combinations of sounds used in the language. Yet close observation of native speakers suggests a great deal of sociolinguistic variation. There are obvious regional differences in the way French is pronounced in various parts of France and other parts of the French-speaking world. There are also differences in the pronunciation of individuals and groups of speakers, which correlate with personal factors and the nature of the communicative situation (see Chapter 5). The first problem, then, in describing the pronunciation of French is deciding which variety to base the description on.

For many Francophones nowadays the point of reference is the variety spoken in and around Paris. Indeed, the political, economic and (much lamented) cultural domination of the capital, *le parisianisme*, has made Paris a focus that now attracts people from all parts of France for a few years or more of their working lives, although many of them subsequently return to their region of origin. This creates a 'melting pot' where different geographical varieties of French meet, mingle and influence one another, to form a kind of neutral French, difficult to identify regionally, and widely relayed to other parts of the French-speaking world, both by the media and by the flow and counterflow of 'provincials' to and from the capital. So when speakers pass judgement on their own or others' 'accent', 'careful' or 'sloppy

speech', or adjust their own performance, they seem to be implicitly, or even explicitly, conscious of the existence of an ideal spoken standard, from which deviations from the norm are identified and assessed.

Consequently, our point of reference is this variety, not that of the inhabitants of a particular province, nor that of native Parisians, but the variety that has emerged out of the mutual contacts and influences between the provinces and the capital. This is the variety the French themselves are aware of, which they strive to master in order to get on in the world, and hold up as a model. Finally, it is the variety which commands not only the widest acceptability but also the highest degree of intercomprehension.

2   The representation of sound

Describing and studying the sounds of a language objectively and precisely presupposes that we can do so unambiguously. In particular, we need a notation system in which a given sound is associated with a given symbol, and vice versa. We might think that a highly literate society like that of France, which has long had a writing system, would already possess such a tool. However, this isn't the case. While sounds are the basic units represented by the Roman letters used in the French writing system, there is no systematic correspondence between orthography and pronunciation.

2.1   *The orthographic representation of sound*

Written French uses an inventory of twenty-six letters (or graphemes), of which six, *a, e, i, o, u* and *y*, represent vowels, and twenty, *b, c, d, f, g, h, j, k, l, m, n, p, q, r, s, t, v, w, x* and *z*, represent consonants. The use of **diacritics**, that is, symbols added to certain letters, such as the acute (´), grave (`) and circumflex (^) acents, as well as the diaeresis (¨) and cedilla (ₐ) provide a further thirteen graphemes, namely *é, à, è, ù, â, ê, î, ô, û, ë, ï, ü* and *ç*. Two digraphs (pairs of letters used in combination with each other) are also available, namely *œ*, as in *œuf* or *cœur*, and the very rare *æ*, as in *Ænone*. Some of these simple graphemes also appear in complex combinations of two or more letter-symbols, of the type *ai, ain, au, eau, gn, ch* and *ph*. Considering the total number of distinct letters (eighteen vowels and twenty-one consonants), there seem to be more than enough to represent the thirty-seven French speech sounds we'll be describing later (2: 3.5). Yet relating orthography to pronunciation is no easy matter, as we'll see.

2.2   *From sounds to letters*

We saw in 1: 3.2 that the French writing system is an old one, whose conventions began to be fixed around the fourteenth century. Since the system has remained extremely conservative, many subsequent changes in pronunciation are not represented in modern orthography. Consider, for instance, *Les poules du couvent couvent*. In *poules* or *couvent*, *ou* reflects a thirteenth-century diphthong which both reader and writer nowadays equate with a single vowel sound. Additionally, the orthographic representation of the sentence provides the reader with grammatical information, such as the plural marker -*s* in *poules*, or the verbal ending -*ent*. The orthography also has to select, from a variety of possibilities, spellings for the vowels in *lES* and *couvENT* (noun), while in a different grammatical context (verb) the same *ENT* written sequence will not be reflected in speech, just as *ES* in *poulES* is not, while it is in *lES*. In conclusion, while some elements of the code do represent pronunciation (such as *l* or *v*), orthographic conventions provide much additional (etymological or grammatical) information, which is not linked to sound.

A further function of French spelling is apparent in sets of words with the same pronunciation (homophones):

ver, vers, vair, verre, vert
père, pair, paire, pers, perd, perds
seau, sceau, sot, saut

Here, the written code operates according to a differentiating principle, which allows words with identical pronunciations to be distinguished in their written forms. French orthography therefore fulfils several functions in addition to transcribing sounds. Indeed, it appears more concerned with indicating etymological, grammatical and semantic information than with reflecting pronunciation.

2.3 From letters to sounds

It isn't always easy to deduce the pronunciation of French words and phrases from spelling. With consonants, doublets sometimes correspond to a single sound, as in *verre* and *ver*, sometimes to different sounds, as in *rose* and *rosse*. Further, written symbols, particularly consonants, are often unrealised in speech, as in *verT*, *Homme*, *poiDS* and *fusiL*. In the phrase *Si six scies scient six citrons*, the first six syllables are pronounced identically, for, in phonetic terms, *si* = *scie* = *ci* and the final consonants *x*, *s* and *nt* are silent.

The spoken realisation of certain letters may also depend on the formality or informality of the occasion. Consider, for example, the optional realisation of orthographic *e* (*e-muet*) in *la petite*, where both [lapətit] and [laptit] are possible in speech, or the pronunciation of word-final consonants. Orthography provides scant clues as to whether or not final -*s* is pronounced, to convey different meanings, in sentences, such as *J'en veux plus* [plys] versus *Je n'en veux plus* [ply].

Yet another problem lies in the different pronunciations determined by context, for example whether the word is taken in isolation or ends an utterance, or, alternatively, whether it's linked, phonetically and grammatically, via its final consonant to a following word. Compare the different pronunciations of the adjective *grand* in the following contexts. Note that the underlining here indicates linkage, and that the | indicates the absence of linkage. Finally, the square brackets indicate the consonant sounds that are pronounced, and the Ø, those that aren't.

il est grand	Ø	*versus*	elle est grande	[d]
mon grand ami	[t]		ma grande amie	[d]
mes grands amis	[z]		mes grands	héros	Ø

We conclude, then, that Standard French orthography isn't at all suitable to cope with individual (idiolectal) pronunciations, geographical variations (regional accents) or even stylistic variation in the speech of individual speakers.

2.4   Regular correspondences between letters and sounds

The discussion so far may have implied that French orthography is of little use in the representation of sound. Yet this would be a somewhat over-hasty conclusion, for there are, in fact, certain regular correspondences between letters or complex graphemes and sounds. Taking a particular letter, we can, by establishing the relative frequencies of certain phonetic values in precise contexts, extract its basic phonetic value, as opposed to its positional value, where certain precise letter sequences correspond to a different sound in limited contexts. In other environments, particularly word-finally, the letter may also have a null value, as seen earlier. Table 2.1, for the letter *g* and the sound [g], illustrates some of these points (see Léon 1966 for further examples).

Before the vowel letters *a*, *o*, *u*, the phonetic value of the letter *g* is [g], as in *gare*, *gomme* and *ambigu*. Before *i* and *é*, as in *gélatine* and *gilet*, or when *ge* is followed by *a* or *o*, its value is [ʒ], as in *Georges* and *mangeant*. The same pattern is found with consonant clusters (such as *lg*, *rg* and *dg*), as in *belge*, *courge* and *budget*. With consonant clusters like *gl*, *gr* and *gn*, *g* has the value [g], as in *églantine*, *diagnostic* and *agrandir*. The graphy *gn* may have the value [gn], but it only occurs in a few specialised scientific terms, *stagnation* for instance. More often, the sequence represents the nasal sound [ɲ], as in *agneau*, *montagne* and *vigne*.

The combination *gu* followed by *i* or *e* again corresponds to [g], as in *gui*, *guerre*, *Guillaume*, *bague* and *fatigue*. It may also combine with *h* in foreign names (like *Ghiberti*) or in place names, and maintain the same value (*Enghien*). The letter *h*, silent in speech, blocks the pronunciation [ʒ], which would be normal for a *g* + *i* sequence. Other *gu*+ vowel sequences exist with *a*, representing [ga] in verb endings, as in *navigua* and *fatigua*, but [gwa] in place names, as in *Guadeloupe* and *Guatemala*. In a few cases,

Table 2.1

Graphy	Example	Value	Other values
g+a	gare	g	
g+o	gomme		
g+u	ambigu		
g+u+i	gui		linguistique [gɥi]
g+u+a	fatigua		Guadeloupe [gwa]
gh	Enghien	g	
gn	stagnation		vigne [ɲ]
g+C	églantine		
c	second		
g+i	gilet	ʒ	
g+e	gélatine		
gg+e	suggérer	gʒ	
C+g+e	orge		
final g	long	Ø	gag, gong [g]

Note
C = consonant.

gui corresponds to [gɥi], as in *linguistique, aiguille* and *ambiguïté*. As for *gg*, which appears only in medial position, as in *suggérer*, this corresponds to [gʒ]. Finally, note that, at the end of a word, the letter *g* is normally silent, as in *long, bourg* and *sang*, unless it appears in a foreign word like *Zadig* and *gong*, and that another, very limited, possible representation of [g] is the letter *c*, as in *second* and its derivatives, or *zinc* (but note *zingueur*).

This type of analysis shows that the primary phonetic value of the letter *g* is the sound [g]. Its other values, or positional phonetic values, are dictated by specific contexts, and are less frequent. The letter *g* word-finally can also have a null phonetic value, or be combined with another letter to represent a different sound within the system. Finally, and in an even more restricted way, [g] may be an idiosyncratic value of a different letter altogether, as in *second*. Such an analysis (which could be undertaken for all of the symbols used in the conventional alphabetic writing system) illustrates that there are some underlying correspondences with sound, which can be expressed in terms of the primary phonetic value of the letter as opposed to (more limited) positional values.

3   The representation of sound through phonetic notation

However, since French orthography has many different functions, the relationship between spelling and pronunciation is fairly complex. Conventional spelling is therefore less than ideal for our purposes, whether we are attempting to indicate the pronunciation of a word in a dictionary, or describe the sounds of French objectively and unambiguously. This is why we need to resort to a different system of notation and representation, one in which, for both reader and writer, sounds and letters enjoy a one-to-one relationship.

3.1 Syllables and speech sounds

When we speak, we don't pronounce sounds in isolation, but in a continuous chain. However, to describe a language and understand the essential features of its pronunciation, we need to break this continuous chain of sounds into smaller units, just as, to extract meaning from sound, we must break down the flow of sounds into smaller parts which we relate to words or phrases. There is evidence (for instance, from other writing systems and children's rhyming games) that most people are able to break down a word or sentence into syllables, and that they perceive the syllable as the natural minimum unit of speech. So the syllable can be said to constitute a basic unit of perception (for the listener) and production (for the speaker).

Although a syllable is the minimum utterance in language, and nothing less than a syllable can be pronounced (for instance, *Ah?*, *où* and *y*), the syllable is itself a complex unit, in which three main phases can be distinguished, namely the onset, the nucleus and the coda. One way to represent a syllable visually, taking the word *terre*, is as follows:

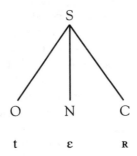

3.2 Syllabic segmentation

Given a word like *université*, French speakers will, without much hesitation, agree that it contains five syllables, and syllabify it in the following way (note that the full stop is used as a convention to mark syllable boundaries).

u.ni.ver.si.té

How is this division into syllables, or syllabic segmentation, accomplished? Note that some sounds are more prominent than others. These are, for instance, the sounds represented by *u* and *i*, where the passage of air is not constricted. These sounds are called **vowels**, whereas the sounds represented by the letters *v*, *n*, *s*, *t* and *r* involve some constriction of the passage of air in the mouth, and are called **consonants** (see 2: 5). Note, also, that a vowel may stand alone to form a syllable, as in *u* above, whereas consonants and **glides** (the final sound of *feuiLLE*, for example) cannot (2: 14). We therefore conclude that a syllable necessarily contains a vowel (its nucleus), optionally preceded or followed by a consonant or glide.

In *université*, there are five vowels and, therefore, five syllables. A sequence such as *Comment allez-vous?* illustrates not only the close relationship between the number of syllables in a word and the number of pronounced vowels, but also, how, in French, syllabic segmentation in speech occurs usually within an utterance, and not merely within an isolated word. Here, again, we identify five syllables, namely:

Co.mmen.ta.llez.vous

Syllabic segmentation in French is fairly straightforward:

- When two vowels are separated by one consonant, the consonant 'belongs to' the second vowel; it is then the onset of the second syllable, hence *animal* is syllabified *a.ni.mal*.
- When two vowels are separated by two consonants, as in *absent* and *obtus*, the first consonant 'belongs to' the first vowel (it's the coda of the first syllable), while the second is the onset of the second syllable, giving *ab.sent* and *ob.tus*.
- However, if the second consonant of a cluster is *r* or *l*, the entire cluster 'belongs to' the second syllable, as in *fai.blesse*, *com.prend*, *a.cro.ba.tie* and *e.ffluve*.
- With intervocalic clusters of three (or, more rarely, four) consonants, such as *obscur* and *abstrait*, syllabic segmentation gives *ob.scur* and *ab.strait* (and not *abs.trait* or *abst.rait*). As Valdman (1976: 86–9) demonstrates, medial consonants are assigned to the following syllable on condition that they form an acceptable onset. Hence, *ob.scur*, since *sc* is a possible onset, as in *scolaire* and *scandale*.

We see, then, that syllables fall into two categories with respect to whether or not they have a coda. Open syllables don't have a coda; they end in a vowel, as in *u.ni.(ver).si.té*, which contains four open syllables. Closed syllables end in one or more consonants, and thus do have a coda, for instance *ver* in *uniVERsité*, or *par* (one closed syllable). In continuous speech in French, there is a predominance of open syllables over closed syllables (Wioland 1991: 55).

This excursion into syllabic segmentation has shown, first, that while speech may be organised into syllables, the syllable is sometimes rather too large and complex a unit on which to base our description. Second, since within each syllable we can distinguish three, or even four, kinds of sound, on the basis of how they are produced or how they behave in the syllable, these smaller units, known as speech sounds (or **segments**), may be useful as a starting point for the description.

3.3   Sounds, phonemes and allophones

Like all languages, French uses a fixed and restricted number of speech sounds out of the almost unlimited number that humans can produce, and organises them in a unique way. These speech sounds can be analysed and described in terms of how they are produced, which is the domain of **phonetics**. Thus, a 'voiced uvular fricative' is a kind of consonant, and the term 'high front rounded vowel' describes a vowel sound. But behind the objective phonetic reality of speech sounds, which may vary considerably depending on context or speaker, there lies an abstract system, unique to each language, in which speech sounds are organised to produce meaning. When we communicate we are able, using subtle phonetic differences, to distinguish between words and, hence, meanings. The aim of **phonology** is to identify the sounds, called **phonemes**, which have this distinctive function in the language. We can test whether a phonetic distinction between two sounds is contrastive (or phonemic) by looking at word pairs (minimal pairs) which differ by a single segment only. For example, in the words *pain* and *bain*, the initial consonants function contrastively, since, in substituting one for the other, we signal a different meaning. The consonants /p/ and /b/, which contrast in a variety of positions in French words, as in *abbé* and *happé*, *rab* and *rap*, are therefore phonemes of French that are said to be in parallel distribution in the language. A phoneme is a minimal unit of a language which provides meaningful contrast; it is represented between slashes.

A second type of sound is the **allophone**. Spoken language isn't a succession of separate units, but rather a continuous chain. Further, the pronunciation of one sound may be influenced by a preceding or, more usually, a following sound. Consequently, a phoneme isn't always pronounced the same way everywhere it occurs. Consider the *r*- sounds in *rat*, *bras* and *par*. Phonetically, these sounds are a voiced uvular fricative, a voiceless uvular fricative and a voiced uvular approximant respectively. (Note that they are all uvular.) Examining the context in which they appear, it's apparent that these three sounds systematically occur in different environments; that is, they have a specific distribution. For instance, the uvular approximant appears word-finally, in *par*, or before a consonant, as in *arbuste*. Further, no context exists in which more than one type of *r*-sound occurs; that is, they are in complementary distribution. Yet, from the perspective of French speakers (who master all three *r*-sounds when acquiring the language), while the *r*-sounds may be phonetically distinct, they are somehow 'different versions of the same thing', and incapable of signalling differences in meaning. The differences are then said to be non-distinctive and non-functional, and the three *r*-sounds are context-sensitive **allophones** of a single /ʀ/ phoneme. As we identify and classify the speech sounds of Standard French, we shall be looking at both their phonetic features and their phonemic status.

3.4 Phonetic notation

Based on how it's articulated, we described one French *r*-sound in 2: 3.3 as a 'voiced uvular approximant'. Alternatively, we could use a shorthand phonetic notation, that is, a conventional system of symbols which unambiguously represent individual speech sounds.

The notation system we'll be using here employs symbols from the International Phonetic Alphabet, devised by the International Phonetic Association (IPA). It is intended not only to be a genuine general phonetic alphabet, but also to provide, for any language, letter-symbols for each distinctive sound, resorting as far as possible to the ordinary letters of the Roman alphabet. The IPA phonetic alphabet is thus an economical system of representing speech sounds in writing, and of indicating fairly unambiguously how they are pronounced. In order to differentiate phonetic notation from conventional spelling in the body of the text, the phonetic symbols are placed in square brackets, as in *gâteau* [gato].

Phonetic notation can be used either to identify a speech sound in isolation or to record whole utterances or parts of utterances (known as phonetic transcription). Thus, it's a means of capturing, in a way which conventional orthography cannot, some of the distinctive features of spoken utterances. For example, it enables us to reflect a pronunciation of *au revoir* as [oʀvwaʀ], with the usual absence of *e-muet*, or linking phenomena of the type *un animal horrible* [œ̃nanimalɔʀibl], as opposed to the absence of such linkages in *les héros* [leeʀo] versus *les héroines* [lezeʀoin]. However, in addition to the basic symbols for the standard pronunciation, a number of diacritics and other symbols are also available to indicate the fine details of pronunciation in regional varieties (see Chapter 5), or suprasegmental features such as intonation and stress (2: 16). A transcription with fine phonetic detail is called a narrow transcription. When referring to sounds that distinguish meaning, the phonemes, we shall, by convention, enclose the transcription in slashes.

In describing Standard French we'll, first, examine thirty-seven speech sounds under the headings of consonant (eighteen), vowel (sixteen) and glide (three). Then, for each category, we'll consider whether these are all phonemes of French, for, as we shall see, not all French speakers make all of the distinctions available.

3.5   *The phonetic symbols used for the description of French*

Table 2.2 illustrates the IPA symbols used to represent the consonants, together with three words showing the distribution of the sounds in different positions.

If we ignore the double consonants in conventional spelling, most of the symbols [p, t, k, b, d, g, m, n, f, v, z, l] correspond to those in the orthography. The *r*-sound of Standard French may be represented by the symbol [ʁ], but this is often replaced by a small upper-case *r* [ʀ] for reasons of typographical convenience. Let's review briefly the other symbols which require some practice before they can be used fluently.

- Note that the hard *c*-sound is represented as [k], as in *cor* [kɔʀ], *acquérir* [akeʀiʀ] and *sec* [sɛk], while [s] represents orthographic *s* in *sa* [sa], but *c* in *préciser* [pʀesize] and *pince* [pɛ̃s]. In turn, [z] represents *s* in *préciser*, but *z* in *zéro* [zeʀo] and *gaz* [gaz].
- The symbol [ʃ], shaped like an elongated *s*, represents the *ch* sequence in *chat* [ʃa], *acheter* [aʃ(ə)te] or *cache* [kaʃ].
- The symbol [ʒ] often corresponds to orthographic *j*, as in *jeu* [ʒø] or *ajouter* [aʒute], but can also correspond to *g*, as in *âge* [aʒ].
- Two further symbols require explanation: [ɲ], an *n* with a descending tail on the left, represents the sound conveyed orthographically by the sequence *gn*, as in *agneau* [aɲo] and *peigne* [pɛɲ]. As for [ŋ], an *n* with a descending tail on the right, this is found in English words like 'bring', orthographically represented by the sequence *ng*. It appears in French,

Table 2.2

Consonants	Initial	Medial	Final
[p]	Pie	aPPorter	hanaP
[t]	THé	ôTer	ceTTe
[k]	Cor	aCQUérir	seC
[b]	Bar	aBorder	courBe
[d]	Dos	aDorer	corDe
[g]	Gare	éGarer	fiGUe
[m]	Mer	adMirer	albuM
[n]	Nu	aNNée	toNNe
[ɲ]	GNole	aGNeau	peiGNe
[ŋ]			swiNG
[f]	PHare	eFFrayer	œuF
[s]	Su	préCiser	pinCe
[ʃ]	CHat	aCHeter	caCHe
[v]	Valise	éViter	laVe
[z]	Zéro	suppoSition	roSe
[ʒ]	Jeu	aJouter	âGe
[l]	Lait	aLLer	peLLe
[ʀ]	Rond	duRer	paR

both in loan words from English and in neologisms incorporating the written sequence *-ing*, such as *le footing* [futiŋ], *le zapping* [zapiŋ] and *le lifting* [liftiŋ].

Moving on, Table 2.3 lists the IPA symbols used to represent French vowels, and makes immediately apparent the discrepancy between the representation of vowels in the orthography, which recognises six basic symbols for vowels, and the range of as many as sixteen actual vowel sounds. Some of the IPA symbols don't appear in the orthography [ɛ, ø, ɔ, ə, ɛ̃, ɑ̃, ɔ̃, œ̃]; others, such as [y], have different values in the orthography and the phonetic notation.

- The symbols [i, e, a] represent the vowels in words like *lit* [li], *les* [le] and *la* [la].
- The symbol [y], on the other hand, represents the vowel *u*, as in *une* [yn] or *rue* [ʀy], while, somewhat confusingly, [u] represents the orthographic sequence *ou*, in words like *où* [u] and *roue* [ʀu].
- The sounds represented in the orthography as *o* or *au* are represented in the IPA system by [ɔ], 'open *o*', as in *Paul* [pɔl] or *sotte* [sɔt], and [o], 'closed *o*', as in *Paule* [pol] or *sot* [so]. Similarly, the phonetic alphabet distinguishes the two French *a*-sounds, namely the sounds which, for some speakers, distinguish pairs of words like *Anne* [an] and *âne* [ɑn], or *malle* [mal] and *mâle* [mɑl].
- The symbol [ɛ] represents the sound often spelt *è*, as in *père* [pɛʀ], or *-ais/-ait* in verb endings, as in *vais* [vɛ], *allait* [alɛ] or, initially, in *aime* [ɛm].
- Other new symbols include [ø], a slashed *o*, generally written *eu*, as in *feu* [fø], or sometimes *eux*, as in *eux* [ø] and *heureux* [øʀø]. The symbol

Table 2.3

Vowels	Initial	Medial	Final
[i]	île	stYle	épI
[e]	Été	fidÉlité	blÉ
[ɛ]	AIme	pÈre	lAIt
[a]	Anne	avAler	sofA
[y]	Une	sUr	reçU
[ø]	HEUreux	malhEUreux	fEU
[œ]	HEUre	mEUbler	
[ə]		mainTEnant	quE
[u]	hoUle	doUter	coUp
[o]	AUteur	impOsant	pOt
[ɔ]	Or	parasOl	
[ɑ]	Âne	pÂte	appÂt
[ɛ̃]	IMpossible	amINcir	enfIN
[œ̃]	UN	emprUNter	parfUM
[ɔ̃]	hONte	remONter	allONs
[ɑ̃]	ENnui	amANde	enfANt

[œ] corresponds to a more open vowel, orthographically represented by *eu* or *œu*, as in *heure* [œʀ] and *cœur* [kœʀ].

- Four of these symbols, namely [ɛ, œ, ɔ, ɑ], also have versions with a tilde (˜) above them, namely, [ɛ̃, œ̃, ɔ̃, ɑ̃], which indicates their particular quality as **nasal** vowels. In the production of these sounds, air escapes through both the nose and the mouth, instead of through the mouth only, as with the other, **oral** vowels. In the orthography, the nasal vowels appear as one or more vowel letters, followed by *m* or *n*, as in *main* [mɛ̃], *parfum* [paʀfœ̃], *bon* [bɔ̃], *enfant* [ɑ̃fɑ̃] and *faim* [fɛ̃].

Finally, Table 2.4 lists the symbols for the three sounds known as **glides**, and some examples of words in which they are found.

- Orthographically, [j], which is similar to the first sound in 'yes' in English, can correspond to the written sequence *i* + vowel in *lion* [ljɔ̃] or *y* in *Lyon* [ljɔ̃], or even *ille* or *il*, as in *paille* [paj], *œil* [œj].
- The symbol [w] corresponds to the spelling *ou* before a pronounced vowel, as in *oui* [wi], *oi(s)*, as in *foi* [fwa] or *trois* [tʀwa], *oin* in *loin* [lwɛ̃] and, occasionally, as *oê* or *oe*, as in *poêle* [pwal], or even *w* in borrowed words, as in *sandwich* [sɑ̃dwitʃ] and *tramway* [tʀamwɛ].
- As for the symbol [ɥ], a letter *h* rotated 180°, this corresponds orthographically to the vowel *u* followed by another vowel, in words like *huit* [ɥit] and *tuer* [tɥe].

It's clear from the examples in Tables 2.2–4 that, while the orthography is potentially ambiguous, phonetic transcription allows those ambiguities to be resolved. Thus, [ləpuldykuvɑ̃kuv] is a much more reliable representation of pronunciation than *Les poules du couvent couvent*.

4 The physical production of speech sounds

Before describing how the individual speech sounds of French are pronounced, and classifying them so that they can be distinguished one from another (2: 5; 2: 8; 2: 14), we'll consider how speech sounds are produced in general. The study of how speakers produce speech sounds is called articulatory phonetics.

Most commonly, speech sounds are produced using an airstream, expelled from the lungs, and modified by the action of the **speech organs**. Speech is

Table 2.4

Glides	Initial	Medial	Final
[j]	Yéti	biLLet	paYe
[ɥ]	HUIt	lUI	
[w]	OUi	LOUis	

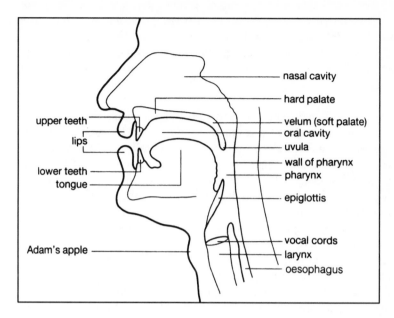

Figure 1 The vocal tract

therefore normally produced while exhaling. As the airstream passes through the **vocal tract**, it's modified by the movement of various parts of the vocal tract (the lips or tongue, for instance) which are brought into contact, or into close proximity, with one another. Figure 1 illustrates the vocal tract from the larynx to the lips and/or nostrils. The articulatory features used to classify speech sounds relate to the way the airstream is modified between the lungs and the open air. Traditionally, speech sounds are classified into two main categories, namely **consonants** (such as [p, t, k]) and **vowels** (such as [i, o, a]). In terms of articulation, the major distinction between conso-nants and vowels is that vowels involve no obstruction of the airstream, while, with consonants, the airstream is obstructed or impeded at some point by the articulators (see 2: 4.3), resulting in audible friction. A third category of sounds, which share characteristics of both vowels and consonants, are **glides** (also sometimes known as semi-consonants or semi-vowels). Let's consider the principal positions where the escape of the airstream can be modified to produce consonants and vowels.

4.1   The vocal cords

The vocal cords are important in distinguishing between speech sounds. Most speech sounds are produced with air, from the lungs, rising through the trachea (or wind-pipe) to the **larynx** (behind the Adam's apple). This is where the vocal cords are located, a complex muscular structure through which the air passes to reach the throat. In normal breathing, the vocal cords are drawn apart, and the airstream can pass freely through the space in between, known as the **glottis**. The vocal cords/glottis are the first point at which the airstream can be modified to produce different speech sounds.

- The vocal cords may be partially drawn together, and the pressure of the escaping air may cause them to vibrate. This vibration is called **voicing**, and sounds produced in this way are called **voiced** sounds. If you touch your Adam's apple and pronounce the consonant [z], as in *déSert*, you should feel the vocal cords vibrating through your fingertips. Voicing is also produced in the articulation of the initial consonants *Bas*, *Dos* and *Gare*, as well as vowels, like [a].
- When the glottis is open, there is no appreciable vibration of the vocal cords as the air passes through. Speech sounds produced this way are called **voiceless**. Voiceless sounds include the consonants [s] in *deSSert*, as well as [p] in *Pas*, [t] in *Tas* and [k] in *Cas*.
- Finally, the glottis may close briefly to temporarily block the escape of the airstream. If the airstream is then suddenly released, the sound produced is called a **glottal stop**, represented by the symbol [ʔ]. This sound momentarily interrupts and then resumes an utterance, and, in French, is used in certain contexts, notably to signal emphasis, as we'll see later.

The phonetic feature of voicing allows an initial classification between the voiced and voiceless speech sounds of French. There are six voiceless consonants in French, namely [p, t, k, f, s, ʃ]; the rest are all voiced.

Finally, note that the frequency at which the vocal cords vibrate, and, therefore, the pitch of the speech sound, can be adjusted. The greater the tension of the vocal cords, the higher the frequency of the vibration, and the higher the pitch. We'll see later that pitch variations produce what is called the **intonation** of utterances, and that intonation can play an important linguistic role (2: 16.3).

4.2   The supraglottal cavities

The supraglottal cavities are the pharynx, the oral cavity and the nasal cavity (Figure 1). Having passed through the glottis into the pharynx, the airstream has two possible routes outside the body, namely, via the **nasal cavity** and out through the nostrils, or via the **oral cavity** and out between the lips. The escape of the airstream can be modified here, too, and further distinctions between speech sounds can be made. First, escape of the airstream through the oral and/or nasal cavities can be totally obstructed, in the former case, for example, by closure of the lips, or, in the latter case, by the **velum** (or soft palate), situated behind the hard palate, and ending with the **uvula** at the back of the throat. The velum can be raised or lowered by muscular action. When it's raised, it comes into contact with the back of the pharynx, and blocks off the escape of the airstream through the nose. This is called velic closure. The airstream can then escape through the oral cavity only. If the velum is allowed to fall, some of the air escapes through the nasal cavity. We can therefore distinguish between **oral** sounds (the air escapes through the mouth only) and **nasal** sounds (the air escapes partly, or wholly, through the nose).

4.3   The oral cavity

When the air enters the oral cavity, the airstream may again be modified at various points (at the lips, for example) and in various ways. Within the oral cavity, speech organs called **articulators** can be configured in various ways to affect the airstream. They can be divided into passive articulators, which do not move, most of which are attached to the upper jaw, namely the upper lip and teeth and the roof of the mouth (itself divided into **alveolar ridge**, hard palate and velum), and the active articulators, principally the lower lip and the tongue. The tongue itself can be divided into the tip (or **apex**), the front (or **blade**) and the back (or **dorsum**). The uvula may also be included, as a semi-active articulator, where it can be made to vibrate rapidly against the back of the tongue, as with certain *r*-sounds. In order to classify French speech sounds further, let's return to the traditional categories of sounds we noted in 2: 4 and consider, in turn, consonants, vowels and glides.

5   The classification of French consonants

Aside from the presence versus absence of voicing (2: 4.1), to which we return in 2: 5.3, two further criteria are needed to classify French consonants. These are **place of articulation** and **manner of articulation**.

5.1   Place of articulation

We noted earlier (2: 4) that consonants involve total or partial obstruction of the airstream in the oral cavity. This results either from bringing the tongue into (near) contact with a passive articulator, or from contact between active articulators such as the lips or the teeth and lips. So the place of articulation of a consonant relates to where in the oral cavity the airstream is modified, and which articulators are involved in its production.

Figure 2 illustrates the various places of articulation, together with the names of the articulators and the corresponding terms relevant to the description of French consonants.

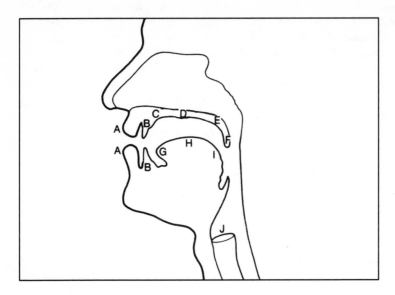

Figure 2 Articulators and places of articulation

Articulators	*Places of articulation*
A lips	bilabial or labial
B teeth	dental
C alveolar ridge	alveolar
D hard palate	palatal
E soft palate (velum)	velar
F uvula	uvular
G tongue tip (apex)	apical
H blade of the tongue	coronal
I back of the tongue (dorsum)	dorsal
J vocal cords (glottis)	glottal

We can now classify the consonants given in small capitals in the following words according to their place of articulation:

Pas, Bas, Ma	BILABIAL: the lips are brought together.
Fou, Vous	LABIO-DENTAL: the lower lip is brought into contact with the upper teeth.
Tu, Du, Nu, Lu	DENTAL: the tip of the tongue comes into contact with the upper teeth.
Sot, Zoo	ALVEOLAR: the tip and/or blade of the tongue is/are brought against the alveolar ridge.
CHou, Joue	PALATO-ALVEOLAR: the tongue is more retracted in the oral cavity than for [s] or [z], and lies just behind the alveolar ridge.

aGNeau   PALATAL: the front part of the back of the tongue is placed against the hard palate.

Car, Gare, swiNG VELAR: the back of the tongue comes into contact with the velum.

Rat   UVULAR: a constriction is formed between the back of the tongue and the velum/uvula.

5.2 *Manner of articulation*

The manner of articulation of a consonant relates to how the airstream is impeded or obstructed as it passes through the vocal tract. Consonants produced by momentarily blocking the airstream at some point in the oral cavity are called **stops**. The bilabial consonants [p] and [b], as in *pas* and *bas*, are articulated by blocking, then releasing, the airstream, using the lips; [p] and [b] are therefore bilabial stops. The consonants [k] and [g], as in *cou* and *goût*, are also stops, but differ from [p] and [b] in having a velar place of articulation, and are therefore velar stops. Finally, [t] and [d], as in *tout* and *doux*, are dental stops. These six consonants are all oral stops, since the interruption of the airstream is accompanied by velic closure (2: 4.2), that is, the air cannot escape through the nose.

The consonants [m], [n], [ɲ] and [ŋ] are also stops (bilabial, dental, palatal and velar, respectively), but the oral closure is not accompanied by velic closure. In other words, while the air is prevented from escaping through the mouth, it can escape via the nasal cavity.

In contrast to the oral and nasal stops, the initial consonants in *fou* [fu], *vous* [vu], *sou* [su], *zazou* [zazu], *chou* [ʃu] and *joue* [ʒu] don't involve a complete obstruction of the airstream in the mouth. Rather, a constriction is achieved by the close proximity of the articulators. The airstream is forced through the partially obstructed vocal tract and escapes through the middle of the mouth with audible friction. These six consonants are therefore called **fricatives**. There are two labio-dental ([f] and [v]), two alveolar ([s] and [z]) and two palato-alveolar fricatives ([ʃ] and [ʒ]).

In addition to stops and fricatives, note the uvular [ʀ] of Standard French, which some speakers produce with distinctly audible friction, as the tongue is retracted to the back of the mouth, and narrows the passage of the airstream between the tongue and the soft palate. For other speakers, the constriction is too slight to produce friction, in which case [ʀ] is called an **approximant** (2: 3.3).

The initial sound in *lu* is often grouped together with the *r*-sounds under the heading of approximants since, as a rule, it is pronounced without friction. However, [l] is articulated in a different way. The tongue is placed behind the upper front teeth (hence its label: dental or dental-alveolar), and causes an obstruction of the airstream in the centre of the oral cavity. Nevertheless, the air can escape over the sides of the tongue.

Table 2.5

	Voiced	Voiceless
oral stops	b d g	p t k
nasal stops	m n ɲ ŋ	
fricatives	v z ʒ	f s ʃ

Table 2.6

Place of articulation \ Manner of articulation	Stop	Fricative	Nasal	Approximant	Lateral
bilabial	p b		m		
labio-dental		f v			
dental	t d		n		
alveolar		s z			l
palato-alveolar		ʃ ʒ			
palatal			ɲ		
velar	k g		ŋ		
uvular				ʀ	

The consonant is therefore called a lateral consonant, as opposed to all the other consonants which are central.

5.3   Voicing

The presence or absence of voicing, that is vibration of the vocal cords (2: 4.1), is the final criterion we need to distinguish between the three pairs of oral stops and the three pairs of fricatives (see Table 2.5). The difference between [p] and [b] (which have the same manner and place of articulation) is that the vocal cords don't vibrate during the production of [p], which is voiceless, while they do with [b], which is voiced. On the basis of these three criteria (place of articulation, manner of articulation, voicing), we can summarise, as in Table 2.6, the distinct phonetic features of French consonants. However, this table calls for three remarks:

1   Where two symbols appear in the same cell, the voiceless consonant is on the left, the voiced on the right.
2   The symbol [ʀ] represents the urban pronunciation of Standard French, although several other *r*-sounds exist, in particular, the apico-alveolar [r], produced by rapid vibration of the tongue tip against the alveolar ridge, prevalent in many rural areas of France (notably in the south), as well as outside France, for example in Quebec.
3   The table includes both a velar and a palatal nasal consonant. The palatal nasal [ɲ] predates the Old French period, and occurs medially in words like *mignon* and *craignons*, and in a few instances initially, as

in *gnon*. It has been noted, in particular by Walter (1982), that many French speakers now pronounce this sound as [nj], as in *minier*. Others use [ɲ] in word-final contexts only, as in *hargne*, using [nj] elsewhere. It's clear from the table that this is the only palatal stop (the other nasals, namely [m], [n] and [ŋ], share a place and manner of articulation with corresponding oral stops). The velar nasal stop [ŋ], originally introduced into French via English loan words, therefore finds a natural place within the system of French consonants, alongside the velar oral stops [k] and [g]. This is also suggested, not only by the fact that [ŋ] is readily used by French speakers in English loan words, such as *parking* and *shopping*, but also by the fact that the suffix *-ing* (with a velar nasal pronunciation) now has some autonomy within French morphology, and appears in new words, for example *zapping*, *pressing* and *brushing*, which either don't exist in English, or have a different meaning.

All these consonants, with the exception of [ɲ] and [ŋ], are undisputably phonemes within French phonology, since they all contrast meaningfully in parallel distribution, and differ from each other by at least one phonetic feature. For instance, the bilabial /p/, /b/ and /m/ contrast with the dental /t/, /d/ and /n/, and /p/ contrasts with /b/ in terms of voicing. However, the status of the palatal and velar nasals is much more debatable, since not all speakers have them both in their consonant system. This is why we refer to a potential maximum system of eighteen consonant segments and a system of sixteen phonemes.

6 Consonants in contact: assimilation

The term **assimilation** refers to the way, in connected speech, sounds 'take on' phonetic features of neighbouring sounds, either in the context of single words or across word boundaries. In French, this phonological phenomenon affects the articulation of consonants in particular, principally with regard to voicing. Assimilation can be seen as a process of economy of effort, in which speakers anticipate what they are going to say next, with the result, for example, that, where one voiced and one voiceless consonant meet, one will take on the characteristics of the other, and they will both be pronounced as voiced or voiceless consonants, depending on the circumstances. Assimilation may be **regressive** (or **anticipatory**), which is the most common type of assimilation in French, or **progressive**.

6.1 Assimilation of voice

French possesses two sets of (oral) stops and fricatives, which contrast with each other with regard to voicing: /b, d, g, v, z, ʒ/ are voiced, /p, t, k, f, s, ʃ/ are voiceless. These are therefore the consonants most likely to be affected by assimilation when they come together in connected speech.

In French, assimilation is most often regressive; that is, the coda of one syllable is influenced by the onset of the following syllable (2: 3.1). For instance, in *un coup de pied*, where, in informal styles, the voiced /d/ of *De* immediately precedes the voiceless /p/ of *Pied*, /d/ tends to devoice under the influence of /p/, as in [kut.pje]. Similarly, in *aneCDote*, voiceless /k/ may be pronounced as voiced [g], as in [a.nɛg.dɔt]; in *oBTenir*, voiced [b] in contact with voiceless [t] may devoice, as in [ɔp.tə.niʀ]. More often, and especially within a phrase, assimilation is incomplete, and the assimilated consonant is either a voiceless consonant with the weak articulation of a voiced consonant or, conversely, a voiced consonant with the stronger artic-ulation of a voiceless one. So, in *obtenir*, rather than the complete loss of the voiced/voiceless contrast, there may be a reduced contrast, marked only by the difference in articulatory tension between [b] and [t]. Devoicing of [b] is marked by the diacritic [̥]: [ɔb̥təniʀ]; and voicing of a [k], as in *anec-dote*, is marked by [̬]: [anɛk̬dɔt].

In the following examples, assimilation affects consonants with the same place and manner of articulation:

voiceless + voiced = voiced		voiced + voiceless = voiceless	
un groupe binaire	pb	une robe propre	b̥p
une miette de pain	t̬d	une grande théière	d̥t
un coq gaulois	k̬g	un gag connu	g̥k
un chef victorieux	f̬v	une brève folie	v̥f
un olibrius zélé	s̬z	une rose saffran	z̥s
une bâche jaune	ʃ̬ʒ	une loge chauffée	ʒ̥ʃ

Assimilation also affects consonants which differ in respect of place and manner of articulation, as well as voicing, as in:

on se voit	s̬v	il n'y a pas de quoi	d̥k
une tasse de thé	s̬t	pas de problème	d̥p

In progressive assimilation, which is much less frequent in French, a preceding sound has an assimilatory effect on a following sound, as in the pronunciation of *cheval* or *cheveu* as [ʃv̥al] and [ʃv̥ø]. A voiceless allophone of /m/ can also occur word-finally, through progressive assimilation after /s/, as in *asthme* [asm̥]. Similarly, the nasals and liquids /m, n, l, ʀ/, as well as the glides /j, ɥ, w/, devoice when they follow a voiceless consonant, both in the onset and in the coda, as in:

plat	[pl̥a]	peuple	[pœpl̥]
tri	[tʀ̥i]	patrie	[pa.tʀ̥i]
pneu	[pn̥ø]	quoi	[kw̥a]

Note that in the initial syllable of an utterance, the voiceless consonant assimilates the voiced, either by regressive or progressive assimilation. See, for instance, the regressive assimilation in:

je trouve [ʒətʀuv]   in rapid speech [ʃtʀuv]
je suis   [ʒəsɥi]   in rapid speech [ʃɥi]

6.2 Manner of articulation

In rapid speech, assimilation may also affect manner of articulation. For instance, under the influence of a following nasal, an oral stop, whether voiced or voiceless, nasalises. Thus, *une heure et demie* can be pronounced as [ynœʀɛnmi], *ma langue maternelle* as [malɑ̃ŋmatɛʀnɛl].

Assimilation provides one example, by no means unique, of the influence of neighbouring sounds upon each other. We return to this in 2: 15.1–5.

7 The pronunciation of double consonants and final consonants

In this section we deal, first, with the pronunciation of two-consonant clusters represented orthographically by identical letters (2: 7.1–3). Then, in 2: 7.4, we consider final consonants. In both cases, we note those instances where a difference in pronunciation plays a demarcative role.

7.1 Double-consonant clusters requiring different pronunciations

There are numerous double consonants in French orthography. Indeed, all the consonant letters, except *h*, *j*, *k*, *q*, *v* and *w*, may be doubled. While, in almost all cases, the two identical consonant letters in the spelling don't indicate a different pronunciation, a few are pronounced differently in different contexts:

- *cc* stands for [ks] before *e* or *i*, as in *accès* [aksɛ] and *accident* [aksidɑ̃], and [k] before *a*, *o* and *u*, as in *occasion* [ɔkazjɔ̃], *accord* [akɔʀ] and *occupation* [ɔkypasjɔ̃];
- *gg*, as noted earlier (2: 2.4), stands for [gʒ] before *e*, as in *suggérer* [sygʒeʀe] and its derivatives; otherwise, it stands for [g], as in *toboggan* [tɔbɔgɑ̃] or *Maggie* [magi];
- word-internally, when following a consonant-letter, *ill* usually corresponds to [ij], as in *fille* [fij] and *bille* [bij]. This also applies to verbs ending in *-iller*, such as *habiller* [abije] and *pétiller* [petije] (but note *distiller* [distile]). The pronunciation [ij] also applies to words ending in *-illard* or *-illon*, such as *billard* [bijaʀ], *vieillard* [vjejaʀ], *carillon* [kaʀijɔ̃] and *Villon* [vijɔ̃]. Less commonly, *ill* after a consonant corresponds to [il], as in *Lille* [lil], *ville* [vil] and *village* [vilaʒ];
- *rr*, again, is usually pronounced [ʀ], as in *arriver* [aʀive], *horrible* [ɔʀibl] and *Arras* [aʀas]. For an exception, see 2: 7.2.

7.2   Compulsory pronunciation of geminate consonants

Geminate (or long) consonants are articulated longer than usual, without an intervening release. The extra length is indicated by the symbol [ː], after the relevant consonant. There are two contexts in French where geminate consonants are necessary. First, orthographic *rr* in the future and conditional forms of *mourir* and *courir* requires a lengthened articulation to distinguish these forms from those of the imperfect (see Table 2.7). However, geminate pronunciations don't appear in other future and conditional verb forms containing orthographic *rr* where the imperfect, future and conditional tenses use different stems: for instance, *pouvoir* and *voir*; hence, *je pourrai* [puʀe] and *je verrais* [veʀɛ] (3: 3.2).

The second context where a geminate pronunciation is compulsory isn't signalled in the orthography by a double letter, but, rather, occurs following the phonological deletion of the vowel known as *e-muet* or **schwa** (2: 9). If *e-muet* is deleted and two identical consonants are thereby brought together within a word or utterance, they are realised together as a single geminate consonant, as in the following examples.

Geminate consonants within words

elle procuRERa	[pʀɔkyʀːa]
deuxièMEMent	[døziɛmːɑ̃]
sainTETé	[sɛ̃tːe]
là-DEDans	[ladːɑ̃]

Geminate consonants across words

une noix	[ynːwa]	*versus*	une oie	[ynwa]
tu me mens	[tymːɑ̃]		tu mens	[tymɑ̃]
Il est de Douai	[ilɛdːwe]		il est doué	[ilɛdwe]

Other examples are *Veux-tu te taire?* [vøtytːɛʀ] and *pas ce soir* [pasːwaʀ]. In some very common words and in very casual delivery, other vowels may occasionally be deleted (see 5: 8.2.1), leading to lengthening of the consonants brought together, as in *maman* [mːɑ̃] and *à tout à l'heure* [atːalœʀ].

Table 2.7

Future [ʀː]	Conditional [ʀː]	Imperfect [ʀ]
je mourrai [muʀːe]	je mourrais [muʀːɛ]	je mourais [muʀɛ]
il courra [kuʀːa]	il courrait [kuʀːɛ]	il courait [kuʀɛ]

7.3 Optional pronunciation of geminate consonants

Since the early part of the twentieth century, many observers of the language (Nyrop 1930, Martinet 1945, Walter 1976) have noted an increasing tendency to pronounce geminate consonants in words with the prefixes *-im*, *-in*, *-il*, *-ir*, when the base itself begins with the same consonant, as in:

IMmangeable	[ẽmː]	IMmature	[imː]
INné	[inː]	INnomable	[inː]
ILlégal	[ilː]	ILlimité	[ilː]
IRrésistible	[iʀː]	IRréel	[iʀː]

This is characteristic of the speech of many broadcast journalists, politicians and other 'professional speakers', who tend to pronounce double consonant-letters as geminates. The most favoured contexts are the nasals [m, n] and the liquids [l, ʀ], as in *grammaire* [ɡʀamːɛʀ], *annexe* [anːɛks], *horrible* [ɔʀːibl] and *allô!* [alːo]. These appear to be 'spelling pronunciations', as, for some speakers, virtually any double orthographic consonant may attract a geminate pronunciation. These pronunciations are, however, generally felt to be affected or pedantic.

Finally, there are two cases of geminate consonants which don't correspond to a written sequence of two identical consonants:

- The first context relates to words with emphatic stress. As we'll see later (2: 16.2), emphatic stress attaches particular prominence to the first consonant-initial syllable of a word. One way of marking the disruption of the usual word-final stress in French for expressive purposes is the lengthening of this consonant, as in *c'est atroce* [a.tːʀɔs] and *fantastique!* [fːɑ̃.tas.tik].
- Second, a geminate may occur (again, unmotivated by the orthography), when, and only when, the verb is preceded by the elided object proform *l'* (which replaces *le* and *la* before vowel-initial verbs), leading to gemination of the [l]. While this is not obligatory, and is indeed rare in spontaneous connected speech, it may, in careful diction, serve to clarify possible misunderstandings in pairs, such as:

[lːa]	je l'arrange	[la]	je la range
	tu l'apprends		tu la prends
	nous l'apportons		nous la portons

In conclusion, we observe that geminate consonants in French are rare in the pronunciation for they are compulsory only in two contexts. In the contexts where they are optional, their existence is primarily linked to stylistic or individual choices.

7.4   *The pronunciation of final consonants*

The pronunciation of word- or utterance-final consonants in French is
rather complex, since, although many words end in a consonant in the
orthography, these aren't always pronounced. A useful general rule is that
if the word ends in one or more written consonants followed by *e* (*e-muet*),
the consonant will be pronounced, as in *trait* [tʀe] versus *traite* [tʀɛt]. So

Table 2.8

Grapheme	Usually pronounced	Exceptions	Showing variation
B	*Jacob, snob*	after m: *plomb*	

C	*avec, caduc, Marc*
	ending – VC or VCC:
	  cognac, troc, turc
	zinc [zɛ̃g]
		estomac, tabac, marc,
		  porc, escroc, accroc,
		  caoutchouc
		nasal vowel + C:
		  blanc, tronc
			donc

F	*golf, neuf*	*clef, nerf*	*cerf*
L	*avril, persil, Brésil*	*fusil, outil, gentil, cul,* *saoul*	*nombril, sourcil*

Table 2.9

Grapheme	Usually pronounced	Exceptions
K	*tank, bifteck*	
Q	*cinq, coq*	
V	*Kiev, Tel Aviv*	

R	*par, tour, sur*
	er = [ɛʀ] *mer, fer*
	er = [œʀ] (rare)
	eur = [ø] *Monsieur*
	borrowings: *gangster, révolver,*
	  leader
		er = [e] in -*er* verb infinitives
		boucher, banquier, entier, léger,
		  premier, dernier

M	learned words: *minimum,*
	  radium, géranium, album
		combines with previous V to form
		  a nasal vowel: *Adam, parfum,*
		  faim

N	scientific words ending C + en:
	  gluten, abdomen, pollen
	borrowings from English: *gin,*
	  (blue) *jean*
		usually combines with previous V
		  to form a nasal vowel: *paysan,*
		  païen, fin, un, foin, bon, examen

verb endings and the final consonants of masculine adjectives are, for the most part, silent. Also, the presence or absence of a final consonant in the pronunciation plays an important role in differentiating between masculine and feminine forms of adjectives, as in *grand* [ɡʀɑ̃] versus *grande* [ɡʀɑ̃d], and third person singular/plural present tense verb forms, as in *elle vend* [ɛlvɑ̃] versus *elles vendent* [ɛlvɑ̃d]. Grammatical markers of plurality on nouns and adjectives are also silent in the word taken in isolation, but see 2: 15.3–4 for the fate of word-final consonants within a phrase.

Although the presence of an orthographic *e* indicates that a word-final consonant is likely to be pronounced, its absence does not reliably signal that the written consonant will be silent. To try to clarify matters, Tables 2.8 and 2.9 indicate final consonant-letters that are usually pronounced (with exceptions to the general rule), Table 2.10 indicates those that are usually silent (also with exceptions) and Tables 2.11 and 2.12 deal with the more complex cases of final *s* and final *t*. In each table, the final column gives examples of words where the pronunciation is currently in a state of flux. (Note that the abbreviation C stands for consonant, V for vowel.)

Table 2.10

Grapheme	Usually silent	Exceptions	Showing variation
D	*sourd, vieillard, Périgord, nord*	*sud* foreign names: *Donald* borrowings: *bled, fjord*	
G	after r: *bourg* after n: *long, sang, shampooing*	*bang, gong, gang, gag, grog, zigzag* *-ing* words [ŋ]: *camping, jogging*	*joug, legs*
H	after vowel (rare): *Allah* ch = [k] *varech* ch = [ʃ] *Auch, Foch, match, sandwich* th = [t] *mammouth*	*almanach* [almana]	
P	*trop, beaucoup*	*cap* borrowings: *stop, top, handicap* interjections: *hop*	
X	*prix, paix, noix, Sioux*	x = [ks] *onyx, lynx* x = [s] *six, dix*	
Z	*riz, assez, chez, rez-de-chaussée, raz-de-marée, Saint-Tropez*	*gaz, La pointe du Raz* [ʀaz] foreign words: *fez, jazz* z = [s] *quartz, Metz* [mɛs]	

Table 2.11 Final s

Always silent	Exceptions
in adjectives: *gros, gras*	
in adverbs and prepositions: *sous, dans*	*jadis*
in nouns ending in vowel + *is*: *Anglais, Louis, engrais, bois*	
as a plural marker on adjectives and nouns in verb endings: *vends*	

Usually silent	Exceptions
pronouns and nouns ending in *-ous*: *nous, vous*	*couscous*
nouns ending in *-as*: *cas, pas, repas, ananas*	*as, atlas*
nouns ending in *-ns*: *dépens, encens*	*sens*
nouns ending in *-rs*: *secours, velours*	*mars, ours*

Always pronounced	Exceptions
nouns ending in *-us*: *autobus, cactus, campus, lapsus*	*abus, jus, talus, obus*

Table 2.12 Final t

Always silent
as part of verb ending: *chantait, est, fait*

Usually silent	Exceptions
in endings:	
-ait: *souhait*	*en fait*
-et: *replet*	*net*
-at: *chat*	*mat*
-aut: *saut*	
-oit: *droit*	
-ot: *sot*	*dot*
-uit: *fruit*	
nouns and adjectives ending in *-it, -out, -ut*: *bandit, récit, habit, début, salut, bout, goût*	*août, but* (some variation)
after nasal vowel: *lent, gant*	
after *r*: *art, vert*	*flirt, yaourt* (some variation)

Usually pronounced	Exceptions
Nouns, adjectives ending in *-ct*: *intellect, verdict, strict, correct, compact*	*distinct, succinct*
After *l, p, s*: *volt, concept, ouest*	*exact, suspect* (some variation: [kt] or silent)
foreign words, scientific terms ending in *-it, -ut, -out*: *déficit, transit, azimut, brut, scout, knout*	

- With a number of vowel +s endings it isn't easy to predict whether or not the s will be pronounced, since almost as many examples can be found requiring final s to be pronounced as requiring it to be silent. However, a general rule that scientific words, foreign words and mono-syllabic words are more likely to have a pronunciation of final s does hold true more or less.

- Note that *tous* and *plus* are pronounced differently, depending on their grammatical function, as in:

Ils parlent tous	[tus]	tous les deux	[tu]
J'en veux plus	[plys]	Je (n')en veux plus	[ply]

- According to prescriptive tradition, the word *os* 'bone(s)' is pronounced [ɔs] in the singular and [o] in the plural. Similarly, *mœurs* 'morals', 'customs', can only be used as a plural, and is pronounced [mœʀ]. Both seem to be shifting towards a systematic pronunciation with final s.

Although a large number of word-final orthographic consonant-letters aren't pronounced, it would be hasty to conclude that French is a language in which final orthographic consonants are predominantly silent (even if they are silent to a much greater extent than in many other languages).

The instances of fluctuating usage given in the tables underline the fact that some items which are exceptions to the general 'rule' for a particular final consonant are tending to move towards the 'regular category'. For instance *nombril* and *sourcil* are clearly joining the much more numerous category of words ending in an [il] pronunciation. Items such as *cerf* and *os*, where the presence of the consonant formerly marked the singular/plural contrast, are adopting a single form with pronunciation of the final conso-nant. Similarly, the distinction between *donc* [dɔ̃k], as an adverb meaning 'consequently', as opposed to the intensifying [dɔ̃], as in *Dis donc!*, seems well on the way to being lost, in favour of the generalised consonant-final pronunciation.

The examples of words such as *legs* and *joug*, for which the prescribed pronunciations were formerly [lɛ] and [ʒu], and the two current pronunci-ations of the nouns *août, but, coût* and *fait*, suggest that, particularly with monosyllabic words, the pronunciation of final consonants is on the increase. On the one hand, this may be seen by native speakers as a way to reduce the number of homophones and clarify meaning (consider, for instance, *août* [ut], and *coût* [kut], otherwise indistinguishable in pronunciation from *ou* and *où* [u], or from *cou, coud* and *coup*, respectively [ku]). On the other, many borrowed lexical items, notably from English, are in the form of closed monosyllables, as in *star, spot, cross, stress, bled, oued* and *fjord*, which may also contribute to the prevailing trend in French.

8   The classification of French vowels

In comparison with other languages, French has an impressive range and number of vowels. The maximum system for French comprises seventeen units (as opposed, for instance, to seven in Italian, six in Catalan and five in Spanish). We shall look, in turn, at the way vowels are produced and classified (2: 8.1–6), before turning to more detailed consideration of their articulatory characteristics (2: 8.7), and the special case of *e-muet*.

8.1   *The production and classification of vowels*

We saw earlier (2: 4) that a major difference in the way consonants and vowels are produced is that in the production of vowels the airstream passes freely through the oral cavity. Vowels are also normally produced with vibration of the vocal cords; that is, they are voiced. As a consequence, in classifying vowels, different criteria are required from those used to classify consonants. The criterion of voicing is, here, irrelevant, and we cannot speak in terms of manner and place of articulation in quite the same way as we did for consonants, since vowels are produced with 'open approximation' of the articulators, involving little or no contact.

The distinctive quality of each vowel results, instead, from the general shape of the mouth and throat, depending partly on the position of the tongue in the mouth and partly on the shape of the lips. The position of the tongue in the mouth, whether front or back in the horizontal dimension, whether high or low in the vertical dimension, and the shape of the lips, whether **spread** (unrounded) or **rounded** (when the corners are brought forward), provide three articulatory features for classifying vowels, namely tongue position (**vowel fronting** and **vowel height**) and **lip rounding**. The fourth parameter, orality or nasality, relates to whether or not the air can escape through the nose (2: 4.2).

8.2   *Oral vowels and nasal vowels*

The four **nasal** vowels constitute a distinctive feature of the French vowel system. They are produced with the velum lowered, thus allowing air to escape through both the nasal and oral cavities, while, for oral vowels, the velum is raised, and the airstream escapes through the mouth, only. The four nasal vowels of French are illustrated and contrastive in *hein?* [ɛ̃], *un* [œ̃], *on* [ɔ̃] and *an* [ɑ̃].

8.3   *The vowel area*

The area that the tongue can move around in to articulate vowels is limited by two factors. First, it is not physically possible to move the highest point of the tongue beyond certain points forward in the mouth, or downwards. Second, if the tongue is drawn back too far towards the soft or hard palate,

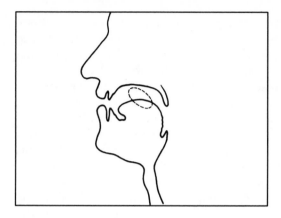

Figure 3 The vowel area

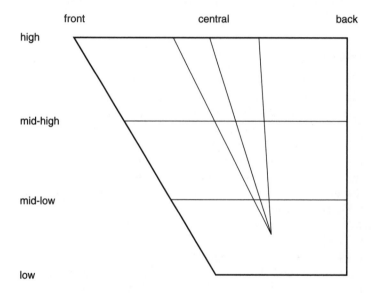

Figure 4 Vowel trapezium

audible friction results, so that a fricative rather than a vowel is produced. The vowel area, represented by an elliptical line in Figure 3, shows the limits within which the tongue changes position in relation to various points in the mouth when vowels are being produced. This rather awkward shape is conventionally represented in a diagram which, for the sake of simplicity, is reduced to a geometric trapezium, where the angled left side represents the front of the mouth, the perpendicular side on the right, the back (see Figure 4).

8.4   Tongue position

The tongue can assume a number of positions within the mouth, but one constant feature is that, when vowels are produced, the blade of the tongue is always convex. To classify vowels, it is therefore sufficient to consider the position of the highest point of the tongue within the oral cavity on two planes, namely the horizontal and the vertical. Determining the position of the highest point will indicate fairly accurately the position of the tongue as a whole, since the tip and back of the tongue slope away from it.

On the horizontal axis, vowels are classified from the front to the back of the mouth, using three conventionally determined points, namely **front**, **central** and **back**. The vertical axis (the height of the tongue) distinguishes four positions, labelled *high, mid-high, mid-low* and *low*. (The terms *close, half close, half open* and *open* are sometimes used as alternatives, when the aperture of the jaw, rather than the height of the tongue, serves as the basis for the terminology.) Let's now take a closer look at these conventional points of the horizontal and vertical axes, and see how they can be used to classify and describe the vowels of French.

8.4.1   The horizontal axis

Consider the following set of words, containing three different oral vowels, namely *lit* [li], *lu* [ly] and *loup* [lu]. As you move from [i]/[y] to [u], note that the tongue moves back within the mouth, from a position where its tip lies just behind the lower front teeth, for [i] and [y], to one where it's too far back to come into contact with the teeth at all, in the case of [u]. The vowels [i] and [y] are front vowels, and [u] is a back vowel.

Similarly, if you pronounce in turn *les* [le], *leu* [lø], *serre* [sɛʀ], *sœur* [sœʀ] and *la* [la], and then *lot* [lo], *sort* [sɔʀ] and *las* [lɑ], you can feel the tongue move from a front position for [e, ø, ɛ, œ, a] to a back position for [o, ɔ, ɑ]. In particular, if you pronounce *leu* [lø] followed by *lot* [lo], or *sœur* [sœʀ] followed by *sort* [sɔʀ], note that the vowels [o] and [ɔ] are arrived at from [ø] and [œ], merely by moving the tongue back in the oral cavity.

What of the nasal vowels? Again, if we compare the tongue positions required for the pronunciation of *hein?* [ɛ̃] and *un* [œ̃], as opposed to *an* [ɑ̃] and *on* [ɔ̃], we note that, for the first pair, the tongue is further forward in the mouth than for the second. We can illustrate the result of using the

Table 2.13

Front oral vowels	Back oral vowels
i, y, e, ø, ɛ, œ, a	u, o, ɔ, ɑ
Front nasal vowels	Back nasal vowels
ɛ̃, œ̃	ɔ̃, ɑ̃

parameter of vowel fronting as in Table 2.13. We now see that there are considerably more front vowels than back vowels in French.

8.4.2 *The vertical axis*

On the vertical axis, four major points are used to classify vowels, corresponding to the height of the tongue within the vowel area, starting from the highest position, high or close (closest to, but not in contact with, the roof of the mouth), down through mid-high (half close), to mid-low (half open) and low (open), where the tongue lies at its lowest point in the mouth. This parameter is sometimes referred to as aperture since vertical tongue position correlates with the degree of opening of the mouth.

Taking the four back oral vowels we described earlier, we can illustrate the parameter of tongue height by pronouncing, in succession, the words *pou* [pu], *pot* [po], *Paul* [pɔl] and *pâle* [pɑl]. With the vowel [u], the tongue is close to the roof of the mouth, whereas with [a], it assumes a low position. Note the correlation between a high tongue position and a small mouth aperture, and between a low tongue position and a large mouth aperture. Passing from the vowel [ɑ], with maximum aperture and minimal tongue height, to [u], which has minimal aperture and maximum tongue height, and gradually bringing the lower jaw closer to the upper, note that, in pronouncing the intermediate vowels [ɔ] and [o], the lower jaw assumes two intermediate positions between those for [u] and [ɑ].

With the front vowels, note that the pronunciation of the vowels [i] and [y] in *pu* [py] and *pie* [pi] doesn't involve a change in jaw aperture or tongue height: [u] is a high (back) vowel, while [y] and [i] are both high (front) vowels. The same similarity in the degree of aperture can be observed by pronouncing, in sequence:

pot	[po]	peu	[pø]	mes	[me]
Paul	[pɔl]	peur	[pœʀ]	mai	[mɛ]
pâle	[pɑl]	pas	[pa]		

Similarly, the four nasal vowels of French can be classed as front mid-low in *lin* [lɛ̃] and *l'un* [lœ̃], back mid-low in *long* [lɔ̃] and low in *lent* [lɑ̃].

The second stage of classification based on tongue height is summarised in Table 2.14.

Table 2.14

	Front oral		Front nasal		Back oral	Back nasal
high/close	i	y			u	
mid-high/half close	e	ø			o	
mid-low/half open	ɛ	œ	ɛ̃	œ̃	ɔ	ɔ̃
low/open	a				ɑ	ɑ̃

8.5   Lip position

The final feature needed to classify the vowels fully, and show all the principal articulatory features which distinguish one from the other, is the position of the lips, which also modifies the quality of the vowel sound produced.

It is generally thought to be sufficient to consider two main postures for the lips: that is, the rounded position where the corners of the lips are brought forward, and the **unrounded** or **spread** position where the corners of the lips are pulled back, as if for a smile.

The unrounded or spread position is illustrated by the vowels in *mie*, *mes* and *mère*. The vowel [i] is distinguished from [y] in *mu* by the fact that [y] is rounded. The same distinction can be made between the unrounded [e] in *mes* and the rounded [ø] in *peu*, and between the unrounded [ɛ] in *mère* and the rounded [œ] in *peur*. The back vowels [u, o, ɔ], as well as the nasals [œ̃, ɔ̃], are also rounded, whereas the vowels [a, ɑ, ɛ̃, ɑ̃] are fairly neutral with regard to this parameter.

8.6   Summary

Our description and classification of French vowels in summarised in Table 2.15.

Figure 5 shows all the French vowels on the conventional trapezium representing the vowel area.

8.7   Articulatory characteristics of French vowels

Particular difficulties in the pronunciation of French vowels may arise for the non-native speaker from the specific articulatory characteristics discussed in 2: 8.7.1–3:

8.7.1   Lip rounding

As Table 2.15 illustrates, one of the most distinctive features of the French vowel system is the number of rounded vowels. Indeed, a total of eight

Table 2.15

	Front vowels				Back vowels			
	Oral	Nasal	Oral	Nasal	Oral	Nasal	Oral	Nasal
	Unrounded		Rounded		Unrounded		Rounded	
high/close	i		y				u	
mid-high/half close	e		ø				o	
mid-low/half open	ɛ	ɛ̃	œ	œ̃			ɔ	ɔ̃
low/open	a				ɑ	ɑ̃		

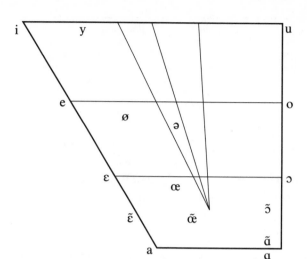

Figure 5 The vowels of French

vowels involve some degree of lip rounding. More significant, however, is the existence of a series of front rounded vowels, which don't feature in English or in most Romance languages, and therefore require special attention from the non-native speaker.

8.7.2   Vowel quality

An important difference between English and French vowels is that French vowels don't undergo vowel reduction. In French, irrespective of whether the syllable is stressed or unstressed (2: 15), the vowel is produced with the same articulatory strength in all instances. In other words, French vowels always retain their full quality, whatever their position in the word or utterance. In a word like *illicite* [ilisit], the vowel [i] has the same quality in all three syllables, as do, for example, the [a] vowels in *cascade* [kaskad] and [o] in *Kosovo* [kosovo]. (For the pronunciation of final orthographic *e*, see 2: 9.2.1.) The vowels therefore require firm and constant muscular tension, in particular with regard to lip rounding, during their entire articulation. Indeed, lip rounding for rounded vowels tends to be anticipated when uttering the previous consonant (if any), and it, too, is articulated with rounded lips, as shown in Table 2.16.

8.7.3   Vowel length

In many languages, a distinction in vowel length (or quantity) plays an important role, and the difference between a long and a short vowel can

Table 2.16

With lip rounding throughout				With spread lips throughout	
pu	[py]	pou	[pu]	pis	[pi]
lu	[ly]	loup	[lu]	lit	[li]
su	[sy]	sous	[su]	si	[si]

distinguish meanings (as in English the difference between 'ship' and 'sheep'). In modern Standard French, vowels are relatively short, especially in final open syllables (those ending in a vowel) and, with one exception, vowel length today plays no distinctive role.

DISTINCTIVE VOWEL LENGTHENING

This exception relates to the distinction between [ɛ] and a lengthened [ɛː] (the colon-like symbol placed after the vowel symbol indicates lengthening). This distinction, noted by Martinet (1990), is now somewhat residual, and is unknown among younger Parisian native speakers. Yet for a small number of speakers the contrast serves to distinguish between pairs of words, such as:

[ɛ]	belle (adjective)	[ɛː]	bêle (verb)
	fait		fête
	mettre		maître
	bette		bête
	tette		tête

COMPULSORY VOWEL LENGTHENING

There are certain specific cases where vowels are automatically lengthened. Since these are determined by the phonetic context and are totally predictable, differences in meaning won't result from this feature alone. Two conditions must be met for vowel lengthening to occur. First, the vowel must be stressed (lengthening affects the vowel contained in the last syllable of a word or group; see 2: 15); second, the syllable must end in a consonant. Vowel lengthening affects neither [e] nor [ə].

Certain vowels are regularly lengthened when followed by any consonant. These are the nasal vowels [ɛ̃, œ̃, ɔ̃, ɑ̃] and the oral vowels [ø, o, ɑ], as in:

pince	[pɛ̃ːs]	pense	[pɑ̃ːs]
ponce	[pɔ̃ːs]	humble	[œ̃ːbl]
pâle	[pɑːl]	pôle	[poːl]
meute	[møːt]		

All vowels are subject to lengthening under stress and when they occur in a syllable closed by [ʀ, z, ʒ, v, vʀ], as in *cher* [ʃɛːʀ], *onze* [ɔ̃ːz], *rouge* [ʀuːʒ], *chèvre* [ʃɛːvʀ] or *brève* [bʀɛːv].

In addition to cases of compulsory lengthening, which serve no distinctive purpose in the language, there are cases of optional lengthening of any vowel occurring in a stressed syllable, regardless of the consonant which closes the syllable, when the word is placed under emphatic stress, as in the exclamation *Qu'elle est bête!* [bɛːt]. For further discussion of emphatic stress see 2: 16.2.

9   The special case of *e-muet*

Rounding off this survey of French vowels, we must mention one rather exceptional case, variously called *e-muet*, *e-caduc*, *e-instable* or **schwa**, which raises a number of questions relating to its identification, behaviour and status within the inventory of French vowels.

9.1   *Identifying* e-muet

Orthographically, the most frequent context of *e-muet* is the spelling *e*, without an accent, at the end of many monosyllabic words, notably *je*, *me*, *te*, *se*, *le*, *ce*, *de*, *ne* and *que*, and the prefixes *de-* and *re-*. In polysyllabic words it's found in initial, medial and final syllables, as in:

rEvenir	dEssus	rEsEmer
prestEment	fEnêtrE	mElon
maintEnant	chEmisE	rEtour
chantEnt	joliE	grisE
parlEs	pEtit	prEmier

In addition to *e*, *e-muet* is also represented by *on* in *Monsieur* and *ai* in *faisan*, as well as the verb forms *faisons*, *faisant*, *faisais* and so on.

The traditional term, *e-muet*, highlights the unique behaviour of this vowel within French phonology: either it's pronounced as a full vowel or, under certain precise circumstances, it disappears entirely. While the label *e-muet* isn't entirely satisfactory, since there are many instances when it's clearly not mute, we'll retain the term because of its widespread use.

In phonetic terms, *e-muet* is a mid-central vowel (neither front nor back, neither high nor low), requires minimum articulatory effort, and is represented in the IPA system by [ə]. However, many Parisian speakers pronounce *e-muet* as a front vowel, like [ø] or [œ] (see Walter 1977: 50). As for its phonemic status within French, since [ə] doesn't contrast meaningfully with any other vowel, it must be considered an allophone of /ø/ or /œ/, rather than a phoneme.

9.2   The distribution of e-muet

When considering the behaviour of *e-muet*, remember, first, that utterances aren't normally single syllables but, rather, a succession of larger rhythmic units or groups. On average, these contain between three and seven syllables and are usually indicated by a following pause (see 2: 15). Second, remember also that the disappearance of [ə] means the disappearance of a syllable, and the coming together of previously separate consonants. In French, as in all other languages, there are constraints on the number of consonants that may cluster together, and also on the nature of permissible consonant clusters (see Valdman 1976: 86–9). This is a major factor in the apparently erratic behaviour of *e-muet*. As we shall see, there are some basic patterns in the behaviour of *e-muet* in different positions within the group.

9.2.1   *Phrase-final* e-muet

At the end of a group, or in the last syllable of a word before a pause, final orthographic *e* isn't usually pronounced in Standard French:

Ouvrez la porte!	[pɔʀt]
Où sont mes chaussettes?	[ʃosɛt]

However, where *le, ce* or *que* are (exceptionally) in a stressed position, the vowel needs to be pronounced, either as [ø] or [œ].

Qu'est ce que tu veux? dis-lE!	[dilø/œ]
Pourquoi pas? Parce quE!	[paʀskø/œ]
Sur cE, elle est sortie	[syʀsø/œ]

9.2.2   *E-muet in group-initial syllables*

As a general rule, *e-muet* is pronounced in the first syllable of the group, as in *QuE dis-tu?* [kədity], *sElon lui* [səlɔ̃] and *dE telle sorte* [dətɛlsɔʀt] although in items such as cE and jE, followed by a stop, [ə] is frequently dropped in more informal styles, as in *cE que tu dis* [skətydi] and *jE pense* [ʒpɑ̃s]. However, deletion of *e-muet* is subject to a couple of constraints. First, while it's possible if one consonant only precedes:

dEmain matin	[dmɛ̃]
nE fais pas ça!	[nfɛpasa]

it isn't, if two consonants precede:

prEmièrement	[pʀəmjɛʀmɑ̃]
prEnez note	[pʀəne]

Second, the consonant cluster formed as a result of the loss of e-muet must be pronounceable. Thus, [ə] won't be deleted if it produces a consonant cluster which doesn't normally occur in initial position, or brings together two identical consonants:

- clusters of oral stops, such as [db] or [pt], as in dEpuis [dəpɥi], dE quoi a-t-elle peur? [dəkwa];
- a pair of identical consonants, such as jE joue [ʒəʒu], cEci dit [səsidi], lE long du canal [ləlɔ̃];
- a cluster comprising a consonant and a glide, as in jE lui parle [ʒəlɥi], lE pion [ləpjɔ̃];
- e-muet will be pronounced if the second syllable of the group also contains e-muet, as in revenez me voir [ʀəvne] or je ne peux pas [ʒənpøpa].

9.2.3 E-muet in medial syllables

In a medial syllable within a word or group, e-muet isn't pronounced if only one consonant precedes, as in subitement [sybitmɑ̃], maintenant [mɛ̃tnɑ̃] or samedi [samdi]. However, e-muet is pronounced if preceded by two (pronounced) consonants, as in prestement [pʀɛstəmɑ̃], mercredi [mɛʀkʀədi] or propreté [pʀɔpʀəte]. Note, also, that quelque and presque, followed by a consonant, retain their [ə] when they modify the following word, as in quelques journaux [kelkəʒuʀno] and presque jamais [pʀɛskəʒamɛ]. This is traditionally known as la loi des trois consonnes (Grammont 1894), an appealingly simple rule which states that e-muet is always pronounced where deletion would otherwise bring three consonants together.

However, la loi des trois consonnes isn't totally satisfactory (see Spence 1982). In il sera [ilsra] and elle fera [ɛlfʀa], [ə] deletes, even though this results in a cluster of three consonants. Similarly, in word-final position, when e-muet is preceded by two consonants but followed by a word with a single initial consonant, it may also be deleted, as in Force-toi un peu! [fɔʀstwa].

Also problematic are those contexts where e-muet isn't deleted when preceded by one consonant only. It isn't deleted after a single consonant when followed by a sequence of a liquid ([l] or [ʀ]), the glide [j] and a vowel, since this would result in a consonant–liquid–glide–vowel sequence, not generally tolerated. This accounts for [ə] being present in words like atelier [atəlje], chapelier [ʃapəlje] and Richelieu [ʀiʃəljø]. (Note the contrast between nous serions [səʀjɔ̃] and nous aiderions [ɛdəʀjɔ̃], on the one hand, where e-muet is pronounced, and nous serons and nous aiderons, on the other, where it isn't.)

Finally, in some polysyllabic words, [ə] seems to have stabilised during the course of the twentieth century, as in rebelle, melon, querelle, menu and velu (Walter 1990).

9.3   E-muet *in consecutive syllables*

Where a sequence of consecutive syllables contains [ə], at most every second *e-muet* can be deleted. With a sequence of two such syllables within a single word, it's the second which is deleted, as in *chevelure* [ʃəvlyʀ].

When [ə] occurs in successive syllables across an utterance, the overall pattern of *e-muet* deletion is sensitive to the consonant clusters created by deleting each successive [ə]. Consider, for example, the phrase *Je le dis* [ʒələdi]. Deleting both [ə] results in an unacceptable consonant cluster, namely [ʒldi]. However, since deletion of *e-muet* is optional, it may apply in the first or second syllable in the sequence, rather than both, giving [ʒlədi] or [ʒəldi], respectively. In *Je te le dis* [ʒətələdi], either the first and third *e-muet* can be deleted, or else the second can be, giving [ʒtəldi] and [ʒətlədi], respectively.

The behaviour of [ə] in the negative particle *ne* depends on the context in which it appears. In *Je ne te le dis pas* [ʒənətələdipa], where a sequence of four syllables contain *e-muet*, deletion is more likely to produce [ʒəntəldipa] than [ʒnətlədipa], since the [ə] of *ne* is particularly susceptible to deletion in such a context (4: 12). In contrast, in the initial syllable of an utterance, the [ə] of *ne* will be pronounced, as in *Ne me dis pas* [nəmdipa].

Note, finally, that *ce que* and *parce que* tend always to be pronounced as [skə] and [paʀskə], respectively, at least before consonant-initial words (on elision see 2: 15.2).

9.4   E-muet *within a word-group*

Note an interesting constraint on the behaviour of [ə] in compounds like:

porte-clé	[pɔʀtəkle]	porte-bagage	[pɔʀtbagaʒ]
porte-carte	[pɔʀtəkaʀt]	porte-monnaie	[pɔʀtmɔnɛ]
garde-boue	[gaʀdəbu]	garde-barrière	[gaʀdbaʀjɛʀ]
morte-née	[mɔʀtəne]	morte-saison	[mɔʀtsɛzɔ̃]

Here, the final *e-muet* (of the first part of the compound) is pronounced when the second part of the compound is monosyllabic, but deleted when followed by a polysyllabic word. As suggested by Léon (1966), the determining factor appears to be rhythm.

A context in which [ə] can be pronounced in informal speech is totally unmotivated by the orthography. Here, [ə] acts as a sort of 'lubricant', or avoidance strategy, in contexts where, within a word group, the two final consonants of one word and the initial consonant of the next are brought together in a three-consonant cluster, as in *match nul* [matʃənyl], *un verdict surprenant* [vɛʀdiktəsyʀpʀənɑ̃] or *un short rose* [ʃɔʀtəʀoz].

Finally, note the pronunciations of *à quaTRe Pattes* [akatpat], *une auTRe Fois* [ynɔtfwa] and *un souFFLe D'air* [ɛ̃sufdɛʀ], which are very typical of fairly informal styles or rapid speech. What's going on is that, following deletion of final [ə] (in *quatrE*, *autrE* and *soufflE*), leaving word-final sequences of a consonant + liquid immediately before a consonant-initial word, the liquid then disappears, too. Some aspects, then, of the behaviour of *e-muet* are determined by stylistic factors, and we return to these in Chapter 5 (5: 8.1.1; 5: 8.2.1; 5: 8.3.1).

10   The mid vowels

In articulatory terms, there are six mid vowels in French, namely three mid-high vowels [e, ø, o] and three mid-low vowels [ɛ, œ, ɔ]. These six vowels function phonologically in pairs, distinguished by the feature of aperture, the front unrounded vowels [e] and [ɛ], the front rounded vowels [ø] and [œ] and, finally, the back rounded vowels [o] and [ɔ].

While the high vowels /i, y, u/ are phonemes in French (they contrast meaningfully in all positions, and differentiate a great number of words or phrases), the distribution of the mid vowels is subject to certain conditions which reduce their contrastiveness. As we'll see, in certain contexts, one member of each pair must occur, rather than the other. This, in turn, raises the question of their phonemic status in French.

The main factor in the distribution of the mid vowels is syllable structure, that is, whether they occur in an open or closed syllable, and whether or not the syllable is final. Additionally, the quality of certain vowels in unstressed syllables is sometimes altered to match that of the vowel in the stressed final syllable. This is called **vowel harmony** (2: 10.4).

10.1   The distribution of the front rounded mid vowels [œ] and [ø]

In final open syllables, such as *peu* [pø], *nœud* [nø], *bœufs* [bø] and *douloureux* [du.lu.ʀø], mid-high [ø] can appear, while mid-low [œ] cannot. In final closed syllables, [œ] is much more frequent, notably before [ʀ], as in *fleur* [flœːʀ], *pleure* [plœːʀ] and *beurre* [bœːʀ], and when it precedes the consonants:

b	in	club	[klœb]
f	in	neuf	[nœf]
j	in	deuil	[dœj]
l	in	seul	[sœl]
bl	in	meuble	[mœbl]
gl	in	aveugle	[a.vœgl]
pl	in	peuple	[pœpl]
v	in	neuve	[nœːv]
vr	in	œuvre	[œːvʀ]

Mid-high [ø] will appear before [z], as in *creuse* [kʀøːz], *heureuse* [ø.ʀøːz] or *menteuse* [mãtøːz] (with compulsory vowel lengthening; 2: 8.7.3), as well as in final syllables closed by [t] or [tʀ]. Note, however, that only four such

Table 2.17

Final open S	Final closed S	Non-final open S	Non-final closed S
[ø]	[ø]	[ø]	–
–	[œ]	–	[œ]

lexical items are in general use, namely *(é)meute* [(e)mø:t], *neutre* [nø:tR] and *feutre* [fø:tR].

In non-final position, it's syllable structure that's relevant: mid-high [ø] occurs in open syllables, while mid-low [œ] occurs in closed syllables, particularly before [R]:

[ø]		[œ]	
peuplier	[pø.pli.je]	pleurnicher	[plœR.ni.ʃe]
jeudi	[ʒø.di]	Meursault	[mœR.so]
Eugénie	[ø.ʒe.ni]	heurter	[œR.te]
Europe	[ø.Rɔp]	meurtrir	[mœR.tRiR]

This distribution pattern could be summarised as shown in Table 2.17 (note that S = syllable). This table shows a pattern of complementary distribution, in which the only context where the vowels potentially contrast meaningfully is in final closed syllables. However, the fact that the potential contrast is only exploited in two pairs of words, belonging to different syntactic categories, namely *jeune* (adjective) [ʒœn] versus *jeûne* (noun) [ʒø:n] and *veulent* (verb) [vœl] versus *veule* (adjective) [vø:l], suggests that there is a single phoneme, namely /Ø/, which is realised as [ø] or [œ], depending on the nature of the syllable in which it occurs.

10.2   The distribution of the back rounded mid vowels [ɔ] and [o]

In final open syllables, the back rounded mid vowels are non-contrastive; the mid-high vowel [o] can appear, as in *beau* [bo], *mot* [mo], *bouleau* [bu.lo] and *métro* [me.tRo], while mid-low [ɔ] cannot. If the vowel occurs in a final closed syllable, its quality is determined by the nature of the coda (2: 3). In a syllable closed by [z], mid-high [o] alone is found (again, lengthened), as in *cause* [ko:z], *dose* [do:z], *repose* [Rə.po:z] and *rose* [Ro:z]. However, in a syllable closed by [R, g, ɲ], mid-low [ɔ] occurs:

porc	[pɔ:R]	bogue	[bɔg]	cogne	[kɔɲ]
bord	[bɔ:R]	vogue	[vɔg]	trogne	[tRɔɲ]
fort	[fɔ:R]	dogue	[dɔg]	grogne	[gRɔɲ]

In non-final syllables, mid-low [ɔ] is more common, as in *soleil* [sɔ.lɛj], *monastère* [mɔ.na.stɛ:R], *corbeille* [kɔR.bɛj], *momie* [mɔ.mi] and *monnaie*

Table 2.18

Final open S	Final closed S	Non-final open S	Non-final closed S
[o]	[o]	[ɔ]	–
–	[ɔ]	–	[o]

[mɔ.nɛ]. However, when followed by [z], mid-low [o] occurs, as in *osier* [o.zje], *oseille* [o.zɛj], *Joseph* [ʒo.zɛf] and *groseille* [gʀo.zɛj]. This pattern of distribution is summarised in Table 2.18.

Contrastive distinctions between [o] and [ɔ] occur in final syllables, closed by consonants other than [ʀ, g, ɲ] only:

Beauce	[bos]	bosse	[bɔs]
côte	[kot]	cotte	[kɔt]
heaume	[om]	homme	[ɔm]
saule	[soːl]	sol	[sɔl]
Paule	[poːl]	Paul	[pɔl]
fausse	[foːs]	fosse	[fɔs]
paume	[poːm]	pomme	[pɔm]
(le) nôtre	[noːtʀ]	notre	[nɔtʀ]
vôtre	[voːtʀ]	votre	[vɔtʀ]
taupe	[toːp]	top	[tɔp]

Since there exists, therefore, a context in which the two sounds occur and contrast, that is, they are in parallel distribution, we conclude that there are two phonemic back rounded mid vowels in French, namely mid-high /o/ and mid-low /ɔ/.

10.3 The distribution of the front unrounded mid vowels [e] and [ɛ]

The only context for a distinction between [e] and [ɛ] is in final open syllables:

les	[le]	lait	[lɛ]
pré	[pʀe]	prêt	[pʀɛ]
thé	[te]	taie	[tɛ]
allée	[ale]	allait	[alɛ]
chanté	[ʃɑ̃te]	chantait	[ʃɑ̃tɛ]
poignée	[pwaɲe]	poignet	[pwaɲɛ]

The same opposition distinguishes first person singular verb forms in the following tenses:

[e]	j'ai (present indicative)	*versus*	[ɛ]	j'aie (present subjunctive)
	j'irai (future)			j'irais (conditional)
	j'allai (past historic)			j'allais (imperfect)

In a final closed syllable, no contrast is possible, and [ɛ] alone occurs:

bête	[bɛːt]	belle	[bɛl]
crête	[kRɛːt]	net	[nɛt]
dette	[dɛːt]	maire	[mɛːR]
treize	[tRɛːz]	perdre	[pɛːRdR]
sept	[sɛt]	j'espère	[ʒɛspɛːR]

This distribution pattern is also illustrated by the vowel alternations in masculine and feminine forms of adjectives and nouns, the former regularly having [e] in open final position, the latter [ɛ] in closed final position (3: 4.2):

dernier	[dɛR.nje]	dernière	[dɛR.njɛːR]
léger	[le.ʒe]	légère	[le.ʒɛːR]
jardinier	[ʒaR.di.nje]	jardinière	[ʒaR.di.njɛːR]

The same [e]/[ɛ] alternation occurs in forms of verbs ending orthographically in *e* + consonant + *er*, depending on whether the vowel occurs in a closed or open syllable (3: 1.1):

céder	[se.de]	je cède	[sɛd]	nous cédons	[se.dɔ̃]
mêler	[me.le]	je mêle	[mɛl]	nous mélons	[me.lɔ̃]
abréger	[a.bRe.ʒe]	j'abrège	[a.bRɛːʒ]	nous abrégeons	[a.bRe.ʒɔ̃]

Abbreviated words may also show the same pattern:

dernier, la der [dɛːR], as in 'la der des der' (the war to end all wars)
bénéfice [be.ne.fis], le bénef [be.nɛf]
agrégation [a.gRe.ga.sjɔ̃], l'agreg [a.gRɛg]

In non-final syllables closed by [R], mid-low [ɛ] occurs, as in *perdition* [pɛR.di.sjɔ̃], *perdu* [pɛR.dy], *fermeté* [fɛR.mə.te] and *merci* [mɛR.si]. However, if the non-final syllable is open, mid-high [e] occurs. This distribution is summarised in Table 2.19. The table shows that [e] and [ɛ] are contrastive in final open syllables. Given that, as we've seen, this contrast is widely exploited, we conclude that these sounds are distinct phonemes in French.

Comparing Tables 2.17–19 brings out a general tendency in the phonology of mid vowels; namely, the mid-low vowels [ɛ, œ, ɔ] tend to

Table 2.19

Final open S	Final closed S	Non-final open S	Non-final closed S
[e]	–	[e]	–
[ɛ]	[ɛ]	–	[ɛ]

occur in closed syllables, while the mid-high vowels [e, ø, o] tend to occur in open syllables.

10.4 Vowel harmony

In non-final syllables, particularly in rapid, spontaneous speech, the quality of a mid vowel in an unstressed syllable may be influenced by the quality of the vowel in the final (stressed) syllable. This is called **vowel harmony**. For instance, the mid-low back vowel [ɔ] may raise to [o], under the influence of a mid-high vowel in the final syllable:

dormir	[dɔr.mir]	*but*	dodo	[do.do]
moteur	[mɔ.tœr]		moto	[mo.to]
automobile	[ɔ.tɔ.mo.bil]		auto	[o.to]

Similarly, the front rounded mid-high vowel [œ] tends to close to [ø] if it precedes [ø]:

peur	[pœːr]	peureux	[pø.rø]
heur	[œːr]	heureux	[ø.rø]

The front unrounded mid vowels are more susceptible to the effects of vowel harmony. Mid-low [ɛ] will raise to [e] before [i, e, y] (themselves high or mid-high vowels), and, conversely, mid-high [e] may lower to [ɛ], where a low or mid-low vowel occurs in the following syllable:

aigre	[ɛgr]	aigri	[e.gri]
aimé	[e.me]	aimant	[ɛ.mã]

However, vowel harmony doesn't affect vowels in closed syllables:

perd	[pɛːr]	perdu	[pɛr.dy]
perce	[pɛrs]	percé	[pɛr.se]
ferme	[fɛrm]	fermé	[fɛr.me]

10.5 Variation in the mid vowel system

While the distribution of the mid vowels described here reflects the pronunciation of Standard French, this is one area of phonology where there is considerable variation. As we'll see in Chapter 5, there are various regional varieties of French, notably the southern varieties, where the distribution of the mid vowels is different. To be precise, the mid-low vowels systematically occur in closed syllables, while the mid-high vowels occur in open syllables. Hence, southern varieties of French have three phonemic mid vowels, rather than the standard five.

11   The nasal vowels

French nasal vowels pose a number of problems for native speakers of English, with respect to both their production and their recognition. In this section we consider, first, the representation of nasal vowels in the orthography. Then, we examine the contrastive role of nasality in French. Finally, we address the question of [œ̃].

11.1   Nasal vowels and orthography

The first problem with regular orthography is distinguishing nasal vowels from oral vowels followed by a nasal consonant.

Orthographically, nasal vowels are represented by the sequence of one or more vowel-letters, followed by n (or m, if followed by b or p) (except for *bonbon*), as in mAIN, pIN, plOMB and IMpossible. These orthographic sequences represent nasal vowels word-finally only, except when followed by a written consonant-letter other than m or n. This is the case, for instance, in bON, brIN, AdAM, essAIM, parfUM, grAND and lONG.

In contrast, a vowel has an oral pronunciation if it's followed orthographically by n or m, and these consonants are themselves followed by another vowel (pronounced or not). The alternation between word-final nasal vowels and word-internal oral vowels (followed by nasal consonants) is illustrated in the following pairs:

vin	[ɛ̃]	*versus*	[i]	vinaigre
un	[œ̃]		[y]	unique
bon	[ɔ̃]		[ɔ]	bonhomme

In other words, a vowel-letter followed by a nasal consonant-letter (m or n) is pronounced as a nasal vowel [ɛ̃, œ̃, ɔ̃, ɑ̃] when:

(i) the nasal consonant is word-final, or;
(ii) word-internally, the nasal consonant is followed by an oral consonant which is the onset of the next syllable, as in *impossible* [ɛ̃.po.sibl] or *honteux* [ɔ̃.tø].

A vowel appearing before one or two nasal consonant-letters, followed by another vowel, is pronounced as an oral vowel:

| inné | [ine] | elles tiennent | [tjɛn] |
| homme | [ɔm] | femme | [fam] |

A few special cases deserve closer examination:

- [ɑ̃] The prefixes *en-* and *em-*, followed by p, b or m, retain their nasal pronunciation, even when followed by a vowel or the nasal consonants *n* or *m*. Hence, *emmener* [ɑ̃məne] and *emporter* [ɑ̃pɔʀte], *ennui* [ɑ̃nɥi] and *ennuyer* [ɑ̃nɥie], as opposed to *ennemi* [ɛnmi] or *gemme* [ʒɛm].

- [ɛ̃] The prefixes *in-* or *im-* follow the general pattern, and are realised as an oral vowel followed by a nasal consonant, namely [in], before a vowel-initial root. However, with consonant-initial roots, these prefixes correspond to the nasal vowel [ɛ̃]. Before a liquid (*l* or *r*), the prefix is realised as [i]:

inhérent	[ineʀɑ̃]	inoubliable	[inubliabl]
inactif	[inaktif]	inexplicable	[inɛksplikabl]
inconvenant	[ɛ̃kɔ̃vnɑ̃]	impossible	[ɛ̃pɔsibl]
incalculable	[ɛ̃kalkylabl]	immangeable	[ɛ̃mɑ̃ʒabl]
illisible	[ilizibl]	illégitime	[ileʒitim]
irrésistible	[iʀezistibl]	irréel	[iʀeɛl]

- [ɔm] The pronunciation [ɔm] applies to words ending in orthographic *um*, such as *rhum* [ʀɔm], *album*, *maximum*, *géranium* and *référendum*. (The word *parfum* is exceptional, and ends with the nasal vowel [œ̃].)
- [im, em, am] These pronunciations correspond to word-final orthographic *im*, *em* and *am* in borrowed words, for instance *intérim* [ɛ̃teʀim], *idem* [idem] and *macadam* [makadam].
- [ɛ̃] Finally, orthographic *en* may correspond to a pronunciation of [ɛ̃], rather than [ɑ̃], in scientific terms, foreign words and some place names:

Benjamin	[bɛ̃ʒamɛ̃]	appendicite	[apɛ̃disit]	Agen	[aʒɛ̃]
Rubens	[ʀybɛ̃s]	pentagone	[pɛ̃tagɔn]	Amiens	[amjɛ̃]

11.2 The contrastive role of nasality in French

The phonetic difference between an oral and a nasal vowel is contrastive in French, that is, it allows meaning distinctions to be made:

motte	[mɔt]	*versus*	monte	[mɔ̃t]
las	[lɑ]		lent	[lɑ̃]
dais	[dɛ]		daim	[dɛ̃]

Further, the alternation between a nasal vowel, on the one hand, and an oral vowel followed by a nasal consonant, on the other, can distinguish masculine from feminine forms in morphologically related nouns, pronouns and adjectives, as in *paysan/paysanne*, *cousin/cousine*, *mien/mienne* and *certain/certaine*.

With a number of verbs, these alternations also distinguish singular from plural forms in the present indicative, and the singular forms of the present indicative from those of the subjunctive, in verbs like *tenir*, *venir* and *prendre* (3: 3.2). The same oral/nasal vowel alternations occur in derivationally

Table 2.20

Noun	Verb	Adjective	Adverb
[ɔ̃] nasal V	[ɔ] oral V	[ɑ̃] nasal V	[a] oral V
pardon	pardonner	brillant	brillamment
bouton	boutonner	patient	patiemment
savon	savonner	constant	constamment

related words, for example nouns and their related verbs, or adjectives and derived adverbs (see Table 2.20).

Similarly, nouns derived from stems, to which a suffix has been added, exhibit the same pattern of alternation between oral and nasal vowel:

an	[ɑ̃]	annuel	[a]
son	[ɔ̃]	sonorisation	[ɔ]
bain	[ɛ̃]	baignade	[ɛ]
parfum	[œ̃]	parfumeur	[y]
un	[œ̃]	unité	[y]
matin	[ɛ̃]	matinée	[i]

Note how, in these examples, the mid-low and low vowels, namely [ɛ, ɔ, a], alternate with their corresponding nasal vowels, namely [ɛ̃, œ̃, ɔ̃, ɑ̃], whereas the high vowels [i] and [y], which don't have corresponding nasal vowels, alternate with the nearest available nasals, namely [ɛ̃] and [œ̃], respectively.

11.3   The nasal vowel [œ̃]

There are numerous minimal pairs in French, in which the meaning distinction rests upon the contrast between the three nasal vowels [ɛ̃], [ɑ̃] and [ɔ̃] and their oral counterparts, for example *paix* [pɛ], *pain* [pɛ̃], *pan* [pɑ̃], *pas* [pa], *conte* [kɔ̃t], *cote* [kɔt]. This justifies concluding that these three nasal vowels are distinct phonemes. In contrast, there are a number of reasons *not* to conclude that [œ̃] is an independent phoneme in French. First, [œ̃] is one of the rarest French vowels (see Valdman 1976: 65), appearing in very few words, the most common being the indefinite article *un* (others are *aucun, quelqu'un, untel, brun, chacun, lundi, emprunt(er), parfum, commun, à jeûn*). Second, in the pronunciation of the majority of speakers today, the nasals [œ̃] and [ɛ̃] are not distinguished. Third, there are no more than a few minimal pairs solely distinguished by a contrast between nasal [ɛ̃] and nasal [œ̃], and the ones that do exist, such as those below, are hardly likely to cause a serious breakdown of communication if they are articulated in the same way, since the members of each 'pair' belong to different syntactic categories.

empreinte (noun) [ɛ̃]	emprunte (verb) [œ̃]
brin	brun
hein	un
des fins	défunt
Agen	à jeûn

Recall that the only articulatory feature distinguishing [ɛ̃] from [œ̃] is lip rounding ([œ̃] is rounded, [ɛ̃] is unrounded). Since the most common word containing this vowel, namely *un*, is usually an indefinite article, and unstressed, it tends to lose its lip rounding and be almost indistinguishable from [ɛ̃]. Thus, for the vast majority of speakers of Standard French today (notably Parisians), there are three phonemic nasal vowels only.

12   Front [a] and back [ɑ]

As with [ɛ] versus [ɛː] and [ɛ̃] versus [œ̃], the contrast between the two low vowels, namely front [a] versus back [ɑ], is now rather uncommon. Note that 95 per cent of French *a*-sounds are front vowels, and that contrastive distinctions between the two *a*-sounds, indicating distinctions in meaning, are therefore few in number.

For the purposes of recognition, the phonetically back vowel [ɑ], traditionally, appears mostly in monosyllables, such as *pas*, or under stress, as in *il est las!* [ileˈlɑ]. It often occurs, with lengthening, before [z], as in *phase* [fɑːz], and sometimes occurs after [w] in a few monosyllables ending with orthographic *oix*, *oie* or *oi*, as in *voix* [vwɑ], *soie* [swɑ] and *foi* [fwɑ]. The most common orthographic representations suggesting a back [ɑ] prounciation are *a* and *as*. Note, however, that the noun *bras* is pronounced [bʀɑ], and that a front [a] pronunciation is usual for the second and third person endings of the past-historic and the third person of the imperfect subjunctive verb forms.

Not only is [ɑ] the less frequent member of the pair, but there are only a few pairs of words in which the [a] versus [ɑ] distinction is contrastive, for example:

[a] matin	*versus*	[ɑ] mâtin
battons		bâton
lacer		lasser
Anne		âne
malle		mâle
patte		pâte
tache		tâche

Small wonder, then, that the distinction between the two *a*-sounds shows considerable individual and regional variation. Many observers of the contemporary language (Walter 1988) forecast the eventual disappearance of the contrast from Standard French, in favour of a single central low vowel closer to [a]. Meanwhile, while production of back [ɑ] isn't essential for non-native speakers of French, recognition is useful, and can offer interesting insights into styles (see 5: 8.1).

13   Minimal versus maximal vowel system

In the preamble to this description of the contemporary French vowel system, we spoke of a maximum system of seventeen units. The ensuing discussion has suggested that the loss of the lengthened [ɛː], the instability of back [ɑ], the almost complete disappearance of nasal [œ̃] and the realisation of *e-muet* as [ø] or [œ], all point to a general tendency within the language towards a reduction of the vowel system. Not surprisingly, the most vulnerable vowels are those which offer fewest meaningful contrasts with their phonetically closest neighbours. We can therefore talk of a minimal French system of thirteen phonemic vowels, those that are maintained by all Standard French speakers, while some speakers, depending on age, sex, socio-economic status, education, geographical provenance and so forth, may, in addition, make one or more of these optional contrasts.

14   The glides of French

As mentioned in 2: 4, glides are speech sounds which share articulatory characteristics of both vowels and consonants, but which, unlike vowels, cannot stand alone to form a syllable. The Standard French sound system includes three glides [j, w, ɥ], two of which, namely [j, w], exist in many other languages, including English (the initial sound of 'you' or 'we', for instance), whereas [ɥ] is rather unusual, and doesn't even figure in some varieties of French. In this section we consider the articulatory characteristics of glides, their orthographic representation, their distribution and their relationship to the high vowels.

14.1   *Articulatory characteristics*

From an articulatory point of view, a parallel can be drawn between the three glides and the corresponding high oral vowels:

[j]	as in *lieu* [ljø]	with	[i]	as in *lit* [li]
[ɥ]	as in *lui* [lɥi]	with	[y]	as in *lu* [ly]
[w]	as in *Louis* [lwi]	with	[u]	as in *loue* [lu]

The glide [j] is pronounced with the tongue raised towards the hard palate, as far forward as possible without creating friction. Since it's pronounced without lip rounding, it's called a front unrounded glide, just as [i] is a front unrounded oral vowel. Comparing the pronunciation of *lit* [li] with that of *lier* [lje], the position of the lips and tongue are identical; the difference is that the tongue is more raised in the case of the glide. Conversely, if *lier* is deliberately pronounced with two syllables, the vowel in the first syllable is naturally realised as [i], again suggesting a close relationship between the two.

The phonetic feature of lip rounding is what distinguishes [ɥ] from [j]. Recall that this is also the distinctive feature between [i] and [y]. Thus, just as [y] is a front rounded oral vowel, [ɥ] is a front rounded glide. The close relationship between [y] and [ɥ] can be illustrated by pronouncing, first, *nu* [ny] and *su* [sy], and, second, *nuée* and *suer*, initially as two syllables, [ny.e] and [sy.e], and then more rapidly, as one syllable, [nɥe] and [sɥe].

The third glide, [w], is articulated a similar way to the vowel [u], where the lips are strongly rounded (just as for [ɥ]), but with the tongue raised towards the soft palate. The sound [u] is a back rounded oral vowel and, similarly, [w] is a back rounded glide. Whereas [j] and [ɥ] differ with regard to lip rounding, [ɥ] and [w] differ in relation to tongue position (fronting). Compare the pronunciation of *lui* [lɥi], with rounded lips and the tongue forward, and *Louis* [lwi], with the same lip position but a back tongue position.

14.2 The representation of glides in the orthography

Tables 2.21–23 show the most frequent orthographic representations of the glides.

As always, a word of caution about assuming that the correspondence between spelling and pronunciation is totally regular. For instance, although the most common pronunciation of *ill* after consonants is [ij], as in *fille* (see Table 2.21), in a limited number of cases this orthography may represent [il], as in *mille* [mil]. Also, in a small number of foreign place names or borrowings, the orthographic sequences *ay* and *oy*, followed by a pronounced vowel, correspond to the sounds [aj] or [ɔj], as in *Himalaya* [imalaja] and *coyote* [kɔjɔt].

The brief list in Table 2.22 shows that the vowel which most frequently appears after orthographic *u* giving rise to the glide pronunciation [ɥ] is [i]. The glide is never found with [y], nor with the back vowels [ɔ, o, u, ɔ̃]. In a few words where *u* follows the consonant-letter *g* or *q* and precedes *i*, it's pronounced [ɥ], as in *linguistique* [lɛ̃gɥistik], *ambiguïté* [ãbigɥite], *aiguille* [egɥij], and in technical words such as *équidistant* [ekɥidistã].

In a handful of words only, the spellings *oê*, *oe* and *oue* represent [wa], namely, *poêle* [pwal], *moelle* [mwal] and *couenne* [kwan]. Also, in a few foreign or learned words where the letter *u* follows *g* or *q* and precedes *a*, the sequence represents [gwa] and [kwa], as in *Guatemala* [gwatemala], *jaguar* [ʒagwaːʀ], *aquarium* [akwaʀjɔm] and *quadrupède* [kwadʀypɛd]. (See Table 2.23.)

Table 2.21   The glide [j]

	Spellings	Initially	Medially	Finally
[j]	*i* or *y* before pronounced V	hier	Lyon	
		y a-t-il	bien	
	ill after vowel		ailleurs	aille
			souiller	feuille
	il after vowel			ail, œil
[ij]	*ill* = [ij] after glide		cuiller	
	after consonant		piller	famille
			briller	fille
	ay = [e/ɛj] before vowel		balayer	paye
	oy = [waj]		nettoyer	
	uy = [ɥij]		ennuyer	

Table 2.22   The glide [ɥ]

	Spellings	Initially	Medially
[ɥ]	*u* + pronounced vowel	huile	Suède
		huître	Don Juan
		huée	suis
			juin
			bruit

Table 2.23   The glide [w]

	Spellings	Initially	Medially
[w]	*ou*	oui	Louis
	+ pronounced V		jouer
	oi/oy = [wa]	oiseau	loi
	+ pronounced V	oiseux	noyer
	oin = [w]	oindre	loin
	+ pronounced V		témoin
	w in borrowed words	week-end	sandwich, kiwi

14.3   The distribution of glides

Tables 2.21–23 show how, in contrast to vowels, glides can't form the nucleus of a syllable; glides occur in the same positions in syllables as consonants do, that is in onset and coda position, before or after an accompanying vowel. However, closer examination reveals that the three glides don't all enjoy the same range of distribution.

The glide [j] may appear in almost any context where a consonant is possible, that is in syllable-initial position, either word-initially or word-internally, as in *yaourt* [jauʀ(t)], and syllable-final position, as in *œil* [œj], or indeed after a consonant, as in *bien* [bjɛ̃].

In contrast, [ɥ] and [w] cannot occupy all consonant positions. Crucially,

Table 2.24

[j]	[jː]
present	imperfect subjunctive
nous cueillons [kœjɔ̃]	cueillions [kœjːɔ̃]
nous travaillons [tRavajɔ̃]	travaillions [tRavajːɔ̃]

they are always followed by a vowel, and therefore don't appear syllable-finally. The glide [ɥ] can occur word-initially, as in *huit* [ɥi(t)] and *huile* [ɥil], but more commonly occurs between a consonant (cluster) and the letter *i*, as in *suis* [sɥi] and [bRɥi]. It also occurs between a single consonant and the vowels [e, a, ɑ̃], as in *nuée* [nɥe], *nuage* [nɥaːʒ] and *Don Juan* [ʒɥɑ̃].

The glide [w] has the same distribution as [ɥ]. It's syllable-initial in *oui* [wi] and *whisky* [wiski], and can follow one or more onset consonants, as in *loi* [lwa] and *trois* [tRwa]. It never occurs syllable-finally.

14.4 Alternations between glides and high vowels

In a small number of words, the glide [j] and the vowel [i] are meaningfully contrastive after a vowel:

abbaye	[abei]		abeille	[abɛj]
pays	[pei]		paye	[pɛj]
piller	[pije]		pied	[pje]

(Note, though, that in the first two pairs the vowel also alternates.) Some speakers also maintain an opposition between [j] and a long, or geminate form, [jː], to distinguish the first person plural present tense forms from imperfect and subjunctive forms, as shown in Table 2.24.

Normally, when a vowel-initial suffix is added to a word ending in a high vowel such as [i], the high vowel becomes a glide such as [j], in a process called gliding. Two high vowels in hiatus are thereby reduced to a glide + vowel sequence, resulting in a monosyllabic pronunciation, a phenomenon called synaeresis, as in:

lit	[li]	*versus*	liant	[ljɑ̃]
scie	[si]		scier	[sje]
école	[ekɔl]		écolier	[ekɔlje]

After a consonant + liquid cluster, gliding doesn't occur; [i] is retained, and a transition jod ([j]) is inserted between [i] and the following vowel. This results in a bisyllabic pronunciation, a phenomenon known as diaeresis:

Table 2.25

	CGV	CLGV	V+
[i]	–	+	+
[j]	+	–	+

riant	[ʀjɑ̃]	*versus*	brillant [bʀi.jɑ̃]
liez	[lje]		pliez [pli.je]
riez	[ʀje]		criez [kʀi.je]

Finally, gliding doesn't occur with prefixes, in compounds, or across word boundaries, for example *elle y habite* [ɛl.i.a.bit], *anti-aérien* [ɑ̃.ti.a.e.ʀjɛ̃] and *demi-écrémé* [də.mi.e.kʀe.me]. Note, though, that in the common phrase *il y a, y a* is often realised as [ja].

The alternation between [i] and [j] is summarised in Table 2.25. Recall that, while VG and CGV sequences are possible within a single syllable, CLG sequences are pronounced as CL [i] + GV across syllable boundaries (where C = consonant, G = glide, V = vowel, L = liquid (l/ʀ) and +/– signal the contexts where the vowel or the glide are present or absent). Note the pattern of parallel distribution; meaningful contrasts can hinge on the vowel-versus-glide distinction post-vocalically. The speech sounds /i/ and /j/ must therefore both be considered phonemes of French.

With the alternation between [y] and [ɥ], in contrast, no morphologically related, minimal pairs are distinguished by this contrast. Also, as we saw earlier, the glide [ɥ] and the vowel [y] cannot alternate after a vowel, since [ɥ] cannot appear syllable-finally. The only opposition, therefore, will occur before a vowel. For example, suffixation causes [y] to glide to [ɥ] syllable-internally after a single consonant:

pue [py]	puer [pɥe]
sue [sy]	suer [sɥe]

However, after a consonant + liquid cluster, suffixation doesn't trigger gliding, as in *glue* [gly] versus *gluant* [glyɑ̃].

As for the distribution of [ɥ], the essential factors are the number of preceding consonants and the nature of the following vowel. If the following vowel is [i], orthographic *u* will be realised as [ɥ], whether it's preceded by one or two consonants, as in *nuit* [nɥi], *bruit* [bʀɥi] and *pluie* [plɥi]. However, if the following vowel isn't [i], the number of preceding consonants becomes relevant, in that, with a single preceding consonant, the glide is used in a monosyllabic pronunciation, as in *nuée* [nɥe], *nuage* [nɥaːʒ] and *ruelle* [ʀɥɛl], while, with two consonants, the vowel [y] appears in a bisyllabic pronunciation, as in *cruel* [kʀy.ɛl], *cruauté* [kʀy.ote] and *truelle* [tʀy.ɛl].

Table 2.26

	C or CC + [i]	CC + V (≠ [i])	CV (≠ [i])
[y]	–	+	–
[ɥ]	+	–	+

Summarising, the glide [ɥ] appears in all contexts, and allows synaeresis before [i], and, if only one consonant precedes, before a vowel other than [i]. However, the vowel [y] appears with diaeresis, if two consonants precede, and a vowel other than [i] follows (see Table 2.26). This pattern of complementary distribution suggests that [ɥ] is an allophone of /y/, whose occurrence is determined by context.

With the alternation between the vowel [u] and the glide [w], there are again no examples of words whose meaning is differentiated by the contrast between them. Further, [w] cannot appear unless it's followed by a vowel within the same syllable, regardless of the number of preceding consonants. Thus, the vowel appears before a single consonant, or syllable-finally, whereas the glide appears before a vowel only, as in *oui* [wi] and *trois* [tʀwa] versus *tout* [tu] and *troupe* [tʀup].

Here, too, suffixation triggers gliding, resulting in alternations in which the vowel [u] is replaced by the glide [w]:

noue	[nu]	*versus*	nouer	[nwe]	nouant	[nwɑ̃]
joue	[ʒu]		jouer	[ʒwe]	jouant	[ʒwɑ̃]

But, once again, gliding is blocked when [u] is preceded by a consonant + liquid cluster, and the vowel [u] remains:

trou	[tʀu]	trouer	[tʀu.e]
clou	[klu]	clouer	[klu.e]

In this case, consonant + liquid + [w] is possible before [a, ɛ̃], but not before a different vowel. Hence, the pronunciations *froid* [fʀwa] and *groin* [gʀwɛ̃] are fine, but not [bʀwɛt] for *brouette*, which is realised as [bʀu.ɛt], that is, as two syllables. The distribution of the glide and vowel is summarised in Table 2.27. Once again, we have a pattern of complementary distribution. This suggests that these speech sounds are allophones of a single phoneme; [u] appears before consonants, [w] before vowels.

Table 2.27

	+ consonant/Ø	+ vowel
[u]	+	–
[w]	–	+

While the description in this section summarises the situation in contemporary Standard French, the behaviour of individual speakers does show some variation. For instance, the lengthened [j:] in verbs isn't always maintained. Variation also occurs with gliding. In the context of the liquid [l], gliding is fairly regular, less so in the context of [ʀ]. Finally, gliding of [i] is more common than [u] and [y].

As we've seen, the three glides are closely related to vowels, but, like consonants, they are non-syllabic. We return to the properties of glides word-initially in the discussion of linking phenomena in 2: 15.2.2; 2: 15.3.2 and 2: 15.5.1.

15   Syllables and sense groups

Spoken utterances are more than a succession of individual vowels and consonants. Vowels and consonants occur within a prosodic pattern, and are organised into larger units, from the syllable, at one end of the scale, to the utterance, at the other, which essentially corresponds to the grammatical unit called the sentence. Unlike written sentences, lengthy utterances are usually divided by pauses, due to the physiological need to draw breath at intervals. The resulting groups are called breath groups. However, breath groups are rather large, and, depending on the meaning to be conveyed, speakers subdivide them further, into smaller units called sense groups, corresponding generally to grammatical boundaries, so that words which are grammatically and semantically connected aren't separated. Pauses can therefore play a significant role in the language by defining the grammatical and lexical boundaries of the various parts of the message.

Connected speech by native French speakers is a regular succession of syllables uttered at a rather staccato and steady rate until a pause is reached. The syllables are produced with very little perceptible variation in rhythm. For this reason, French is called a syllable-timed language, since the basic rhythm is imposed by the syllable. Another feature of French is that not only are the syllables of roughly equal duration, but, in order to indicate sense group boundaries, French uses rhythmic stress, placed on the last syllable of a word or group (termed from this perspective rhythmic group or stress group). This means that, in a string of syllables, only the final pronounced syllable before a pause will be stressed, that is, have a vowel which is slightly longer and more prominent than the others. In isolated words, stress in French is fixed according to this invariable rule, no matter how many syllables there are in the word:

> pend [pɑ̃] – one stressed syllable
> dépend [de.pɑ̃] – two syllables with stress on [pɑ̃]
> dépendant [de.pɑ̃.dɑ̃] – three syllables with stress on [dɑ̃]
> indépendamment [ɛ̃.de.pɑ̃.da.mɑ̃] – five syllables with stress on [mɑ̃]
> indépendamment de moi [ɛ̃.de.pɑ̃.da.mɑ̃.də.mwa] – seven syllables
> with stress on [mwa]

Similarly, within long utterances, stress falls on the (highlighted) final syllable of each group:

Voilà huit JOURS | que j'atTENDS | un coup de téléphone de MaRIE.

Consider also how meaning changes depending on the pauses and stress placement in:

Souvent Madame Bovary   [su.'vɑ̃ | ma.dam.bo.va.'ʀi]
Souvent Madame Beau varie [su.'vɑ̃ | ma.dam.'bo | va.'ʀi]

Thus, the type of stress which in French affects the last syllable of a sense group or utterance is referred to as grammatical or phrasal stress, since it has a demarcative function.

15.1 Syllables and linking phenomena

The fact that French speakers organise utterances prosodically in sense groups means that, within the groups, syllabic division occurs across word boundaries. Indeed, since there's group stress, rather than word stress as in English for instance, there are no clear word boundaries in connected speech in French. It's important to be aware that the word, in its orthographic sense, isn't a phonological entity in French, particularly with respect to features of connected speech, such as linking phenomena and intonation patterns.

We noted in 2: 3.2 that open syllables are very prevalent in French. Within a word, if a consonant follows a vowel, it's likely to attach to the following vowel, as the onset of the next syllable. Syllabic division like this within the sense group results in various kinds of linking phenomena, namely elision, *enchaînement* and liaison, which we'll examine in turn, on the understanding that the unit in which they occur is the sense group. Indeed, within the sense group, these linking phenomena can be seen as a strategy to maintain the favoured syllable structure, namely sequences of CV syllables. With liaison in particular, we'll see, too, that the spoken form of a word may vary depending on the environment in which it appears, and, to some extent, depending on the sociolinguistic characteristics of the speakers and the style.

15.2 Elision and non-elision

15.2.1 Elision

Elision is the easiest linking phenomenon to identify, since generally it's clearly indicated in the orthography. Elision is the disappearance of certain vowels, namely [ə, a, i], followed, within a sense group, by a vowel-initial word. Consequently, the stranded consonant attaches to the initial vowel of the following word by a process called resyllabification. Elision is a fairly restricted phenomenon, since only three vowels can be elided, and even with these it doesn't always happen.

As we saw in 2: 9, elision most commonly targets [ə], particularly in the monosyllabic words *je, me, te, le, se, ce, de, ne* and *que* (as a complementiser or in conjunctions such as *bien que, lorsque* and so on) when followed by a vowel-initial word. The (non)-occurrence of elision is indicated orthographically by alternations, such as *je/j', me/m', ce/c'*, as in C'*est une chemise* D'*homme, quoi* QU'*elle fasse, parce* QU'*il a ri* and *jus*QU'*en 1914*. Elision also targets the vowel [a] in the feminine definite article *la* and the direct object proform *la*, as in L'*artiste* L'*a chantée*. More restricted still is the elision of [i], which only occurs when *si* precedes the proforms *il/ils*. It doesn't occur with other vowel-initial proforms or proper nouns:

s'il vient	[sil]	*but*	si elle vient	[si.ɛl]
s'ils étaient	[sil]		si Isabelle était	[si.i.za.bɛl]

These elisions occur systematically and in all styles, but in rapid colloquial delivery the vowel [y] may also be elided. Since the negative particle *ne* is also frequently omitted in the spoken language (4: 12), Standard French *tu n'as qu'à* may be realised as [taka]. Similarly, *Tu as vu?* may be pronounced as [tavy], and TU (N')AS PAS *5 francs?*, as [tapa].

Again, in a fairly informal style, the vowel [ɛ] in the frequent presentative *c'est* may be elided, as in *c'est un idiot* [stɛ̃nidjo], as well as certain discourse markers like *mais, enfin* and *puis* (5: 7.3; 5: 7.6), as in [mɑ̃fɛ̃] and [pi]. Elision may also concern consonants as we mentioned in 2: 9.4. In speech, following the deletion of *e-muet* (2: 9.4), the liquids [l] and [ʁ], which are often relatively weakly articulated, can be elided, as in *une autre fois* [ynotfwa] and *quelque chose* [kɛkʃoz]. Finally, note that consonants brought into contact as a result of elision may be subject to assimilation (2: 6).

15.2.2   Non-elision

Since elision suppresses one vowel before another, it obviously doesn't take place before consonant-initial words, hence l'*élève* versus *le garçon*. Nor does it take place before some glide-initial words which behave as if they were consonant-initial, or before words starting with what is traditionally called *h-aspiré*.

In 2: 14.1 we saw that glides are like vowels in terms of their articulation. However, with respect to linking phenomena within a group, glide-initial words don't all behave the same way. Some glide-initial words behave like vowel-initial words and tolerate linking phenomena like elision; others behave like consonant-initial words, and don't:

l'oiseau	[lwazo]	*but*	le whisky	[ləwiski]
l'ouest	[lwɛst]		le week-end	[ləwikend]
l'huile	[lɥil]		le huit	[ləɥit]
l'iode	[ljɔd]		le yoga	[ləjoga]

While this contrast is, ultimately, an idiosyncratic property of glide-initial words, it's probably fair to say that glide-initial words are treated as if they were consonant-initial (with no elision) if they are still felt to be 'foreign' or intrusive, and treated as vowel-initial (with elision) if they are well integrated in the lexicon of French.

Table 2.28 Selected *h-aspiré* words

Masculine nouns	Feminine nouns	Adjectives	Verbs
le haddock	la haie	haineux	haïr
le hameau	la haine	handicapé	hanter
le handicap	la halte	hardi	harceler
le hangar	la hanche	hasardeux	hasarder
le harcèlement	la hantise	hâtif	(se) hâter
le hareng	la hardiesse	haut	(se) hausser
le haricot	la harpe	hautain	heurter
le harpon	la hâte	hideux	hurler
le hasard	la hausse	hiérarchique	
le haut	la hauteur	hollandais	
le hautbois	la hiérarchie		
le hayon	la Hollande		
le hérisson	la Hongrie		
le héros	la honte		
le hêtre	la horde		
le hockey	la hotte		
le homard	la houle		
le hoquet	la housse		
le hurlement	la huée		
le hors d'œuvre	la hutte		

(For a very comprehensive list of *h-aspiré* words, see Fouché 1959.)

Another category of words resistant to linking phenomena (elision in particular) comprises the so-called *h-aspiré* words. In isolation, there's no phonetic distinction between *harpe* [aʀp], *hérisson* [eʀisɔ̃] and *haut* [o], on the one hand, and *habit* [abi], *héritier* [eʀitje] and *homme* [ɔm], on the other. All are orthographically *h*-initial, yet phonetically vowel-initial. However, *habit*, *héritier* and *homme* are called *h-muet* words, while *harpe*, *hérisson* and *haut* are *h-aspiré* words. These traditional labels obviously mean nothing with regard to the standard pronunciation of the word in isolation; the difference is that, in a possible linking context, *h-muet* words tolerate linking, while *h-aspiré* words don't:

L'homme est à L'hôpital D'Haumont.

but   LE hasard a fait que LA harpe de ma tante a été retrouvée dans LE hangar.

While it's impossible to tell, orthographically, whether an *h*-initial word belongs to one category or the other, *h-aspiré* words are generally borrowings from languages other than Latin and Greek. Note the absence of elision with recent introductions from English, such as *le hamburger*, *le hardware* and *la hype*. Note, also, the even smaller number of words which don't allow linking phenomena, which may or may not have an initial orthographic *h*, particularly numerals, *un*, *huit*, *onze* and *onzième*.

Table 2.28 gives a sample of *h-aspiré* words grouped in lexical categories. Note that if a word belongs to the *h-aspiré* category, its derivatives will generally do so, too, with the salient exception of *le héros* [ləeʁo] (*h-aspiré*), but *l'héroine* [leʁoin] and *l'héroisme* [leʁoism] (*h-muet*).

15.3   Enchaînement *and* non-enchaînement

15.3.1   Enchaînement

Enchaînement is also a linking phenomenon which reorganises syllable structure. A pronounced consonant which is word-final in isolation attaches itself to a following vowel-initial word, as the onset of its first syllable. Like elision, *enchaînement* occurs within the sense group. In the utterance *Une automobile* [y.nɔ.tɔ.mo.bil] *par accident* [pa.ʁak.si.dã] *a renversé cet homme* [sɛ.tɔm], there are three contexts for *enchaînement*, since the final consonants of *une*, *par* and *cet* are pronounced in the word in isolation and, here, are followed by a vowel-initial word. However, there's no *enchaînement* across sense group boundaries, as shown in [pa.ʁak.si.dã.(*t)a.ʁã.vɛʁ.se] (where the asterisk indicates that this form isn't acceptable in normal discourse).

All word-final pronounced consonants (2: 7.4) are subject to *enchaînement*, but with words ending in orthographic *rs* or *rt*, pronounced [ʁ], the *enchaînement* consonant is [ʁ], as in *il dort encore* [dɔ.ʁã.kɔʁ] and *elle est toujours en retard* [tu.ʒu.ʁã.ʁtaʁ].

15.3.2   Non-enchaînement

In 2: 15.2.1 we saw that *h-aspiré*, and, in some cases, glides, block elision. Similarly, they block *enchaînement*. Note, in particular, how the feminine indefinite article *une* is realised with the pronunciation of a final schwa which prevents the consonant from attaching itself to the initial vowel of the following word:

c'est une_orange	[y.nɔ.ʁã:ʒ]	*versus*	c'est une honte [y.nə.ɔ̃t]
la petite_amie	[pti.ta.mi]		la petite hutte [pti.tə.yt]

15.4   Liaison

Liaison is a particular case of *enchaînement*, to the extent that here, too, a word-final consonant is attached to a following vowel-initial syllable. However, there is a subtle difference. In the case of *enchaînement*, the re-syllabified consonant would also be pronounced in the word in isolation. In the case of liaison, in contrast, the resyllabified consonant would *not* be pronounced in the word in isolation, or before a consonant-initial word, even though it's present in the orthography.

For example, consider the adjective *petit(s)*, pronounced [pti] or [pəti] in isolation, and before a consonant-initial word within a group, as in *Elle a un petit garçon* [pti.gaʀ.sɔ̃] and *Elle a deux petits chiens* [pti.ʃjɛ̃]. In contrast, in *Elle a un petit ami* [pti.ta.mi] and *Elle a deux petits enfants* [pti.zɑ̃.fɑ̃], the final written consonant is pronounced and attaches to the next syllable.

As with *enchaînement* and elision, liaison takes place within the sense group, and is blocked by some glides and *h-aspiré*.

15.4.1   Liaison consonants

Very few consonants are affected by liaison. The most common by far are [z, t, n]; [p, ʀ, g] occasionally occur with *trop, beaucoup, long, léger, premier, dernier*, as well as -*er* infinitives.

Usually, the liaison consonant is self-evident from the orthography. However, the liaison consonant [t] sometimes corresponds to orthographic *d*, as in the adjectives *grand* and *second*, the conjunction *quand* and the present tense of -*re* verbs:

un gran<u>d h</u>omme	[gʀɑ̃.tɔm]
ven<u>d-il</u> du pain?	[vɑ̃.til]
quan<u>d elle</u> est rentrée	[kɑ̃.tɛl]

Liaison with [n] is triggered by words ending in a nasal vowel. This is common with the article *un*, the subject proform *on*, the possessives *mon*, *ton* and *son*, the proform/preposition *en*, the adjectives *bon, certain, ancien* and *plein*, and, to a lesser extent, with the adverb *bien* and *rien*. Note that *dans, sans* and *tant*, which in isolation all end in a nasal vowel, link with their orthographically final consonant, as in *tanT et plus* [tɑ̃.te.plys], *sanS œufs* [sɑ̃.zø] and *danS une heure* [dɑ̃.zy.nœːʀ].

The most common linking consonant is [z], usually represented ortho-graphically as *s*, as in *un gros obus* [gʀo.zo.by], *des petits animaux* [pti.za.ni.mo], but sometimes as *x* or *z*, as in *en piteux état* [pi.tø.ze.ta]. Its frequency is due to its prevalence as the plural marker for determiners, adjectives and nouns, as in *leS uns et leS autres* [le.zœ̃.e.le.zotʀ] and *quelqueS ancienS amis* [kɛl.kə.zɑ̃.sjɛ̃.za.mi].

15.4.2   *Liaison and vowel quality*

Since liaison modifies syllable structure, that is turns a closed syllable into an open one, it can have an effect on vowel quality, as in *le premieR acte* [pʀə.mjɛ.ʀakt], where the vowel [e] of *premier* which, in isolation or utterance-finally, is in a final stressed syllable, lowers in unstressed position.

Further, in a number of words, a final nasal vowel tends to denasalise in liaison contexts, as in *le Moyen-Age* [mwa.jɛ.naːʒ], *le plein emploi* [plɛ.nɑ̃.plwa], *un ancien élève* [ɑ̃.sjɛ.ne.lɛv] and *un certain effet* [sɛʀ.tɛ.nɛ.fɛ]. Just as [ɛ̃] denasalises to [ɛ], [ɔ̃] frequently also denasalises in the adjective *bon* and the possessives *mon*, *ton* and *son*, as in *un bon ami* [bɔ.na.mi] and *mon équipe* [mɔ.ne.kip].

15.5   *Liaison contexts*

Having considered liaison in phonetic terms, the major question remains of when and where liaison occurs. Unfortunately, with liaison the question isn't as straightforward as it is with elision and *enchaînement*, which are compulsory, provided the basic conditions are met. With liaison, in contrast, there is an element of speaker choice. This means that, besides those contexts where liaison is either compulsory or impossible on syntactic grounds, there is a grey area, where liaison is optional and there is individual or stylistic variation. Table 2.29 summarises the situation with 'compulsory', 'optional' and 'impossible' liaisons (see also Encrevé 1988).

Two major principles can be used as a guide to when or where to effect a liaison linkage. First, the closer the syntactic links within a phrase, the more

Table 2.29   Liaison contexts

Compulsory	Optional	Impossible
NOUN PHRASE: determiner	plural noun +	singular noun +
+ noun		
+ proform		
+ adjective + noun		
VERB PHRASE: conjunctive proform +	verb +complement	
proform + verb		
verb + proform		
	PREPOSITION +	
	ADVERB +	et +
SET PHRASES		SET PHRASES
		h-aspiré words
		(some) glides
		un, huit, onze

the liaison is likely to be compulsory, since liaison is a marker of cohesion within a sense group. Second, liaison much more commonly marks plurality, and links a monosyllabic word to a longer word, rather than the reverse.

15.5.1   Impossible liaison contexts

Liaison doesn't occur in the following circumstances.

- Across a pause, or sense group boundary:

  Quand | est-il venu?
  Ils se sont levés | à cinq heures du matin.

- When a word needs to be isolated in a sentence for emphasis or clarity. This applies particularly to numbers, quotes and exclamations:

  J'ai dit | oui.
  Il a cent | un ans.

- Before *h-aspiré* and some glide-initial words:

  Les | yuccas ont-ils des fleurs?
  des | hauts et des bas
  Les | hérissons sont carnivores.

- With the conjunction *et*, since it links one sense group to another, rather than two words:

  un homme et | une femme
  Elle est rentrée et | elle a dévoré deux croissants et trois tartines.

- The absence of liaison may also signal a singular interpretation, whereas, with the liaison, a plural would be understood:

  Elle donne | un bonbon   *versus*   Elles donnent un bonbon
                                           [dɔn.tœ̃.bɔ̃.bɔ̃]
  l'Anglais | adorable   des Anglais adorables
                                           [de.zɑ̃.glɛ.za.dɔ.ʁabl]

- In some set phrases, such as *nez à nez* [ne.a.ne], *une fois ou l'autre* [yn.fwa.u.lotʁ] and *de part en part* [də.pa.ʁɑ̃.paːʁ], liaison is also impossible.

15.5.2   Compulsory liaison contexts

Liaisons always occur in the following circumstances.

- Before the noun: liaison occurs between a determiner and a following noun, proform or prenominal adjective:

  un enfant, les autres, un ancien ami

- Around the verb: liaison occurs between a verb and the accompanying proforms, as well as between the proforms themselves:

  on y va, nous allons, allez-y, nous en avons

- After the adverbs and prepositions *en, dans, sans, sous, chez* and *très*:

  sans un sou, chez eux, très unis

- In set phrases: the liaison consonant [z] occurs in:

  Champs-Elysées, Etats-Unis, de plus en plus, de temps en temps, le cas écheant, etc.

- The liaison consonant [t] occurs in:

  mot à mot, petit à petit, tout à coup, tout à fait, fait accompli, etc.

15.5.3   *Contexts for optional liaisons*

- In the noun phrase: between a plural noun and a following adjective:

  des parlementaires européens, des personnes âgées

- In the verb phrase: between the verb and a following past participle, determiner, infinitive, adjective or adverb:

  c'était ici, il est important, je vais essayer, nous sommes arrivées, c'est un ami

- After the monosyllabic adverbs *pas, trop* and all polysyllabic adverbs, such as *extrêmement, beaucoup* and the conjunction *mais*:

  Je suis extrêmement énervée, mais enfin je vais mieux

- In a small number of set phrases: à bras ouverts, de long en large (realised as [k] or [g]). See Fouché (1959) for other examples.

Liaison is possible in all the above contexts, but speakers may vary quite widely in their practice for stylistic and sociolinguistic reasons. Since the seventeenth century, and especially since the advent of universal education, grammarians and teachers have presented liaison as one of the most salient marks of *le bon Usage* in spoken French. Correct use of optional liaisons, which require careful monitoring (and a knowledge of spelling conventions!), signals mastery of the system, and even a superior education or social status. Liaison therefore occurs more frequently in formal discourse, and can vary quite widely in individual speakers, depending on whether they are communicating in an informal personal situation or a more formal context. There's also evidence to suggest that other factors, such as age, gender and level of education, affect speakers' use of liaison.

16   Suprasegmentals: stress and intonation

In this final section, we briefly consider what are technically called supraseg-mental features. So far we've concentrated on articulatory features, that is the production of segments of syllables. However, an utterance is more than a mere succession of articulations. The meaning of an utterance is also conveyed by variations in loudness or in the general melody added to, or superimposed upon, the sequence of speech sounds, hence the term supraseg-mentals. The two aspects we'll examine are stress and intonation.

16.1   *Grammatical stress*

Listening to connected French speech, stress can be perceived as the extra prominence of a particular syllable, marked principally in terms of the length of the final vowel. From the perspective of the speaker, stress is produced using more breath force to produce a louder sound. We saw earlier how one type of stress, grammatical stress, is used in French to mark the boundaries of words in isolation or of sense groups, and how speakers have no choice about which syllable the stress falls on. If the utterance comprises a single sense group, it's the final syllable that bears stress; if it contains several sense groups, the strongest grammatical stress falls on the final syllable of the final group (since it marks a complete break in the syntax), and weaker gram-matical stress marks the end of each sense group within the utterance.

16.2   *Emphatic stress*

In addition to invariable grammatical stress, another kind of stress is used to draw the listener's attention to a particular element of the sentence. This is known as emphatic stress or lexical stress, a kind of 'phonetic under-lining' for a word. As with grammatical stress, a syllable with emphatic stress will be given greater prominence, but the greater breath force will be attributed to a syllable which wouldn't normally bear stress, so as to highlight the item in question. In fact, it's often more perceptible in French than grammatical stress, both because it's stronger and because of its different placement.

Generally speaking, the syllable in a word that can bear emphatic stress is the first consonant-initial syllable. In monosyllables, there's obviously no choice, and that syllable will bear the emphatic stress, as in *c'est FOU!* [sɛ."fu]. (Note that emphatic stress is transcribed by the symbol " before the relevant syllable.) If the first syllable of a polysyllabic word is consonant-initial, this will be the stressed syllable:

CArrément idiot! ["ka.ʀe.mɑ̃.ti.djo]

If the first syllable is vowel-initial, it's usually the second syllable that receives emphatic stress:

aBSOlument pas! [a."ḅsɔ.ly.mɑ̃.pa]

However, the first syllable of a vowel-initial word may receive emphatic stress if a linking consonant is present, as in the phrase *c'est* INacceptable [sɛ."ti.nak.sɛp.tabl].

Under emphatic stress, a vowel may be pronounced more loudly and the initial consonant may be geminated (that is, have a lengthened articulation):

Quel imBÉcile! [kɛ.lɛ̃."bːe.sil]

Note, also, that in words where the first vowel is an *e-muet*, which might under ordinary circumstances be deleted (in *la fenêtre*, for example), under emphatic stress that vowel will be retained:

J'ai dit: Fermez la FEnêtre, pas la porte! [la."fə.nɛtʀ]

Words which lend themselves most readily to emphatic stress are obviously those with a strong lexical meaning, that is some verbs, and, more especially, adjectives and adverbs. However, in contrastive contexts, almost any item can be stressed:

Ce n'est pas UNE voiture, c'est LA voiture!
[sə.nɛ.pa."yn.vwa.tyːʀ.sɛ."la.vwa.tyːʀ]

16.3   Intonation

Apart from the basic rhythm of a sentence – the syllable timing of French (2: 15) – and the intensity or loudness of certain syllables induced by stress, an additional layer of information about the message the speaker is trying to convey is provided by the **intonation** of an utterance.

When we speak, the vocal cords are in constant vibration as we utter voiced sounds: the frequency or rate of vibration of the vocal cords varies according to their tension and the force of the airstream, and determines the pitch of the voice which, in the course of an utterance, is in constant fluctuation. This variation in pitch follows regular melodic patterns which are common to speakers of a particular language, and play an important linguistic role, since they are as much a part of the language as the individual speech sounds. Intonation also plays an important non-linguistic role, since it enables speakers to convey their mood, attitudes or emotions to the listener. Intonation has several functions. First, it has a grammatical function indicating syntactic boundaries within an utterance, and clarifying meaning. Consider, for instance, how a different patterning of groups, on which the intonation will be superimposed, changes the meaning of the following:

Si tu me donnes le numéro aujourd'hui | je téléphonerai à Marie

versus   Si tu me donnes le numéro | aujourd'hui je téléphonerai à Marie

Intonation also serves a modal function. Depending on the intonation pattern used by the speaker, a sentence like *Il fait beau aujourd'hui* will be variously interpreted as a statement, a question or an exclamation. Finally, intonation can have an expressive function, conveying the attitudes and emotions of the speaker (irony, indignation, happiness, etc.). In the following sections, we concentrate on the grammatical and modal functions of intonation.

16.4 Basic intonation patterns of French

We shall briefly consider here, at the risk of considerable oversimplification, the four main intonation patterns for French in relation to the type of utterance in which they occur. To illustrate these, as a convention, two parallel lines are used to indicate the normal pitch range of an individual voice, and a continuous line placed between them gives the general pattern of intonation.

RISING-FALLING INTONATION

This applies mainly to statements of fact, from a bisyllabic utterance such as *J'arrive*, to one containing several sense groups (or, more strictly speaking, rhythmic groups). In a simple statement, there's a rising pitch at the end of each group except for the last, which is pronounced with falling pitch. The final syllable of the last sense group will be on a low pitch, falling below the normal speaking range; this is the audible clue that the utterance is complete. In a sentence, such as *Le chien a aboyé toute la nuit*, we identify two groups on syntactic and semantic grounds. The first has a rising intonation, the second the falling intonation described above:

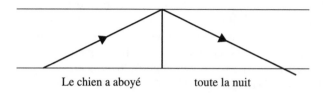

Le chien a aboyé   toute la nuit

The same sentence could be elaborated upon, as in *Le chien de notre voisin a encore aboyé toute la nuit*. In this case, the utterance could be divided into four sense groups, the first three having the rising intonation appropriate to an unfinished statement, the final group, the falling intonation marking completion. For successive rising intonations, the first syllable in each group will start on a slightly higher pitch than the previous one, until the upper limit of the range is reached:

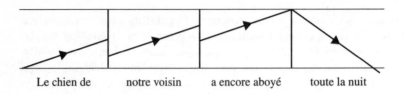

Le chien de   notre voisin   a encore aboyé   toute la nuit

FALLING INTONATION

This intonation pattern suggests that the utterance is complete, and the speaker has nothing more to say. This is typical of constituent questions containing interrogative phrases like *comment, quand, où, qui, que* and *pourquoi*, as in *Pourquoi donc?*, *Que faites-vous?* and *Tu en veux combien?* (4: 1.5). The first syllable starts off on a pitch slightly above the normal speaking range. If the question contains more than one rhythmic group, each one starts on a slightly higher pitch than the end of the previous group.

A falling intonation is also characteristic of imperatives, conveying requests, instructions and orders (4: 1.5). In imperative utterances, the voice rises slightly on the final syllable of each group, except for the last, as in *Taisez-vous!*, *Passez me voir demain!*, *Prenez d'abord un café!*

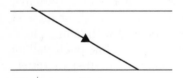

RISING INTONATION

This intonation pattern suggests that the utterance is incomplete, that the speaker is hesitating before finishing what he or she wants to say, or is waiting for some response from the listener. Thus, this pattern will be used for: unfinished sentences (1); yes–no questions with subject–clitic inversion (2); and, more typically in spoken French, those with the overt structure of a declarative sentence (3) (4: 1.5). These generally have a rising pitch on the last stressed syllable of the group. If there's more than one group, each begins on a lower pitch than the end of the previous one, and the intonation peak is reached at the end of the final group (5). Finally, rising intonation may convey, for example, doubt or incredulity on the part of the speaker (4). Here, the first syllable starts off on a note which is at the bottom of the normal speaking range and remains within the band of the normal speaking range for the unfinished statement, whereas for the questions, the final intonation peak rises slightly above.

(1) Je voudrais ... (un kilo de pommes).
(2) As-tu fini?
(3) Le chat est dehors?
(4) Maintenant? ('I can hardly believe my ears!')
(5) Tu est sûre que tu n'as pas laissé tes clés dans la voiture?

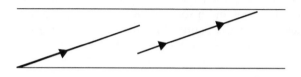

LEVEL INTONATION

Information which is presented as an aside, or an additional piece of information outside the main statement, is often presented on a level pitch starting from the end of the previous intonation contour:

Son frère, celui qui est en Amérique, est malade.
Tu t'en vas, Marie?
Arrête, Simon.

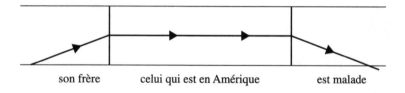

son frère   celui qui est en Amérique   est malade

17 Final remarks

In this review of the sounds of French, we have described not only the repertoire of speech sounds in modern Standard French (phonetics), but also the way they are articulated and combined within a speech sound system by which meaning is conveyed (phonology). We've also suggested that the system described is a somewhat idealised construct, since it constitutes both a pedagogic norm and a consensus view of the usage of a prestigious minority of French speakers. Yet variation has been seen to exist within the system, and we explore this further in Chapter 5. Meanwhile, in Chapters 3 and 4, respectively, we consider how French speech sounds are combined into words, and words into sentences.

Further reading

On general phonetics and the pronunciation of French, see Delattre (1966), Fouché (1959), Armstrong (1982), Tranel (1987), Price (1991), Wioland (1991) and Valdman (1993). As general introductions to phonology, see Lass (1984), Carr (1993). Trask (1996a) is particularly useful for terminology.

More specifically on the phonology of French, see Schane (1968), Valdman (1976), Durand (1990). On changes in the behaviour of *e-muet*, see Walter (1990). Encrevé (1988) presents a summary on work on liaison, its relevance to phonological theory and a sociolinguistic survey of liaison in the speech of politicians and media figures. See also Gadet (1989) on liaison and assimilation. On intonation, see Di Cristo (1998).

3 French word structure

Having discussed French phonology, we move on to the basic linguistic units of French grammar. In Chapter 4 we see words combined into **phrases** and **sentences** (**syntax**). But, first, we need to understand how words are formed. The study of word formation is called **morphology**. This chapter is about French morphology. In Chapter 2 we saw that French phonology follows certain principles. In this chapter we'll see that French word structure respects certain principles, too. Our aim is to set out as explicitly as possible what these principles are. A recurrent theme of our discussion here (and in Chapter 4) is that words don't all behave alike; that is, words belong to different word classes, or **categories**. We'll see that the morphological behaviour of a word depends primarily on the category it belongs to.

Before we start, and in case you doubt that words *do* have internal structure, or that they *are* formed according to principles, compare the words in (1) with the *non*-words (asterisked) in (2). Without our even thinking about what's 'wrong' with (2), the mere fact that these aren't French words is proof that morphology isn't random.

(1) a. utile b. utilité(s) c. utilitaire d. utilitarisme
(2) a. *(s)téutile b. *utilismeté c. *utilaire d. *téutilarisme

Each word in (1) contains a basic meaningful unit, namely *utile*, called a **root**. In (1b–d) various endings (**suffixes**) have been added to form more complex words. The *non*-words in (2) illustrate two strict principles of suffixation. First, suffixes are endings: that is, they follow the root; they cannot precede (see (2a, d)). Second, suffixes attach in a certain order; they cannot be mixed up and attached randomly (see (2b, c)). We conclude therefore that word formation follows principles.

After introducing the basic concepts of morphology (3: 1), especially the distinction between inflectional and derivational processes (3: 1.3), we move on to examine **inflectional morphology** in three categories, namely **adjectives** (3: 2), **verbs** (3: 3) and **nouns** (3: 4). Finally, we briefly address **derivational morphology** (3: 5). In Chapter 2 we found that French spelling inadequately represents spoken language; in this chapter, it will again be necessary to distinguish orthography from pronunciation.

1   Word classes and morphemes

Here, we explore morphological variation in three word classes. Consider the nouns in (3):

(3) La jeune AVOCATE voit la grande ÉGLISE.

In addition to their dictionary meaning (*une avocate* is a legal representative, *une église* a place of worship), these words also bear the grammatical features **number** and **gender**. With its final orthographic -*e* and its pronounced final consonant, *avocate* [avɔkat] has **feminine** gender. This contrasts with **masculine** *avocat* [avɔka], which lacks the pronounced final consonant and the -*e*. In French, gender is a binary feature; that is, it has two possible values (unlike German, for example, where gender has three possible values, namely masculine, feminine and neuter). The labels masculine and feminine are used for the two values of the gender feature in French because nouns referring to human males tend to have masculine gender, while those referring to females tend to be feminine, as in *avocat/avocate*. However, the link between grammatical gender and biological sex shouldn't be taken too far. French grammar requires all nouns to have a gender (some words, for example *après-midi*, exceptionally, are either masculine or feminine, and words like *délice*, even more exceptionally, are masculine in the singular and feminine in the plural), and there's often no real motivation in the dictionary meaning of words for them having one gender or the other. Mostly, the gender of Modern French nouns is a historical relic. This is the case, for instance, with the noun *église*, which is feminine because it derives etymologically from a noun which was feminine in Latin. Further, gender doesn't always follow sex. While the gender of nouns like *enfant* is determined by the biological sex of the referent, the nouns *victime*, *personne* and *vedette* have feminine gender, irrespective of whom they refer to (3: 4.1.2).

Gender isn't the only grammatical feature associated with French nouns. A second is **number**, which, like gender, is binary; nouns are either **singular** or **plural**. Generally, singular nouns refer to just one entity, while plurals refer to more than one. Most French nouns are marked plural by final orthographic -*s*, while singular nouns have no overt number marking.

We conclude, then, that French words can be analysed in terms of smaller units. Words have different spoken and written forms depending on their grammatical features. The orthographic form of the word *avocates* can be divided into at least three smaller units, as in (4):

(4) $[_3 [_2 [_1 \text{ avocat-}]\text{-e-}]\text{-s}]$

First, there's the root (bracket 1), the 'core' which gives the word its dictionary meaning. Suffixation then adds an ending (bracket 2) indicating (feminine) gender. (Absence of orthographic *-e* would have indicated masculine gender.) Finally, a second suffix is added (bracket 3) indicating (plural) number. (Absence of orthographic *-s* would have indicated singular number.)

With adjectives, we again find variation in word form relating to gender and number. However, whereas a noun's gender is an idiosyncratic property to be learned with the word (recall that *église* is feminine for historical reasons) and its number depends on its referent, the gender and number of an adjective are determined via **agreement** with the noun it describes. In (3) the adjectives *grande* and *jeune* are feminine and singular, not because of any inherent properties, but because they describe the feminine singular nouns *église* and *avocate* respectively, and agree with their gender and number. If we replace *église* and *avocate* with *bâtiments* and *avocates*, the form of the adjectives changes, too. (The asterisk against (5a) indicates ungrammaticality.)

(5) a. *Les JEUNE avocates voient les GRANDE bâtiments.
    b. Les JEUNES avocates voient les GRANDS bâtiments.

Turning finally to verbs, we see, for example, that *voir* has the forms *voit* in (3) and *voient* in (5). While both describe an event taking place at the time of utterance (they are **present** tense verb forms; 4: 15.1), they differ with respect to certain grammatical features. Just as the form of an adjective is determined by (agrees with) the number and gender of the noun it qualifies, so, too, the form of a **finite verb** is determined by the **person** and number features of its **subject** (4: 1.1). The form *voit* appears in (3) because the subject is the third person singular *la jeune avocate*; *voient* appears in (5) because *les jeunes avocates* is third person plural.

In summary, words like *avocates*, *grande* and *voit* are bundles of linguistic information. Besides its dictionary meaning, each contains units of grammatical meaning. In the case of nouns and adjectives this relates to gender and number; in the case of finite verbs it relates to subject agreement features and tense. Units of meaning, whether dictionary meaning or grammatical meaning, are called **morphemes**, and are the minimal unit of grammatical analysis. Interestingly, in the same way that phonemes can be realised as different allophones (2: 3.3), morphemes can be realised in different ways, too. The different realisations of a morpheme are called its **allomorphs**. We'll see allomorphic variation at various points in this chapter.

1.1 Root, suffix and prefix

Having identified morphemes as the minimal units of grammatical analysis, we now consider how they are realised in French words. In (6) we've repeated the morphological analysis of the noun *avocates*:

(6) morpheme: root   gender   number

                    | | |

    word: $[_3 \, [_2 \, [_1$ avocat-] -e-]   -s]

This shows that the word *avocates* comprises three morphemes: namely, a root, indicating the dictionary meaning of the word, to which have been added, in sequence, gender and number suffixes. Compare *avocates* with *avocat*, which is interpreted as masculine and singular, despite the lack of overt suffixes. This shows that morphological information can be given by the *absence* as well as the presence of overt marking. Non-overt morphemes are called **null morphemes**; they have **zero realisation**. The morphological structure of *avocat* is in (7), where Ø represents a null morpheme:

(7) morpheme: root   gender   number

                    | | |

    word: $[_3 \, [_2 \, [_1$ avocat-] -Ø] -Ø]

Like (6), the representation in (7) shows that *avocat* comprises a root and two suffixes. Gender and number are null morphemes, and the word is interpreted as masculine (or unknown) singular.

Not all morphemes are roots and suffixes; some morphological processes add morphemes *before* the root:

(8) a. ex-étudiant   b. amoral

Here, *ex-* and *a-* precede the roots *étudiant* and *moral*, and are called **prefixes**.

So far, identifying the root has been straightforward. Yet this isn't always the case. Sometimes the root itself is morphologically complex. For instance, the written form of *étudiantes* could be analysed as the root *étudiant*, the gender suffix *-e* and the plural suffix *-s*. However, *étudiant* can itself be analysed as the verbal root *étudi-* and the suffix *-ant*. So there are two types of root, namely simple roots (like *avocat*), which can't be analysed further, and complex roots (like *étudiant*), which can. This shows that word formation processes interact; that is, a complex unit which is the *output* of one morphological process can serve as the *input* (the root) of another. (See also *-ifier/-iser*-suffixation and *-ication*-suffixation in 3: 5.2.1.)

1.2   *Transparent word forms and suppletion*

In 3: 1.1 we saw morphologically complex words analysed as roots and (possibly null) prefixes/suffixes. Unfortunately, morphological analysis isn't always as straightforward as with the written form of *avocates*, where there's a neat one-to-one relationship between each morpheme and the constituent parts of the word. For example, the pronunciation of *avocates*, [avɔkat], isn't as morphologically informative as the orthography. This is because in spoken

French (liaison contexts notwithstanding; 2: 15.4) plural number is generally a null morpheme.

Further, morphological analysis of some words, even in their written form,
is less than straightforward. Consider forms of the **imperfect** tense (4: 15.1;
4: 15.4) of *donner*:

(9) (je) donnais, (tu) donnais, (il/elle) donnait, (ils/elles) donnaient

Orthographically, the root *donn-* is followed by the suffixes *-ais*, *-ait* and
-aient, which we can further analyse as *-ai-*, marking tense, and *-s*, *-t* and
-ent, marking subject agreement. However, we run into problems with *(nous)
donnions* and *(vous) donniez*, where the tense suffix is *-i-*, instead of *-ai-*. To
solve the problem, we can exploit the notion of allomorphic variation. We
can say that the imperfect tense morpheme has two allomorphs, one of
which, *-ai-*, appears in stressed syllables, the other, *-i-*, in unstressed syllables (2: 16).

The morphological analysis is less straightforward when we consider the
pronunciation of the six forms:

(10) [dɔnɛ], [dɔnɛ], [dɔnɛ], [dɔnjɔ̃], [dɔnje], [dɔnɛ]

Four of the pronunciations are identical ([dɔn-ɛ]), and it's difficult to say
whether the suffix [-ɛ] marks tense or subject agreement. Plausibly, it marks
both simultaneously; that is, the suffix [-ɛ] here is the result of **fusion**.
Ambiguities resulting from suffixes like [-ɛ] will generally be resolved by
context, for example the subject of the sentence. In 3: 3.2 we analyse the
morphology of French verbs following Martinet (1969), and make wide use
of fusional suffixes simultaneously marking subject agreement and tense.

In the imperfect paradigm of *donner*, while it wasn't always possible to
distinguish different suffixes, it was none the less possible to distinguish the
root (i.e. *donn-* [dɔn-]) from the suffixes. In some cases, however, even this
isn't easy. Sometimes, the combination of the root and its suffix(es) defies
morphological analysis, as in the three forms *beau* [bo], *bel* [bɛl] and *belle*
[bɛl]:

(11) a. un BEAU discours
      b. un BEL homme
      c. une BELLE affaire

Here, a transparent root-plus-suffix analysis isn't possible. All that these
three adjective forms have in common is their initial [b-], hardly a
convincing candidate root morpheme. Further, such an analysis would mean
that the masculine gender morpheme has two allomorphs, [-o] and [-ɛl],
while feminine gender has a single form, [-ɛl], identical to one of the masculine forms. Alternatively, we can adopt the approach we used for (10),

where we analysed the suffix [-ɛ] as fusional. We can conclude that the adjective forms [bo], [bɛl] and [bɛl] are suppletive forms, that is, forms which are related in dictionary meaning but which don't show their morphological relation transparently.

1.3 Inflectional and derivational morphology

Apart from prefixation, the morphological processes we've seen so far have taken a root and added grammatical meaning in the form of a suffix. We saw number and gender marking on nouns and adjectives, as well as subject agreement and tense marking on finite verbs. Morphological processes adding grammatical meaning are called **inflectional morphology**. Apart from the meaning added, inflectional morphology can be recognised in two other ways. First, it doesn't change category: *avocates* and *avocat* are both nouns; *grand* and *grande*, adjectives; *donnais* and *donnions*, verbs. Second, inflectional morphology is **productive**, generally applying in all suitable contexts (but see suppletion in 3: 1.2). For example, plural marking on nouns with orthographic final -*s* is productive, and therefore inflectional, because almost 99 per cent of French nouns have orthographically distinct plural and singular forms. Similarly, most adjectives have distinct orthographic masculine/feminine singular/plural forms. Gender and number marking are therefore productive, and therefore inflectional.

Unlike inflectional morphology, some morphological processes *do* add more than grammatical meaning, *do* change the category of the root, and are *not* productive. Consider (12)–(13):

(12) a. rival → rivalité   b. fatal → fatalité
     c. brutal → brutalité   d. légal → légalité
(13) a. jouer → joueur   b. danser → danseur
     c. casser → casseur   d. promener → promeneur

The meanings of the words in each pair are clearly related, and it makes sense to attribute this to the fact that the pairs contain the same root. The second word is derived from the first by a morphological process, which we can represent as here:

(14) a. root: rival-/fatal-/brutal-/légal-   b. suffix: -ité
(15) a. root: jou-/dans-/cass-/promen-   b. suffix: -eur

These processes differ from inflectional morphology. First, they change the category of the root. In (14) suffixation of -*ité* turns adjectives into nouns; in (15) -*eur* turns verbs into nouns. Second, the meaning that these suffixes add is more than mere grammatical information like number and gender. In (14) the derived nouns denote the abstract quality of the meaning expressed in the adjectival root; in (15) they denote the **agent** of the action expressed by the verbal root (*un casseur* is someone who breaks things, that is the agent of *casser*). The processes in (14)–(15) differ from inflectional morphology in a third way, too. Recall that inflectional morphology is productive. We can predict with almost 100 per cent certainty that *-ons* attaches to finite verbs whose subject is *nous*. In fact, there's only one exception, namely *sommes*. In contrast, we can't predict with much certainty at all that the suffixes in (14) and (15) will attach to a given adjectival or verbal root, to derive related nouns. For example, they don't attach to the roots in (16) and (17):

(16) a. bleu → *bleuité
    b. seul → *seulité
    c. lent → *lentité
(17) a. fixer → *fixeur
    b. exprimer → *exprimeur
    c. partir → *parteur

Our comparison of the two types of morphology is summarised in (18):

(18) *Inflectional morphology*   *Second type of morphology*
    (i) grammatical meaning   (i′) not grammatical meaning
    (ii) applies in almost all cases   (ii′) limited in its application
    (iii) doesn't modify category   (iii′) can modify category

Whereas inflectional morphology derives different forms of the same word, the second type of morphology derives different words, and is called **derivational morphology**.

We turn, finally, to words which are the output of a combination of *both* derivational *and* inflectional processes. It's usually possible to distinguish derivational morphemes from inflectional ones. Quite apart from the fact that inflectional and derivational morphology have the distinctive properties shown in (18), this is because, as we noted earlier with respect to (2), suffixes are attached in strict order. More precisely, derivational suffixes are attached first, inflectional suffixes last. Where a root like *rival-* is followed by both kinds of suffix, the derivational ones are closer to the root than the inflectional ones:

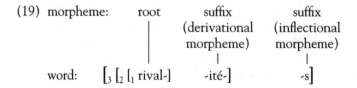

(19) morpheme: root   suffix   suffix
                    (derivational   (inflectional
                    morpheme)   morpheme)
     word: $[_3 [_2 [_1$ rival-]   -ité-]   -s]

In the words in (20) the derivational suffixes are in small capitals, the inflectional ones, italics:

(20)   a. rival-IS-*i-ons*   b. absurd-ITÉ-*s*   c. hollywood-IEN-*s*

Now we're familiar with the concepts of morphological analysis, we can examine the inflectional morphology of three categories (3: 2–4). In 3: 5 we briefly explore derivational morphology.

2   The morphology of French adjectives

We noted in 3: 1 that inflectional morphology marks French adjectives for number and gender. Since French orthography frequently fails to reflect pronunciation, we'll consider the written and oral realisation of this feature separately.

2.1   Written adjectival morphology

Orthographically, most French adjectives are complex words comprising the root (*grand-*, *vert-*, *joli-*, etc.), the gender morpheme and the number morpheme.

2.1.1   The regular pattern

Let's examine the most widespread orthographic pattern for marking gender and number agreement on French adjectives. First, consider gender. Nouns (and adjectives which agree with them) are either masculine or feminine. Orthographically, gender agreement is typically realised as in (21).

(21)   a. Le garage$_{masc}$ est $[_2 [_1$ grand-$]$ -Ø$]_{masc}$
      b. La chemise$_{fem}$ est $[_2 [_1$ vert-$]$ -e$]_{fem}$

Where an adjective qualifies a masculine noun, gender agreement is non-overt. In abstract terms, gender agreement takes place and the morpheme marking gender agreement is present (the adjective is after all understood as qualifying a masculine noun), but it has a zero realisation. Where an adjective qualifies a feminine noun, it's clear that gender agreement takes place, since it's overt, in the form of final orthographic -*e*. In conclusion, gender (realised as -Ø or -*e*) is the first inflectional suffix attached in the orthography to the adjectival root.

The second inflectional suffix attached to an adjectival root in the orthography is number, the distinction between singular and plural. Plural number is realised orthographically by the suffix -*s*. Singular number, like masculine gender, has a zero realisation. The written morphology of the adjectives *grands* and *verte* is represented in (22):

(22)   a. Les garages$_{masc/pl}$ sont $[_3 [_2 [_1$ grand-$]$ -Ø-$]$ -s$]_{masc/pl}$
      b. La chemise$_{fem/sg}$ est $[_3 [_2 [_1$ vert-$]$ -e-$]$ -Ø-$]_{fem/sg}$

The above pattern of orthographic gender and number marking on adjectives might be termed 'regular' written adjectival morphology. Common
adjectives which follow it are *prêt, idiot, bleu, vrai, meilleur, joli, supérieur,
petit, menu* and *fort*, as well as the past participles *donné, vendu* and *fini*.
The pattern applies unless it's overridden: (a) by an orthographic convention; (b) to reflect a phonological pattern; or (c) as a consequence of a
more radical morphological process.

2.1.2   Deviations due to orthographic convention

The pattern of written adjectival morphology in 3: 2.1.1 is sometimes disregarded due to orthographic convention. For example, one convention
disallows orthographic *-ee-* sequences. Adjectives like *triste*, whose roots end
in orthographic *-e*, cannot therefore mark feminine gender agreement by
final orthographic *-e*, since this would produce the proscribed *-ee-* sequence,
as in **tristee(s)*. Instead, the form *triste(s)*, with a single *-e*, is maintained
in the feminine. Masculine and feminine gender therefore both have zero
realisations. Common adjectives which behave this way are *jeune, rouge,
jaune, passable, (im)mobile, terrible, proche, (im)possible, probable, aimable, tran-
quille, valable, paisible* and *sage*.

A similar problem is posed by adjectives like *gris*, whose root ends in
-s, because an orthographic convention disallows word-final *-ss* sequences.
The form *gris* is therefore maintained in the masculine plural, instead of
the proscribed **griss*. Note that the problem doesn't arise with the feminine plural form, since the orthographic realisation of the gender morpheme
-e, prevents the word-final *-ss* sequence from forming:

(23) a. la chatte gris**E**   b. les chattes gris**ES**

In the same orthographic class as *gris* is *ras*, as well as the past participles
pris and *mis*.

A convention proscribing *-xs* sequences similarly explains the forms of
the adjective *heureux*, whose root ends in orthographic *-x*: *heureux* (masc/sg),
heureux (**heureuxs*) (masc/pl), *heureuse* (fem/sg) and *heureuses* (fem/pl).
Other adjectives in this class include *pieux, malheureux* and *peureux*. Note
the similar, but not identical, pattern of *jaloux/ jalouse(s), doux/douce(s),
roux/rousse(s)* and *faux/fausse(s)*.

Finally, the feminine written forms of the adjectives *long* [lɔ̃], *oblong* [ɔblɔ̃],
public [pyblik], *turc* [tyʁk] and *grec* [gʁɛk] also deviate slightly from the pattern
in 3: 2.1.1. This is due to a convention which prevents orthographic *-ge-* and
-ce- from representing [g] and [k], respectively. Although the regular pattern
of feminine gender agreement marking produces **(ob)longe(s), *publice(s),
turce(s) and **grece(s)*, these forms fail to respect the convention. With
*(ob)longe(s), orthographic *-u-* is inserted before the feminine suffix *-e*. This
avoids the orthographic sequence *-ge-*, which conventionally represents [ʒ], as

in *allonger* [alɔ̃ʒe]. The orthographic sequence -*gue*- conventionally represents [g], as in *fatigue* [fatig], and is therefore appropriate for *(ob)longue(s)* [(ɔb)lɔ̃g] (2: 2.4). With **publice(s)*, **turce(s)* and **grece(s)*, the problems posed by the orthographic sequence -*ce*- are avoided by the feminine forms *publique(s)*, *turque(s)* and *grecque(s)*, which are homophonous with the masculine forms.

2.1.3   *Phonologically motivated deviations*

Other exceptions to the pattern of written adjectival morphology in 3: 2.1.1 reflect not orthographic convention but morpho-phonological phenomena. For example, with some adjectives, the stressed vowel has a different quality depending on whether it occurs in a closed or open syllable (3: 2.2), and this difference is marked in the orthography, too. The pattern is found with *er*-final adjectives like *léger*, whose masculine and feminine forms are [leʒe] and [leʒɛʀ], respectively. Final [ʀ] in the feminine closes the final syllable, and changes the quality of the stressed vowel from [e] to [ɛ] (2: 10.3). This contrast is represented orthographically by the alternation -*e*-/-*è*-, as in *léger(s)/légère(s)*. Adjectives behaving this way include *premier(s)/première(s)* and *dernier(s)* /*dernière(s)*. The same orthographic pattern is also triggered in *complet(s)/complète(s)*, *secret, discret, inquiet, replet* and *concret*, with final [t]. However, these cases must be attributed to analogy, since there's no phonological difference between the quality of the stressed vowel, for example, [kɔ̃plɛ]/[kɔ̃plɛt].

Adjectives whose roots end in orthographic -*el*, -*eil*, -*en*, -*et* and -*on* follow the regular pattern with their masculine forms, but in the feminine the final orthographic consonant of their root is doubled before -*e* is added, for example *solennel(s)* (masc) versus *solennelle(s)* (fem), *vermeil(s)/vermeille(s)*, *ancien(s)/ancienne(s)*, *cadet(s)/cadette(s)* and *bon(s)/bonne(s)*. A similar pattern is found with the adjectives *nul/nulle, gentil/gentille* [ʒɑ̃ti]/[ʒɑ̃tij], *bas/basse, gras/grasse, las/lasse* and *sot/sotte*, although their roots end in different orthographic sequences. This orthographic irregularity is only partly attributable to a phonological process. In some cases the quality of the stressed vowel is different in the masculine and feminine forms, for example [ɑ̃sjɛ̃] versus [ɑ̃sjɛn] *(ancien(ne))*, and we can think of the consonant doubling as an attempt to reflect this in the orthography. (Recall the discussion of *léger* above.) However, elsewhere, for example, *solennel* [sɔlanɛl] versus *solennelle* [sɔlanɛl], there is no phonological motivation for the consonant doubling, which must therefore be analogical.

Finally, there's a small group of adjectives like *beau* with two orthographic masculine singular forms, reflecting a (historical) phonological alternation. We find *beau* before a consonant, *bel* before a vowel (3: 1.2):

(24) a. ce BEAU garçon   b. ce BEL homme

Adjectives in this class are *fou(s)/fol/folle(s)*, *nouveau(x)/nouvel/nouvelle(s)*, *mou(s)/mol/molle(s)* and *vieux/vieil/vieille(s)*.

2.1.4   Morphologically motivated deviations

A final category of deviations from the pattern of written adjectival morphology in 3: 2.1.1 is morphologically motivated. Adjectives ending in -eur are a particularly interesting case, and can be divided into three classes depending on how feminine gender agreement is marked. (They all mark plural number agreement in the regular way.)

First, there are adjectives like *supérieur* and *meilleur* where -eur is part of a simple root and feminine gender agreement is marked in the regular way by orthographic -e. Second, there are adjectives like *trompeur, menteur* and *flatteur* with complex roots where -eur is a derivational suffix attached to a verbal root, such as *tromp-, ment-* and *flatt-* (see (41) in 3: 5). Here, the suffix has a suppletive feminine form -euse (instead of -eure), as in *trompeuse, menteuse* and *flatteuse*. Finally, there are adjectives like *consolateur, destructeur* and *révélateur*, also with complex roots, but where the derivational suffix -eur attaches to a special root. Note that *consolat-, destruct-* and *révélat-* aren't the roots of *consoler, détruire* and *révéler* (3: 3). Here, the suffix -eur has a suppletive feminine form -rice, as in *consolatrice, destructrice* and *révélatrice*.

A slightly less complex case relates to adjectives whose root ends with -al. These can be divided into two groups, those which follow the regular pattern, such as *glacial(e)(s), fatal(e)(s), natal(e)(s), naval(e)(s), tonal(e)(s)* and *bancal(e)(s)*, and the numerically larger irregular group, like *loyal*. While the feminine forms *loyale(s)* follow the regular pattern, the masculine forms *loyal/loyaux* do not (see 4: 2.4; see also Rickard 1989: 66–7). Other adjectives following this pattern are *rival/rivaux, brutal/brutaux, général/généraux, spécial/spéciaux, normal/normaux, occidental/occidentaux* and *royal/royaux*.

Finally, some residual irregular written feminine forms which are morphologically motivated (3: 2.2) are *blanc(s)/blanche(s), sec(s)/sèche(s), frais* (both sg and pl)/*fraîche(s), vif(s)/vive(s)* and *franc(s)/franche(s)*. Note *favori(s)/favorite(s)*, where not only -e, but also a preceding -t appear in the feminine forms.

2.1.5   Morphologically invariant adjectives

Before we leave written adjectival morphology, note the small number of adjectives which are invariant. Some, for example *standard, chic* and *snob*, are borrowings from other languages which have not been regularised. Others include compound adjectives, especially compound colour terms, such as *bleu foncé, bleu ciel* and *bleu vert*, which can best be analysed as elliptical forms. The phrase *une chemise bleu clair* is thus derived from *une chemise D'UN bleu clair*, in which *bleu* is a masculine noun qualified by *clair*. Colour terms like *orange, paille* and *marron* are actually nouns and also invariant.

2.2   Oral adjectival morphology

Having considered written adjectival morphology, we now turn to oral forms, that is, how they are pronounced. These are considered separately, since, as we saw in 2: 2.2, French orthography is an unreliable reflection of pronunciation. With adjectives, pronunciation differs most noticeably from orthography in that singulars and plurals aren't generally distinguished:

(25) a. le GRAND [gʀɑ̃] chat   b. les GRANDS [gʀɑ̃] chats
      c. la GRANDE [gʀɑ̃d] chatte   d. les GRANDES [gʀɑ̃d] chattes
      e. le pré VERT [vɛʀ]   f. les prés VERTS [vɛʀ]
      g. l'herbe VERTE [vɛʀt]   h. les herbes VERTES [vɛʀt]

In each singular/plural pair the written forms differ, but the pronunciations are identical. From the perspective of pronunciation, it looks as if number can be ignored. However, there are good reasons not to ignore number in oral adjectival morphology. First, singular and plural are distinguished orally in adjectives such as *royal* and *principal* (3: 2.1.4):

(26) a. cet ami ROYAL [ʀwajal]   b. son livre PRINCIPAL [pʀɛ̃sipal]
      c. ces amis ROYAUX [ʀwajo]   d. ses livres PRINCIPAUX [pʀɛ̃sipo]

Second, singular and plural are distinguished in phonological contexts such as liaison; compare *le seul ami* [ləsœlami] with *les seuls amis* [lesœlzami] (2: 15.4). Number cannot therefore be ignored, and we analyse the oral plurals of *grand* as in (27a–d).

(27)

		root	gender	number
a.	les GRANDS garages	gʀɑ̃-	-Ø	-Ø
b.	les GRANDS hommes	gʀɑ̃-	-Ø	-z
c.	les GRANDES fenêtres	gʀɑ̃-	-d-	-Ø
d.	les GRANDES ardoises	gʀɑ̃-	-d-	-z

Turning to gender, compare the masculine and feminine forms of *grand* and *vert* in (28). Note that feminine gender isn't realised the same way in both cases.

(28)

		root	gender
a.	le GRAND garçon	gʀɑ̃-	-Ø
b.	la GRANDE fille	gʀɑ̃-	-d-
c.	le tableau VERT	gɛʀ-	-Ø
d.	la table VERTE	gɛʀ-	-t-

It seems that feminine gender agreement can be marked by suffixation of a variety of consonants. In (28b) it's [d]; in (28d) [t]. Further examples of this variability are given in (29):

(29) [blã/blãʃ], [fɔʀ/fɔʀt], [gʀo/gʀos], [du/dus], [øʀø/øʀøz], [pəti/pətit], [ɛ̃tɛliʒã/ɛ̃tɛliʒãt], [kuʀ/kuʀt], [almã/almãd], [fo/fos], [ãglɛ/ãglɛz], [fʀɛ/fʀɛʃ], [famø/faməz], [o/ot]

Adjectives which mark feminine gender agreement like this are called class one adjectives. Let's think about what's going on. We had to conclude that feminine agreement is variable, because we analysed the word-final consonant as a suffix rather than part of the root. But this isn't the only way to deal with the phenomenon. We might assume instead that the consonant which appears at the end of the feminine (but not the masculine) is in fact part of the root. The root would then resemble the feminine form, and the morphological process relating the feminine and masculine forms would not be 'add a (phonetically variable) consonant *to* the root to form the *feminine*', but rather '*subtract* the final consonant *from* the root to form the *masculine*'. Such an approach avoids the variability of the suffix.

Not all adjectives are class one adjectives. Several are phonologically invariable both for number and gender (liaison effects notwithstanding). These are called class two adjectives, and are illustrated in (30):

(30) a. le joli [ʒɔli] chat   b. les jolis [ʒɔli] chats
     c. la jolie [ʒɔli] chatte   d. les jolies [ʒɔli] chattes

Outside liaison contexts (2: 15.4), all four forms of *joli(e)(s)* are homopho-nous, despite the orthographic variation. Class two adjectives generally end in orthographic -*é*, -*i* or -*u*, such as *aisé(e)(s)* [eze] and *carré(e)(s)* [kaʀe]; *poli(e)(s)* [pɔli], *irréfléchi(e)(s)* [iʀefleʃi] and *étourdi(e)(s)* [etuʀdi]; *menu(e)(s)* [məny], *ingénu(e)(s)* [ɛ̃ʒeny] and *cornu(e)(s)* [kɔʀny] (NB: *favori* [favɔʀi]/*favorite* [favɔʀit] is exceptional here).

The behaviour of a third class of adjective differs quite radically. Class one and two adjectives have a single oral root, and morphological processes derive the masculine and feminine forms from that root. In contrast, class three adjectives have suppletive masculine and feminine roots, and might be called double-rooted adjectives. These adjectives can be divided into subgroups. In subgroup one adjectives like *rival* and *brutal* have both a masculine and a feminine root, and the masculine root has distinct singular and plural forms:

(31)		Singular	Plural
	masculine root	[ʀival]	[ʀivo]
	feminine root	[ʀival]	[ʀival]

In subgroup two morphologically complex adjectives like *consolateur(s)*/ *consolatrice(s)* comprise a root and a derivational suffix with suppletive masculine and feminine forms:

Table 3.1

Class 1	morpheme:	root	gender	number
	word:	[gʀɑ̃]	-∅-/-d-	-∅/-∅ (-z)

Class 2	morpheme:	root	gender	number
	word:	[məny]	-∅-/-∅	-∅/-∅ (-z)

Class 3		singular	plural	
Subgroup 1	masculine root:	[ʀival]	[ʀivo(z)]	
	feminine root:	[ʀival]	[ʀival(z)]	
Subgroup 2	masculine root:	[kɔ̃sɔlatœʀ]	[kɔ̃sɔlatœʀ]	
	feminine root:	[kɔ̃sɔlatʀis]	[kɔ̃sɔlatʀis]	
Subgroup 3	masculine root:	[mu]+C [mɔl]+V	[mu(z)]	
	feminine root:	[mɔl]	[mɔl(z)]	

(32) root + masculine suffix   [kɔ̃sɔlat-œʀ]
      root + feminine suffix   [kɔ̃sɔlat-ʀis]

Finally, subgroup three includes adjectives like *beau* with suppletive masculine forms which appear in prevocalic contexts, as shown in (33).

(33)   Singular   Plural
      masculine root   [bo] + C   [bo]
                          [bɛl] + V
      feminine root   [bɛl]   [bɛl]

Other members of subgroup three are *nouveau* [nuvo/nuvɛl], *mou* [mu/mɔl], *fou* [fu/fɔl] and *vieux* [vjø/vjɛj].

Our analysis of French oral adjectival morphology is summarised in Table 3.1. (The appearance of [-z] indicates liaison.)

3 The morphology of the French verb

We now turn to verbs, whose forms are of two types. A verb form can be **finite**, that is, marked for tense (4: 15.1) and mood (4: 15.3). The verb form *lise*, for example, is marked for present tense and subjunctive mood. Alternatively, a verb form can be **non-finite**, in which case it isn't marked in this way. The participles *lu* and *lisant* and the infinitive *lire* are non-finite verb forms.

Apart from tense and mood marking, finite verb forms also **agree** with the **person** and **number** of their subject (4: 1.1). The morpheme person has three possible values in French, namely first, second and third. First person subjects include the speaker (*je/nous*). Second person subjects don't include the speaker, but do include the addressee (*tu/vous*). Finally, third person subjects include neither the speaker nor the addressee (*il/elle/ils/elles*) (4: 4.3). As we saw in 3: 2, number has just two possible values, namely singular and plural. The singular subject pronouns are *je*, *tu* and *il/elle*; the plural ones, *nous*, *vous* and *ils/elles*. Tense, mood and subject agreement marking on finite verbs is illustrated in (34) with the future indicative of *donner*.

(34) *Singular*   *Plural*
   1 (je) donnerai   (nous) donnerons
   2 (tu) donneras   (vous) donnerez
   3 (il/elle) donnera   (ils/elles) donneront

A set of word forms related by inflectional morphology like this is called a (written) **paradigm** (see also the oral paradigm in (10) in 3: 1.2).

The sound changes from Latin to Modern French (Chapter 1) have made French verb morphology opaque in many cases. Written morphology in Modern French reflects pronunciation in the twelfth century, that is, when orthographic conventions were first established. Nine centuries of change mean that there's now considerable divergence between written and oral verb morphology. We saw from the discussion of the oral morphology of the imperfect tense in (10) in 3: 1.2 how a fully transparent analysis cannot always be achieved. In 3: 3.1 we give a conventional, albeit incomplete, analysis of French written verb morphology. In 3: 3.2 we turn to oral verb morphology.

3.1 Written verb morphology

French verbs are traditionally divided into three groups, called **conjugations**, on the basis of their written morphology. The written morphology of the three conjugations is dealt with in 3: 3.1.1–3. While classifying verbs on the basis of their written morphology brings out certain regular patterns, it's not without its weaknesses. For example, some irregularities within the first conjugation are the consequence of orthographic convention only, and mask an underlying linguistic regularity. Written morphology also fails to recognise a major distinction within the traditional second conjugation. Finally, the third conjugation is, in many ways, a waste paper basket into which all verbs are thrown which don't fit into the first or second conjugation. As we'll see in 3: 3.2, a number of the weaknesses of the analysis of written verb morphology disappear when we consider oral forms, instead.

3.1.1 First conjugation verbs

The written paradigms of most first conjugation verbs (*-er* verbs) conform to the pattern illustrated with *donner* in Table 3.2. The compound tenses (4: 15.2) combine an auxiliary and the past participle, for example *j'ai donné* (compound-past), *j'avais donné* (pluperfect) and *j'aurai donné* (future-perfect).

Table 3.2   Donner

Present	Imperfect	Past-historic	Future
donne	donnais	donnai	donnerai
donnes	donnais	donnas	donneras
donne	donnait	donna	donnera
donnons	donnions	donnâmes	donnerons
donnez	donniez	donnâtes	donnerez
donnent	donnaient	donnèrent	donneront

Present subjunctive	Imperfect subjunctive	Imperative	Participles
donne	donnasse		
donnes	donnasses	donne	
donne	donnât		donnant
donnions	donnassions	donnons	donné
donniez	donnassiez	donnez	
donnent	donnassent		

While written morphology in the first conjugation is highly regular, the regularity isn't perfect. The first two deviations are due to orthographic convention. Consider, first, a verb like *manger*, whose root ends with *-g*, representing [ʒ]. Now, convention allows *-g-* to represent [ʒ] only if it's followed by orthographic *-i* or *-e* (see Chapter 2, Table 2.1, and the discussion of the written morphology of *(ob)long* in 3: 2.1.2). A problem therefore arises with the suffixes *-ons* and *-ais*, whose initial letter is *-o-/-a-*. Adding these suffixes directly to the root would produce the orthographic sequences *-ga-* and *-go-*, which represent [ga] and [go], respectively. To overcome the problem, orthographic *-e-* is inserted after *-g-*. So, instead of **mangons* and **mangant*, which would be pronounced [mãgɔ̃] and [mãgã] respectively, we find *mangeons* and *mangeant*. Recall (2: 2.4) that the orthographic sequence *-gi-* represents [ʒi]; the suffixes *-ions* and *-iez* are therefore unproblematic, and no orthographic *-e-* is inserted. The full set of paradigms for *manger* is set out in Table 3.3. The forms to be attentive to are highlighted. Verbs with *-g*-final roots, which follow the pattern of *manger* in Table 3.3, include *changer, diriger, héberger, mélanger, loger, partager, ravager, exiger, purger, nager, venger, protéger* and *vendanger*.

The second deviation from the pattern in Table 3.2 due to orthographic convention concerns verbs like *placer*. Further, while the orthographic nature of the deviation is slightly different from the one in Table 3.3, the motivation is identical. In the case of verbs like *manger*, the verbal root ends in *-g-*, which cannot represent [ʒ] when followed by *-a-* or *-o-*. Instead, *-e-* is inserted. In the case of verbs like *placer*, the root ends in *-c-*, which, similarly, cannot represent [s] when followed by *-a-* or *-o-*. Consequently, where *-e-* is inserted in verbs like *manger*, some orthographic modification is needed with verbs like *placer*. However, in the case of verbs like *placer*, rather than inserting *-e-*, the letter *-c-* is changed to *-ç-*. The full set of

Table 3.3   Manger

Present	Imperfect	Past-historic	Future
mange	MANGEAIS	MANGEAI	mangerai
manges	MANGEAIS	MANGEAS	mangeras
mange	MANGEAIT	MANGEA	mangera
MANGEONS	mangions	MANGEÂMES	mangerons
mangez	mangiez	MANGEÂTES	mangerez
mangent	MANGEAIENT	mangèrent	mangeront

Present subjunctive	Imperfect subjunctive	Imperative	Participles
mange	MANGEASSE		
manges	MANGEASSES	mange	
mange	MANGEÂT		MANGEANT
mangions	MANGEASSIONS	MANGEONS	mangé
mangiez	MANGEASSIEZ	mangez	
mangent	MANGEASSENT		

Table 3.4   Placer

Present	Imperfect	Past-historic	Future
place	PLAÇAIS	PLAÇAI	placerai
places	PLAÇAIS	PLAÇAS	placeras
place	PLAÇAIT	PLAÇA	placera
PLAÇONS	placions	PLAÇÂMES	placerons
placez	placiez	PLAÇÂTES	placerez
placent	PLAÇAIENT	placèrent	placeront

Present subjunctive	Imperfect subjunctive	Imperative	Participles
place	PLAÇASSE		
places	PLAÇASSES	place	
place	PLAÇÂT		PLAÇANT
placions	PLAÇASSIONS	PLAÇONS	placé
placiez	PLAÇASSIEZ	placez	
placent	PLAÇASSENT		

paradigms for *placer* is set out in Table 3.4. The forms to be attentive to are highlighted. Verbs with -c-final roots which follow the pattern of *placer* in Table 3.4 include *annoncer, influencer, renoncer, balancer, lancer, divorcer, remplacer, fiancer, sucer, tracer, nuancer, prononcer, rincer, grincer, commencer, glacer* and *désamorcer*.

Verbs like *manger* and *placer* aren't the only deviations from the pattern in Table 3.2. However, other deviations can partly be explained in linguistic terms rather than on the basis of mere orthographic convention. To be precise, as we'll see in 3: 3.2.2, a number of first conjugation verbs have two oral roots, a phenomenon known as **stem alternation**. In other words, depending on syllabification and stress patterns, the root of these verbs is pronounced in

Table 3.5   Céder

Present	Imperfect	Past-historic	Future
CÈDE	cédais	cédai	céderai
CÈDES	cédais	cédas	céderas
CÈDE	cédait	céda	cédera
cédons	cédions	cédâmes	céderons
cédez	cédiez	cédâtes	céderez
CÈDENT	cédaient	cédèrent	céderont

Present subjunctive	Imperfect subjunctive	Imperative	Participles
CÈDE	cédasse		
CÈDES	cédasses	CÈDE	
CÈDE	cédât		cédant
cédions	cédassions	cédons	cédé
cédiez	cédassiez	cédez	
CÈDENT	cédassent		

two different ways. (This is unlike what we saw with *changer* and *placer*, whose roots are always pronounced the same way but have different orthographic forms.) Of relevance here is that these pronunciation differences are reflected in the orthography. There are two kinds of alternation. First, there are verbs like *céder*, which has the two roots: [sɛd-] (which occurs when the final syllable of the root is closed, as in [ʒə.sɛd]) and [sed-] (which occurs when the final syllable of the root is open, as in [nu.se.dɔ̃]). This difference in pronunciation is reflected in the orthography, as in *je cÈde* versus *nous cÉdons*. The full set of paradigms for *céder* is set out in Table 3.5, where the forms with -*è*- are highlighted. Verbs with oral stem alternation which follow the pattern of *céder* in Table 3.5 include *accélérer, accéder, célébrer, considérer, coopérer, compléter, espérer, digérer, exagérer, récupérer, pénétrer, régler, répéter, posséder, réitérer, inquiéter, révéler, précéder, suggérer, préférer, libérer, tolérer* and *interpréter*.

A different stem alternation is exemplified by *lever*, which has the two roots [lɛv-] (which occurs when the final syllable of the root is closed, as in [ʒə.lɛv]) and [ləv-] (which occurs when the final syllable of the root is open, as in [nu.lə.vɔ̃]). Again, this oral difference is reflected in the orthography, as in *je lÈve* versus *nous lEvons*. The full set of paradigms for *lever* is set out in Table 3.6, in which the forms with -*è*- are highlighted. Verbs with oral stem alternation which follow the pattern of *lever* in Table 3.6 include *peser, semer, mener, relever, promener, enlever, amener, acheter, crever* and *déceler*.

As a further example of the mismatch between orthography and pronunciation, compare the pattern in Table 3.6 with that of verbs like *jeter*. Despite having two oral roots, namely [ʒɛt-] and [ʒət-], and exactly the same kind of stem alternation as *lever*, the orthographic representation of the stem alternation is different. Roots with [ə] retain their final single consonant, while roots with [ɛ] have their final consonant doubled. The

Table 3.6   Lever

Present	Imperfect	Past-historic	Future
LÈVE	levais	levai	LÈVERAI
LÈVES	levais	levas	LÈVERAS
LÈVE	levait	leva	LÈVERA
levons	levions	levâmes	LÈVERONS
levez	leviez	levâtes	LÈVEREZ
LÈVENT	levaient	levèrent	LÈVERONT

Present subjunctive	Imperfect subjunctive	Imperative	Participles
LÈVE	levasse		
LÈVES	levasses	LÈVE	
LÈVE	levât		levant
levions	levassions	levons	levé
leviez	levassiez	levez	
LÈVENT	levassent		

Table 3.7   Jeter

Present	Imperfect	Past-historic	Future
JETTE	jetais	jetai	JETTERAI
JETTES	jetais	jetas	JETTERAS
JETTE	jetait	jeta	JETTERA
jetons	jetions	jetâmes	JETTERONS
jetez	jetiez	jetâtes	JETTEREZ
JETTENT	jetaient	jetèrent	JETTERONT

Present subjunctive	Imperfect subjunctive	Imperative	Participles
JETTE	jetasse		
JETTES	jetasses	JETTE	
JETTE	jetât		jetant
jetions	jetassions	jetons	jeté
jetiez	jetassiez	jetez	
JETTENT	jetassent		

full set of paradigms for *jeter* is set out in Table 3.7, in which the forms with consonant doubling are highlighted. Verbs with oral stem alternation which follow the pattern of *jeter* in Table 3.7 include *appeler, atteler, feuilleter, grommeler, jumeler, ficeler, projeter, cacheter* and *voleter*.

3.1.2   Second conjugation verbs

Most second conjugation verbs (*-ir* verbs) conform to the pattern illustrated by *finir* in Table 3.8. However, *haïr* [aiʀ] has three exceptional present tense forms, namely *(je) hais, (tu) hais* and *(il/elle) hait* (all [ɛ]). Otherwise, the written morphology of *haïr* is regular.

Table 3.8 Finir

Present	Imperfect	Past-historic	Future
finis	finissais	finis	finirai
finis	finissais	finis	finiras
finit	finissait	finit	finira
finissons	finissions	finîmes	finirons
finissez	finissiez	finîtes	finirez
finissent	finissaient	finirent	finiront

Present subjunctive	Imperfect subjunctive	Imperative	Participles
finisse	finisse		
finisses	finisses	finis	
finisse	finît		finissant
finissions	finissions	finissons	fini
finissiez	finissiez	finissez	
finissent	finissent		

More radical deviations from the pattern in Table 3.8 are the paradigms of common verbs like *dormir, tenir, sentir, venir, sortir* and *partir*, illustrated in (35).

(35) (je) dors   (tu) dors   (il/elle) dort
      (nous) dormons   (vous) dormez   (ils/elles) dorment

3.1.3 *Third conjugation verbs*

With third conjugation verbs (-*re* verbs), irregularity increases. The regular pattern is usually exemplified with *vendre* (see Table 3.9). Verbs which follow the pattern of *vendre* in Table 3.9 include *attendre, descendre, correspondre, perdre, mordre, défendre, rendre, prétendre, étendre, tordre* and *dépendre*.

However, many -*re* verbs, for example *être, rompre, prendre* and *joindre*, don't follow this pattern. Some grammarians have proposed a fourth conjugation containing the irregular verbs from the second and third conjugations, but linguistically this amounts to an admission of failure, since the whole point of a conjugation is to capture general patterns.

The analysis of the written morphology of French verbs in this section has shown the inadequacy of traditional classifications on the basis of infinitival endings. For example, the orthographic irregularity exhibited by verbs like *changer* and *placer* hides an underlying regular pattern. Further, even where the irregularity was linguistically motivated, it wasn't represented consistently in the orthography (cf. *levons/lève* versus *jetons/jette*). An arguably more satisfying approach to verb morphology considers oral rather than written forms.

Table 3.9 Vendre

Present	Imperfect	Past-historic	Future
vends	vendais	vendis	vendrai
vends	vendais	vendis	vendras
vend	vendait	vendit	vendra
vendons	vendions	vendîmes	vendrons
vendez	vendiez	vendîtes	vendrez
vendent	vendaient	vendirent	vendront

Present subjunctive	Imperfect subjunctive	Imperative	Participles
vende	vendisse		
vendes	vendisses	vends	
vende	vendît		vendant
vendions	vendissions	vendons	vendu
vendiez	vendissiez	vendez	
vendent	vendissent		

3.2 Oral verb morphology

In 3: 3.1.1–3 we discussed the written morphology of three verb conjugations, and concluded that such an approach was inadequate in a number of respects. In this section, we avoid the problems of orthography and consider the spoken language instead, using an analysis based on Martinet (1969).

Concentrating on oral patterns, we find verb morphology considerably more regular than written patterns suggest. However, we must recognise that some tenses, for example the imperfect subjunctive and the past-historic, have virtually disappeared from spontaneous spoken French, and accept that a plausible analysis of oral verb morphology doesn't need to deal with them. We will therefore only consider those finite and non-finite forms which occur in the spoken language.

In the approach adopted here, French verbs have two parts, namely a lexical root and one of the grammatical suffixes in Table 3.10. The suffixes remain constant (with the rare exception of infinitives and past participles) for all verb conjugations. The variation concerns the number of roots a verb has, and the way the roots interact with the suffixes. (In a number of cases the number of roots a verb has is increased because of the idiosyncratic behaviour of past participles.)

The suffixes in Table 3.10 are fusional (3: 1.2). They mark (non-)finiteness and, where appropriate, subject agreement. The numbers 1, 2 and 3 refer to first (*je*), second (*tu*) and third (*il/elle*) person singular; 4, 5 and 6 to first (*nous*), second (*vous*) and third (*ils/elles*) person plural. Recall that Ø indicates a null morpheme.

Table 3.10   The oral inflectional morphology of the French verb

Infinitive		-e, -R, -iR, -waR (depending on the verb)
Present	1, 2, 3, 6 4 5	-Ø -ɔ̃ -e*
Imperfect	1, 2, 3, 6 4 5	-ɛ -jɔ̃ -je
Future	1, 5 2, 3 4, 6	-Re -Ra -Rɔ̃
Conditional	1, 2, 3, 6 4 5	-Rɛ -Rjɔ̃ -Rje
Present subjunctive	1, 2, 3, 6 4 5	-Ø -jɔ̃ -je
Imperative	2 4 5	-Ø -ɔ̃ -e
Present participle		-ɑ̃
Past participle		-e, -y, -Ø, -i (depending on the verb, the feminine and plural can take an additional -t and/or -z; on past participle agreement see 4: 7.5)

*The verbs *dire*, *faire* and *être* take the suffix [-t] or -Ø, rather than [-e].

3.2.1   Verbs with one root

The suffixes in Table 3.10 attach to one of the verb's roots. This is illustrated in Table 3.11 with *chanter*, which only has one root, namely [ʃɑ̃t-] (see Table 3.2 in 3: 3.1.1). Given the redundancy in Table 3.11 (the root never varies), we can represent the same information more economically, as in Table 3.12, in which the root is given just once, and the suffixes from Table 3.10 are numbered alongside.

3.2.2   Verbs with two roots

For verbs with two roots, the table needs to indicate which suffixes attach to which root. One class of two-root verbs includes *jeter*, *lever* and *acheter*

Table 3.11

Infinitive	Present	Imperfect	Future	Conditional	Subjunctive	Imperative	Participles
	ʃãt+Ø	ʃãt+ɛ	ʃãt+ʀe	ʃãt+ʀɛ	ʃãt+Ø		
	ʃãt+Ø	ʃãt+ɛ	ʃãt+ʀa	ʃãt+ʀɛ	ʃãt+Ø	ʃãt+Ø	
	ʃãt+Ø	ʃãt+ɛ	ʃãt+ʀa	ʃãt+ʀɛ	ʃãt+Ø		ʃãt+ã
ʃãt+e	ʃãt+ɔ̃	ʃãt+jɔ̃	ʃãt+ʀɔ̃	ʃãt+ʀjɔ̃	ʃãt+jɔ̃	ʃãt+ɔ̃	ʃãt+e
	ʃãt+e	ʃãt+je	ʃãt+ʀe	ʃãt+ʀje	ʃãt+je	ʃãt+e	
	ʃãt+Ø	ʃãt+ɛ	ʃãt+ʀɔ̃	ʃãt+ʀɛ	ʃãt+Ø		

Table 3.12

	Infinitive	Present	Imperfect	Future	Subjunctive	Imperative	Participles
[ʃãt-]	-e	123456	123456	123456	123456	245	-e/-ã

Table 3.13

Infinitive	Present	Imperfect	Future	Conditional	Subjunctive	Imperative	Participles
	pɛz+Ø	pəz+ɛ	pɛz+ʀe	pɛz+ʀɛ	pɛz+Ø		
	pɛz+Ø	pəz+ɛ	pɛz+ʀa	pɛz+ʀɛ	pɛz+Ø	pɛz+Ø	
	pɛz+Ø	pəz+ɛ	pɛz+ʀa	pɛz+ʀɛ	pɛz+Ø		pəz+ã
pəz+e	pəz+ɔ̃	pəz+jɔ̃	pɛz+ʀɔ̃	pɛz+ʀjɔ̃	pəz+jɔ̃	pəz+ɔ̃	pəz+e
	pəz+e	pəz+je	pɛz+ʀe	pɛz+ʀje	pəz+je	pəz+e	
	pɛz+Ø	pəz+ɛ	pɛz+ʀɔ̃	pɛz+ʀɛ	pɛz+Ø		

Table 3.14

	Infinitive	Present	Imperfect	Future	Subjunctive	Imperative	Participles
[pɛz-]		1236		123456	1236	2	
[pəz-]	-e	45	123456		45	45	-e/-ã

(see Tables 3.6 and 3.7 in 3: 3.1.1). Their behaviour is illustrated with *peser*, with the roots [pɛz-] and [pəz-], shown in Table 3.13.

Once again, given the redundancy in Table 3.13, we can represent the same information more economically, as in Table 3.14. Verbs behaving like *peser* include *amener* [amɛn-]/[amən-], *jeter* [ʒɛt-]/[ʒət-], *promener* [pʀɔmɛn-]/[pʀɔmən-] and *rappeler* [ʀapɛl-]/[ʀapəl-]. (On schwa deletion see 2: 9.2.)

Another class of two-root verbs includes regular -*ir* verbs like *finir* (see Table 3.8 in 3: 3.1.2). *Finir* has two roots, namely [fini-] and [finis-], to which the suffixes in Table 3.10 attach as in Table 3.15. Verbs behaving like *finir* include *éclaircir*, *élargir* and *abasourdir*. Slightly different two-root verbs are *conduire* [kɔ̃dɥi-]/[kɔ̃dɥiz-], *produire* [pʀɔdɥi-]/[pʀɔdɥiz-], *dire* [di]/[diz-], *cuire* [kɥi-]/[kɥiz-] and *construire* [kɔ̃stʀɥi-]/[kɔ̃stʀɥiz-]. These differ

Table 3.15

	Infinitive	Present	Imperfect	Future	Subjunctive	Imperative	Participles
[fini-]	-R	123		123456		2	-Ø
[finis-]		456	123456		123456	45	-ɑ̃

Table 3.16

	Infinitive	Present	Imperfect	Future	Subjunctive	Imperative	Participles
[kɔ̃dɥi-]	-R	123		123456		2	-Ø
[kɔ̃dɥiz-]		456	123456		123456	45	-ɑ̃

Table 3.17

	Infinitive	Present	Imperfect	Future	Subjunctive	Imperative	Participles
[pɛʀ-]		123				2	
[pɛʀd-]	-R	456	123456	123456	123456	45	-y/-ɑ̃

Table 3.18

Infinitive	Present	Imperfect	Future	Conditional	Subjunctive	Imperative	Participles
	li+Ø	liz+ɛ	li+ʀe	li+ʀɛ	liz+Ø		
	li+Ø	liz+ɛ	li+ʀa	li+ʀɛ	liz+Ø	li+Ø	
	li+Ø	liz+ɛ	li+ʀa	li+ʀɛ	liz+Ø		l+y
li+ʀ	liz+ɔ̃	liz+jɔ̃	li+ʀɔ̃	li+ʀjɔ̃	liz+jɔ̃	liz+ɔ̃	liz+ɑ̃
	liz+e	liz+je	li+ʀe	li+ʀje	liz+je	liz+e	
	liz+Ø	liz+ɛ	li+ʀɔ̃	li+ʀɛ	liz+Ø		

from verbs like *finir* in the final consonant of their long root, namely [z] instead of [s] (see Table 3.16).

Ecrire is another two-root verb which patterns with *finir* and *conduire* in Tables 3.15 and 3.16, but its roots are [ekʀi-] and [ekʀiv-]. Finally, *perdre* also has two roots, but the suffixes in Table 3.10 attach to the roots slightly differently (see Table 3.17). Verbs patterning like *perdre* include *attendre*, *défendre*, *entendre*, *rendre*, *répondre*, *vendre*, *tendre*, as well as *battre*, whose roots are [ba-] and [bat-].

3.2.3   Verbs with three roots

As we move on to verbs with more roots, we find fewer verbs but steadily more idiosyncratic behaviour. *Lire* is an example of a three-root verb; it patterns as in Table 3.18.

Table 3.19

	Infinitive	Present	Imperfect	Future	Subjunctive	Imperative	Participles
[li-]	-R	123		123456		2	
[liz-]		456	123456		123456	45	-ã
[l-]							-y

Table 3.20

	Infinitive	Present	Imperfect	Future	Subjunctive	Imperative	Participles
[mɛ-]		123				2	
[mɛt-]	-R	456	123456	123456	123456	45	-ã
[mi-]							-Ø/-z

Table 3.21

	Infinitive	Present	Imperfect	Future	Subjunctive	Imperative	Participles
[mœR-]		1236			1236	2	
[muR-]	-iR	45	123456	123456	45	45	-ã
[mɔR-]							-Ø/-t

The same information is given in Table 3.19, which shows that, its past participle aside, *lire* follows the pattern in Tables 3.15 and 3.16. The verbs *plaire* [plɛ-]/[plɛz-]/[pl-] and *taire* [tɛ-]/[tɛz-]/[t-] also pattern like *lire*.

The verb *mettre* has three roots, too, and Table 3.20 shows how they interact with the suffixes in Table 3.10. As indicated in Table 3.10, given that past participles sometimes have to be marked for agreement (3: 2.2; 4: 7.5), the phonetic nature of this agreement marking needs to be specified. Note that, its past participle aside, *mettre* follows the pattern in Table 3.17. Below are further examples of three-root verbs which behave like *mettre*. In each case, we give the three roots, indicate the root and suffix which combine to form the past participle and, where appropriate, the consonant to be added to the past participle to mark feminine gender agreement: *vivre* [vi-]/[viv-]/[vek-] (+[y]+Ø), *suivre* [sɥi-]/[sɥiv-]/[sɥivi] (+Ø), *offrir* [ɔfʀ-]/[ɔfʀi-]/[ɔfɛʀ-] (+Ø+[t]$_{fem}$), *ouvrir* [uv-]/[uvʀi-]/[uvɛʀ-] (+Ø+[t]$_{fem}$), *croire* [kʀwa-]/[kʀwaj-]/[kʀ-] (+[y]+Ø), *dormir* [dɔʀ-]/[dɔʀm-]/[dɔʀmi-] (+Ø), *sentir* [sã-]/[sãt-]/[sãti-] (+Ø), *partir* [paʀ-]/[paʀt-]/[paʀti-] (+Ø), *servir* [sɛʀ-]/[sɛʀv]/[sɛʀvi-] (+Ø).

Other three-root verbs differ slightly in having stem alternation; that is, the same vowel doesn't appear in all three roots, for example *plaindre* [plɛ̃]/[plɛɲ-]/[plɛ̃d-] and *mourir* [mɔʀ-]/[muʀ-]/[mœʀ-]. The interaction of these roots with the suffixes in Table 3.10 is set out in Table 3.21.

Table 3.22

Infinitive	Present	Imperfect	Future	Conditional	Subjunctive	Imperative	Participles
	dwa+Ø	dəv+ɛ	dəv+Re	dəv+Rɛ	dwav+Ø		
	dwa+Ø	dəv+ɛ	dəv+Ra	dəv+Rɛ	dwav+Ø	dwa+Ø	
	dwa+Ø	dəv+ɛ	dəv+Ra	dəv+Rɛ	dwav+Ø		dəv+ã
dəv+waR	dəv+ɔ̃	dəv+jɔ̃	dəv+Rɔ̃	dəv+Rjɔ̃	dəv+jɔ̃	dəv+ɔ̃	d+y
	dəv+e	dəv+je	dəv+Re	dəv+Rje	dəv+je	dəv+e	
	dwav+Ø	dəv+ɛ	dəv+Rɔ̃	dəv+Rɛ	dwav+Ø		

3.2.4   Verbs with four roots

Four-root verbs include *devoir*, with the roots [dwa-]/[dəv-]/[dwav-]/[d-] and the distribution in Table 3.22. *Recevoir* and *apercevoir* also behave like *devoir*. *Paraître* is a four-root verb, too, but its distribution differs slightly from that of *devoir* (see Table 3.23).

Other four-root verbs are *tenir* [tjɛ̃-]/[tən-]/[tjɛn-]/[tjɛ̃d-], *venir* [vjɛ̃-]/[vən-]/ [vjɛn-]/[vjɛ̃d-], *voir* [vwa-]/[vwaj-]/[ve-]/[v-], *valoir* [vo-]/[val-]/[vaj-]/[vod-] and *boire* [bwa-]/[byv-]/[bwav-]/[b-].

3.2.5   Verbs with five roots

Five-root verbs include *prendre* (see Table 3.24). *Apprendre*, *reprendre* and *comprendre* also behave like *prendre*. Other five-root verbs are *savoir* [sɛ-]/ [sav-]/[so-]/[sa-]/[s-], *faire* [fɛ-]/[fəz-]/[fɔ̃-]/[fəR-]/[fas-] and *vouloir* [vø-]/[vul-]/ [vœl-]/[vud-]/[vœj-].

3.2.6   Verbs with six roots

This 'group' contains only one verb, *aller*, whose roots are [vɛ-]/[va-]/[al-]/ [vɔ̃-]/[i-]/ [aj-] (see Table 3.25).

3.2.7   Verbs with seven roots

This group contains just two verbs, namely *pouvoir* [pø-]/[puv-]/[pœv-]/ [pu-]/[pɥis-]/[p-]/[pɥi-] and *avoir* [e-]/[a-]/[av-]/[ɔ̃-]/[o-]/[ɛj-]/[Ø-]. (Note that [Ø] represents a null morpheme; here, it relates to the verb form *ont*, analysed as [Ø+ɔ̃].)

3.2.8   Verbs with nine roots

This 'group' contains the most irregular French verb of all, *être*, which has the paradigms shown in Table 3.26.

Table 3.23

	Infinitive	Present	Imperfect	Future	Subjunctive	Imperative	Participles
[paʀɛ-]		123				2	
[paʀɛs-]		456	123456		123456	45	-ã
[paʀɛt-]	-ʀ			123456			
[paʀ-]							-y

Table 3.24

	Infinitive	Present	Imperfect	Future	Subjunctive	Imperative	Participles
[pʀã-]		123				2	
[pʀən-]		45	123456		45	45	-ã
[pʀɛn-]		6			1236		
[pʀãd-]	-ʀ			123456			
[pʀi-]							-Ø/-z

Table 3.25

	Infinitive	Present	Imperfect	Future	Subjunctive	Imperative	Participles
[vɛ-]		1					
[va-]		23				2	
[al-]	-e	45	123456		45	45	-ã/-e
[vɔ̃-]		6					
[i-]				123456			
[aj-]					1236		

Table 3.26

Infinitive	Present	Imperfect	Future	Conditional	Subjunctive	Imperative	Participles
	sɥi+Ø	ɛt+ɛ	sə+ʀe	sə+ʀɛ	swa+Ø		
	e+Ø	ɛt+ɛ	sə+ʀa	sə+ʀɛ	swa+Ø	swa+Ø	
	ɛ+Ø	ɛt+ɛ	sə+ʀa	sə+ʀɛ	swa+Ø		ɛt+ã
ɛt+ʀ	sɔm+Ø	ɛt+jɔ̃	sə+ʀɔ̃	sə+ʀjɔ̃	swa+jɔ̃	swaj+ɔ̃	ɛt+e
	ɛt+Ø	ɛt+je	sə+ʀe	sə+ʀje	swa+je	swaj+e	
	sɔ̃+Ø	ɛt+ɛ	sə+ʀɔ̃	sə+ʀɛ	swa+Ø		

3.2.9 How to justify this approach

The approach to French oral verb morphology in 3: 3.2.1–8 is based on the observation that, generally, verb forms reliably comprise a root followed by a suffix from Table 3.10, marking (non-)finiteness and subject agreement. While this approach led us to conclude that French verbs have as many as nine roots, it can be justified by the interesting insights it uncovers, insights which remain hidden in the analysis of written verb morphology. Most importantly, an approach to verb morphology based on pronunciation avoids all the problems posed by orthographic convention we saw in 3: 3.1. Consequently, more verbs have fewer roots (that is, are more regular), and, indeed, by far the largest group of verbs is the one with a single oral root. As Martinet (1969) himself says, 'L'unicité du radical représente un idéal qui se trouve réalisé dans la grande majorité des verbes français.' Further, as already noted, in several cases (see Tables 3.19–24) the idiosyncratic behaviour of past participles means that the number of oral roots a given verb has is higher than it would otherwise be.

A second reason to think that the approach adopted here is along the right lines comes from the observation that those verbs with the largest number of roots, the most irregular verbs *être*, *aller* and *avoir*, are the most frequently occurring verbs in the spoken language. Children learning French as their first language therefore have a lot of exposure to these multi-root verbs, and are able to master the highly irregular forms.

Additional, and related, evidence in support of this approach to oral verb morphology comes from the 'errors' that young children acquiring French as their mother tongue make when conjugating verbs. Many 'errors' amount to attempts to regularise the verb paradigm, that is, to reduce the number of roots a verb has. Young Francophone children sometimes produce forms like **mouru* (instead of *mort*), **je mourirai* (*je mourrai*), **peindu* (*peint*), **je vas* (*je vais*), **vous faisez* (*vous faites*) and **vous disez* (*vous dites*). Indeed, morphologically complex verbs based on highly irregular verbs are sometimes more regular than the verbs they are based on, for example *vous contredisez* (**contredites*). Further, some regional varieties of French have regularised aspects of verb morphology (5: 3.4; 5: 4.1.2).

Finally, this approach allows us to distinguish between two types of infinitive in French, namely infinitives ending in [-e], by far the largest and most productive group, as well as the one tending to have a single root, and infinitives ending in [-ʀ], which might be taken by the learner as a signal that the verbs have more than one root.

4   Nominal morphology

As was the case with our discussion of adjectives (3: 2) and verbs (3: 3), our treatment of the inflectional morphology of French nouns needs to distinguish orthography (3: 4.1) from pronunciation (3: 4.2). A significant feature of both written and oral nominal morphology is the parallel with the morphology of adjectives.

4.1   Written nominal morphology

4.1.1   The straightforward cases

The most transparent pattern of written noun morphology follows that of adjectives (3: 2.1.1). For example, nouns like *avocat* (3: 1) are overtly marked, not only for number (singular versus plural), but also for gender (masculine versus feminine), as in *avocat, avocate, avocats, avocates*. The feminine plural form can be analysed in terms of the overtly realised morphemes shown in (36).

(36) morpheme:　　root　　gender　　number
　　　　　　　　　│　　　│　　　│
　　　word:　　avocat-　-e-　　-s

Such transparent gender and number marking is actually quite exceptional, even in written French, and in the next two sections we consider other orthographic realisations of gender and number.

4.1.2　Gender

In some cases, the orthographic realisation of gender on nouns is more straightforward than the pattern in 3: 4.1.1, in that the nouns concerned are invariant for gender. Nouns like *le/la concierge* and *le/la prof* fall into this category. A different but superficially similar situation involves pairs of nouns, such as *le/la mémoire*, where a change of gender isn't overtly marked on the nouns themselves, but nevertheless serves to indicate a change of meaning. Often, these meanings are clearly related, for example *le/la critique* and *le/la réglisse*, but this isn't always the case, as in *le/la page* and *le/la somme*.

In other cases, deviation from the pattern in 3: 4.1.1 involves increased complexity. Some words have orthographic forms which, like those of *avocat*, vary for gender (and number), but where feminine gender marking is more complex than the addition of orthographic *-e* (for similar patterns in written adjectival morphology see 3: 2.1.3):

(37)　a. Roots whose final consonant doubles: *chat/chatte,*
　　　　　chien/chienne, paysan/paysanne, etc.
　　　b. Roots whose final vowel changes: *fermier/fermière,*
　　　　　infirmier/infirmière, etc.
　　　c. Roots whose final consonant changes: *loup/louve*.

More complex feminine suffixes are illustrated in (38) (for similar patterns in written adjectival morphology see 3: 2.1.4):

(38)　a. *-esse*, as in *prince/princesse, âne/ânesse, prêtre/prêtresse,*
　　　　　poète/poétesse, Suisse/Suissesse;
　　　b. *-eresse*, alternating with masculine *-eur*, as in *bailleur/*
　　　　　bailleresse, défendeur/défenderesse, chasseur/chasseresse,
　　　　　pécheur/pécheresse;
　　　c. *-rice*, alternating with masculine *-eur*, as in *instituteur/*
　　　　　institutrice;

    d. *-euse*, alternating with masculine *-eur*, as in *joueur/joueuse*;

    e. *-elle*, alternating with masculine *-eau*, as in *chameau/ chamelle*.

Elsewhere, with pairs designating kinship terms, or the two sexes of the same species, there's no real morphological relationship at all, as in *père/mère*, *frère/sœur*, *bélier/brebis*, *porc/truie*, etc. (Young French speakers sometimes also make the mistake of thinking that *la souris* is the feminine of *le rat!*)

Finally, a number of words designating professions don't have generally accepted feminine forms (Walter 1988: 308), for example *professeur* (NB: *le/la prof*), *peintre*, *auteur*, *écrivain*, *ingénieur* and *médecin*, which are all grammatically masculine. (Note, though, the Canadian French feminine forms *professeure*, *auteure* and *écrivaine*; 5: 4.1.3.) The traditional way of forming the feminine equivalent of these terms is *un professeur femme*, *un peintre femme* or *une femme professeur*, *une femme peintre*. Note a similar process with animals, *une gazelle mâle*, *une souris mâle*, etc.

In summary, gender distinctions aren't always overtly marked in the same way. Sometimes the masculine has a zero realisation ($\emptyset$), while the feminine is overtly marked; in other cases, both masculine and feminine are marked distinctly. However, the vast majority of nouns don't mark gender in any straightforward way. Although there are orthographic generalisations allowing gender to be predicted (Tucker *et al.* 1977), we could treat most French nouns as fusional morphemes, comprising the root and the gender morpheme, especially where the gender isn't semantically motivated. For example, with nouns like *église* or *toit* we might propose the morphological analysis shown in (39).

(39) morpheme: root gender number   morpheme: root gender number

                 \ / | \ / |

    word: église   -$\emptyset$/-s   word: toit   -$\emptyset$/-s

Note that the gender of animate nouns can't always be predicted, for instance *la sentinelle*, *la victime*, *la brute*, *la dupe*, *la personne*, *le témoin*, *le bébé* (3: 1) and, for professional titles, *Madame le juge*, *Madame le ministre* (although, increasingly, *la ministre* and *la députée* are accepted).

4.1.3   Number

As we saw in 3: 4.1.1, number is almost always marked on French nouns orthographically as a null morpheme ($\emptyset$) for singular and a final *-s* for plural, as in *le toit* versus *les toits* (for similar patterns with adjectives see 3: 2.1.1). Nevertheless, there are a couple of common exceptions, which are, again, similar to what we saw in the context of written adjectival morphology in 3: 2.1.2–5.

First, nouns whose roots already end in orthographic -*s* don't take plural -*s*, for example *les rubis, les Anglais, les mois, les fois, les poids, les pois* and *les bras* (3: 2.1.2). Second, nouns whose roots end in orthographic -*x* and -*z* behave like those whose roots end in -*s*, and don't vary orthographically for number, for example *les noix, les nez, les croix, les voix* and *les gaz* (3: 2.1.2).

Third, nouns whose roots end in -*eau* form their plural with orthographic -*x*, rather than -*s*, for example *les châteaux, les gâteaux* and *les bateaux*. Nouns whose roots end in -*ou* are less straightforward. Seven of them take orthographic -*x* in the plural, namely *les bijoux, les cailloux, les choux, les genoux, les hiboux, les joujoux* and *les poux*. All others form their plural with orthographic -*s*, for example *les trous, les sous, les verrous* and *les fous*.

Fourth, as with adjectives, nouns whose roots end in orthographic -*al* generally form their plurals with -*aux*, for example *le cheval/les chevaux* and *le caporal/les caporaux*. There are, however, a number of exceptions which take the regular orthographic -*s* plural marker, for example *les bals, les festivals* and *les carnavals*. Similarly, there are eleven (often archaic) nouns whose roots end in orthographic -*ail* and which also form their plurals with -*aux*, for example *travail/travaux, vitrail/vitraux, corail/coraux, bail/baux* and *émail/émaux*. Others take -*s*, for example *les détails* and *les portails*. The noun *ail* is unusual in having two plurals, namely *les aulx* ([o]) and *les ails* ([aj]).

Finally, the pair *l'œil* and *les yeux*, though related etymologically and in meaning, may best be learnt as two separate forms.

4.2 Oral nominal morphology

In their oral morphology, too, French nouns are very similar to adjectives (3: 2.2), and we'll limit ourselves to a brief overview. Starting with gender, there are three patterns. First, some nouns are invariable for gender, for example *le/la concierge* [kɔ̃sjɛʀʒ]. Second, some nouns have roots on which masculine gender has a zero realisation, while feminine gender is realised as a single consonantal suffix (possibly with a modification in the quality of the stressed vowel), for example [ʃa]/[ʃat], [fɛʀmje]/[fɛʀmjɛʀ], [vwazɛ̃]/ [vwazin], [lu]/[luv], [ʃjɛ̃]/[ʃjɛn]. Third, some masculine/feminine pairs can be analysed as morphologically complex, comprising a root and a derivational suffix with suppletive masculine and feminine forms, for example [ʒwœʀ]/[ʒwøz] and [ɛ̃stitytœʀ]/[ɛ̃stitytʀis]. These three patterns are summarised in Table 3.27.

With respect to number, there's very little oral morphology, and, liaison contexts aside (2: 15.5), the vast majority of nouns are invariable (for the realisation of number on nominals see 4: 2). The only real exception relates to nouns with fusional forms, that is a singular and a plural root, for example *le travail* versus *les travaux* (see (40)).

(40) morpheme: singular root   plural root
      word: [tʀavaj]   [tʀavo]
                 [ʃəval]   [ʃəvo]

Table 3.27

	Morpheme:	Root	Gender
Group 1	word:	[kɔ̃sjɛʀʒ]	-Ø/-Ø
Group 2	word:	[ʃa] [lu] [ʃjɛ̃]	-Ø/-t -Ø/-v -Ø/-n (+denasalisation)
	Complex root:	*Root + masculine*	*Root + feminine*
Group 3	word:	[ɛ̃stitytœʀ] [ʃamo]	[ɛ̃stitytʀis] [ʃamɛl]

5   A brief introduction to derivational morphology

In 3: 1.3 we distinguished between inflectional and derivational morphology, and in 3: 2–4 we reviewed inflectional morphology with adjectives, verbs and nouns. So far, we've only briefly considered derivational morphology, as illustrated in (41):

(41) a. tricher → tricheur
  b. vendre → vendeur
  c. porter → porteur

The nouns *tricheur*, *vendeur* and *porteur* are related to the verbs *tricher*, *vendre* and *porter* respectively, in the sense that the nouns denote the **agent** of (the person who carries out) the action expressed by the verb. Contrasting the morphological processes illustrated in (41) with those in 3: 2–4, we can say, for example, that while *avocat*, *avocats*, *avocate* and *avocates* are in an intuitive sense all grammatically triggered different forms of the same word, the verb *tricher* and the noun *tricheur* are distinct words. (See (18) in 3: 1.3.)

Space limitations prevent us from detailing derivational morphology. Instead, we briefly review the topic, discussing the lexicon in 3: 5.1, derivational processes in 3: 5.2 and **compounding** in 3: 5.3.

5.1   The lexicon

Fluent language users know a large number of words. 'Knowing a word' means knowing how to pronounce it in context, knowing what it means, knowing whether (and how) it varies morphologically, and knowing how it can combine with other words. This knowledge is stored in the speaker's mental dictionary, or **lexicon**. The lexicon provides a speaker with the idiosyncratic information needed to use words appropriately.

The lexicon also contains morphological knowledge allowing speakers to use new words. For example, by understanding the meaning and morphological structure of *francophone*, we also understand words like *anglophone*, *russophone*, *danophone*, *norvégiophone* and *lusophone*, even if we haven't heard these words before, and even if they don't all appear in dictionaries. We can do this because we 'know' a morphological process which attaches the suffix *-phone* to a root denoting a language, and derives an adjective describing individuals who speak that language.

The lexicon is the most innovative part of language; it's always open to change, and adapts itself to cultural and social evolution. Creating new words (neologisms), and changing the meaning of existing ones, are often responses to extralinguistic factors. As we embark on the twenty-first century, we have only to think of the technological developments of the twentieth century to appreciate how languages have had to respond. Examples of lexical innovation can be seen in fields such as aviation, computing, the discovery of space, even economics (*la stagflation*, *les délits d'initié*) and cultural terms, such as *le magnétoscope*, *l'aéroglisseur*, *le livre de poche* and *spationaute*.

The diversity of word formation processes makes the French lexicon appear superficially highly heterogeneous. However, careful scrutiny reveals that there's actually a good deal of regularity beneath the surface. The use of derivational processes like prefixation and suffixation is discussed in 3: 5.2, while compounding is dealt with in 3: 5.3. Yet another way of enriching the lexicon is to borrow directly from other languages, a phenomenon which has been much criticised in official quarters in France (1: 7), especially where the borrowing has been from English, for example *le roller-skate*, *l'internet*, *le hot-dog*, *le irish coffee*, *le chewing-gum*, *le foot(ball)*, *le top* (top ten, etc.), *le management*, *un check-up*, *le bestseller*, *un scoop* and *le fairplay* (5: 8.2.3). English has also had a direct influence on the French lexicon, for example the word *opportunité* strictly speaking means 'opportuneness' or 'timeliness', but is increasingly used with the meaning of the English word *opportunity* (1: 7). Despite paranoia about what English is doing to French, note that borrowings and neologisms still draw heavily from Latin and Greek roots (see Wise 1997: ch. 3) and from migrant languages (5: 8.3.3), for example Arabic *le couscous* and *le méchoui*.

Also noteworthy, finally, in French is the use of acronyms as roots in the derivational process. For example, the initials of the trades union *la Conféderation générale du travail* give the acronym CGT [seʒete] as well as the root in *un cégétiste* (a member of the CGT). Similarly, the acronym SMIC [smik] (*salaire minimum interprofessionnel de croissance*) is the root of *smicard* (someone on the minimum wage), and RMI [ɛʀɛmi] (*revenu minimum d'insertion*) is the root of RMiste (sic) (someone on welfare or income support) (3: 5.2.1).

5.2   *Some derivational processes in Modern French*

5.2.1   *Derivational suffixes*

* [$_{suffix}$ [$_{root}$ X] -ment]

This derives an adverb from an adjectival root. A traditional problem for
the formal analysis of this process is how to describe the adjectival root to
which the suffix attaches. Derived adverbs like *relativement* and *purement*
suggest that the process uses feminine forms of adjectives. This is problematic if feminine forms are first derived from masculine ones:

$$\begin{array}{ccc} \text{root} & \text{inflection} & \text{derivation} \\ (42) \ \big[\ \big[\ \big[\ \text{pur-} \ \big] & \text{-e-} \ \big] & \text{-ment} \big] \end{array}$$

The problem is that this analysis runs counter to the generalisation (3: 1.3)
that processes of derivational morphology precede processes of inflectional
morphology. However, if we accept the alternative approach to the inflectional morphology of adjectives (3: 2.2), whereby final consonants are
deleted from adjectival roots to derive masculine forms, we could take the
'feminine' form to be the root. Then, suffixation of *-ment* directly to the
adjectival root is unproblematic and the following forms can be accounted
for:

(43) a. clairement   b. mûrement   c. postérieurement
     d. proprement   e. franchement

However, this analysis still fails to account for the derivation of *-ment*
adverbs from adjectives ending in orthographic *-ent* and *-ant*. If the 'feminine' root were used, we would expect the following ungrammatical forms
to be grammatical:

(44) a. *suffisantement   b. *bruyantement   c. *évidentement

Instead, the grammatical forms are:

(45) a. suffisamment   b. bruyamment   c. évidemment

A full explanation of what's going on here would take us into the realms
of French historical phonology and morphology, in particular the development of nasal vowels, which is beyond the scope of this book.

   With respect to the distinction between inflectional and derivational
morphology in 3: 1.3, and in particular the criteria in (18), suffixation of
-ment to an adjectival root clearly satisfies criterion (iii′) for derivational
morphology, in that it turns an adjective into an adverb. It also satisfies

criterion (ii′) by not being totally productive, as demonstrated by the non-existence of the following:

(46) a. *permanentement   b. *permanemment   c. *mixtement
     d. *modalement   e. *efféminément

The suffix *-ment* which derives an adverb from an adjectival root shouldn't be confused with the suffix *-ment* which derives a masculine abstract noun from a verbal root. This process derives a noun expressing the result of, or an attitude associated with, the meaning of the verbal root:

(47) a. égarer → [$_{\text{suffix}}$ [$_{\text{root}}$ égare-] -ment]
     b. effarer → effarement
     c. abattre → abattement
     d. écœurer → écœurement
     e. décourager → découragement

- [$_{\text{suffix}}$ [$_{\text{root}}$ X] -isme] and [$_{\text{suffix}}$ [$_{\text{root}}$ X] -iste]

The suffixes *-isme* and *-iste* can be considered together since, generally speaking, where one is possible, the other is too. The suffix *-isme* derives a masculine noun denoting a school of thought, while *-iste* attaches to the same root to derive a noun denoting a follower of that school of thought (the gender of the derived noun ending in *-iste* depends on the sex of the referent).

(48) a. commun → [$_{\text{suffix}}$ [$_{\text{root}}$ commun-] -isme], [$_{\text{suffix}}$ [$_{\text{root}}$ commun-] -iste]
     b. capital → [$_{\text{suffix}}$ [$_{\text{root}}$ capital-] -isme], [$_{\text{suffix}}$ [$_{\text{root}}$ capital-] -iste]
     c. idéal → [$_{\text{suffix}}$ [$_{\text{root}}$ idéal-] -isme], [$_{\text{suffix}}$ [$_{\text{root}}$ idéal-] -iste]

The creativity of derivational morphology can be illustrated by the variety of roots available, for example names and phrases:

(49) a. Mitterrand → [$_{\text{suffix}}$ [$_{\text{root}}$ mitterrand-] -isme],
        [$_{\text{suffix}}$ [$_{\text{root}}$ mitterrand-] -iste]
     b. Thatcher → [$_{\text{suffix}}$ [$_{\text{root}}$ thatchér-] -isme],
        [$_{\text{suffix}}$ [$_{\text{root}}$ thatchér-] -iste]
     c. Le Pen → [$_{\text{suffix}}$ [$_{\text{root}}$ lepén-] -isme], [$_{\text{suffix}}$ [$_{\text{root}}$ lepén-] -iste]
     d. Jospin → [$_{\text{suffix}}$ [$_{\text{root}}$ jospin-] -isme], [$_{\text{suffix}}$ [$_{\text{root}}$ jospin-] -iste]
     e. je m'en fous → [$_{\text{suffix}}$ [$_{\text{root}}$ je m'en fou(t)-] -isme],
        [$_{\text{suffix}}$ [$_{\text{root}}$ je m'en fou(t)-] -iste]

- [$_{\text{suffix}}$ [$_{\text{root}}$ X] -ation]

This process derives an abstract feminine noun, generally from a verbal root:

(50) a. exciter → [$_{\text{suffix}}$ [$_{\text{root}}$ excit-] -ation]
b. importer → [$_{\text{suffix}}$ [$_{\text{root}}$ import-] -ation]
c. préparer → [$_{\text{suffix}}$ [$_{\text{root}}$ prépar-] -ation]
d. orienter → orientation
e. provoquer → provocation
f. inciter → incitation
g. recommander → recommandation

The process isn't fully productive, though, and the following don't exist (although other suffixation processes are available):

(51) a. tolérer → *tolération (*but*: (in)tolérance)
b. assurer → *assuration (*but*: assurance)

Sometimes, the form of the root or the suffix deviates slightly from the pattern above:

(52) a. introduire → *introduiration (*but*: introduction)
b. interroger → *interrogeation (*but*: interrogation)
c. adopter → *adoptation (*but*: adoption)

- [$_{\text{suffix}}$ [$_{\text{root}}$ X] -ifier]

This process generally derives verbs from adjectives:

(53) a. solide → [$_{\text{suffix}}$ [$_{\text{root}}$ solid-] -ifier]
b. pur → [$_{\text{suffix}}$ [$_{\text{root}}$ pur-] -ifier]
c. simple → [$_{\text{suffix}}$ [$_{\text{root}}$ simpl-] -ifier]
d. vif/vive → [$_{\text{suffix}}$ [$_{\text{root}}$ viv-] -ifier]

It isn't fully productive:

(54) a. gris → *grisifier   b. froid → *froidifier   c. sûr → *sûrifier

The form of the root isn't always as expected:

(55) a. clair → clarifier (*clairifier)
b. glorieux → glorifier (*glorieusifier)

The output from this suffixation process can provide the input for a further process, deriving abstract feminine nouns through suffixation of -cation (3: 1.1):

(56) a. simplifier → [$_{\text{suffix}}$ [$_{\text{root}}$ simplifi-] -cation]
    b. purifier → purification
    c. vivifier → vivification

- [$_{\text{suffix}}$ [$_{\text{root}}$ X] -iser]

This process turns an adjectival root into a verb:

(57) a. verbal → [$_{\text{suffix}}$ [$_{\text{root}}$ verbal-] -iser]
    b. immobile → [$_{\text{suffix}}$ [$_{\text{root}}$ immobil-] -iser]
    c. stérile → [$_{\text{suffix}}$ [$_{\text{root}}$ stéril-] -iser]
    d. viril → [$_{\text{suffix}}$ [$_{\text{root}}$ viril-] -iser]

Once again, the output from this process can provide the input for a further process, deriving abstract feminine nouns through suffixation of *-(is)ation* (3: 1.1):

(58) a. verbaliser → [$_{\text{suffix}}$ [$_{\text{root}}$ verbalis-] -ation]
    b. immobiliser → immobilisation
    c. stériliser → stérilisation
    d. viriliser → virilisation

- [$_{\text{suffix}}$ [$_{\text{root}}$ X] -age]

Suffixation of *-age* onto a verbal root derives a masculine noun which denotes the unfolding of the action described by the verb:

(59) a. pétrir (pétrissant) → [$_{\text{suffix}}$ [$_{\text{root}}$ pétriss-] -age]
    b. modeler → modelage
    c. mixer → mixage
    d. élaguer → élagage
    e. marier → mariage

Again, this process isn't fully productive:

(60) a. donner → *donnage (*but*: donation)
    b. noyer → *noyage (*but*: noyade)
    c. humilier → *humiliage (*but*: humiliation)

5.2.2 *Derivational prefixes*

Prefixes are morphemes which attach before the root. While derivational suffixes sometimes alter the category of the root, prefixes do not. However, like derivational suffixes, prefixes aren't fully productive.

- [_{prefix} in- [_{root} X]]

This prefix attaches to an adjectival root to derive its **antonym**, that is an adjective with the opposite meaning. For instance, *discipliné* means the opposite of *indiscipliné*, derived by prefixation of *in-*. Here are some further examples of *in-* prefixation:

(61) a. conscient → [_{prefix} in- [_{root} conscient]]
      b. contestable → incontestable
      c. certain → incertain
      d. actif → inactif
      e. apte → inapte
      f. direct → indirect

Note that the pronunciation of the prefix *in-* varies depending on whether the root is vowel- or consonant-initial. For example, compare [inaktif] with [ɛ̃kɔ̃testablə]. In other cases the prefix-final nasal [-n] assimilates to the root-initial consonant (2: 11.1):

(62) a. *inlisible → illisible [ilizibl]
      b. *inrésolu → irrésolu [iʀezɔly]
      c. *inrésistible → irrésistible [iʀezistibl]
      d. *inmobile → immobile [imɔbil]

There are also cases where, in purely orthographic terms, the prefix-final -n assimilates to a root-initial bilabial (although this makes no difference to pronunciation in the modern language):

(63) a. *inpoli → impoli
      b. *inbuvable → imbuvable
      c. *inbattable → imbattable

Orthographic forms like *impoli* and *imbuvable* are historical relics, and probably reflect pronunciation in the twelfth century when the first orthographic conventions were laid down for French. Subsequent phonological change, namely the development of nasal vowels, has resulted in the loss of the nasal consonant in these words.

- [_{prefix} re- [_{root} X]]/[_{prefix} ré- [_{root} X]]/[_{prefix} r- [_{root} X]]

The prefix *re-/ré-/r-* attaches to a verb, often to derive another verb expressing repetition of the action denoted by the original verb. For instance, *rappeler* can mean 'to call again'. However, this prefix can have other effects on meaning. For example, it can have the sense of 'to return (to an original state)', as in *renvoyer*, which can mean 'to send back', and *repayer*, which means 'to pay back' rather than 'to pay again'. In fact, another possible interpretation of *rappeler* is 'to return someone's call' or 'to call back'. Note also the (non-standard) form *rerentrer*, in which prefixation has applied twice, first giving the meaning 'to go back inside', and second giving the meaning 'to go back inside again'. Finally, this process can highlight the completion of a process, as in *réunir*, *ramasser* and *raccourcir*.

(64) a. boucher → [$_{prefix}$ re- [$_{root}$ -boucher]]
   b. fermer → refermer ('to put the lid back on')
   c. s'habiller → se rhabiller ('to put one's clothes back on')
   d. chauffer → réchauffer ('to warm up')
   e. dire → redire

• [$_{prefix}$ mé- [$_{root}$ X]]

The prefix *mé-* attaches to noun and verb roots to derive a word which expresses the idea of an unsatisfactory entity or state of affairs. For instance, *se fier* means to trust, while *se méfier* means to mistrust. Here are some further examples:

(65) a. compte → [$_{prefix}$ mé- [$_{root}$ compte]]
   b. juger → méjuger
   c. connaissance → méconnaissance
   d. priser → mépriser

There are also at least two adjectives to which this prefixation process can apply, namely *content* and *connu*, which are related to *mécontent* and *méconnu*.

Other prefixes are *a-*, as in *moral* → *amoral*, *co-* as in *opérer* → *co-opérer*, *auteur* → *co-auteur*, *dé-* as in *mettre* → *démettre*, *non-* as in *existence* → *non-existence* and *pré-* as in *natal* → *prénatal* and *budget* → *prébudget*.

5.3 Compounding

The final process of derivational morphology we shall consider is **compounding**, that is, the creation of new lexical items from those which already exist in the language. An example of a compound is *le porte-bonheur*, made up of two separate lexical items, namely the verb *porte* and the noun *bonheur*. Here, the meaning of the compound is clear from the meaning of the two individual parts of the compound. However, such semantic transparency isn't always the case, as with *le garde-fou* and *le pare-brise*.

In the twentieth century, compounding was a common means of enriching the French lexicon, and words of almost all classes combined to form compounds. Examples of the most common patterns are listed below (note that orthographic plurals aren't always predictable, neither is the use of hyphenation):

(66) Noun + noun
    a. l'autoradio (les autosradios)
    b. le camion-citerne (les camions-citernes)
    c. le timbre-poste (les timbres-poste)
    d. le tapis-brosse (les tapis-brosses)
    e. le bébé-éprouvette (les bébés-éprouvettes)
    f. l'appui-main (les appuis-main(s))
       also l'appuie-main (les appuie-main(s))
    g. l'auto-école (les auto-écoles)
    h. le canapé-lit (les canapés-lits)
    i. la femme médecin (les femmes médecin)
    j. le médecin femme (les médecins femme)

(67) Verb + noun
    a. le porte-savon (les porte-savons)
    b. le porte-monnaie (les porte-monnaie)
    c. le porte-objet (les porte-objets)
    d. l'arrache-clou (les arrache-clous)
    e. le trouble-fête (les trouble-fête)
    f. l'aide-mémoire (les aide-mémoire)
    g. le chauffe-eau (les chauffe-eau)
    h. l'ouvre-bouteille (les ouvre-bouteilles)

(68) Verb + preposition + noun
    a. le tape-à-l'œil (les tape-à-l'œil) (note that this can also be
       used as an adjective as in *les politiques creuses mais tape-*
       à-l'œil de l'actuel gouvernement)
    b. le touche-à-tout (les touche-à-tout)

(69) Noun + preposition + noun
    a. l'arc-en-ciel (les arcs-en-ciel)
    b. le haut-de-forme (les hauts-de-forme)
    c. le cul-de-sac (les culs-de-sac)
    d. le coup de poing (les coups de poing)

(70) Adjective + noun
    a. la basse-cour (les basses-cours)
    b. le rond-point (les ronds-points)
    c. le faux-monnayeur (les faux-monnayeurs)

(71) Noun + adjective
    a. le sang-mêlé (les sang-mêlé)
    b. l'amour-propre (les amours-propres)
    c. le cul-terreux (les culs-terreux)

(72) Preposition + noun
    a. l'avant-bras (les avant-bras)
    b. l'après-demain (les après-demain)
    c. l'après-midi (les après-midi)
    d. l'après-guerre (les après-guerres)
    e. l'à-coup (les à-coups)
    f. le sans-abri (les sans-abri)
    g. l'à-côté (les à-côtés)

Recognising a compound isn't always straightforward, and particularly common compounds can soon come to be perceived as single words, for example *le passeport*. Further, in some apparent compounds, it's not always clear whether or not both parts of the compound actually are independent words, for example *anti-* in *antigel, anti-nucléaire, anticorps* and *antisocial*, as well as *archi-* in *archicélèbre, archiconnu* and *archiplein*.

6 Final remarks

In this study of French word formation we've seen how words often have a complex internal structure. Words are structured bundles of information called morphemes, some of which are grammatical (number and gender morphemes in the case of nouns and adjectives; (non-)finiteness, number and subject agreement morphemes in the case of verbs) and some of which are lexical; they refer to entities, concepts, emotions and so on in the real world. We've also briefly introduced processes of derivation, that is, processes available to speakers for enriching and adapting the lexicon to meet their changing needs. An important thread running through most of this chapter has been the need to distinguish written from oral morphology, that is orthography from pronunciation. Now that we are familiar with how French words are formed, the next step is to examine how they can be combined to form phrases and sentences. This is the topic of Chapter 4.

Further reading

For general introductions to word formation, see Aitchison (1987), Anderson (1988), Bauer (1988), Katamba (1993), Radford *et al.* (1999: chs 9, 10), Wise (1997). On French word formation, see Harris (1988: sec. 3), Spence (1996: chs 7–10), Thiele (1987). On orthography, see Catach (1993, 1995). On gender, see Corbett (1991), Gervais (1993), Spence (1996: ch. 13). On the gender of professional titles, see Brick and Wilks (1994), Muller (1994). On number, see Spence (1996: ch. 12). On verbal morphology, see Foley (1979), Gertner (1973), Lanly (1977), Picoche (1979). On the reduction of verbal irregularity, see Walker (1995). On nominal morphology, see Dubois (1965). On derivational morphology and lexical innovation, see Ball (1990), Corbin (1987), George (1993), Mitterand (1968), Noreiko (1993), Wise (1997: ch. 6). On prefixation, see Amiot (1995), Peytard (1975).

4 The sentence structure of French

In Chapter 3 we analysed French words as grammatical units with an internal structure in which a root, suffixes, etc. combine, following regular patterns. Of course, when we speak, we don't usually say isolated words. We usually utter **phrases** or **sentences** containing *a number of* words:

(1) a. Bonne chance!　　b. Très intéressant.　c. A votre santé!
(2) a. J'ai faim.　　　　b. Où va-t-elle?　　c. Tais-toi!

The utterances in (1) are short multi-word phrases, those in (2) are sentences. A sentence is a particular kind of phrase (4: 1.1). A phrase is a sequence of words which, *taken together*, form a linguistic unit. Consider, for example, (1c) *à votre santé*. These three words form a phrase because, together, they *mean* something. In contrast, the words *à votre* don't form a phrase because, together, they *don't* mean anything.

In this chapter we investigate the structure of multi-word phrases and sentences, like those in (1) and (2). As with words (see (2) in Chapter 3), we discover that phrases and sentences, too, have a regular internal structure. So, while (3a) is a grammatical sentence, (3b, c) are not (as indicated by the preceding asterisk):

(3) a. Les deux jeunes filles regardent les petits chats.
　　b. *Deux filles jeunes les regardent chats les petits.
　　c. *Filles les deux regardent jeunes petits les chats.

The sentence in (3a) differs from the *non*-sentences in (3b, c), in that the words in (3a) have been combined following the patterns of French phrase and sentence structure, while those in (3b, c) have not. The study of patterns of phrase and sentence structure is called **syntax**. This chapter is about French syntax.

To understand syntax fully, we need to bear in mind the major insight of Chapter 3, namely that different words belong to different **categories**. The major categories we've seen are **noun**, **verb** and **adjective**; another important category is **preposition**. In Chapter 3 we saw that a word's morphology is largely determined by its category. In this chapter we'll see that the way a word can combine with other words to form phrases or sentences – its syntax – is, similarly, largely determined by its category.

1 Verbal structures

1.1 Verbs, subjects and complements

We have described sentences as a particular kind of phrase. Sentences generally contain a particular kind of verb and a **subject**. Let's consider the verb first. While the examples in (4) are sentences (the verb is highlighted), the examples in (1) don't contain a verb, and therefore aren't sentences, but phrases.

(4) a. Nous PARTONS.
b. Tu DISAIS des bêtises.
c. Pierre et Yvette DONNÈRENT le cadeau à Marie.
d. Chaque enfant OBÉIRA à son père.

In each sentence in (4) the verb is preceded by a phrase (*nous*, *tu*, *Pierre et Yvette* and *chaque enfant*). Further, the form of the verb (3: 3) is determined by grammatical features of this phrase, namely its **person** and **number** features. In (4a) *nous* is first person plural, in (4d) *chaque enfant*, third person singular. In each case the verb has the corresponding form (*partONS* and not, for example, *partEZ*; *obéirA* and not *obéirAI*). In other words, there's morpho-syntactic **agreement** between the verb and the preceding phrase. The phrase whose number/person features determine verb morphology like this is called the **subject**; a verb which agrees with the number/person features of its subject is called a **finite verb**. In (4) *nous*, *tu*, *Pierre et Yvette* and *chaque enfant* are the subjects, *partons*, *disais*, *donnèrent* and *obéira*, the finite verbs.

Subjects play an important role in sentences, and their absence generally leads to ungrammaticality, in English as in French; just as a finite verb is essential to a sentence, so, too, is a subject. The importance of subjects in sentences can be understood in terms of what sentences are *for*. Sentences are often used to say something about something/someone. The subject is essential because it's the something/someone that the sentence says something about.

This special function of subjects allows us to understand a puzzling fact. While sentences require a finite verb and a subject in order to be grammatical, they vary as to whether they require other phrases. Look at what follows the finite verb in the sentences in (4). The verb *partir* isn't followed by anything; *dire* and *obéir* are followed by one further phrase (*des bêtises* and *à son père*, respectively); and *donner* is followed by *two* further phrases (*le cadeau* and *à Marie*). Moreover, the presence of these further phrases is compulsory; without them, the sentences in (4b–d) would be ungrammatical. (For discussion of optional phrases see 4: 11.) To understand these differences we need to look at the verbs one by one.

The sentence in (4a) contains the subject *nous* and (a form of) the verb *partir*, only. The subject is what the sentence is about, and *partir* 'says something' about the subject. No other phrases are needed. Verbs like *partir*, which, on their own, can 'say something' about a subject, are called **intransitive verbs**. Other intransitive verbs are *venir*, *aller*, *arriver*, *rire*, *sourire* and *dormir*.

In contrast to (4a), the sentences in (4b–d) contain more than a subject and a verb. In addition to the subject *tu* and the verb *dire*, (4b) contains an obligatory further phrase, namely *des bêtises*, known as a **direct object**. Unlike *partir*, *dire* cannot, on its own, 'say something' about the subject; it's only with the help of a direct object that *dire* 'says something' about the subject. Phrases such as direct objects are called **complements**, because they 'complement' the verb. In (4b) the direct object *des bêtises* 'complements' the verb by indicating what was said. French direct objects differ from subjects in two ways (but see 4: 7.2). First, subjects usually precede the finite verb, while direct objects usually follow. Second, a finite verb agrees with its subject, but not with its direct object. Verbs like *dire* which take a direct object are called **transitive verbs**. Other transitive verbs are *couvrir*, *dévorer*, *raconter* and *caresser*.

A different pattern is illustrated in (4c). In addition to a subject and the verb *donner*, the sentence contains *two* further phrases, namely *le cadeau* and *à Marie*, both of which 'complement' the verb. The first of these, *le cadeau*, is a direct object (it indicates what was given, just as *des bêtises* in (4b) indicates what was said). The second complement, *à Marie*, is called an **indirect object** (it indicates who *le cadeau* was given to). French indirect objects are similar to direct objects in that they follow the verb and don't determine verb morphology. They differ from direct objects in being introduced by a preposition, often *à* (4: 2.4). Verbs like *donner* which take *both* a direct *and* an indirect object are called **ditransitive verbs**. Other ditransitive verbs are *offrir* and *proposer*.

A different pattern again, finally, is illustrated in (4d), in which *obéir* takes an indirect object only. Verbs which take an indirect, but not a direct, object are called **indirect transitive verbs**. The indirect object is *à son père* and, as in (4c), is introduced by the preposition *à*. Other indirect transitive verbs are *convenir*, *plaire* and *nuire*.

1.2   Subcategories of verb and the minimal sentence

In 3: 3 we used *morphological* criteria to distinguish verbs from nouns and adjectives. We also used morphological grounds to distinguish different *types* of verbs (called conjugations), for example *-er* and *-ir* verbs. In 4: 1.1 we saw that, in their *syntactic* behaviour, too, not all verbs behave in the same way; they belong to different syntactic **subcategories**. A verb's subcategory corresponds to the nature of the complement(s) it minimally needs to form a phrase which 'says something' about the subject in a **minimal sentence**. A minimal sentence is one which contains no more than is necessary to achieve grammaticality, namely a subject, a finite verb and its complements (if it has any). Given that the verb is the most important element, or **head**, of that part of the sentence which 'says something' about the subject (the verb is, after all, what determines the nature of any complements), the phrase containing the verb and any complements is called a verb phrase, or VP for short. The VP in (4c) comprises a verb and two complements:

(5) Pierre et Yvette [$_{VP}$ [$_V$ donnèrent] [le cadeau] [à Marie]].

The VPs in (4b, d) comprise a verb and a single complement:

(6) a. Tu [$_{VP}$ [$_V$ disais] [des bêtises]].
    b. Chaque enfant [$_{VP}$ [$_V$ obéira] [à son père]].

Finally, the VP in (4a) comprises a bare verb (with no complements at all):

(7) Nous [$_{VP}$ [$_V$ partons]].

Given that the verb, together with any complements, forms a VP, we can revise our analysis of sentence structure. Rather than saying that a sentence comprises a subject, a verb and its complements, we can say that a sentence comprises a subject and a VP. The subject expresses what the sentence is about; the VP, what's being said about it. This generalisation applies to all the sentences in (4). The different patterns we've discussed don't therefore concern *sentence* structure as such, but rather *VP* structure. The VP contains a bare verb in (7), and a verb and a number of complements in (5) and (6). Crucially, VP structure is determined by the subcategory of its head, the verb.

We've ignored subjects in our discussion of VPs because subjects are crucially different from complements. First, French finite verbs agree with their subject but not with their complement(s). Second, a sentence always has exactly one subject, yet the number and nature of a verb's complements vary depending on its subcategory. Finally, the subject usually precedes the verb, while complements usually follow. In summary, then, there are good reasons for distinguishing subjects from complements; the verb and its complements form a phrase, VP, which excludes the subject. Of course, this is what we would expect: the subject expresses what the sentence is about, and the VP expresses what the sentence says about the subject.

Returning to direct objects, so far we've described them as postverbal phrases unmarked by a preposition like *à*. Yet not all the highlighted phrases in (8) are direct objects.

(8) a. Le chat tuera L'OISEAU.
   b. Vous pesez QUATRE-VINGTS KILOS.
   c. Je pars LA SEMAINE PROCHAINE.

A simple test shows whether or not a postverbal phrase is a direct object: direct objects undergo **pronominalisation** with (can be replaced by) forms such as *le/la/les* or *en* (4: 4.1). In (8) the postverbal phrases aren't all direct objects, since they don't all pronominalise:

(9) a. Le chat LE tuera.
   b. *Vous LES pesez.
   c. *Je LA pars.

We return to the postverbal phrases in (8b, c) in 4: 11. (The example in (8b) contrasts with *Vous pesez LES POMMES* where pronominalisation is possible – *Vous LES pesez* – because the postverbal phrase here is indeed the direct object.)

   In summary, we've seen that different verbs behave syntactically in different ways. Crucially, while a sentence generally needs a subject, irrespective of the nature of the verb heading the VP, whether or not complements are needed depends on the subcategory of the verb. Subjects are therefore distinguished from complements. In turn, within the class of complement, direct objects are distinguished from indirect objects. A cover label which we can use for all these concepts, and which will prove useful later, is **argument**. Subjects, direct objects and indirect objects are all arguments of the verb.

(10)
   Arguments
   ⎰ Subjects
   ⎱ Complements
      ⎰ Direct objects
      ⎱ Indirect objects

1.3   *Verbs which belong to more than one subcategory*

In 4: 1.1–2 we saw different verbs behaving syntactically in different ways, and we introduced the notion subcategory. In fact, some verbs seem to belong to more than one subcategory. For example, a number of transitive verbs have intransitive uses, too:

(11) a. Le chat TUE la souris. / L'alcool TUE.
   b. Marie VOIT le château. / Marc VOIT.
   c. Paul MANGE des cacahuètes. / Pauline MANGE.
   d. Les enfants CHANTENT des chansons. / Les enfants
      CHANTENT.

These sentences have subtly different interpretations depending on whether the verbs are used transitively or intransitively. The intransitive use of *voir* relates to being sighted (as opposed to being blind), whereas its transitive use relates to (a) specific instance(s) of seeing something. This semantic difference determines which subcategory the verb belongs to, that is whether complements are needed.

1.4 A final verbal subcategory: copulas

Before ending our discussion of types of verb, there's one final subcategory we need to mention, highlighted in (12):

> (12) a. Marie SERA la directrice de l'école.
> b. Jean et Yves DEVIENDRONT vos meilleurs amis.

Verbs like *être* and *devenir* are called **copulas**. Despite superficially resembling transitive verbs (they are followed by what look like direct objects), copulas are different in that they function like grammatical 'glue': in (12a, b) they hold together the subject (*Marie* and *Jean et Yves*, respectively) and another phrase (*la directrice de l'école* and *vos meilleurs amis*, respectively) which describes the subject. In fact, evidence suggesting that the verbs in (12) aren't transitive (and, consequently, that the postverbal phrases aren't direct objects) comes from facts about pronominalisation (4: 4.1). We saw in (9a) in 4: 1.2 that direct objects can pronominalise as agreeing pronouns. In (13) *la* and *les* agree with *cette tarte* and *toutes les infos*, respectively.

> (13) a. Marc mangera CETTE TARTE. → Marc LA mangera.
> b. Chris écoute TOUTES LES INFOS. → Chris LES écoute.

While pronominalisation is possible with copulas like *être* and *devenir* (unlike what we saw in (9b, c)), in the **standard language**, the pronoun *doesn't* agree in number/gender with the phrase it replaces, and is always *le*. This is shown in (14), in which the postcopular phrases from the examples in (12) have been pronominalised. Note that, although the replaced phrase is feminine in (14a) and plural in (14b), the corresponding pronoun is *le* in both cases:

> (14) a. Marie LE sera.   b. Jean et Yves LE deviendront.

We return to copulas in 4: 3.2.

In summary, we've seen that French verbs belong to different subcategories, heading different kinds of VP. Ultimately, the shape of the minimal sentence is determined by the subcategory of the verb. The concept of minimal sentence is a crucial one, and we see in 4: 11 that optional phrases providing supplementary information can be added to a minimal sentence, but that these optional phrases aren't as closely associated with the verb as its complements.

1.5 Types of sentence

Having looked at types of verb in 4: 1.1–4, we now turn to types of sentence. Before reading on, go back to the sentences in (2) and think about how they differ.

Sentences don't all serve the same purpose. For example, a sentence can make a statement:

(15) a. L'éléphant demandait une cigarette à la girafe.
b. Les élèves préparent leurs devoirs.

These are called **declarative sentences**, and are the type of sentence we concentrated on in 4: 1.2. Note that they have the characteristic sentence structure of a subject followed by a VP. Another kind of sentence is one which asks a question:

(16) a. Est-il content?   b. A qui parlent mes parents?

These are called **interrogative** sentences. The interrogative in (16a) is a **yes–no interrogative/question**, which invites a 'yes' or 'no' answer. In contrast, the interrogative in (16b) is a **constituent question**. Here, 'yes' or 'no' would be an inappropriate reply; instead, some specific information is required. Both interrogatives in (16) have a special structure; for example, the finite verb precedes, rather than follows, the subject (4: 6.2.2; 4: 7.2). Interrogatives don't always have a special structure, though. A question can have the structure of a declarative and be marked as an interrogative by a rising **intonation** on *banque* (2: 16.3).

(17) Tu vas à la banque?

Rather than making a statement or asking a question, a sentence may express the speaker's emotion, surprise or excitement:

(18) a. Quel beau chat dort sur ton lit!
b. Comme ils sont aimables aujourd'hui!

These are called **exclamatives**. Finally, a sentence may express a command and, again, have a special syntactic form. These are called **imperatives**:

(19) a. Partons!   b. Préparez vos devoirs!   c. Viens ici!

(Note that imperatives don't contain an overt subject.)

Each of these four sentences types (declarative, interrogative, exclamative and imperative) can vary with respect to a feature called **polarity**. Compare the examples in (20), which have **negative** polarity, with the ones above, which have **positive** polarity:

(20) a. Le chat NE dort PAS.
     b. NE sortez PAS!
     c. N'est-il PAS content?
     d. Comme ils NE sont PAS aimables aujourd'hui!

These sentences are negative due to the presence of the highlighted negative markers. We return to **negation** in 4: 12.

In summary, sentences can be declarative, interrogative, exclamative or imperative, and can have positive or negative polarity.

1.6 Basic sentence patterns

The word order in the declarative sentences in 4: 1.1–5 is known as **unmarked word order**, namely:

(21) [s subject VP]

In turn, unmarked VP structure follows the pattern in (22):

(22) [vp verb (direct object) (indirect object)]

The (round) brackets show that direct and indirect objects are optional (depending on the subcategory of the verb), but that when they do appear, the unmarked order is for both to follow the finite verb, and for the indirect object to follow the direct object. Unmarked word order is found in sentences which aren't being used to create any particular effect, such as contrast or stress. It's illustrated in the examples in (23):

(23)

Subject	[vp Verb	Direct object	Indirect object]
a. Marie	donne	un cadeau	à Pierre.
b. Les élèves	arrivent.		
c. Les enfants	obéissent		à leur père.
d. Le touriste	regarde	l'église.	

Sentences can have a **marked word order** for various reasons. The relative order of the direct and indirect object can change if the direct object is heavy (= relatively long):

(24)

Subject	[vp Verb	Direct object	Indirect object]
Marie	donne	à Pierre	un très beau cadeau qui a coûté très cher.

Unmarked word order can also be disturbed as a consequence of sentence type: in interrogatives the finite verb can precede the subject, as in (16a), repeated here:

(16) a. *Verb*   *Subject*   *Adjective*
         Est-   il   content?

Other phrases can appear sentence-initially, too, as in (16b), repeated here:

(16) b. *Indirect Object*   *Verb*   *Subject*
         A qui   parlent   mes parents?

In fact, these are complex phenomena, and we return to them in 4: 7. Finally, word order can be varied for special effect, for example to add particular emphasis to certain phrases within the sentence, and we consider examples of this in 4: 8.

2   Nominal structure

In 4: 1 we saw that sentences have an internal structure, comprising a subject and a VP. VP structure is determined by the subcategory of its head, the verb. The sentence in (3a), repeated here, comprises a subject (*les deux jeunes filles*) followed by a VP comprising a transitive verb (*regardent*) and a direct object (*les petits chats*).

(3) a. [Les deux jeunes filles] [$_{VP}$ [$_V$ regardent] [les petits chats]].

Like the sentence itself, the subject and direct object have an internal structure, too. In (3b, c) we saw that words within a sentence can't be randomly reordered without producing ungrammaticality, and the same is true of words within the subject or the direct object:

(25) a. *deux les filles jeunes   b. *petits chats les
     c. *filles deux les jeunes   d. *chats les petits

The subject and direct object in (3a) are centred on the nouns *filles* and *chats*. Indeed, the basic meaning of (3a) could be conveyed in economical (but ungrammatical) telegram-like style as *filles regardent chats*, retaining just the noun in each case. In 4: 1.2 we introduced the term verb phrase, VP, to refer to the phrase in the sentence headed by the verb. Since *les deux jeunes filles* and *les petits chats* are (a) phrases (sequences of words which form a meaningful unit) and (b) headed by nouns, we can call them noun phrases, or NPs.

(26) a. [$_{NP}$ les deux jeunes [$_N$ filles]]   b. [$_{NP}$ les petits [$_N$ chats]]

Often, a noun denotes a person, place or thing. But this isn't always the case (e.g. *amour*, *clarté* and *chômage*), and it's better to think of morpho-syntactic behaviour rather than meaning. A word is a noun, not because of what it means, but because of how it behaves; it has nominal morphology (3: 4) and heads an NP. To take the parallel with verbs one step further, we can distinguish between different *subcategories* of noun. For example, **proper nouns** – the names of people, places and products, such as *Pierre*, *Paris* and *Adidas* – can be distinguished from **common nouns**, which express more general notions, for example *fille*, *amour* and *œuf*.

In 4: 2.1 we consider an important characteristic of French NPs which contrasts with English NPs, namely the fact that they generally contain a grammatical word called a **determiner**, a word like *le*, *une*, *ces*, *votre*, *plusieurs* and *quel*. In 4: 2.2 we explore the different kinds of French determiner. In 4: 2.3 we integrate adjectives and *tout(e)(s)* into NP structure, and in 4: 2.4 we introduce prepositions.

2.1 Noun phrases and determiners

To understand the structure of the NPs in (26), we need to look at the words appearing with the noun. While proper nouns can appear alone in an NP, common nouns normally cannot. Consequently, while a bare proper noun can be an argument (see (10) in 4: 1.2), a bare common noun cannot:

(27) a. [$_{NP}$ [$_N$ PASCALE]] frappe [$_{NP}$ [$_N$ REX]].
   b. *[$_{NP}$ [$_N$ FILLE]] frappe [$_{NP}$ [$_N$ CHIEN]].

The sentence in (27b) is ungrammatical because bare common nouns in French are unable to refer to something in the non-linguistic world. While the word *chien* denotes the class of canine entities, it can't refer to any particular dog, or indeed to dogs in general, and it can't appear in an NP on its own and function as an argument. Thus (27b) becomes grammatical if we add a certain type of grammatical word to each bare noun.

(28) a. LA FILLE frappe UN CHIEN.   b. QUELLE FILLE frappe LE CHIEN?
   c. SA FILLE frappe CE CHIEN.   d. CETTE FILLE frappe SON CHIEN.

Words like *la/le*, *un*, *ce(tte)*, *quelle* and *son/sa* turn a bare non-referring noun into an NP which *does* refer and which can function as an argument. These words are called **determiners**. Unlike English NPs, French NPs headed by common nouns generally contain a determiner:

(29) a. CATS rarely drink BEER.
   b. *CHATS boivent rarement BIÈRE.
   c. LES CHATS boivent rarement DE LA BIÈRE.

There are, however, three exceptional contexts in which bare common nouns do occur in French. The first is fixed expressions, in which bare nouns appear as pseudo-direct objects, such as *avoir PEUR/FROID/CHAUD/ FAIM/SOIF/RAISON/TORT, faire FORTUNE/SCANDALE, poser PROBLÈME, faire PARTIE de qqch, avoir BESOIN de qqch, mettre FIN à qqch, donner SOIF à qqn, faire ATTENTION à qqch.* These can be compared to expressions like *to take PLACE.* The second exception is **coordinated** nouns (4: 13):

> (30) a. ÉTUDIANTS ET LYCÉENS ont manifesté dans les rues de Paris.
>   b. Apprenant à ma sœur LECTURE, ÉCRITURE, CALCUL, je
>   connus dès l'âge de six ans l'orgueil de l'efficacité (Beauvoir).

Finally, in appositive contexts, nouns can appear without a determiner:

> (31) Mon voisin, CHEF DE RAYON CHEZ DARTY, est parti en vacances.

The idea that determiners turn non-referring nouns into referring NPs helps us understand why French NPs can't contain *more* than one determiner:

> (32) a. *LA UNE fille   b. *LES MES histoires
>   c. *UN CE garçon   d. *UN MON fils

Once an NP is able to refer it doesn't need an additional determiner.

Finally, note that the determiner often agrees with the gender/number of the head noun (see 4: 1.1 for agreement between subjects and finite verbs).

In summary, French NPs contain a head noun together, in the case of common nouns, with a determiner (Det):

> (33) [$_{NP}$ Det N]

Sometimes, there's agreement between the determiner and the noun. Before considering NP structure in more detail, let's look at the subcategories of determiner.

2.2   *Kinds of determiner*

- **Articles**: four kinds of article are usually recognised.

Definite articles – *le, la, les* – often allow the NP to refer to a specific and/or familiar entity. For example, in (34) the subject NP refers to a specific girl familiar to both speaker and hearer.

> (34) LA fille est arrivée.

French definite articles also have a generic use, which has no direct equivalent in English. Compare (35a) with the potentially synonymous (35b):

(35) a. LE vin coûte cher.   b. Wine is expensive.

The NPs *le vin* and *wine* don't refer to any specific (kind of) wine; they
refer to wine in general. The French NP contains a definite article, the
English NP does not. (See also (29) in 4: 2.1.) Similarly, abstract concept
nouns need a definite article in French, but not in English:

(36) a. LA haine   b. hatred

Indefinite articles – *un(e)*, *des* (= *de* + *les*) – are used to introduce unfamiliar NPs into the discourse.

(37) DES filles sont arrivées.

The **partitive article** – *du* (= *de* + *le*), *de la*, *de l'*, *des* (= *de* + *les*) – is a
combination of the preposition *de* (4: 2.4) and a definite article. NPs
containing the partitive article refer to 'a part of' or 'some (unspecified
quantity) of' whatever is denoted by the noun. For instance, the NP DU
pain refers to 'some of the bread'. Similar meanings are expressed by DE
L'eau, DES *oranges* and DE LA *crème*. (NB: the form *des* can be an indefinite or partitive article.)

The definite/generic and indefinite articles agree with their head nouns,
as does the partitive article. In contrast, the final article – *de* – does not.
This article is used in two major contexts, but is restricted to direct object
NPs. First, it appears in negative sentences (4: 12):

(38) a. Je n'ai pas mangé DE pain.   b. Personne n'a plus D'amis.

Second, it appears with certain displaced **quantifiers**, such as *beaucoup* and
trop (see below and 4: 8.1):

(39) a. Ils ont beaucoup vu DE films.   b. J'ai trop mangé D'ail.

This article isn't sensitive to the number/gender of the head noun; the
contrast between *de* and *d'* is strictly phonological and sensitive to whether
the following word is vowel- or consonant-initial (2: 9.2).

- **Demonstrative determiners:** *ce* (*cet*), *cette*, *ces*.

These agree with the noun in number and gender. They function similarly to
definite articles but can additionally indicate location in space (*ce bâtiment*),
time (*cette année*) or the general discourse (*ces hypothèses*). Together with *-ci*

and *-là*, historically derived from the locative adverbs *ici* and *là*, they can distinguish between proximity and distance, as in *cette porte-ci* and *ce jour-là*.

• **Possessive determiners** are set out in Table 4.1.

Table 4.1

Singular:	mon/ma	ton/ta	son/sa	notre	votre	leur
Plural:	mes	tes	ses	nos	vos	leurs

These determiners express possession as in:

(40) a. MES filles   b. SON livre   c. SA glace

As for agreement between the determiner and the head noun, French possessive determiners behave quite differently from their English counterparts. French possessive determiners are sensitive to features of the *possessed noun* in a way that their English counterparts are not; conversely, English possessive determiners are sensitive to features of the *possessor* in a way that their French counterparts are not. In French the form of the possessive determiner depends on the number/gender of the possessed noun, as in (40). This is another case of agreement between the determiner and the noun. Depending on whether the possessed noun is masculine singular, feminine singular or indeed plural, the determiner indicating possession by the speaker is *mon*, *ma* or *mes*. In English *my* is used throughout.

In contrast, possession by a singular third person is marked in English by a determiner which is sensitive to whether the *possessor* is human or not, and, if it is human, whether it's male or female. Possession by a non-human singular third person is marked by *its*; possession by a human singular third person is marked by *his* or *her*, depending on sex. None of these forms is sensitive to any property of the possessed noun. The linguistically most sensible way of explaining this difference is to assume that in French there's a single **morpheme** (3: 1) for possession by a singular third person (irrespective of its gender or animacy) with three **allomorphs** (*son*, *sa* and *ses*) allowing agreement with the noun (similarly with the singular first and second person, as shown in Table 4.1), while in English there are three distinct morphemes – *his*, *her* or *its* depending on the grammatical properties of the possessor – and no allomorphy determined by agreement with the noun.

• In syntactic terms **quantifiers** indicate quantity within an NP.

They form quite a heterogeneous group and are dealt with together here because of their common function. For example, *quelques* is a determiner in (41a) but looks like an adjective in (41b). (Recall that NPs are limited to one determiner. If *ces* is a determiner in (41b), then *quelques* must be something else, e.g. an adjective (4: 3).)

(41) a. QUELQUES moments   b. ces QUELQUES moments

Similarly the French numerals are determiners in DEUX *hommes*, TROIS *histoires* and QUATRE *enfants*, but look like adjectives in *les* DEUX *hommes*, *ces* TROIS *histoires* and *mes* QUATRE *enfants*. In contrast, *plusieurs* is only ever a determiner, as in PLUSIEURS *bêtises*. It cannot be used adjectivally, **les PLUSIEURS bêtises*.

Quantifiers with particularly quirky behaviour are those followed by the article *de* (see above), as in *beaucoup de bêtises, peu de, trop de, tant de, autant de, énormément de* and *pas mal de*. As was noted above, some of these quantifiers can be displaced (4: 8.1); see (39). As final evidence for the arbitrary nature of this subcategory, the interrogative quantifier *combien de* could equally well be included here or under the next heading.

• The **interrogative determiners** are *quel(le)(s)* and *combien de*.

Note that, while *quel(le)(s)* agrees with its noun, as in QUELLES *filles*, *combien de* behaves like the other quantifiers occurring with *de*, and does not.

2.3 *More complex NPs*

We can now look in more detail at NP structure, which we left in 4: 2.1 with the schema in (33), namely [$_{NP}$ Det N]. More needs to be said, since NPs can, for example, contain adjectives and relative clauses. We look at the syntax of relative clauses in 4: 7.3–4. Adjectives follow three general patterns when used **attributively**, that is, within NPs. (More general issues are addressed in 4: 3.) First, a small group of usually short adjectives can appear *pre*nominally:

(42) a. mon GROS chat   b. les JOLIES PETITES JEUNES filles
     c. cette BELLE PETITE voiture   d. un BON PETIT VIEUX
                                          camembert

Other prenominal adjectives are *long, haut, mauvais* and *nouveau*.
    In contrast, most adjectives appear *post*nominally:

(43) a. les livres MODERNES   b. un homme SÉRIEUX

Adjectives expressing nationality (*français, anglais* and so on), colour (*bleu, gris* and so on) and shape (*rond, ovale, carré* and so on), as well as verbal participles (*apprécié, éclatant* and so on) (3: 3), are usually postnominal.
    Finally, a small number of adjectives can be *either* pre- *or* postnominal, but have subtly different meanings depending on where they occur:

(44) a. les TRISTES parents   b. les parents TRISTES
     c. la PAUVRE Française   d. la Française PAUVRE
     e. un GRAND homme   f. un homme GRAND

A significant generalisation can be captured here. In *postnominal* position, as in (44b, d, f), these adjectives retain their usual dictionary meaning. For example, *les parents tristes* denotes parents who are sad, and *un homme grand* denotes a man who's tall. In *prenominal* position, as in (44a, c, e), in contrast, the interpretation isn't always easy to predict, and often represents more of a subjective or emotive judgement on the part of the speaker. For example, *les tristes parents* denotes parents whom the speaker in some way pities, while *un grand homme* denotes someone who, in the view of the speaker, is a great man. Other adjectives which can either precede or follow the noun – and have subtly different meanings – are *seul*, *brave*, *méchant*, *propre*, *certain* and *ancien*.

In summary, we can make the following generalisation about the position of attributive adjectives within NPs. In the unmarked case, they are postnominal. In marked cases, namely where they give a subjective rather than an objective judgement, or belong to a small, restricted class, they can be prenominal.

We can now modify the schema in (33), as shown in (45). (The adjectives (A) are in (round) brackets because they are optional. The asterisk here indicates that more than one adjective can appear in these positions.)

(45) [$_{NP}$ Det (A)* N (A)*]

A further modification needs to be made to accommodate *tout(e)(s)*, which can precede some determiners:

(46) a. TOUS mes amis
     b. TOUTES les histoires
     c. TOUTE cette crise

Because of its position, *tout(e)(s)* is called a **predeterminer** (PreDet). Like adjectives, predeterminers are optional:

(47) [$_{NP}$ (PreDet) Det (A)* N (A)*]

Note that, just like the determiners in (46), adjectives (both pre- and postnominal), as well as predeterminers, agree in number and gender with the noun. This is clear from the examples in (48), which use all the structural positions in the schema in (47):

(48) a. tous mes beaux petits chats noirs
     b. toutes ces belles histoires vraies
     c. tout le bon pain blanc

2.4   NPs and prepositions

The discussion in 4: 2.3 is valid for every NP in French, no matter what its function. Provided the NP follows (47), like *tous mes beaux petits chats noirs* in (48a), it can function as an argument:

(49) a. [_NP_ Tous mes beaux petits chats noirs] dorment.   (subject)
b. J'ai vu [_NP_ tous mes beaux petits chats noirs].   (direct object)
c. J'en ai donné à [_NP_ tous mes beaux petits
chats noirs].   (indirect object)

Recall from 4: 1.1 that indirect objects such as *à tous mes beaux petits chats noirs* in (49c) are NPs introduced by a preposition (in this case, *à*). A phrase comprising a preposition (P) (*de, par, contre, vers, envers, sous, sur, avec*, and so on) followed by an NP is called a prepositional phrase, or PP. PPs have the following structure:

(50) [_PP_ P NP]

The form of a PP in French generally follows the schema in (50) fairly transparently, as in the following examples:

(51) a. [_PP_ sous [_NP_ ces conditions]]
b. [_PP_ à [_NP_ la maison]]
c. [_PP_ dans [_NP_ un quart d'heure]]

However, there are three exceptional contexts in which the internal structure of a PP is less transparent. First, if the preposition is *à* or *de* and the first element in the NP is the definite article *le* or *les*, the preposition and determiner fuse as *au* (= *à* + *le*), *aux* (= *à* + *les*), *du* (= *de* + *le*) or *des* (= *de* + *les*) (4: 2.2):

(52) a. J'ai parlé AU(X) garçon(s).   b. J'ai parlé DU/DES livre(s).

This fusion is best understood from a historical perspective, more particularly as part of the phonological change whereby preconsonantal [l] was first vocalised to [u], and the diphthong then levelled, as in the plurals *chevals* [-als] → *chevaus* [-aus] → *chevaux* [-o]. (See the discussion in 3: 2.1.4 of the regular plurals of nouns and adjectives ending in -*al*.)

The second context in which PP structure is opaque involves the article *des* (= *de* + *les*) (4: 2.2), as in (53a), which, in the written language, usually reduces to *de* in the presence of a prenominal adjective (4: 2.3), as in (53b):

(53) a. DES efforts surhumains   b. DE grands efforts

Finally, where the articles *du, de la, de l'* or *des* (4: 2.2) follow the preposition *de*, the sequence is reduced to *de*. Contrast the ungrammatical examples in (54) with the grammatical ones in (55):

(54) a. *Il est accusé [$_{PP}$ DE [$_{NP}$ DES crimes violents]].
     b. *La baignoire est pleine [$_{PP}$ DE [$_{NP}$ DE L'eau]].

(55) a. Il est accusé DE crimes violents.
     b. La baignoire est pleine D'eau.

3   Adjectival structure

3.1   *The adjective phrase*

So far, we've seen verbs heading VPs, nouns heading NPs and prepositions heading PPs. This is beginning to look like a regular pattern. Equally regular has been the internal structure of these VPs, NPs and PPs. Turning to adjectives (familiar from 4: 2.3 and 3: 2), we find that they head phrases – called adjective phrases or APs – and that AP structure is regular, too.

But why would we want to say that adjectives head APs? After all, the attributive adjectives in 4: 2.3 were single words and didn't look much like phrases. However, we only saw part of the picture there. Adjectives aren't always bare; sometimes they form a meaningful unit with other words, independently of the structure of the NP proper. Adjective meaning can be modified by words like *extrêmement, si, très, peu, tout* and *trop*, to form phrases like TRÈS *beau*, TOUT *petit* and TROP *grand*. (In 4: 10.2 we see adjectives taking complements, too.) We can think of these phrases as APs which contain not only the adjective but the optional preceding modifier, too:

(56) [$_{AP}$ (modifier) A]

Thus, an adjective occupies an AP, even in the absence of a modifier, in the same way that nouns and verbs always occupy an NP or VP respectively, even when there's nothing else in the NP or VP. Consequently, we can revise our NP schema in (47) to take account of the fact that APs rather than mere adjectives can appear within NPs:

(57) [$_{NP}$ (PreDet) Det (AP)* N (AP)*]

In an NP like *tous mes beaux petits chats noirs*, then, each adjective occupies its own AP. This analysis is supported by the fact that the meaning of each adjective can be modified by exploiting the AP structure in (56):

(58) [$_{NP}$ tous mes [$_{AP}$ très beaux] [$_{AP}$ si petits] chats [$_{AP}$ tout noirs]]

The NP in (58) contains both the predeterminer *tout(e)(s)* (4: 2.3) and the AP modifiers *très*, *si* and *tout*.

3.2   The distribution of APs

Having considered AP structure, we turn now to its distribution, that is the positions where APs occur. APs are used in three ways. The first is familiar from 4: 2.3 and (57) in 4: 3.1; APs can be used attributively within NP. The second use of AP is illustrated in the copular sentences here:

(59) a. Marie est [_{AP} (TROP) INTELLIGENTE].
      b. Les élèves semblent [_{AP} (BIEN) MOTIVÉS].
      c. Les nuages deviennent [_{AP} (TRÈS) MENAÇANTS].
      d. Les chats paraissent [_{AP} (TOUT) NOIRS].

Recall from 4: 1.4 that copulas are grammatical 'glue', holding together the subject NP and another phrase which describes it. In the examples in (12) in 4: 1.4 the 'other phrase' was an NP; in the examples in (59) the 'other phrase' is an AP. This is called the **predicative** use of APs, and the adjective again agrees in number/gender with the noun it describes; *intelligente* agrees with *Marie* (feminine singular), *noirs* agrees with *les chats* (masculine plural).

The final use of APs is a slightly different predicative use:

(60) a. Je trouve cette nouvelle [_{AP} (TRÈS) INTÉRESSANTE].
      b. Pierre considère ces cours [_{AP} (TROP) ENNUYEUX].
      c. Nous jugeons nos étudiants [_{AP} (EXTRÊMEMENT) DOUÉS].

The difference between the uses of APs in (59) and in (60) has to do with the grammatical function of the NP described by the AP. In (59) the AP describes a subject NP, while in (60) the AP describes a direct object NP.

To summarise, we've seen: (a) that adjectives head APs; (b) that APs are used attributively and predicatively; (c) that AP structure follows the schema in (56); and (d) that adjectives agree with the noun they describe. We return to AP structure in 4: 10.2–3.

4   Proforms and clitics

In this section we look at **pronominalisation** (the use of **pronouns**). Actually, the term 'pronoun' is imprecise and misleading, and we'll use **proform**, instead. Proforms are linguistic energy-saving devices, a shorthand way of referring to something familiar, for example something which has already been mentioned. Consider the following examples:

(61) a. J'ai vu MARIE. ELLE était radieuse.
   b. J'ai vu L'HOMME À QUI MARIE PARLAIT CE MATIN.
      IL était radieux.

In (61a) the proform is *elle*; it refers back to the NP *Marie* in the previous sentence. In (61b) *il* refers to *l'homme à qui Marie parlait ce matin*. Using proforms, the speaker saves time and effort, not having to repeat *Marie* or *l'homme à qui Marie parlait ce matin* – quite a saving in the second case.

The term 'pronoun' is inappropriate because it implies, wrongly, that forms like *il* and *elle* replace nouns. In fact, in (61) *il* and *elle* replace an entire NP, not just a noun. So we might think of them as pro-NPs. We'll see later that phrases of various categories can be 'pronominalised'. The term proform is therefore a useful cover term for all these forms. We look at non-subject proforms in 4: 4.1 and consider one of their properties, namely cliticisation, in 4: 4.2. We consider subject proforms (like *il* and *elle*) in 4: 4.3. In 4: 4.4 we discuss non-clitic proforms, and briefly review some other proforms in 4: 4.5.

4.1   Non-subject proforms

In (62) *le*, *la* and *les* 'stand for' the direct objects of the transitive verb *saluer*:

(62) a. Nous avons vu PAUL. Pierre voulait LE saluer.
   b. Nous avons vu CHANTAL. Pierre voulait LA saluer.
   c. Nous avons vu PAUL ET CHANTAL. Pierre voulait LES saluer.

Note, first, that these are proforms and not the definite articles discussed in 4: 2.2 (despite being homophonous). There are a number of syntactic and morphological differences between definite articles and these proforms. First, while definite articles occur with nouns within NPs, these proforms occur with verbs inside VPs (4: 4.2). Second, the type of fusion discussed in 4: 2.4, which affects definite articles, doesn't affect these proforms, *J'ai décidé DE LE faire*, **J'ai décidé DU faire*. In conclusion, the forms *le*, *la* and *les* in (62) are direct object proforms and *not* definite articles.

Direct objects aren't unique in being susceptible to pronominalisation. In (63) it's the indirect objects of the verb *parler* that have been pronominalised, as singular *lui* and plural *leur*:

(63) a. J'ai vu PAUL ce matin et je LUI ai parlé.
   b. J'ai vu PAUL ET MARIE ce matin et je LEUR ai parlé.

The proforms in (62) and (63) replace (in)direct objects of the third person. First and second person (in)direct objects can be pronominalised, too, using *me* and *te* (singular), *nous* and *vous* (plural). In contrast to the third person, though, where we saw specialised direct object proforms (*le, la, les*) in (62) and specialised indirect object proforms (*lui, leur*) in (63), the first and second person proforms (*me, te, nous, vous*) can replace *both* direct *and* indirect objects. In (64a) *nous* replaces the direct object (*appeler* is a transitive verb; *on appelle* QUELQU'UN), while in (64b) it replaces the indirect object (*téléphoner* is an indirect transitive verb; *on téléphone* À QUELQU'UN):

(64) a. Pierre NOUS appelle.   b. Pierre NOUS téléphone.

We can see that *nous* replaces different things in (64a) and (64b) from the phenomenon of past participle agreement. We discuss past participle agreement in detail in 4: 7.5 where we see that it is triggered when a *direct object* appears before the past participle. With this characterisation in mind note the difference between (65a) and (65b):

(65) a. Pierre NOUS a appelés.   b. Pierre NOUS a téléphoné.

In both cases, *nous* precedes the past participle, yet only in (65a) is there past participle agreement. This indicates to us that only in (65a) is *nous* the direct object. In (65b), where past participle agreement doesn't take place, *nous* isn't the direct object (it's the *indirect* object, instead). We can generalise our conclusion for (65) and assume that, in (64), too, *nous* is a direct object proform in (a) and an *indirect* object proform in (b).

Other non-subject proforms are *y* and *en*. The proform *y* usually replaces a locative PP, as in (66a), where it replaces *à Paris*. The proform *en* has two sources. First, it can stand for a PP headed by *de*, as in (66b), where it replaces *du livre*. Second, *en* can be related to a quantified indefinite direct object NP (4: 2.2; 4: 7.5), as in (66c).

(66) a. Je vais À PARIS. Tu Y vas aussi?
     b. 'As-tu lu la préface DU LIVRE et le premier chapitre?'
        'J'EN ai lu la préface mais pas le premier chapitre.'
     c. Moi, j'ai vu trois ÉGLISES, mais elle EN a vu deux.

Pronominalisation isn't restricted to non-subject NPs and PPs. The proform *le* can replace phrases of various categories. In (14) in 4: 1.4 we saw it standing for a predicative NP. Further pronominal uses of *le* are given in (67):

(67) a. La mère de Minou était TRÈS MIGNONNE, et Minou
        LE sera aussi.
     b. Je sais QUE MARIE SERA EN RETARD, et tu LE sais aussi.

In (67a) *le* replaces the predicative AP *très mignonne* (4: 3.2); *le* is a pro-AP here. Note that *le* isn't gender- and number-sensitive here; in (67a) *le* replaces a feminine AP but doesn't change its form to *la*. This follows the pattern we saw in (14): *le* isn't gender- and number-sensitive when it replaces a predicative NP either. But it's unlike the behaviour of the definite article *le* (4: 2.2) and the direct object proform *le* (see (62)) which *are* gender- and number-sensitive. In (67b) *le* replaces the entire **subordinate clause** (4: 6) *que Marie sera en retard*; *le* is a pro-clause here.

A final use of the proform *le* (with *faire* as an auxiliary) is illustrated in the **comparatives** in (68) which are not only synonymous but also structurally parallel:

> (68) a. Marie m'embête plus qu'elle (ne) LE FAISAIT l'an dernier.
> b. Marie m'embête plus qu'elle (ne) M'EMBÊTAIT l'an dernier.

The difference is that the VP *le faire* appears in (68a), while the VP *m'embêter* is repeated in (68b). (On this use of *ne* see 4: 12.3.) The use of the verb *faire* allows the proform *le* to stand for the VP *m'embêter*. The value of this auxiliary use of *faire* together with the pro-VP *le* is particularly clear when the VP replaced is long:

> (69) Pierre doit [$_{VP}$ donner cent francs à chacun de ses petits-enfants et arrière-petits-enfants], mais il ne veut pas LE FAIRE.

In 4: 4.2 we consider a salient feature of all these non-subject proforms, namely the fact that they don't occupy the same postverbal position as the phrase they replace.

4.2   Clitic proforms

Before looking at other French proforms, consider a feature of the proforms in 4: 4.1. Compare (70a) and (70b):

> (70) a. Jean voit PAUL.   b. Jean LE voit.

In (70a) the highlighted direct object is an NP in its unmarked *post*verbal position; in (70b) it's a proform in *pre*verbal position. This difference in position is characteristic of the non-subject proforms in 4: 4.1; the proforms are preverbal while the phrases they replace are postverbal. The preverbal position of these proforms is actually just one aspect of what we can describe informally as their phonological and morphosyntactic dependence on the verb. This dependence is captured by the term used to refer to them, namely **clitic proform** or **clitic**. The term clitic comes from the Ancient Greek for 'to lean'; these proforms have 'to lean', or cliticise, onto a verb, hence their characteristic preverbal position. Even after inversion (4: 7.2), non-subject clitic proforms still immediately precede the verb:

(71) a. LA VOIT-il?   b. LE LEUR AVEZ-vous dit?

There are a number of linguistic differences (besides their position with respect to the verb) between clitic proforms and the phrases they replace, and these can all be related to the proforms' dependence on the verb. First, clitics cannot bear independent stress; rather, they form a prosodic unit with the verb they cliticise onto (2: 15). (In fact, clitics are sometimes called unstressed or conjunctive proforms.) In order to say *I can see* HIM, *(but) not* HER clitic proforms cannot straightforwardly be used, and different syntactic structures altogether are needed (4: 8):

(72) a. *Je *le* vois, (mais) pas *la*.
b. *Lui*, je le vois, mais pas *elle*.
c. C'est *lui* que je vois, pas *elle*.

Second, clitic order is rigidly fixed, as in Table 4.2 (on *se* see 4: 5). While the relative position of a direct object NP and an indirect object PP can depart from the unmarked order, as we saw in (24) in 4: 1.6, clitics cannot:

(73) a. Je LE LUI donne.   b. *Je LUI LE donne.

Third, while full phrases can appear on their own in short answers to constituent questions, as in '*Qui vois-tu?*' '*Paul*', clitics cannot: '*Qui vois-tu?*' *'Le.'* Finally, while full phrases can be coordinated (4: 13), as in *Je verrai [NP Paul] et [NP Marie]*, clitics cannot, *Je [le] et [la] verrai*. If non-subject proforms are to be coordinated or used as short answers, a different kind of *non*-clitic proform is used (4: 4.4).

There are two final comments to be made about non-subject clitics. First, in positive imperatives (4: 1.5) they behave somewhat differently from what we've seen so far. Most obviously, they are postverbal, as in *Donnez-le lui!*, rather than *Le lui donnez!* Further, the order and form of the proforms can differ. For example, in preverbal position the first person non-subject clitic proform is *me*, and it precedes *le* (in line with Table 4.2), as in *Vous me le donnez*. Yet in positive imperatives the first person proform is *moi* (4: 4.4), and it follows *le* (at least in the standard language), *Donnez-le moi!* (although in non-standard varieties *Donnez-moi le!* is also heard).

Table 4.2 Non-subject clitics

me				
te	le	lui		
nous	la		y	en
vous	les	leur		
se				

Second, there's one common exception to the generalisation that clitics are dependent on a verb, namely the context of the exclamatives *(re)voici* and *(re)voilà*, which can be preceded by a clitic proform, *Me voici!*, *Les revoilà!*, *En voilà tout un paquet!* The explanation for this is historical. The forms *(re)voici* and *(re)voilà* are derived historically from *voir ici/là*, which, of course, is verbal and, hence, could be preceded by clitic proforms. The modern forms are a vestige of an earlier stage in the development of the language. (Recall from 4: 2.2 that the postnominal restrictors *-ci* and *-là*, used with demonstrative determiners (and demonstrative proforms; see 4: 4.5), are also derived from *ici* and *là*.)

4.3   Subject (personal) proforms

In (61) in 4: 4 *elle* is a feminine, third person singular, subject proform, while *il* is the corresponding masculine/unmarked form. That is, they 'stand for' a third person singular subject NP whose gender is feminine (*elle* stands for *Marie*) or masculine/unknown (*il* stands for *l'homme à qui Marie parlait ce matin*). Corresponding plural proforms are used in the examples below; *ils* is masculine (or mixed, or unknown) plural and *elles* is feminine plural:

(74) a. J'ai vu PAUL ET MARIE hier. ILS étaient radieux.
 b. J'ai vu MARIE ET PAULETTE hier. ELLES étaient radieuses.

The first and second person subject proforms are *je*, *tu*, *nous* and *vous*. These forms are collectively also called **personal proforms**, not because they refer to a person (they can, after all, refer to inanimate entities), but because they encode the person, number (and, in some cases, gender) features of the subject (3: 3).

In 4: 4.1–2 we saw a number of differences between the behaviour of unstressed non-subject proforms and the phrases they replace. These differences were understood in terms of a dependence on the verb, and were captured in the term, clitic, used to refer to the proforms. Interestingly, similar patterns are also found with personal proforms. Rather than behaving like the phrases they replace (namely, subject NPs), personal proforms behave like unstressed non-subject proforms. For this reason, we conclude that, like the non-subject proforms, personal proforms are clitics, too.

First, while a subject NP can be stressed, a personal proform cannot:

(75) a. *Jean* était là, mais *Anne* n'y était pas.
 b. **Il* était là, mais *je* n'y étais pas.

Second, while subject NPs can be coordinated (4: 13), personal proforms cannot (like non-subject clitics):

(76) a. Jean et Marie sont partis.   b. *Il et elle sont partis.

If, for pragmatic or stylistic reasons, a pronominal subject needs to be stressed, separated from the finite verb, or coordinated, a different kind of proform is used (4: 4.4), which, once again, is exactly what we find with non-subject proforms (4: 4.2). Third, while a subject NP can be separated from the finite verb by a parenthetical **adverbial** (4: 11), as in (77a), a personal proform cannot, as shown in (77b), and must immediately precede the verb (like non-subject clitics), as in (77c):

(77) a. Paul, de toute évidence, arrive ce soir.
    b. *Il, de toute évidence, arrive ce soir.
    c. De toute évidence, il arrive ce soir.

Finally, what *can* intervene between the personal proforms and the verb are the non-subject clitics (Table 4.2 in 4: 4.2) and the negative item *ne* (4: 12). In summary, it seems that, like the non-subject proforms in 4: 4.1–2, personal proforms are clitics.

In the rest of this section we look at the subject proforms *on* and impersonal *il*, as well as *ce* and *cela/ça*. Other, more specialised, proforms are discussed in 4: 4.5. We return to the distinction between NP and clitic subjects when we discuss inversion in 4: 7.2.

On is a third person singular proform which can express an indefinite human subject, as in (78), or, often in spoken French, function as an alternative to *nous*, as in (79):

(78) a. ON mange bien dans ce restaurant.
    b. En Angleterre ON prend le thé vers quatre heures.

(79) a. ON a décidé de partir en vacances en Espagne.
    b. ON va donner un cadeau à notre grand-mère.

As an alternative to *nous*, *on* may be found with a feminine (or, less readily, plural) predicative AP or past participle (4: 3.2). It seems that agreement here is with the referent of *on*, rather than its grammatical features.

(80) a. ?ON est très contentS de se voir.
    b. ON a été menacéE par les voleurs.

Impersonal *il* is a subject clitic which doesn't actually refer to anything; it's discussed in detail in 4: 6.3 and 4: 14:

(81) a. IL me semble qu'elle est partie.   b. IL pleuvait ce matin.

The subject clitic *ce* is non-gender-specific (unlike the demonstrative determiner *ce*; 4: 2.2) and always appears with the **copula** *être* (4: 1.4).

Sometimes, it stands for an NP (but see below and 4: 8.3) and, according to conservative grammarians at least, when it does, *être* is followed by another NP, as in the examples in (82):

(82) a. Ecoutez cette chanson, C'est [$_{NP}$ le premier tube de Clo Clo] !
      b. Ecoutez ces chansons, CE sont [$_{NP}$ les plus gros titres de Clo Clo] !

Here *ce* stands for the NPs *cette chanson/ces chansons* and the postcopular phrases are NPs, too (*le premier tube de Clo Clo* and *les plus gros titres de Clo Clo*, respectively). (Note the subject–verb agreement in (82b).)

Where *être* is followed by a phrase other than an NP, such as a predicative AP or a PP, *ce* is replaced by an appropriate personal proform (in this case *elle/elles* because *cette chanson/ces chansons* are feminine NPs):

(83) a. Ecoutez cette chanson, ELLE est [$_{AP}$ terrible] !
      b. Ecoutez ces chansons, ELLES sont [$_{PP}$ au top depuis hier] !

In addition to standing for an NP, *ce* can also stand for vaguer notions, such as the activity denoted by a verbal expression. Here, *être* doesn't have to be followed by an NP:

(84) a. Manger du foie gras, C'est [$_{NP}$ un plaisir inconnu en Angleterre].
      b. Ne fais pas tant de bruit, C'est [$_{AP}$ très énervant].

(85) a. Ah! ce jardin. Comme C'est magnifique!
      b. Les couleurs vives, C'est vulgaire!
      c. Les bonbons! Qu'est-ce que C'est bon!
      d. Les tartes aux pommes, comme C'est bon!

In (84a) *ce* refers to 'eating foie gras', the activity denoted by VP, rather than to foie gras itself; in (84b) *ce* refers to 'making lots of noise'. In (85) *ce* refers not so much to *ce jardin*, *les couleurs vives*, *les bonbons* or *les tartes aux pommes*, as to the broader experience of looking at the garden or the bright colours, or of eating the sweets or the apple tarts. In (84b) and (85) *être* is followed by a predicative AP. We can understand why *ce* isn't replaced by a personal proform here by recalling that personal proforms encode person/number/gender features. Since the abstract notions referred to here don't have these features, a personal proform like *il* can't be used, and the form *ce* is maintained, even though *être* isn't followed by an NP. Note further that the predicative APs in (85) agree with (non-gender-specific) *ce* rather than, for example, *les couleurs vives* and *les tartes aux pommes*.

As mentioned above, the subject clitic *ce* only appears with the copula *être*. In the absence of *être*, non-clitic *cela* (or *ça* in spoken French) is used, instead:

(86) a. Commencer à huit heures, ÇA/CELA m'énerve.
   b. Manger des cuisses de grenouille, ÇA/CELA m'arrive souvent.
   c. Voyager en première classe, ÇA/CELA l'obsède.

(87) a. Les tartes aux pommes, ÇA se mange avec grand plaisir.
   b. Les couleurs vives, ÇA fait vulgaire.

This is generally restricted to spoken registers. The proform *ça* is pejorative when used to refer to people:

(88) a. Tu sais, les voisins, ÇA boit.   b. Pour qui ÇA se prend?

So far, we've seen contexts in which *ce* is used referentially, either referring back to an NP or to more abstract notions. A different use of *ce* is as an informal alternative to impersonal *il* (see above and 4: 14.1):

(89) C'est une grande folie de vouloir être sage tout seul.

This is also the use of *ce* found in **cleft sentences** (4: 8.3). But note that, once again, if a verb other than *être* is used, *ce* is replaced by *cela/ça*:

(90) a. CELA/ÇA me fait plaisir de vous revoir.
   b. CELA/ÇA me choque profondément qu'il ait dit des choses pareilles.
   c. CELA/ÇA m'irrite toujours que les étudiants ne travaillent pas assez.

4.4 Non-clitic proforms

In 4: 4.2–3 we concluded that non-subject proforms like *le*, *leur* and *en*, as well as personal proforms like *il* and *je*, are clitics, that is dependent on a verb. This dependence means that clitic proforms are excluded from certain contexts, for example short answers and coordinated expressions, as well as contexts in which something intervenes between them and the verb, or where they mark a contrast:

(91) a. 'Qui vois-tu?' *'LE.'   b. *Nous LE et LA verrons demain.
   c. *Je LE veux, pas LA.   d. *TU, de toute évidence, pars demain.

The problem with all these contexts is that they require the proforms to bear a kind of stress with which they are incompatible, given that they form a prosodic unit with the verb. While French grammar precludes clitics from appearing in these contexts, it does provide an alternative *non*-clitic set of what are called **disjunctive** personal proforms, ones which *don't* have to appear immediately preverbally, *don't* form a prosodic unit with the verb and, hence, *can* be stressed. (Indeed, they are sometimes called **stressed** or **tonic** proforms.) These are *moi, toi, lui, elle, nous, vous, eux* and *elles*, and can be used as subjects or non-subjects, as in (92):

> (92) a. MOI ET ELLE, de toute évidence, (nous) arrivons ce soir.
>   b. 'Qui vois-tu?' 'LUI.'

Disjunctive proforms obligatorily appear as the pronominal complement of a preposition:

> (93) a. *Jean est arrivé [$_{PP}$ avec LE/LA/ME/LES].
>   b. Jean est arrivé [$_{PP}$ avec LUI/ELLE/MOI/EUX].

They also appear in **cleft sentences** (4: 8.3).

4.5 Other proforms

• **Demonstrative proforms**: *celui, celle, ceux* and *celles*. These are related to the demonstrative determiners (4: 2.2) in 'standing for' an NP containing a demonstrative determiner. However, whereas the demonstrative determiners only *optionally* appear with a restrictor (postnominal *-ci/-là*, a relative clause (4: 7.3–4) or a possessive PP headed by *de*), the demonstrative proforms *necessarily* appear with one:

> (94) Les pantalons? ah! j'aime bien CELUI-CI et CELUI DE TON FRÈRE, mais je n'aime pas du tout CELUI QUE TU M'AS OFFERT.

• **Interrogative proforms**: *qui, quoi, que, lequel, lesquels, laquelle* and *lesquelles* (4: 7.1). *Qui* is used with a human referent:

> (95) a AVEC QUI est-il parti?
>   b. QUI avez-vous vu?
>   c. QUI a parlé?

In contrast, *quoi* and *que* are used with a non-human referent. The behaviour of *quoi* and *que* is actually quite complex and we return to it in 4: 8.4. The interrogative proforms *lequel* etc. are transparent combinations of the definite article and the interrogative determiner *quel(le)(s)*. They differ slightly from *qui/que/quoi* in presupposing a set of possible answers:

> (96) a. Eric et Jean sont là. LEQUEL est arrivé en premier?
>   b. LAQUELLE préfères-tu, la mairie de Paris ou la mairie de Toulouse?
>   c. De tous tes amis, sur LESQUELS peux-tu compter?

• **Relative proforms**: *qui, lequel, laquelle, lesquels, lesquelles, dont* and *où* (NB: on the status of *qui* and *que* in subject and direct object relative clauses see 4: 7.4). The relative pro-NP *qui* has a human interpretation, while *lequel* etc. usually have a non-human one (4: 7.3):

(97) a. l'homme à QUI je parle   b. le banc sur LEQUEL j'étais assis

The relative proform *dont* stands for a PP headed by *de* (4: 2.4), while *où* stands for a locative adverbial (4: 11):

(98) a. l'homme DONT j'ai vu la femme (j'ai vu la femme DE cet homme)
    b. le café OÙ je t'ai rencontré (je t'ai rencontré DANS UN CAFÉ)

• **Adjective phrases and silent nouns.** An AP can't replace a noun, but the presence of an attributive AP (4: 2.3; 4: 3.1) does allow the noun to be omitted (and recovered from context), and so it may look as if the AP has replaced the noun. In the examples below, the silent noun is represented by a dash:

(99) a. Et ces chemises. $[_{NP}$ Les − $[_{AP}$ bleues]] sont belles,
       mais $[_{NP}$ les − $[_{AP}$ blanches]] sont un peu démodées.
    b. $[_{NP}$ Les − $[_{AP}$ très petits]] et $[_{NP}$ les − $[_{AP}$ moyens]] sont ici,
       mais $[_{NP}$ les − $[_{AP}$ très grands]] sont là-bas.

In summary, we've seen that proforms are grammatical energy-saving devices which allow us to refer to familiar concepts without having to repeat ourselves. An important class of proforms are the clitics, which are grammatically dependent on a verb. Other, non-clitic, proforms have specific grammatical functions associated, for example, with interrogative and relative clauses.

5   Reflexive clitics

In 4: 4.1 the first and second person object clitics *me, te, nous* and *vous* were distinguished from the third person object clitics *le, la, les, lui* and *leur*. The first set can stand for *either* a direct object *or* an indirect object. The second set are less flexible; *le, la* and *les* are direct object clitics only; *lui* and *leur* are indirect object clitics only. In fact, this isn't the only distinction between the first set and the second set. First and second person object clitics can be coreferential with (that is, refer to the same real-world entity as) the subject. Consider (100):

(100) a. Je ME lave.   b. Vous VOUS parlez.
      c. Tu T'habilles.   d. Nous NOUS parlons.

In (100a, d) the (in)direct objects of *laver* and *parler* are coreferential with the subjects, and the first person object clitics are used. The same pattern is repeated in (100b, c); the (in)direct objects are coreferential with the subjects, and second person object clitics are used. When these object clitics corefer with the subject, they are called **reflexive clitics**. However, as we shall see in 4: 5.1, this term is vague in an important respect.

In contrast to first and second person object clitics (*me, te, nous, vous*), which can corefer with the subject, third person object clitics (*le, la, les, lui, leur*) cannot. For example, *Jean le lave* cannot mean 'John washes himself'. Similarly, *Jean et Marie leur parlent* cannot mean 'Jean and Marie are talking to each other'. Instead, with *third* person object clitics, coreference with the subject is marked with a *distinct* reflexive clitic, namely *se*. *Se* is very versatile and can stand for a singular or plural, direct or indirect object:

> (101)   a. Il s'est offert un voyage en Inde.   (singular indirect object)
>   b. Elles SE regardent dans le miroir.   (plural direct object)

5.1   Reflexive and reciprocal interpretation

The interpretation of *singular* reflexive clitics is clear and unambiguous. The sentences in (100a, c) describe 'self-washing' and 'self-dressing' events; the sentence in (101a) describes an event of 'giving to oneself'. In contrast, the interpretation of *plural* reflexive clitics isn't so clear. For instance, the sentence in (100d) describes an event in which each of us is talking either to him/herself or to another member of the group. The first case involves a reflexive interpretation of the object clitic; the second involves a **reciprocal** interpretation. The same ambiguity is found in (100b) and (101b). Often, the ambiguity isn't apparent since the context makes it clear which of the two possible interpretations is intended. The clitic *se* presumably has a reciprocal rather than a reflexive interpretation in *Pierre et Marie s'appelleront demain*; after all, what would be the point in Pierre and Marie phoning themselves? However, where there is potential ambiguity, it can be resolved in favour of the reciprocal interpretation by the expressions *l'un(e) (à) l'autre* or *les un(e)s (à) les autres* (NB: à + *les* = *aux*; 4: 2.4). So the sentences in (102) are not even potentially ambiguous; only the reciprocal interpretations are available:

> (102)   a. Nous nous lavons les un(e)s les autres.
>   b. Vous vous parlez les un(e)s aux autres.
>   c. Elles se regardent les unes les autres dans le miroir.

5.2   Pronominal verbs

In 4: 5 and 4: 5.1 we saw reflexive clitics used in contexts such as (100)–(101), where the complement of an (indirect) transitive verb *just*

happens to be coreferential with the subject. A different situation is illustrated in (103):

(103) a. Je ME repens.
      b. Il S'est rappelé son erreur.
      c. Tu T'en vas.

In the relevant uses, these verbs *always* appear with a reflexive clitic (NB:
*Je TE *repens*, *Tu M'en *vas*); they are called **reflexive/pronominal verbs**.
For English speakers, these verbs may seem odd because the clitics *me*,
te and *se* in (103) don't seem like complements which have been pronominalised and cliticised; *Tu t'en vas* doesn't correspond to something along
the lines of *Tu *en vas (à) toi-même*. Rather than complements of the
verb, these reflexive clitics are more sensibly thought of as part and
parcel of the dictionary form of the pronominal verb. Other examples
are *s'apercevoir/s'agir/s'étonner de qqch, se douter/moquer/souvenir de qqch,
s'évanouir, s'envoler, s'enfuir, s'évader, se taire* and *se promener*.
    However, although in *semantic* terms, the reflexive clitic isn't a comple-
ment of the verb, in strictly *syntactic* terms it is. Note the forms of the past
participles in (104):

(104) a. Elles se sont SOUVENUES de la date de mon anniversaire.
      b. Elles se sont RAPPELÉ la date de mon anniversaire.

In (104a) *souvenues* agrees with *elles*; in (104b) *rappelé* does not. Recall
from (64) in 4: 4.1 that a past participle agrees with its *direct object* when
the direct object appears before the past participle. How, then, can we
account for the agreement in (104)? We can assume that, while in both
(104a) and (104b) the reflexive clitic *se* is coreferential with the subject
elles (and is therefore a feminine plural clitic), it's only in (104a) that *se*
stands (in syntactic terms) for the *direct* object of the verb (*souvenir*). In
(104b), in contrast, the reflexive clitic *se* stands for the *indirect* object of
the verb (*rappeler*). So, it's only in (104a) that the direct object precedes
the past participle and triggers agreement. In (104b) it's the indirect object
that precedes the past participle, but since indirect objects don't trigger
agreement, *rappelé* doesn't agree with the clitic. We return to past participle
agreement in 4: 7.5.
    Note also that this analysis explains why the preposition *de* appears in
(104a) but not in (104b). In (104a) the reflexive clitic *se* is the direct
object of the verb (it triggers past participle agreement); *la date de mon
anniversaire* is therefore the indirect object and, accordingly, needs to be
marked by a preposition; hence, the presence of *de*. In (104b) the reflexive
clitic *se* is the indirect object of the verb (it doesn't trigger past participle
agreement); *la date de mon anniversaire* is therefore the direct object, and
no preposition is needed.

5.3   *Pronominal verbs and the passive*

In this section we consider another context in which reflexive clitics are common. First, though, we need to introduce and illustrate the term passive. A sentence whose VP contains a transitive verb can appear in one of two forms. The first is familiar; the subject precedes VP, and VP contains the verb followed by the direct object. These are called **active sentences**:

> (105)   a. Pierre a lu LE LIVRE.   b. Le chasseur a tué L'OISEAU.

These sentences can also appear in a different form:

> (106)   a. LE LIVRE a été lu (par Pierre).
> b. L'OISEAU a été tué (par le chasseur).

There are two relevant features of the examples in (106) which distinguish them from (105). First, the (highlighted) direct objects in (105) have been promoted and become the subjects in (106). Second, the verbs have a particular form, known as **passive morphology**, comprising the auxiliary *être* and the past participle (4: 15.2). The original subjects can optionally appear within an **agent phrase**, a PP headed by *par* (4: 2.4). These are called **passive sentences**.

Interestingly, reflexive clitics appear in sentences which function similarly to passives, and which contain a transitive verb whose direct object has been promoted and become subject:

> (107)   a. On a cassé LA FENÊTRE.
> b. On mange CES BEIGNETS avec plaisir.

> (108)   a. LA FENÊTRE s'est cassée.
> b. CES BEIGNETS se mangent avec plaisir.

In (108) the highlighted direct objects from (107) have been promoted to subject. As for the verb, rather than appearing with passive morphology (like the verbs in (106)), it appears with active morphology and the reflexive clitic *se*.

Sentences like these seem odd to English speakers for the same reason that pronominal verbs seem odd (4: 5.2); the reflexive clitics don't *feel* like complements. It's strange to think of (108a) as **La fenêtre a cassé la fenêtre*, or (108b) as **Ces beignets mangent ces beignets avec plaisir*. We can analyse these forms as we did the pronominal verbs in 4: 5.2. *Semantically*, we can include the reflexive clitic in the dictionary form of the verb. Yet, *syntactically*, we can treat it as the direct object of the transitive verb. We can then account for the agreement in (108a) between the past participle and the reflexive clitic *se* (which is coreferential with the subject *la fenêtre* and therefore feminine singular). The agreement between the past participle and the clitic *se* is a consequence of the fact that, in syntactic terms, the clitic *se* is the direct object of the past participle and precedes it. We return to past participle agreement in 4: 7.5.

6 Subordinate clauses

So far we've looked at simple sentences. In this section, we consider more complex structures which look like small sentences contained within large sentences. Consider the examples in (109):

(109) a. [$_{S1}$ Marie pense [$_{S2}$ que Jean a dit une bêtise]].
　　　b. [$_{S1}$ Jean veut [$_{S2}$ que le train arrive à l'heure]].

The idea that these are sentences within sentences is reflected in the labelled bracketing. S2 is the small sentence contained within S1. A sentence (like S2) which is contained within another is often called an embedded/ subordinate sentence/clause, and a sentence (like S1) which contains another is often called a main/matrix sentence/clause. Here, we shall distinguish between clauses and sentences, and say that each of the examples in (109) is a single **sentence** which comprises two **clauses**, namely a **matrix clause** (S1) and a **subordinate clause** (S2). In the following sections we examine how a subordinate clause is related to the verb in the matrix clause (4: 6.1), different kinds of subordinate clause (4: 6.2), in particular those containing **subjunctive** verbs (4: 6.3–4). (For discussion of other contexts in which subordinate clauses appear see 4: 7.3–4 (relative clauses); 4: 8.3 (cleft sentences); 4: 9 (perception and causative verbs); 4: 10 (nouns, adjectives and prepositions taking complement clauses); 4: 11.3 (adverbial clauses); 4: 14 (impersonal structures).)

6.1 Subordinate clauses as complements of verbs

So far the term **complement** has referred to direct object NPs and indirect object PPs. In fact, NPs and PPs aren't the only complements a verb can take. Think about the relationship between the subordinate clause and the matrix verb in (109a, b). In much the same way that (in)direct objects 'complement' the verb, so in (109a, b) the subordinate clause (S2) 'complements' the matrix verb. This conclusion is supported by the fact that, like direct objects, the subordinate clauses can be pronominalised (4: 4.1).

(110) a. Marie pense QUE JEAN A DIT UNE BÊTISE, mais Anne ne LE pense pas.
　　　b. Jean veut QUE LE TRAIN ARRIVE À L'HEURE, et Pascale LE veut aussi.

Indeed, some verbs, like *dire* and *voir*, take *either* an NP *or* a subordinate clause as their direct object:

(111) a. Pierre DIT [$_{NP}$ des bêtises].
       b. Pierre DIT [$_{S2}$ que Marie sera en retard].

(112) a. Marie VOIT [$_{NP}$ l'église].
       b. Marie VOIT [$_{S2}$ que les chats ont faim].

Subordinate clauses in French are often introduced by a grammatical word called a **complementiser**, which marks the subordinate status of the clause. The subordinate clauses in (109), (111b) and (112b) are all declarative (4: 1.5) and all contain a finite verb (4: 1.1), and the complementiser is *que*. The function of *que* is to introduce a declarative finite subordinate clause.

Where verbs like *dire* are used ditransitively (4: 1.1), that is, with both a direct object and an indirect object, the direct object can still appear as a subordinate clause. The normal order is then for the indirect object to precede the subordinate clause:

(113) Marie [$_{VP}$ dit [$_{PP}$ à Paul] [$_{S2}$ qu'elle ne veut plus le voir]].

Although this doesn't follow the unmarked pattern for VP structure set out in (22) in 4: 1.6, it can be explained in the same way as the marked pattern in (24), namely as a result of the heaviness of the subordinate clause. Indeed, given appropriate intonation, it's possible to maintain the unmarked order:

(114) Marie [$_{VP}$ dit [$_{S2}$ qu'elle ne veut plus le voir] [$_{PP}$ à Paul]].

6.2   Types of subordinate clause

In 4: 6.1 we saw examples of declarative finite subordinate clauses. In this section we consider other types of subordinate clause, namely, *non*-finite declarative subordinate clauses (4: 6.2.1) and *interrogative* subordinate clauses (4: 6.2.2).

6.2.1   Non-finite subordinate clauses

Consider (115a):

(115) a. [$_{S1}$ Marc croyait [$_{S2}$ qu'il avait faim]].
       b. [$_{S1}$ Marc croyait [$_{S2}$ avoir faim]].

The complement of *croire* is a finite declarative subordinate clause, introduced by the complementiser *que* (4: 6.1). The subject of the subordinate clause corefers with the subject of the matrix clause (*il* and *Marc* refer to the same person), and there is an alternative way of expressing (115a), namely (115b). Here, the declarative subordinate clause is *non*-finite (*avoir* is an infinitive, a non-finite verb form). Consequently, *que* doesn't appear. Notice that the non-finite subordinate clause in (115b) doesn't have an overt subject, either; *il* has disappeared (4: 9). Instead, the subject of *avoir faim* is implicit; that is, we know that the subject of *avoir faim* is *Marc* even though the NP *Marc* doesn't appear. In both cases, the subordinate clause is a complement of the matrix verb *croire* and can be replaced by the proform *le*, as in *Marc le croyait*. The contrast between (115a) and (115b) therefore hinges on the finiteness of the verb in the subordinate clause; in (115a) it's finite, in (115b) it's non-finite.

Non-finite declarative subordinate clauses don't all follow the pattern in (115b). There are actually three different patterns. The first is the one illustrated in (115b) in which the subordinate clause isn't introduced by a complementiser at all. Elsewhere, non-finite declarative subordinate clauses are introduced by the non-finite complementisers *de* or *à*:

- Non-finite declarative subordinate clauses introduced by *de*:

  (116) a. [$_{S1}$ Je lui ai dit [$_{S2}$ DE venir]].
       b. [$_{S1}$ Marie a décidé [$_{S2}$ DE partir]].

Other verbs in this class are *accepter, (s')arrêter, brûler, cesser, continuer, craindre, s'efforcer, s'empresser, essayer, s'excuser, se féliciter, se garder, menacer, mériter, oublier, parler, promettre, refuser, regretter, risquer, tenter, venir* and *se vanter*.

- Non-finite declarative subordinate clauses introduced by *à*:

  (117) a. [$_{S1}$ J'arrive [$_{S2}$ À faire mes devoirs]].
       b. [$_{S1}$ Marie continue [$_{S2}$ À travailler]].

Other verbs in this class are *s'abaisser, s'amuser, s'appliquer, apprendre, s'attendre, commencer, consentir, s'employer, s'ennuyer, s'habituer, hésiter, s'intéresser, se mettre, s'obstiner, s'occuper, parvenir, penser, persister, se préparer, se refuser, renoncer, se résigner, se résoudre, réussir, servir, songer* and *tenir*.

- Non-finite declarative subordinate clauses introduced by no complementiser at all:

  (118) a. [$_{S1}$ Je veux [$_{S2}$ partir]].
       b. [$_{S1}$ Marie peut [$_{S2}$ travailler]].

Other verbs in this class are *aimer, aller, compter, croire, devoir, entrer, espérer, faillir, falloir, oser, penser, préférer, savoir, souhaiter* and *venir*.

In summary, subordinate clauses can be non-finite as well as finite. Non-finite subordinate clauses can be introduced by *de* or *à*, or by no complementiser at all.

6.2.2   *Interrogative subordinate clauses*

We now turn to subordinate interrogatives, also known as **indirect questions**. Recall from 4: 1.5 that an interrogative sentence asks a question and often has a special syntactic form. In (16) in 4: 1.5 we distinguished **yes–no questions** from **constituent questions**. In the examples in (119) the matrix clause is a constituent question (there is no subordinate clause). It is interrogative because it contains a (highlighted) **interrogative phrase**:

(119)   a. COMBIEN DE PAIN achète-t-elle?
          b. QUEL CHAPEAU porte-t-il?

Constituent questions can appear in (finite or non-finite) subordinate clauses, too, as the complement of verbs like *demander* and *savoir*:

(120)   a. $[_{S1}$ Je me demande $[_{S2}$ COMBIEN DE PAIN elle a acheté]].
          b. $[_{S1}$ Je sais $[_{S2}$ QUEL CHAPEAU il porte]].

(121)   a. $[_{S1}$ Je me demande $[_{S2}$ COMBIEN DE PAIN acheter aujourd'hui]].
          b. $[_{S1}$ Je sais $[_{S2}$ QUEL CHAPEAU porter]].

These subordinate clauses (S2) aren't introduced by a complementiser because, as constituent questions, their interrogative status is clearly marked by an interrogative phrase (4: 1.5). In yes–no questions, in contrast, interrogative phrases don't appear. Therefore, we expect a complementiser to be needed if a yes–no question appears in a subordinate clause, and this is exactly what we see. However, we don't find *que*, because *que* is a *declarative* complementiser. Instead, the *interrogative* complementiser *si* is used:

(122) $[_{S1}$ Je me demande $[_{S2}$ si tu viendras demain]].

Note the interesting absence in French of sentences along the lines of 'I was wondering whether to leave', that is non-finite subordinate yes–no interrogatives (**Je me demandais si partir*). Why is this? A plausible answer relates to the vital role of complementisers and interrogative phrases in indicating the status of subordinate interrogatives. In subordinate constituent questions a complementiser isn't needed because an interrogative phrase marks both finite – (120) – and non-finite – (121) – subordinate interrogatives. In subordinate yes–no questions, in contrast, there's no interrogative phrase, and a complementiser is needed instead. In *finite* contexts, the finite interrogative complementiser *si* is used, as in (122). But *si* cannot be used in *non*-finite contexts. In fact, there is no non-finite counterpart of *si*. And that's why non-finite subordinate yes–no interrogatives don't exist in French. In order to express the idea in 'I was wondering whether to leave', a *finite* subordinate yes–no interrogative is needed, for example, *Je me demandais si j'allais partir*.

We return to matrix and subordinate interrogatives in 4: 7.1, and consider the marked subject–verb order in (119)–(120) in 4: 7.2.

6.3   Subordinate clauses and subjunctive mood

A specific kind of finite subordinate clause contains **subjunctive** verbs (3: 3). The subjunctive mood (for discussion of the term **mood** see 4: 15.3) is a set, a **paradigm**, of verb forms which contrast with the **indicative** mood in often having a non-assertive or non-factual interpretation. The subjunctive is said to allow the speaker to introduce doubt, uncertainty or attenuation into the declarative strength of a clause, but it's debatable how true this is of Modern French. What is clear is that the subjunctive in French is marked, that is, triggered by some specific feature in the linguistic context. In 4: 6.4 we present a number of grammatical contexts requiring the subjunctive. But first we see some examples of common verbs and expressions which take as their complement a finite subordinate clause containing a subjunctive verb:

VERBS OF WISHING/DESIRE

(123)   a. [$_{S1}$ Je veux [$_{S2}$ que tout le monde SORTE]].
        b. [$_{S1}$ Mon chef souhaite [$_{S2}$ qu'on lui OBÉISSE en tout]].

Other verbs in this class are *aimer (mieux)*, *commander*, *défendre*, *désapprouver*, *désirer*, *empêcher*, *ordonner*, *permettre* and *préférer*.

VERBS OF OPINION AND PERCEPTION

Where the matrix clause is positive and declarative (4: 1.5), the finite subordinate clause contains an indicative verb:

(124)   [$_{S1}$ Je pense [$_{S2}$ qu'elle EST déjà arrivée]].

If the matrix clause is negative or interrogative (4: 1.5), the finite subordinate clause contains a subjunctive verb:

(125)   a. [$_{S1}$ Je ne pense pas [$_{S2}$ qu'elle SOIT déjà arrivée]].
        b. [$_{S1}$ Penses-tu [$_{S2}$ qu'elle SOIT déjà arrivée]] ?

Other verbs which follow this pattern are *admettre, affirmer, annoncer, (s')apercevoir, apprendre, assurer, avertir, avouer, certifier, comprendre, concevoir, constater, croire, dire, douter, nier, parier, promettre, reconnaître, remarquer, se rendre compte, savoir, songer, soupçonner, supposer* and *voir*.

VERBS OF FEELING

Verbs such as *s'étonner, admirer, craindre, regretter* and *se réjouir* take a finite subordinate clause containing a subjunctive verb:

(126) a. [$_{S1}$ Je m'étonne [$_{S2}$ que tu SOIS si content du résultat]].
       b. [$_{S1}$ Pierre craint [$_{S2}$ que Marie (ne) SOIT très malade]].

(On this use of *ne* see 4: 12.3.)

IMPERSONAL STRUCTURES (4: 14)

These are clauses whose grammatical subject is impersonal *il/ce* (4: 4.3):

(127) a. [$_{S1}$ C'est possible [$_{S2}$ que le professeur SOIT malade]].
       b. [$_{S1}$ Il paraît utile [$_{S2}$ que nous RESTIONS encore à l'aider]].
       c. [$_{S1}$ Il semble fâcheux [$_{S2}$ que les livres ne SOIENT pas encore livrés]].

Other expressions in this class are *il est important/impossible/bon/naturel/ heureux/faux/ rare/triste/urgent/honteux/douteux/nécessaire/exclu que, il suffit que, il se peut que, il n'est pas contestable que* and *il s'en faut (de peu) que*.

Other impersonal structures take a finite subordinate clause containing an indicative verb if the matrix clause is positive and declarative, but a subjunctive verb if the matrix clause is negative or interrogative (4: 1.5) (see also the section on verbs of opinion and perception):

(128) a. [$_{S1}$ Il est certain [$_{S2}$ que les touristes SONT arrivés]].
       b. [$_{S1}$ Il n'est pas certain [$_{S2}$ que les touristes SOIENT arrivés]].
       c. [$_{S1}$ Est-il certain [$_{S2}$ que les touristes SOIENT arrivés]] ?

Impersonal expressions in this class include the copular expressions *c'est que, il paraît que,* as well as *il est sûr/clair/incontestable/probable/indiscutable que.*

SEMBLER

The expression *il semble que* takes a finite subordinate clause containing a subjunctive verb:

(129) [$_{S1}$ Il semble [$_{S2}$ que vous AYEZ fait bonne impression]].

However, *il* ME *semble que* takes a finite subordinate clause containing an indicative verb:

(130) [$_{S1}$ Il ME semble [$_{S2}$ que vous AVEZ fait une excellente impression]].

The contrast between (129) and (130) shows that the perspective of the speaker is important in the use of the subjunctive.

ADJECTIVES EXPRESSING FEELINGS (4: 10.2)

(131) a. Mes amis sont [$_{AP}$ heureux [$_{S2}$ que les cours SOIENT suspendus]].
       b. Je suis [$_{AP}$ ravi [$_{S2}$ que tu AIES réussi à vaincre ta peur]].

Other adjectives in this group are *navré*, *fâché*, *désolé*, *irrité* and *surpris*.

NOUNS EXPRESSING FEELINGS (4: 10.1)

(132) [$_{NP}$ Sa crainte [$_{S2}$ que ses fils (ne) FASSENT du bruit]] l'a incité à rester.

(On this use of *ne* see 4: 12.4.) Other nouns in this class are *le désir que*, *l'indignation que*, *la volonté que*, *la joie que* and *le regret que*.

OTHER NOUNS SELECTING THE SUBJUNCTIVE (4: 10.1)

A further class of nouns which often take a finite subordinate clause containing a subjunctive verb includes *le fait que*, *la pensée que*, *l'idée que*, *le doute que* and *la constatation que*:

(133) [$_{NP}$ Le fait [$_{S2}$ que la terre SOIT ronde]] m'effraie.

6.4 The subjunctive in specific environments

In addition to being triggered by lexical items, the subjunctive is found in a number of grammatical contexts. The first concerns relativised NPs (4: 7.3) whose head is modified by a superlative adjective (4: 10.3) or a restrictive adjective like *seul*, *unique*, *premier*, *dernier* and *suprême*:

(134) a. [$_{NP}$ Le PLUS BEAU poème [$_{S2}$ que j'AIE lu]], c'est *Le Loup*.
       b. [$_{NP}$ La SEULE personne [$_{S2}$ qui PUISSE le faire]], c'est Pierre.
       c. [$_{NP}$ Le PREMIER film [$_{S2}$ qu'ils AIENT vu ensemble]], c'était *Titanic*.

In (134a) the head of the relative, *le poème*, is modified by the superlative AP *plus beau*, and the verb in the relative clause is subjunctive. The subjunctive is also found in relative clauses whose head is negative (4: 12) or expresses an idea of doubt or minimum quantity:

(135) a. Je ne connais [$_{NP}$ AUCUN étudiant [$_{S2}$ qui PUISSE maîtriser tout cela]].
b. Il n'y a [$_{NP}$ RIEN [$_{S2}$ que l'on PUISSE faire]].
c. On voit [$_{NP}$ TRÈS PEU de profs [$_{S2}$ qui FASSENT tant de préparation]].
d. Il n'existe [$_{NP}$ PLUS de rivières [$_{S2}$ qui SOIENT libres de pollution]].

There's an interesting semantic difference between the bracketed NPs in (136) and (137):

(136) a. Je cherche [$_{NP}$ une secrétaire [$_{S2}$ qui SAIT parler français]].
b. Où est [$_{NP}$ la robe [$_{S2}$ qui te VA si bien]] ?
c. Je rêve d' [$_{NP}$ une petite maison [$_{S2}$ qui EST au bord de la mer]].

(137) a. Je cherche [$_{NP}$ une secrétaire [$_{S2}$ qui SACHE parler français]].
b. Où trouverons-nous [$_{NP}$ une robe [$_{S2}$ qui t'AILLE si bien]] ?
c. Je rêve d' [$_{NP}$ une petite maison [$_{S2}$ qui SOIT au bord de la mer]].

In (136) the speaker is referring to a particular secretary, a particular dress and a particular house. In (137) the interpretation changes; the speaker isn't looking for any particular secretary, just one who speaks French; no particular dress, just one that suits the addressee; and she isn't dreaming about a particular house, she's just imagining how nice it would be to have a little one by the sea. Of course, the speaker might never find such a secretary, dress or house, and this is precisely what is marked by the subjunctive.

The subjunctive is also found after certain complex complementisers (4: 11.3), such as *bien que* and *quoique*:

(138) a. [$_{S2}$ QUOIQUE tu FASSES des progrès], tu n'es pas prêt à passer l'examen.
b. [$_{S2}$ BIEN QU'il SOIT venu], je ne veux pas le voir.

Note also the following relative structures (4: 7.3) introduced by *quoi que* and *quel(le)(s) que*:

(139) a. [$_{S2}$ QUOI que vous FASSIEZ], elle sera toujours mécontente.
b. [$_{S2}$ QUOI que je DISE], les enfants continuent à jouer dans la rue.

c. [$_{S2}$ QUEL que SOIT le problème], vous pouvez compter sur moi.
d. [$_{S2}$ QUELLES que SOIENT ses excuses], tu dois l'amener avec toi.

In summary, we've seen that sentences can be simple or complex. Complex sentences are subordinate clauses inside matrix clauses. Often, the subordinate clause is a complement of the matrix verb. Subordinate clauses can be finite or non-finite, declarative or interrogative. In marked cases, subordinate clauses contain subjunctive verbs, triggered either by some lexical element, for example a verb of wishing in the matrix clause, or by some grammatical environment such as a superlative adjective within a relativised NP.

7   Sentence structures involving movement

At various points (4: 6.2.2 in particular) we've talked about interrogative sentences (4: 1.5), but we haven't yet examined their internal structure. In this section we do just that, and suggest that some interrogative sentences in French involve 'movement' (4: 7.1). We then go on to show that the idea of movement can illuminate a number of other aspects of French syntax, namely subject–verb inversion (4: 7.2), relative clauses (4: 7.3–4) and, finally, past participle agreement (4: 7.5).

7.1   *Interrogative sentences and movement*

The sentence in (140a) is an **interrogative sentence** (4: 1.5) because the direct object contains the interrogative determiner *quel* (4: 2.2). Phrases like *quel homme* are called **interrogative phrases** (4: 6.2.2). With appropriate intonation (2: 16.3) the sentence in (140a) is an acceptable, if casual, way to ask a question. The same question could also be asked, equally casually, using (140b), in which the interrogative phrase has moved to sentence-initial position. Movement of an interrogative phrase is called **interrogative movement**. A third, more formal, way of asking the question in (140a, b) is (140c). Interrogative movement has taken place here, too, but, in addition, **subject–clitic inversion** has reversed the unmarked order of the subject clitic and the finite verb (4: 7.2).

(140)   a. Tu as vu QUEL HOMME, ce matin, au parc?
                    ↓   (interrogative movement)
         b. QUEL HOMME tu as vu, ce matin, au parc?
                    ↓   (subject–clitic inversion)
         c. Quel homme AS-TU vu, ce matin, au parc?

Direct objects aren't the only kind of interrogative phrase that can undergo movement. Provided it contains an interrogative determiner/proform

(4: 4.5), an indirect object also counts as an interrogative phrase, and can undergo movement. So an alternative to (141a), in which the indirect object contains the interrogative proform *qui*, is (141b), in which *à qui* moves to sentence-initial position. And, once again, interrogative movement can be accompanied by subject–clitic inversion, as in (141c):

(141)   a. Tu as parlé À QUI, ce matin, au parc?
              ↓   (interrogative movement)
        b. À QUI tu as parlé, ce matin, au parc?
              ↓   (subject–clitic inversion)
        c. A qui AS-TU parlé, ce matin, au parc?

In (140b, c) and (141b, c), interrogative movement takes place within a simple sentence (4: 6). However, interrogative movement can take place in complex sentences, too. Recall from 4: 6 that complex sentences are subordinate clauses contained within matrix clauses. In complex sentences, an interrogative phrase can move from within a subordinate clause to sentence-initial position, and, again, subject–clitic inversion is possible:

(142)   a. [$_{S1}$ Tu dis [$_{S2}$ qu'elle a parlé À QUI, ce matin, au parc]] ?
              ↓   (interrogative movement)
        b. À QUI tu dis qu'elle a parlé, ce matin, au parc?
              ↓   (subject–clitic inversion)
        c. A qui DIS-TU qu'elle a parlé, ce matin, au parc?

(143)   a. [$_{S1}$ Tu penses [$_{S2}$ qu'il gagne COMBIEN]] ?
              ↓   (interrogative movement)
        b. COMBIEN tu penses qu'il gagne?
              ↓   (subject–clitic inversion)
        c. Combien PENSES-TU qu'il gagne?

However, an interrogative phrase contained within a subordinate clause doesn't always move to sentence-initial position. Sometimes, it moves to clause-initial position only. Indeed, in (120)–(121) in 4: 6.2.2 we saw this in indirect questions (subordinate interrogatives); (obligatory) interrogative movement is contained entirely within the subordinate clause:

(144)   a. [$_{S1}$ Je me demande [$_{S2}$ À QUI il a parlé]].
        b. [$_{S1}$ Il ne sait pas [$_{S2}$ COMBIEN je gagne]].

Besides direct objects and indirect objects, other interrogative phrases can undergo movement, for example the adverbials (4: 11) *où* (adverbial of place), *quand* (adverbial of time), *comment* (adverbial of manner) and *pourquoi* (reason adverbial):

(145) a. OÙ va-t-on trouver de quoi manger?
b. QUAND arrive le train?
c. Il me demandait [$_{S2}$ COMMENT j'allais].
d. Je ne sais pas [$_{S2}$ POURQUOI il l'a fait].

In the examples so far, interrogative movement targets (in)direct objects or adverbials. What we haven't seen is interrogative movement targeting subjects. If interrogative subjects behave in parallel fashion to interrogative non-subjects, we would expect them to be able to move. However, if we look at *simple* sentences only, it isn't easy to tell whether subjects undergo interrogative movement; the subject of a simple sentence is, after all, usually already in initial position:

(146) a. QUI veut partir?   b. COMBIEN D'ARGENT sera dépensé?

However, we can address the issue by looking at *complex* sentences and the behaviour of an interrogative phrase which is the subject of a *subordinate* clause. This is because the subject of a subordinate clause isn't sentence-initial:

(147) a. [$_{S1}$ Tu dis [$_{S2}$ que QUI veut partir]] ?
b. [$_{S1}$ Tu dis [$_{S2}$ que COMBIEN D'ARGENT sera dépensé]] ?

Now we can test whether the interrogative subject of a subordinate clause can move to sentence-initial position. In fact, (148a, b) show that, if nothing else happens, movement isn't possible, either with or without subject–clitic inversion:

(148) a. *QUI dis-tu que veut partir?   (with subject–clitic inversion)
b. *COMBIEN D'ARGENT tu dis que sera dépensé?
                           (without subject–clitic inversion)

In order to salvage these sentences, the form of the complementiser which introduces the subordinate clause needs to change from *que* to *qui*. This phenomenon is called **masquerade** or ***que/qui* alternation**:

(149) a. [$_{S1}$ Qui dis-tu [$_{S2}$ QUI veut partir]] ?
b. [$_{S2}$ Combien d'argent tu dis [$_{S2}$ QUI sera dépensé]] ?

We conclude, then, that, just like non-subjects, interrogative subjects can and do undergo movement. Further, masquerade is a telltale sign that the subject of a finite subordinate clause has moved. In 4: 7.4 and 4: 8.3 we see other contexts in which masquerade suggests that the subject of a finite subordinate clause has moved. Having considered interrogative movement, we can now address another feature of interrogative clauses, namely subject–verb inversion.

7.2   *Types of subject–verb inversion*

In 4: 7.1 we noted that when an interrogative phrase is moved to sentence-initial position, the unmarked order of subject and verb can be reversed, as in (140c)–(143c). To be precise, we saw interrogative sentences like (150a), in which the subject clitic follows the verb, rather than preceding it. We called this phenomenon **subject–clitic inversion**. In fact, it isn't just subject clitics that can follow the verb in interrogative sentences. In (150b) the subject NP is postverbal, too.

> (150) a. Où va-t-il?   b. Combien d'argent dépense Pierre?

In (150) a complement of the verb is an interrogative phrase (*où* and *combien d'argent*, respectively) which moves to sentence-initial position, and the subject – a clitic in (150a) and an NP in (150b) – is in postverbal position. We might suspect that the same syntactic phenomenon is illustrated in both (150a) and (150b). But this isn't in fact the case, as we can see from (151):

> (151) a. Où EST-IL ALLÉ? b. Combien d'argent A DÉPENSÉ PIERRE?

There are two relevant differences between (150) and (151). The first has to do with the verb. In (150) it's a **simple tense**, while in (151) it's a **compound tense**, that is, the combination of the **auxiliary** *avoir* and a **past participle** (4: 15.2). The second difference relates to the position of the 'inverted' subject. Whereas in (150) the subjects appear to occupy the same position, in (151) they clearly don't; the 'inverted' subject clitic in (151a) follows the auxiliary, while the 'inverted' subject NP in (151b) follows the past participle. In 4: 4.2 we saw a number of differences between subject NPs and subject clitics, and we concluded that subject clitics are dependent on the finite verb, while subject NPs aren't. In (151) we see that this difference surfaces in inversion structures, too. Inverted subject clitics have to appear adjacent to the verb, just like non-inverted subject clitics. In contrast, postverbal subject NPs are independent of the verb, just like non-inverted subject NPs. To distinguish between the two types of inversion illustrated in (151), we shall reserve the term subject–clitic inversion for the inversion in (151a), and use the term **stylistic inversion** for the inversion in (151b).

In the constituent questions in (150) and (151) an interrogative phrase moves to sentence-initial position, and subject–clitic inversion and stylistic inversion are possible, as we've seen. However, this isn't the case in all types of interrogative clause, and we'll mention two here. The first is subordinate interrogatives (indirect questions; 4: 6.2.2), as in (144), in which an interrogative phrase within a subordinate clause moves only as far as clause-initial position (rather than to sentence-initial position). Indirect questions are illustrated without inversion in (152) and (153). In (152) the subject of the subordinate clause is a clitic (*il, elle*); in (153), an NP (*Pierre, Marie*):

(152)　a.　[$_{S1}$ Je me demande [$_{S2}$ COMBIEN D'ARGENT il a gagné]].
　　　　b.　[$_{S1}$ Je ne sais pas [$_{S2}$ QUEL ORDINATEUR elle a utilisé]].

(153)　a.　[$_{S1}$ Je me demande [$_{S2}$ COMBIEN D'ARGENT Pierre a gagné]].
　　　　b.　[$_{S1}$ Je ne sais pas [$_{S2}$ QUEL ORDINATEUR Marie a utilisé]].

In fact, subject–verb inversion is possible here, but only one of the two kinds we've seen. Stylistic inversion is possible, but not subject–clitic inversion. So, the NP subject in (153) can invert, while the clitic subject in (152) cannot:

(154)　a.　*[$_{S1}$ Je me demande [$_{S2}$ combien d'argent A-T-IL gagné]].
　　　　b.　*[$_{S1}$ Je ne sais pas [$_{S2}$ quel ordinateur A-T-ELLE utilisé]].

(155)　a.　[$_{S1}$ Je me demande [$_{S2}$ combien d'argent A GAGNÉ PIERRE]].
　　　　b.　[$_{S1}$ Je ne sais pas [$_{S2}$ quel ordinateur A UTILISÉ MARIE]].

Note that interrogatives like (151b) and (155), in which stylistic inversion has occurred, are potentially ambiguous. For example, (155b) could mean 'I don't know which computer Mary used' or 'I don't know which computer used Mary'. While one of these interpretations is implausible, it isn't difficult to imagine cases, like (156), in which the potential ambiguity could pose communication problems.

(156)　Je ne sais pas quel homme a tué Marie.

This sentence means either 'I don't know which man Marie killed' or 'I don't know which man killed Marie'. Under the first interpretation *quel homme* is the direct object of *tuer* and has moved to clause-initial position; this has been followed by stylistic inversion of *a tué* and the subject *Marie*. Under the second interpretation *quel homme* is the subject of *tuer*, *Marie* is the direct object and no subject–verb inversion has occurred. The difference in meaning is, I think you'll agree, fairly crucial, and it's perhaps for this reason that some speakers avoid stylistic inversion, especially in subordinate interrogatives. Stylistic inversion is nevertheless *possible* in subordinate interrogatives, as in (155), and this contrasts with subject–clitic inversion, which is not, as shown in (154).

The second context which distinguishes subject–clitic inversion from stylistic inversion by allowing one but not the other is yes–no questions (4: 1.5), illustrated without inversion in (157):

(157)　a.　'Il est venu?' 'Oui.'
　　　　b.　'Ils ont trouvé le chemin?' 'Non.'
　　　　c.　'Elle n'est pas contente?' 'Si.'

Unlike the matrix constituent questions in (151) (which allow *both* subject–clitic inversion *and* stylistic inversion), and unlike the subordinate constituent questions in (152)–(155) (which allow stylistic inversion *but not* subject–clitic inversion), yes–no interrogatives allow subject–clitic inversion *but not* stylistic inversion:

(158) a. 'Est-il venu?' 'Oui.'
b. 'Ont-ils trouvé le chemin?' 'Non.'
c. 'N'est-elle pas contente?' 'Si.'

(159) a. *Est venu Pierre?
b. *Ont trouvé Marie et Gilles le chemin?

(Note, also, that stylistic inversion is impossible when the fronted interrogative phrase is *pourquoi*: *Pourquoi sont partis les enfants?*)

But, if the forms in (159) are ungrammatical, how can we ask questions like 'Did Pierre come?' or 'Have Marie and Gilles found the path?'? There are in fact two ways. The first is to use a sentence which superficially has a declarative structure, and to use final rising intonation, as in (160):

(160) a. Pierre est arrivé?

b. Marie et Gilles ont trouvé le chemin?

The second possibility is to use a different type of subject–verb inversion altogether, called **complex inversion**. The 'complex' thing about complex inversion is that it involves *both* a (preverbal) subject NP *and* a (postverbal) subject clitic. Interrogatives with complex inversion corresponding to the ungrammatical (159) are given in (161):

(161) a. Pierre est-il venu?
b. Marie et Gilles ont-ils trouvé le chemin?

Complex inversion is also possible in matrix constituent questions; indeed, it is a less formal alternative to stylistic inversion here:

(162) a. Combien d'argent Pierre a-t-il gagné?
b. Qui Pierre a-t-il vu?

Note, finally, that subject–clitic and complex inversion are also possible in non-interrogative sentences introduced by expressions such as *peut-être*, *sans doute* and *à peine*, as shown here:

(163) a. Sans doute A-T-IL dit cela.

b. Peut-être ne VA-T-ELLE pas venir.
c. A peine Pierre AVAIT-IL vu sa cousine, qu'il a tout compris.

Other sentence-initial phrases which trigger subject–verb inversion are *et encore, tout au plus, encore moins, ainsi, aussi, aussi bien, (tout) au moins, pour le moins, à plus forte raison* and *en vain*. This phenomenon is similar to what happens in English sentences like 'Never in a month of Sundays would I leave him' and 'So does John' in which subject–auxiliary inversion is triggered by sentence-initial phrases like *never in a month of Sundays* and *so*.

7.3 Relative clauses

In 4: 7.1 the movement of interrogative phrases was used to explain the structure of questions. In this section we see that the notion of movement can help us understand the syntax of certain kinds of **relative clauses**, too. The relevant type is illustrated in (164) and (165):

(164) a. [$_{NP}$ La vieille femme [$_{S2}$ QUI EST PASSÉE CE MATIN]] est anglaise.
b. [$_{NP}$ L'étudiant [$_{S2}$ QUE J'AI VU]] est très intelligent.

(165) a. [$_{NP}$ Le gars [$_{S2}$ AVEC QUI JE VEUX ME MARIER]] est parti.
b. [$_{NP}$ La chaise [$_{S2}$ SUR LAQUELLE JE ME SUIS ASSIS]] s'est cassée.

These relative clauses (labelled S2) are subordinate clauses which appear inside an NP headed by a common noun. The relative clause provides extra information about the entity that the NP refers to. (This is why relative clauses can occur with demonstrative proforms; 4: 4.5.) There are two parts to the bracketed NPs in (164) and (165): first, there's the **head** of the structure (*la femme, l'étudiant, le gars* and *la chaise*); second, there's the relative clause (S2) itself.

Let's look at the internal structure of relative clauses in (165). We'll return to (164) in 4: 7.4. The heads of the NPs in (165) are *le gars* and *la chaise*, respectively. The relative clauses are *avec qui je veux me marier* and *sur laquelle je me suis assis*, respectively, in which the initial phrase is a PP containing a preposition (*avec/sur*) and a relative pro-NP (*qui/laquelle*) (4: 4.5) which 'refers back to' the head (*qui* refers to *le gars*; *laquelle* to *la chaise*). Significantly, these PPs intuitively feel like complements of the verb in the relative clause. The PP *avec qui* in (165a) is interpreted as the complement of *me marier* (*on se marie* AVEC QUELQU'UN); *sur laquelle* in (165b) is interpreted as the complement of *s'asseoir* (*on s'assoit* SUR QUELQUE CHOSE). Taking these two ideas into account (that the relative pro-NPs 'refer back to' the head, and that the clause-initial PP is the complement of the verb in the relative clause), we can interpret the sentences in (165) in the following way:

(166) a. Le gars [je veux me marier avec le gars] est parti.
      b. La chaise [je me suis assis sur la chaise] s'est cassée.

How, then, do we relate these intuitions to the actual structures we saw in (165)? This is where the notion of movement comes in. We can account for (165) by appealing to relativisation (a form of pronominalisation) and movement. Recall that pronominalisation avoids repetition of familiar material (4: 4). Relativisation replaces familiar material with a relative proform. Relativisation of the NPs *le gars* and *la chaise* within the subordinate clauses in (166) replaces them with the appropriate relative pro-NPs *qui* (+ human) and *laquelle* (– human, + feminine, + singular), respectively (4: 4.5). Note that these relative pro-NPs are identical to interrogative pro-NPs. We're not surprised, then, to see that PPs containing a relative pro-NP move to clause-initial position, just like interrogative phrases (4: 7.1).

Putting these ideas together, we can think of (165) as involving a two-stage manipulation of (166). First, the NP which is coreferential with the head of the relative is replaced by a relative pro-NP. Second, the PP containing the relative proform is moved to clause-initial position. This is illustrated for (165a) in (167):

(167) a. Le gars [je veux me marier [avec LE GARS]] est parti.
                    ↓   (relativisation)
      b. Le gars [je veux me marier [avec QUI]] est parti.
                    ↓   (movement)
      c. Le gars [[AVEC QUI] je veux me marier] est parti.

Taking the parallel with interrogatives one step further, note that, like interrogative movement (see (142b, c) and (143b, c) in 4: 7.1), movement of a phrase containing a relative proform isn't restricted to a single clause. In (168a), for example, the relative PP *avec qui* moves from within S3 to the beginning of the relative clause S2, and the same thing has happened to *sur laquelle* in (168b). The two steps in the derivation, relativisation and movement, for (168a) are shown in (169).

(168) a. C'est [$_{NP}$ le gars [$_{S2}$ AVEC QUI tu sais [$_{S3}$ que je veux me marier]]].
      b. C'est [$_{NP}$ la chaise [$_{S2}$ SUR LAQUELLE il dit [$_{S3}$ que je me suis assis]]].

(169) a. C'est le gars [tu sais que je veux me marier [avec LE GARS]].
                          ↓   (relativisation)
       b. C'est le gars [tu sais que je veux me marier [avec QUI]].
                          ↓   (movement)
       c. C'est le gars [[AVEC QUI] tu sais que je veux me marier].

Finally, recall that the subordinate constituent questions in (144) in 4: 7.1 weren't introduced by a complementiser. What we see here is that, similarly, the relative clauses (S2) in (165) and (168) aren't introduced by a complementiser, either. In the context of subordinate constituent questions, the *absence* of a complementiser was explained by the *presence* of a clause-initial interrogative phrase, which was enough to mark the status of the subordinate clause. In the context of relative clauses, we might assume that the same function is carried out by the clause-initial relative PP; it marks the subordinate status of the relative clause; hence, the absence of a complementiser.

7.4 Masquerade in relative clauses

Having dealt in 4: 7.3 with relative clauses like (165), and concluded that they involve relativisation and movement, we now return to the relative clauses in (164), repeated here:

(164) a. [$_{NP}$ La vieille femme [$_{S2}$ QUI EST PASSÉE CE MATIN]] est
          anglaise.
       b. [$_{NP}$ L'étudiant [$_{S2}$ QUE J'AI VU]] est très intelligent.

Note, first, the parallel between (164) and (165). Ignoring the fact that relativisation targets different arguments of the verb in the relative clause, the structures are identical. (In (165) it's a PP complement of the verb that's relativised, while in (164a) it's the subject NP (*la vieille femme* is interpreted as the subject of *passer*) and in (164b), the direct object NP (*l'étudiant* is interpreted as the direct object of *voir*).) We might therefore expect the syntactic analysis of (164) to run parallel to (165). We might expect (164) to be the result of a manipulation of (170) involving first relativisation and then movement.

(170) a. La vieille femme [la vieille femme est passée ce matin] est
          anglaise.
       b. L'étudiant [j'ai vu l'étudiant] est très intelligent.

How might this work in detail? One traditional way – which we shall ultimately reject – assumes that clause-initial *que* and *qui* in (164) are relative proforms. We might say, first, that they replace the direct object and subject NPs respectively, and, then, move to clause-initial position. This is illustrated in (171)–(172). Of course, such movement wouldn't actually alter the position of *qui* in (164a), which is already in clause-initial position, but it would move *que* in (164b) from its postverbal position.

(171)   a. La vieille femme [LA VIEILLE FEMME est passée ce matin] est
          anglaise.
                    ↓   (relativisation)
        b. La vieille femme [QUI est passée ce matin] est anglaise.
                    ↓   (movement (no effect))
        c. La vieille femme [QUI est passée ce matin] est anglaise.

(172)   a. L'étudiant [j'ai vu L'ÉTUDIANT] est très intelligent.
                    ↓   (relativisation)
        b. L'étudiant [j'ai vu QUE] est très intelligent.
                    ↓   (movement)
        c. L'étudiant [QUE j'ai vu] est très intelligent.

There are several reasons why this analysis is wrong. First, the relative pro-NP *qui* which we saw in (165a) in 4: 7.3 can only refer to a human NP, hence the distinction in (173):

(173)   a. *la chaise [[sur QUI] je me suis assis]
        b. l'homme [[à QUI] on a parlé]

In contrast, the element *qui* which appears in (164a) isn't sensitive to the [± human] distinction:

(174)   a. la chaise [QUI s'est cassée]   b. l'homme [QUI est venu]

The fact that *qui* behaves differently in these two contexts shows that *qui* isn't actually 'the same thing' in both uses. Given that *qui* clearly *is* a relative pro-NP in (173b), it can't be one in (174).

Second, if *que* in (164b) is a relative pro-NP (as the analysis in (172) suggests), we would expect it to appear within PPs (like the relative pro-NP *qui* in (173b), for example). Yet, this isn't the case:

(175)   a. *l'homme [[à QUE] j'ai parlé]
        b. *l'arbre [[sur QUE] les enfants jouent]

The fact that *que* cannot occur within a relativised PP shows that it isn't a relative pro-NP.

Finally, there's a phonological reason to believe that *qui* in (164a)/(171) isn't a proform (Blanche-Benveniste 1997: 38–9). In subject relative clauses *qui* is prone to phonological reduction before vowels. For example, *qui est* [kiɛ] in (174b) can readily be pronounced as [kjɛ] or [kɛ]. In contrast, where *qui* is a (relative or interrogative) proform, as in (173b), it never reduces;

its [i] vowel is always fully articulated, even if this results in a sequence of two vowels, as in [aki5] (*à qui on*). These distinctive patterns aren't expected if *qui* is a proform in all these contexts. On balance, then, it's unconvincing to conclude that *que* and *qui* in (164) are relative pro-NPs, and so we reject the analysis in (171)–(172).

An alternative way of relating (164) and (170) – one which we shall adopt – is to assume that, rather than being relative pro-NPs, *que* and *qui* in (164) are complementisers. Supporting evidence comes from the masquerade effect (4: 7.1). Recall from (149) that the complementiser *que* is sensitive to whether or not the subject position in the subordinate clause it introduces is empty. If the subject position is filled, the complementiser surfaces as *que*; if the subject position is empty, the complementiser changes to *qui*. This is illustrated in (176):

(176) a. Quel homme politique dis-tu [$_{S2}$ QUE le premier ministre a critiqué] ?
b. Quel homme politique dis-tu [$_{S2}$ QUI a critiqué le premier ministre] ?

In (176a) *quel homme politique* is the direct object of *critiquer*, but has moved to sentence-initial position. The subject position in the subordinate clause is filled (by *le premier ministre*), and the complementiser surfaces as *que*. In (176b), in contrast, *quel homme politique* is the *subject* of *critiquer*. Movement to sentence-initial position therefore leaves an empty subject position in the subordinate clause, and *que* changes to *qui*.

Returning to our relative NPs [$_{NP}$ la vieille femme QUI est passée ce matin] and [$_{NP}$ l'étudiant QUE j'ai vu] in (164), observe the same *que/qui* alternation. Note also that the head of these NPs is associated with the subject of the first subordinate clause (introduced by *qui*) and the direct object of the second (introduced with *que*). In other words, the *que/qui* alternation is sensitive to the same subject/non-subject distinction that it's sensitive to in (176). There, *que/qui* alternation was attributed to whether or not interrogative movement had left an empty subject position in the subordinate clause. It makes sense, therefore, to deal with *que/qui* alternation in relative clauses in the same way. We might assume, then, that in (164a) *qui* is a complementiser which precedes an empty subject position, while in (164b) *que* is a complementiser which precedes a filled subject position.

There's one rather important issue we've not covered yet. If *qui/que* in (164) are complementisers rather than relative proforms, where are the relative proforms? We can answer this question by assuming that the relative NPs exploit a possibility which actually exists in English, too. Consider the English relative NPs in (177):

(177) a. [$_{NP}$ The man [$_{S2}$ WHO(M) I saw this morning]] is French.
b. [$_{NP}$ The man [$_{S2}$ I saw this morning]] is French.

Both NPs contain relative clauses in which the direct object of *saw* has been relativised. In (177a) this can straightforwardly be analysed in terms of a two-stage manipulation of (178):

(178)   The man [I saw the man this morning] is French.

The direct object is first relativised (replaced by the relative proform *who(m)*), then moved to clause-initial position. The parallel example in (177b) shows that the relative proform can be non-overt. The structure of (177b) can therefore be represented as (179), in which the dashes represent the original position of the silent relative proform and the position it moves to:

(179)   [$_{NP}$ The man [$_{S2}$ – I saw – this morning]] is French.

Returning again to the French relative NPs in (164), we can assume that the possibility illustrated in (179) for English is exploited in French too. That is, the relative proforms in (164) are actually silent. The structure of the examples in (164) – following relativisation and movement – is represented in (180), in which the dashes again indicate the original and new positions of the silent relative proform:

(180)   a. [$_{NP}$ La vieille femme [$_{S2}$ – QUI – EST PASSÉE CE MATIN]] est anglaise.
        b. [$_{NP}$ L'étudiant [$_{S2}$ – QUE J'AI VU –]] est très intelligent.

In summary, by assuming that *que* and *qui* are complementisers rather than relative pro-NPs we've been able to analyse the relative clauses in (164) in exactly the same way as the relative clauses in (165), namely in terms of relativisation and movement.

7.5   Past participle agreement

The final syntactic phenomenon we approach from the perspective of movement is past participle agreement, that is, morphological agreement between a past participle and its direct object. We've mentioned the phenomenon already (4: 4.1; 4: 5.2–3), but have delayed discussion until now because it can best be understood in terms of movement. In (181a) ((65a) in 4: 4.1), agreement is triggered because the clitic *nous* is the direct object of the verb *appeler* and has moved to a position preceding the past participle; agreement is absent from (181b) because *nous* is the indirect object of *téléphoner*.

(181)   a. Pierre NOUS a APPELÉS.   b. Pierre NOUS a TÉLÉPHONÉ.

In (182a), similarly, agreement is triggered by *se*, the direct object of *souvenir*; agreement is absent from (182b) because, here, *se* is the indirect object of *rappeler* (the *direct* object of *rappeler* is *la date de mon anniversaire*) (4: 5.2).

    (182) a. Elles SE sont SOUVENUES de la date de mon anniversaire.

                                                                         (= (104))

          b. Elles SE sont RAPPELÉ la date de mon anniversaire.

Finally, in (183), discussed in 4: 5.3, agreement takes place because, in syntactic terms, *se* is the direct object of *casser*.

    (183) La fenêtre S'est CASSÉE.   (= (108a))

What these contexts with past participle agreement have in common (and what we must therefore assume is responsible for triggering the agreement here and not elsewhere) is that the direct object has been replaced by a clitic, and has moved to *preverbal* position. That cliticisation is relevant is supported by minimal pairs like (184) and (185):

    (184) a. Marie a VU la voiture.   b. Marie L'a VUE.
    (185) a. Marie a VU les voitures.   b. Marie LES a VUES.

In (184a) and (185a) the direct object is a postverbal NP and no agreement is triggered. In (184b) and (185b) the direct object has been cliticised, and agreement takes place.

    Note (the traditional view) that the clitic *en* doesn't trigger agreement, even if *en* appears to replace the direct object:

    (186) a. J'ai BU des verres.   b. *J'EN ai BUS.   c. J'EN ai BU.

This is because the proform *en* actually only replaces *part* of the quantified indefinite NP, as is clear from (187):

    (187) J'EN ai bu DEUX.

(See 1: 7 for a less conservative judgement for (186b).)

    In fact, cliticisation of a direct object onto the auxiliary *être* or *avoir* is one of two syntactic mechanisms which trigger past participle agreement. Syntactic movement, as seen in 4: 7.1 and 4: 7.3–4 in the context of interrogative and relative clauses, can also move a direct object to preverbal position. And where it does, past participle agreement is again triggered, as in (188), in which the interrogative phrase *quelles voitures* is moved to sentence-initial position:

    (188) a. Quelles voitures a VUES Marie?   (stylistic inversion; 4: 7.2)
          b. Quelles voitures Marie a-t-elle VUES?

                                      (complex inversion; 4: 7.2)

          c. Quelles voitures a-t-elle VUES?

                                (subject–clitic inversion; 4: 7.2)

Within the relative clauses in (189), the non-overt relative proform has moved to clause-initial position, and agreement is once again triggered.

(189) a. [$_{NP}$ La voiture [$_{S2}$ – que Marie a VUE –]] était noire.
b. [$_{NP}$ Les voitures [$_{S2}$ – que Marie a VUES –]] étaient noires.

Note that the past participle agreement in (189) actually represents solid linguistic evidence that a non-overt relative proform does in fact move to clause-initial position in relative clauses. When we discussed subject and direct object relatives in 4: 7.4, we assumed that the relative proform exists, and moves, since this allowed us to maintain the parallel with our analysis of PP-relatives in 4: 7.3. The past participle agreement which relativised direct objects trigger clearly shows that this is the right analysis.

Often, agreement between the past participle and its preceding direct object has no phonetic effect (all the examples of agreeing past participles in (188)–(189) have the same pronunciation as the non-agreeing form, namely [vy]). Nevertheless, there are cases where past participle agreement can be heard, for example with the past participles *fait*, *mis*, *pris*, *dit* and *peint* (see Table 3.10 in 3: 3.2, as well as Tables 3.20–24):

(190) a. Laquelle de ces tartes as-tu FAITE ([fɛt])?
b. [$_{NP}$ La toile [$_{S2}$ – que Picasso a PEINTE ([pɛ̃t]) –]] a été vendue.

Our generalisation that a past participle only ever agrees with its direct object when its direct object comes before it provides us with further support for a distinction we made in 4: 1.2. We claimed that in (8b), repeated here, the *quatre-vingts kilos* is not the direct object of the verb *peser*.

(8) b. Vous pesez quatre-vingts kilos.

The evidence we used in 4: 1.2 to support this claim came from the unavailability of cliticisation (4: 4.2), as shown in (9b), repeated here:

(9) b. *Vous les pesez.

Significantly, if *quatre-vingts kilos* is relativised, it doesn't trigger past participle agreement either, which is exactly as we expect if it's *not* the direct object of the verb:

(191) [$_{NP}$ Les quatre-vingts kilos [$_{S2}$ – que le colis a PESÉ –]] étaient excessifs.

Other verbs which function like *peser* include *coûter* and *courir*. The postverbal NP here is best analysed as a degree adverbial (4: 11).

(192) a. Ce livre m'a coûté QUATRE CENTS FRANCS.
      b. [$_{NP}$ les quatre cents francs [$_{S2}$ que ce livre m'a COÛTÉ]]

(193) a. J'ai couru UNE DEMI-HEURE avant d'arriver.
      b. [$_{NP}$ la demi-heure [$_{S2}$ que j'ai COURU avant d'arriver]]

However, these verbs do have other, truly transitive, uses in which a preposed direct object does trigger past participle agreement:

(194) a. Ce travail m'a coûté D'ÉNORMES EFFORTS.
      b. [$_{NP}$ les énormes efforts [$_{S2}$ – que ce travail m'a COÛTÉS –]]

(195) a. J'ai couru DES RISQUES pour envoyer ces documents.
      b. [$_{NP}$ les risques [$_{S2}$ – que j'ai COURUS – pour envoyer ces documents]]

(196) a. As-tu bien pesé LES CONSÉQUENCES de tes actions?
      b. Les conséquences de tes actions, les as-tu bien PESÉES?

(For a further case of past participle agreement see 4: 9.1.)

In closing, it must be conceded that past participle agreement is one area where there has never been a reliably close match between what grammarians have laid down and what native speakers actually do. Not only is past participle agreement often phonetically null, even where it is in principle audible it's not consistently marked.

8   More on movement

In this section we examine other contexts in which phrases seem to 'move'. Subsection 4: 8.1 looks at quantifiers; 4: 8.2–3 focus on sentences in which phrases appear to have moved for emphasis. In 4: 8.4 we return to the interrogative proforms *que* and *quoi*, postponed from 4: 4.5.

8.1   *Movement of quantifiers*

Quantifiers express quantity within NPs (4: 2.2). Some function as both determiners and adjectives (QUELQUES *femmes* versus *les* QUELQUES *femmes*); others are only determiners (PLUSIEURS *femmes*); and several occur with the article *de* (BEAUCOUP DE *femmes*). The predeterminer *tout(e)(s)* is quantificational, too (4: 2.3). Although, so far, we've seen quantifiers within NPs, some of them are quite mobile, and can occur outside NPs, too. For example, compare the position of *tout(e)(s)* in (197) and (198):

(197) a. [$_{NP}$ TOUS les garçons] mangent.
      b. [$_{NP}$ TOUTES les filles] ont déjà mangé.

(198) a. [$_{NP}$ Les garçons] mangent TOUS.
       b. [$_{NP}$ Les filles] ont TOUTES déjà mangé.

In (198) *tout(e)(s)* has detached itself from the subject NP and moved to the right of the finite verb. This is called **rightward quantifier floating**. Note that *tout(e)(s)* quantifies the same thing in both (197) and (198), namely *les garçons* and *les filles* respectively. Further, there is agreement in number/gender between *tout(e)(s)* and the head noun in both (197) and (198). Finally, although there are two possible positions for *tout(e)(s)*, only one can be occupied at once:

(199) a. *TOUS les garçons mangent TOUS.
       b. *TOUTES les filles ont TOUTES déjà mangé.

Rightward quantifier floating isn't the only movement that *tout(e)(s)* can undergo. In (200a, b) the direct object *tout* is 'bare', in the sense that, unlike in (197), it's the only element within the NP. Here, rather than appearing in its unmarked postverbal position, [$_{NP}$ tout] has floated left-wards. This is called **leftward quantifier floating**. In fact, movement of *tout* to the left of the past participle or infinitive is not only possible, but actu-ally preferred. Leaving *tout* in the postverbal position, as in (200c, d), is unacceptable or highly marked for most speakers:

(200) a. J'ai TOUT vu.   b. Nous allons TOUT acheter.
       c. ?J'ai vu TOUT.   d. ?Nous allons acheter TOUT.

We might wonder whether *tout(e)(s)* can float leftwards from a direct object NP when it isn't bare. On the face of it, this doesn't appear to be possible:

(201) a. J'ai mangé [$_{NP}$ TOUTE la pomme].
       b. J'ai vu [$_{NP}$ TOUS les étudiants].
       c. *J'ai TOUTE mangé [$_{NP}$ la pomme].
       d. *J'ai TOUS vu [$_{NP}$ les étudiants].

However, when the rest of the NP is cliticised with *le/la/les* (4: 4.1–2) (trig-gering past participle agreement; 4: 7.5), *tout(e)(s)* is 'bare' once again and, consequently, floats to the left of the past participle:

(202) a. Je L'ai TOUTE mangée.   b. Je LES ai TOUS vus.

We conclude therefore that leftward quantifier floating is possible (and pre-ferred) with 'bare' *tout(e)(s)*. Note that, as with rightward quantifier floating, floated *tout(e)(s)* in (202) quantifies the object clitics, there's agreement between them, and *tout(e)(s)* cannot simultaneously occupy both positions:

(203) a. *Je L'ai TOUTE mangée TOUTE.
       b. *Je LES ai TOUS vus TOUS.

What about the other quantifiers? Can they move, too? In fact, we've already seen (4: 2.2) that some quantifiers which occur with *de* can, such as *beaucoup de* and *trop de*. Compare (204a, b) with (204c, d):

(204) a. J'ai lu [$_{NP}$ BEAUCOUP de livres].
       b. Il va voir [$_{NP}$ TROP de musées].
       c. J'ai BEAUCOUP lu [$_{NP}$ de livres].
       d. Il va TROP voir [$_{NP}$ de musées].

In (204a, b) the direct object is quantified by *beaucoup de* and *trop de*; in (204c, d) the quantifier has moved to the left of the past participle/infinitive. Leftward floating of *beaucoup, trop,* etc., is called **remote quantification**. The interrogative quantifier *combien* occurs with *de* and can move, too. There are therefore two ways of questioning a direct object of the form [$_{NP}$ combien de N], one in which the entire NP undergoes interrogative movement, and one in which *combien* alone moves:

(205) a. [$_{NP}$ COMBIEN de livres] as-tu achetés ce matin?
       b. COMBIEN as-tu acheté [$_{NP}$ de livres] ce matin?

Note that the past participle only agrees when the entire direct object moves, not when *combien* alone is moved. (Recall the discussion of *en* in (186) in 4: 7.5.)

8.2 Dislocated structures

In this and the following section, we deal with apparent cases of movement to attain prominence within the sentence. Consider first (206). Note the unmarked word order (4: 1.6); the subject precedes VP, within VP the verb is followed by the direct object and then the indirect object:

(206) [$_{NP}$ Marc et Anne] [$_{VP}$ ont offert [$_{NP}$ un séjour en Inde]
       [$_{PP}$ à Marie]].

We saw in 4: 1.6 that, where the direct object is 'heavy', it can follow the indirect object PP in a marked word order:

(207) [$_{NP}$ Marc et Anne] [$_{VP}$ ont offert [$_{PP}$ à Marie]
       [$_{NP}$ un séjour en Inde]].

Other word orders can be used for emphasis or contrast. In (208) the highlighted phrase has been 'dislocated' to sentence-initial position, and its function within the sentence is indicated by a (highlighted) clitic proform (called a **resumptive proform**):

(208) a. MARC ET ANNE, ILS ont offert un séjour en Inde à Marie.
      b. UN SÉJOUR EN INDE, Marc et Anne L'ont offert à Marie.
      c. (À) MARIE, Marc et Anne LUI ont offert un séjour en Inde.

This is called **left dislocation**. The comma after the dislocated phrase indicates the pause which usually occurs here in speech. (In (208c), where the indirect object is dislocated, the preposition *à* is usually dropped; this isn't a problem since the resumptive proform *lui* clearly shows the function of the dislocated phrase.)

In addition to being left dislocated to sentence-initial position, a phrase can also be *right* dislocated to sentence-*final* position. (In (209c), where the indirect object is right dislocated, the preposition *à* is maintained.)

(209) a. ILS ont offert à Marie un séjour en Inde, MARC ET ANNE.
      b. Ils L'ont offert à Marie, UN SÉJOUR EN INDE.
      c. Ils LUI ont offert un séjour en Inde, À MARIE.

Given appropriate intonation, *multiple* left and right dislocation is also possible, as is *simultaneous* left and right dislocation:

(210) a. MARC ET ANNE, UN SÉJOUR EN INDE, ils l'ont offert à Marie.
      b. (À) MARIE, MARC ET ANNE, ils lui ont offert un séjour en Inde.

(211) a. Ils l'ont offert à Marie, UN SÉJOUR EN INDE, MARC ET ANNE.
      b. Marc et Anne le lui ont offert, UN SÉJOUR EN INDE, À MARIE.

(212) a. MARC ET ANNE, ils l'ont offert à Marie, UN SÉJOUR EN INDE.
      b. UN SÉJOUR EN INDE, Marc et Anne le lui ont offert, À MARIE.

Comparing dislocation with the other apparent instances of movement we've seen, there's one subtle difference. In quantifier floating, as well as the movement in interrogative and relative clauses, the relevant phrase occurs *either* in its original position *or* in its new position, *but not both*. What's different about dislocation is the presence of the resumptive proforms. It looks as though the original position and the new position are *both* filled simultaneously. Consequently, we might question whether movement is really involved here.

The type of emphatic structure illustrated in (213) is a much more clear-cut case of movement, since there's no resumptive proform. Note that the fronted indirect object now doesn't drop its preposition. This makes sense in the absence of a resumptive proform to indicate the function of the fronted phrase:

(213) À MARIE, Pierre et Jeanne ont proposé un voyage en Chine.

8.3 Cleft sentences

Another syntactic device for focusing attention on a particular phrase within a sentence for emphasis or contrast is clefting, illustrated in (214):

(214) C'est [le prof] que [les étudiants aiment le plus].

Cleft sentences have the form *c'est* A *que* B, where A is the phrase to be highlighted and B is a subordinate finite clause out of which A has been moved. There are two reasons to believe that, in (214) for example, [*le prof*] has moved out of [*les étudiants aiment le plus*]. First, the subordinate finite clause (B) is 'missing' a phrase which corresponds to the moved phrase (A) (*les étudiants aiment qui le plus?*). One way of accounting for this is to conclude that *le prof* originates within the subordinate clause and has moved. Second, clefting exhibits the masquerade effect. Recall from 4: 7.1 and 4: 7.4 that, where the subject is moved out of a finite subordinate clause (in the formation of an interrogative or relative clause), the complementiser changes from *que* to *qui*. Significantly, in cleft sentences in which the moved phrase (A) is the subject of the subordinate finite clause (B), the same change takes places:

(215) C'est [$_A$ le prof] QUI [$_B$ passionne les étudiants].

So we conclude that cleft sentences, too, are formed by movement (of A out of B).

If the moved phrase (A) is a non-pronominal NP, then, in formal registers, the form of *être* agrees with it in number; in (216), where the clefted phrase is *les étudiants*, *ce sont* appears instead of *c'est*:

(216) Ce SONT [$_A$ les étudiants] que [$_B$ le prof aime le plus].

In less formal registers, however, agreement doesn't take place and *c'est* is maintained:

(217) C'EST [$_A$ les étudiants] que [$_B$ le prof aime le plus].

If the moved phrase is pronominal (4: 4.4), it is always a disjunctive proform (rather than a clitic) and *c'est* is usually used, irrespective of the singular/plural distinction:

(218) a. C'EST MOI/TOI/LUI/ELLE que/qui . . .
     b. C'EST NOUS/VOUS que/qui . . .
     c. C'EST/CE SONT EUX/ELLES que/qui . . .

8.4   Que *and* quoi

Now that we are familiar with movement, as well as contexts like inter-rogative/relative clauses and cleft sentences where movement takes place, we can return to a topic postponed from 4: 4.5, namely the behaviour of the [– human] interrogative proforms *que* and *quoi*, which is considerably less straightforward than that of the [+ human] proform *qui*. The behav-iour of *qui* in matrix interrogatives is shown in (219). It can function as a direct object, either in its unmarked postverbal position (219a), or in sentence-initial position, following interrogative movement (219b). It can also function as the complement of a preposition, and, once again, the PP can either stay put (219c) or move (219d). Finally, it can function as a subject, either in its unmarked position (219e) or having undergone inter-rogative movement (219f) (triggering *que/qui* alternation):

(219)   a. Nous allons voir QUI?
        b. QUI allons-nous voir?
        c. Elle est partie [avec QUI] ?
        d. [Avec QUI] est-elle partie?
        e. Tu penses [$_{S2}$ que QUI est mort] ?
        f. QUI penses-tu [$_{S2}$ qui – est mort] ?

In subordinate interrogatives (indirect questions), in which interrogative movement necessarily takes place, *qui* can again surface as a subject, a direct object or as the complement of a preposition:

(220)   a. Je ne sais pas [$_{S2}$ QUI est mort].
        b. Je ne sais pas [$_{S2}$ QUI nous allons voir].
        c. Je ne sais pas [$_{S2}$ [avec QUI] elle est partie].

In contrast to the behaviour of *qui*, the behaviour of *que* and *quoi* is more complex. We'll deal with matrix interrogative clauses first. As a direct object, we find *quoi* if interrogative movement doesn't take place – (221a) – but *que* if it does – (221d):

(221)   a. Nous allons voir QUOI?   b. *Nous allons voir QUE?
        c. *QUOI allons-nous voir?   d. QU'allons-nous voir?

As the complement of a preposition, we find *quoi*, irrespective of whether or not the PP moves:

(222)   a. Tu t'es assis [sur QUOI] ?   b. *Tu t'es assis [sur QUE] ?
        c. [Sur QUOI] t'es-tu assis?   d. *[Sur QUE] t'es-tu assis?

A clue to understanding these initial facts comes from a morphological observation. Note the parallel between *que* and *quoi*, on the one hand, and the pairs of clitic (4: 4.2) and disjunctive (4: 4.4) proforms *me/moi, te/toi* and *se/soi*, on the other. We've already seen that clitics (*me, te, se*) behave differently from disjunctive proforms (*moi, toi, soi*); clitic proforms are excluded from contexts in which they would need to bear stress, disjunctive proforms are not. We see in (221)–(222) that *que/quoi* behave in parallel fashion to the clitic/disjunctive proforms. *Quoi* appears as the complement of a preposition and in postverbal position; *que* appears in preverbal position. What this suggests is that *que* is a clitic interrogative proform and that *quoi* is a disjunctive interrogative proform. The disjunctive form *quoi* appears in (221a) because the postverbal position is a stressed position; the form *que* appears in (221d) because, after interrogative movement, it can cliticise onto the verb. The disjunctive form *quoi* appears in (222a, c) because the complement position within PP bears stress, irrespective of whether or not the PP moves. The pattern of behaviour of *que/quoi* therefore follows that of clitic/disjunctive proforms.

Turning to subjects, note first that neither *que* nor *quoi* can function as the subject of a finite clause:

(223) a. *QUOI te fait peur?   b. *QUE te fait peur?

This is expected if *que/quoi* are interrogative equivalents of, for example, *me/moi*. Recall that *me* and *moi* can't function as the subject of a finite clause either (the subject clitic *je* is needed, instead):

(224) a. *MOI te fais peur.   b. *ME te fais peur.
       c. JE te fais peur.

Further, the strategy used to avoid having *que/quoi* in subject position in (223) is the same as the one used to avoid having proforms like *me/moi* in subject position, namely clefting (4: 8.3).

(225) C'est MOI qui te fais peur.

The grammatical equivalents of the ungrammatical examples in (223) are given in (226):

(226) a. C'est quoi qui te fait peur?   b. Qu'est-ce qui te fait peur?

In the **cleft sentence** in (226a), the disjunctive proform *quoi* can appear because, as the complement of *être* rather than the subject of *faire peur*, it bears stress. (See (218) in 4: 8.3.) The complex structure with *que* in (226b) can be analysed as the result of interrogative movement and subject–clitic inversion having applied to (226a), allowing the proform to cliticise onto the verb *être*. In both cases, the need for *quoi* or *que* to appear in subject position is avoided.

We can generalise the cleft sentence analysis of *c'est quoi qui* and *qu'est-ce qui* in the examples in (226) to the three analogical patterns in (227):

(227) a. C'est quoi que tu as vu? → Qu'est-ce que tu as vu?
      b. C'est qui qui est arrivé? → Qui est-ce qui est arrivé?
      c. C'est qui que tu as vu? → Qui est-ce que tu as vu?

In summary, we've seen that the analysis of *que* and *quoi* as clitic and disjunctive non-subject proforms allows us to account for the syntax of matrix constituent interrogatives questioning a [– human] entity, where *qui* can't be used.

We turn now to subordinate interrogatives (indirect questions). We saw in (220) that the behaviour of the [+ human] interrogative proform *qui* is straightforward. Once again, though, the situation with *que/quoi* is more complex. Within an interrogative PP, *quoi* appears, rather than *que*. As before, this is expected since this position bears stress, and clitics are incompatible with stress.

(228) a. *Je ne sais pas [$_{S2}$ [avec QUE] elle est partie].
      b. Je ne sais pas [$_{S2}$ [avec QUOI] elle est partie].

As for subordinate subject and direct object interrogatives, we find that, once again, neither *que* nor *quoi* can appear:

(229) a. *Je ne sais pas [$_{S2}$ QUE/QUOI est mort].
      b. *Je ne sais pas [$_{S2}$ QUE/QUOI nous allons voir].

The forms *que* and *quoi* are excluded from the subject position in (229a) for the same reason that they are excluded from the subject position in matrix interrogatives in (223): like *me/moi*, *que/quoi* are non-subject proforms. As for (229b), *quoi* is excluded because it's unable to undergo movement; meanwhile, *que* is excluded since, although it can move, it needs a verb to cliticise onto. Yet, in the absence of subject–clitic inversion, no verb is available. The grammatical equivalents of (229) are in (230):

(230) a. Je ne sais pas [$_{S2}$ CE QUI est mort].
      b. Je ne sais pas [$_{S2}$ CE QUE nous allons voir].

Note that (230) is characterised by *que/qui* alternation. That is, the complementiser appears as *qui* in the subordinate subject interrogative in (230a), and as *que* in the subordinate object interrogative in (230b). This suggests an analysis in terms of movement, and we might therefore suppose that the subordinate clauses in (230) (labelled S2) have similar structures to subject and object relatives (4: 7.4). That is, in each case, S2 is in fact an NP containing a head, *ce*, and a relative clause (*qui est mort* and *que nous allons voir*, respectively). Within the relative clauses, relativisation and movement take place, triggering masquerade.

Before we leave the murky waters of *que* and *quoi*, note that the analysis of *que* as the clitic equivalent of *quoi* helps us to understand a constraint on complex inversion, the third type of subject–verb inversion we saw in (162) in 4: 7.2, repeated here:

> (162) a. Combien d'argent Pierre a-t-il vu?
> b. Qui Pierre a-t-il vu?

Compare the grammatical (162a, b), in which the sentence-initial interrogative phrases are *combien d'argent* and *qui* respectively, with the almost identical but ungrammatical (231), with sentence-initial *que*:

> (231) *Que Pierre a-t-il vu?

If *que* is a clitic needing to 'lean on' the verb, as we're suggesting, the ungrammaticality of (231) is explained; the presence of *Pierre* between *que* and the verb prevents *que* from cliticising onto the verb. The only kinds of inversion possible here are subject–clitic inversion and stylistic inversion, in which nothing intervenes between the clitic and the verb:

> (232) a. Qu'a-t-il vu?   b. Qu'a vu Pierre?

Summarising, we've seen that movement isn't restricted to interrogatives and relative clauses. We've seen that the syntax of quantifiers, as well as dislocation and clefting, can be understood in terms of movement, too. Finally, the complex behaviour of the [– human] interrogative proforms *que* and *quoi* was explained in part on the basis of movement.

9   Infinitives with overt subjects

A peculiar aspect of French syntax (from an English perspective) is the absence of sentences like (233), non-finite subordinate clauses (4: 6.2.1) with an overt subject:

> (233) a. *Frédérique veut [$_{S2}$ Marie (de) voir Pierre].
> b. *Marc demande [$_{S2}$ Robert (de) partir].

The grammatical counterparts of (233) are in (234):

> (234) a. Frédérique veut [$_{S2}$ que Marie voie Pierre].
> b. Marc demande [$_{PP}$ à Robert] [$_{S2}$ de partir].

In (234a) the subordinate clause is finite (containing a subjunctive verb; 4: 6.3); in (234b) the subordinate clause is still non-finite, but *Robert* is the indirect object of the matrix verb, rather than the subject of the non-finite clause.

However, a small number of verbs look as if they *do* take a non-finite subordinate clause with an overt subject, namely perception verbs and causative verbs, and these are discussed in the next two sections. In neither case are things exactly as they seem.

9.1   Perception verbs

Perception verbs like *entendre, écouter, voir, sentir, apercevoir* and *regarder* look as if their complement is a non-finite subordinate clause with an overt subject:

(235) a. Pierre ENTEND [$_{S2}$ [$_{NP}$ le chien] aboyer].
    b. Ils VERRONT [$_{S2}$ [$_{NP}$ le chien] manger la viande].
    c. Nous avons SENTI [$_{S2}$ [$_{NP}$ l'eau] couler sur nos mains].
    d. Marie REGARDAIT [$_{S2}$ [$_{NP}$ Pierre] donner le cadeau à son fils].

However, although the bracketed NP is *interpreted* as the subject of the infinitive and occupies the canonical preverbal subject position, cliticisation and movement patterns suggest there's more going on than meets the eye. (We shall refer to *le chien*, *l'eau* and *Pierre* in (235) as the **logical subject** of the infinitive.)

Note, first, that, if the (in)direct object of the infinitive in (235d) is pronominalised, it cliticises onto the infinitive:

(236) Marie regardait Pierre LE LUI donner.

In contrast, if the logical subject of the infinitive in (235b) is pronominalised, it cliticises as *le* onto the perception verb (4: 4.1–2). In other words, it behaves as if it were the direct object of the perception verb:

(237) Ils LE verront manger la viande.

Moreover, if *both* the logical subject *and* the direct object of the infinitive in (235b) are pronominalised, there are two possible structures. In (238a), the object cliticises onto the infinitive, while the logical subject cliticises onto the perception verb. Alternatively, both arguments of the infinitive cliticise onto the perception verb, as in (238b) (4: 9.2):

(238) a. Ils LE verront LA manger.   b. Ils LA LUI verront manger.

The order in (238b) suggests that, for cliticisation at least, the two verbs function as one. A similar thing happens obligatorily if the infinitive has no overt logical subject:

(239) a. Je L'ai entendu dire.   b. *J'ai entendu LE dire.

Next, consider (240), in which the matrix perception verb is in a compound tense (comprising the auxiliary *avoir* and a past participle; 4: 7.5; 4: 15.2), and in (240b, c) the logical subject of the infinitive has been moved to the left of the matrix past participle, either by cliticisation onto the matrix auxiliary (*avons*), or by interrogative movement:

(240) a. Nous avons entendu [$_{S2}$ LES JEUNES FEMMES jouer les sonates].
      b. Nous LES avons entenduES jouer les sonates.
      c. QUELLES JEUNES FEMMES avons-nous entenduES jouer les sonates?

Of interest is the past participle agreement that this movement triggers. In 4: 7.5 we saw that past participle agreement is triggered by direct objects only. In triggering agreement in (240b, c), the logical subject of the infinitive is, once again, 'behaving as if it were' the direct object of the perception verb. In contrast, if the direct object of the infinitive moves to the left of the matrix past participle, no agreement is triggered:

(241) Quelles sonates avons-nous ENTENDU les jeunes femmes jouer?

Finally, note that, with intransitive verbs, the logical subject can appear postverbally:

(242) a. Je verrai arriver LE TRAIN.
      b. Pierre entend aboyer LE CHIEN.
      c. Marie a regardé partir LA VOITURE.

In summary, then, while perception verbs are distinctive in French in appearing to take a non-finite subordinate clause with an overt subject, there are a number of syntactic respects in which the overt logical subject of the infinitive actually behaves like an argument of the matrix perception verb.

9.2 Causative verbs

Causative verbs are the second class of verbs which are distinctive in apparently taking a non-finite subordinate clause with an overt subject. There are two causative verbs in French, namely *laisser* and *faire*. The syntactic behaviour of *laisser* is identical to the perception verbs in 4: 9.1. The behaviour of *faire* is more complex, and we can only hope to sketch some of the details here.

First, given a generic interpretation, the logical subject of the infinitive can be implicit rather than overt:

(243) a. Ces médicaments font [$_{S2}$ dormir].
       b. La pub fait [$_{S2}$ dépenser de l'argent].

The sentence in (243a), for example, means that 'These medicines will, in general, send to sleep anyone who takes them', although the idea of 'anyone who takes them' is implicit, rather than appearing as an overt NP.

It's also possible for the logical subject of the infinitive to be overt, and this is where things get complicated. To discuss the possibilities with any clarity, it makes sense to distinguish transitive from intransitive infinitives. We'll start by looking at intransitives. Where the logical subject of an intransitive infinitive is an overt NP, it cannot appear in the regular preverbal position, as shown in (244), and must, instead, appear postverbally, as in (245). This contrasts with the situation we found with perception verbs in (235a) and (242a) in 4: 9.1, where both orders were possible. (Note also the two possible orders in (245b, c).)

(244) a. *Ces médicaments font [$_{S2}$ LES ENFANTS dormir].
       b. *Je ferai [$_{S2}$ MARIE partir en Chine].

(245) a. Ces médicaments font dormir LES ENFANTS.
       b. Je ferai partir en Chine MARIE.
       c. Je ferai partir MARIE en Chine.

If the logical subject of the intransitive infinitive is pronominalised, it appears as a direct object clitic in front of *faire*, as in (246):

(246) a. Ces médicaments LES font dormir.
       b. Je LA ferai partir en Chine.

That is, the logical subject of the intransitive infinitive is behaving 'as if it were' the direct object of causative *faire*. (Compare this with what we saw in (237) in 4: 9.1.) However, unlike what we saw with perception verbs in (240b, c), past participle agreement isn't triggered if *faire* appears in a compound tense and its past participle is preceded by the logical subject of the infinitive:

(247) a. *Ces médicaments LES ont FAIT(E)S dormir.
       b. *Je L'ai FAITE partir en Chine.
       c. *QUEL(LE)S ENFANTS ces médicaments ont-ils FAIT(E)S dormir?
       d. *QUELLE FILLE ai-je FAITE partir en Chine?

(248) a. Ces médicaments LES ont FAIT dormir.
       b. Je L'ai FAIT partir en Chine.
       c. QUEL(LE)S ENFANTS ces médicaments ont-ils FAIT dormir?
       d. QUELLE FILLE ai-je FAIT partir en Chine?

In summary, then, if the subordinate infinitive is intransitive, its logical subject can be non-overt (implicit) or overt. If it's non-overt, as in (243), it has a generic interpretation. If it's an overt NP, as in (245), it must follow the infinitive; if it's an overt pronominal, as in (246), it cliticises onto the causative verb *faire*, as if it were the direct object of *faire*. Yet *unlike* direct objects, the logical subject of the infinitive never triggers past participle agreement on *faire*, as shown in (247)–(248).

Turning now to subordinate infinitives which are transitive, we find some initial similarities, but some complications later. Similarly to what we saw with intransitive infinitives, the logical subject of a transitive infinitive can be implicit rather than overt.

(249) Elle a fait peindre sa cuisine.

However, if the logical subject of the infinitive is overt, the situation is less straightforward than what we saw with intransitive infinitives. First of all, if the logical subject of the infinitive is an NP, it cannot appear preverbally:

(250) a. *J'ai fait [$_{S2}$ LE CHIEN manger la viande].
       b. *Pierre a fait [$_{S2}$ LE MAÇON construire sa maison].

Once again, the logical subject of the infinitive has to be postverbal. However, unlike the situation in (245), the logical subject cannot appear postverbally as a bare NP. This is because the direct object of the infinitive is already a postverbal bare NP. If the logical subject were to appear in postverbal position, too, there would be no way of telling the two apart:

(251) *Elle a fait appeler sa mère son père.

Rather, the logical subject of the infinitive is positioned after the direct object, and is contained within a PP headed either by *à* or by *par*:

(252) a. J'ai fait manger la viande [$_{PP}$ AU CHIEN/PAR LE CHIEN].
       b. Pierre a fait construire sa maison [$_{PP}$ AU MAÇON/PAR LE MAÇON].

There's a subtle meaning distinction which hinges on which type of PP is used here. The difference in meaning can be illustrated by the following translations; with *au* (= *à* + *le*) *maçon* (252b) means *Pierre had the builder build his house*, with *par le maçon* it means *Pierre had his house built by the builder*. That is, (252b) with *à* tells us what Pierre did to the builder (he made him build a house), while with *par* it tells us what Pierre did to the house (he had it built by the builder). We might, therefore, assimilate the use of the PP headed by *par* in (252) to the agent phrase headed by *par* in the context of passives (4: 5.3). In passive sentences, the agent phrase is optional, and this is also the case here with the PP headed by *par*.

Consider, finally, contexts in which arguments of the transitive infinitive are pronominalised. If the logical subject of the infinitive is pronominalised, it cliticises onto the causative verb *faire*, just as we saw above with intransitive infinitives, and with perception verbs in 4: 9.1. However, rather than appearing as a direct object clitic, it appears as an indirect object clitic:

(253) Je LUI ai fait manger la viande.

In fact, this isn't so surprising given that, in the structure preceding pronominalisation and cliticisation, the logical subject was contained within a PP headed by *à*. Further, the interpretation of (253) is the same as the interpretation of (252a) with *à*, rather than *par*. The versions of (252a, b) with *par* don't actually have equivalents in which the logical subject of the infinitive is cliticised. We can take this as further evidence that the PP headed by *par* here is indeed the same agent phrase we find in passives, since the agentive PP in a passive doesn't have a clitic alternative, either.

As for the complements of the infinitive, if these are cliticised, they precede the verb *faire* rather than the infinitive. Thus in the sentence *J'ai fait manger la viande au chien* the phrases *au chien* and *la viande* can be pronominalised, as in (254), in which *la* refers to *la viande*, and *lui*, to *au chien*, and the order is as in Table 4.2 in 4: 4.2:

(254) Je la lui ai fait manger.

Summarising, we've seen two contexts, namely perception and causative verbs, in which non-finite subordinate clauses seem to appear with an overt subject. Although the details differ in each of these two cases, it should be clear that things aren't entirely as they seem, and the logical subject of the infinitive behaves in a number of respects like an object of the matrix perception/causative verb.

10 Further types of complementation

Our interest in complements ((in)direct objects) has so far related to verbs. Yet, there's no principled reason why complements should be restricted to verbs. In this section we see that nouns (4: 10.1) and adjectives (4: 10.2) can take complements, too. In 4: 10.3–4 we see two final contexts in which complements are found.

10.1 Complements of nouns

The most clear-cut cases of nouns taking complements are those derived from verbs, called **deverbal nouns**, which often take complements corresponding to an argument of the verb they are derived from. Consider (255):

(255) a. J'ai oublié [_{NP} l'arrivée [_{PP} de Pierre]].
     b. Vous apprécierez [_{NP} la lecture [_{PP} de ce livre]].

These bracketed NPs are headed by deverbal nouns. The noun *arrivée* is derived from the verb *arriver*; *lecture*, from *lire*. Note that the NPs each contain a PP headed by *de*, too, and that the NP within the PP corresponds to an argument of the verb that the noun is derived from. In (255a) the PP contains *Pierre*, corresponding to the subject of *arriver*. In (255b) it contains *ce livre*, corresponding to the direct object of *lire*. So we conclude that these PPs are complements of the deverbal nouns.

In addition to expressing an argument of a deverbal noun, a PP headed by *de* can express a more general notion of possession or association:

(256) a. [_{NP} les livres [_{PP} DE Marie]]   b. [_{NP} le centre [_{PP} DE Rouen]]
     c. [_{NP} le train [_{PP} DE dix heures]] d. [_{NP} la ville [_{PP} DE Paris]]

Summarising, we've seen that, depending on the head noun, an NP-internal PP headed by *de* can express a possessor/associate or an argument of the head noun. In fact, such a PP can be ambiguous. Consider the interpretation of the two NP-internal PPs in (257):

(257) [_{NP} la photographie [_{PP} DE Jean] [_{PP} DE Marie]]

Either PP could refer to the *owner* of the photograph (possessor), the person who *took* the photograph (subject) or the person *in* the photograph (object). So the NP could have any one of six potential meanings! Thankfully, context usually provides clues as to which potential meaning is intended, and serious misunderstanding isn't a problem.

Moving away from PPs headed by *de*, an NP-internal PP can be headed by various prepositions, as in (258):

(258) a. [_{NP} Ses idées [_{PP} SUR la vivisection]] m'étonnent.
     b. [_{NP} Le chemin [_{PP} À TRAVERS le bois]] est bloqué.
     c. [_{NP} L'homme [_{PP} À CÔTÉ DE moi]] dormait.

In fact, complements of nouns aren't even always PPs. Just as some verbs can take a clausal complement (4: 6.1), so, too, can some nouns:

(259) [$_{NP}$ Le fait [$_{S2}$ que la terre soit ronde]] n'étonne plus personne.

Noun complement clauses also occur with nouns like *l'idée, la pensée, la constatation, le désir, la crainte* and *l'espoir* (4: 6.3). Note that some of these are deverbal nouns, and that the verbs that they are derived from also take a complement clause (e.g. the noun *pensée* is derived from the verb *penser* which takes a complement clause). In (259) the noun complement clause is finite; in (260) it's infinitival:

(260) a. [$_{NP}$ Le fait [$_{S2}$ d'avoir dit cela]] n'implique pas que je suis d'accord.
       b. [$_{NP}$ L'idée [$_{S2}$ de devoir corriger tous ces devoirs]] me pèse.

10.2   *Adjectives and their complements*

In the same way that nouns can take a PP or clausal complement, so, too, can adjectives. The preposition which heads the PP is determined by an idiosyncratic property of the adjective, but *de* is common:

(261) a. Je suis [$_{AP}$ content [$_{PP}$ de mes progrès]].
       b. Pierre est [$_{AP}$ fier [$_{PP}$ de ses amis]].
       c. Les dépenses sont [$_{AP}$ supérieures [$_{PP}$ aux crédits]].
          (NB: *à* + *les* = *aux*.)
       d. La mienne est [$_{AP}$ semblable [$_{PP}$ à la tienne]].

Other adjectives whose complement PP is headed by *de* are *amoureux, jaloux, satisfait, sûr, certain, digne, anxieux, heureux, responsable, soucieux* and *plein*, as well as past participles like *aimé, apprécié* and *estimé*. Adjectives whose complement PP is headed by *à* are much rarer, for example, *identique, inférieur, égal, propre* and *étranger* and the past participles *décidé, disposé, résolu, préparé* and *ouvert*.

Some adjectives, for example *sensible, long, lent, unanime, seul, prêt, premier, second, prompt* and *contraire*, take clausal complements, both finite (262) and non-finite (263):

(262) a. Je suis [$_{AP}$ content [$_{S2}$ que tu sois venu]].
       b. Nous sommes [$_{AP}$ sûrs [$_{S2}$ que vous serez reçus à l'examen]].

(263) a. Je suis [$_{AP}$ certain [$_{S2}$ d'être venu]].
       b. Nous sommes [$_{AP}$ sûrs [$_{S2}$ d'être reçus à l'examen]].

Similar adjectives are *certain que, heureux que, satisfait que, froissé que*, etc. (see 4: 6.3 on the subjunctive in subordinate sentences).

10.3 Comparative and related structures

Another adjectival structure involving complements is illustrated in (264):

(264) a. Ces articles sont plus intéressants QUE LES AUTRES.
     b. Marie est aussi intelligente QUE MYRIAM.
     c. Le chat est moins obéissant QUE LE CHIEN.

Strictly speaking, though, the highlighted phrases aren't complements of the adjective, but rather complements of the combination of the modifier (*plus*, *moins*, *aussi*) and the adjective. These structures are called **comparatives**, for obvious reasons. Note that the combination of the modifier and the adjective sometimes has a synthetic form, such as *meilleur* (= *plus bon*), *pire* (= *moins bon*) and *moindre* (= *plus petit*).

Related to comparatives are **superlatives**:

(265) a. Cette étudiante est LA PLUS INTELLIGENTE de la classe.
     b. Le chien est l'animal LE PLUS OBÉISSANT de tous.
     c. Cet étudiant est LE MOINS INTELLIGENT de la classe.
     d. Le chat est l'animal LE MOINS OBÉISSANT de tous.

Once again the superlatives of *bon* and *petit* have synthetic forms, *le/la/les meilleur(e)(s)*, *le/la/les pire(s)* and *le/la/les moindre(s)*:

(266) a. Ces pommes sont LES MEILLEURES du monde.
     b. Ses films sont LES PIRES de tous.

10.4 Sentential complements introduced by prepositions

We saw in 4: 6.1 that some transitive verbs can take either a direct object NP or a finite subordinate clause (*dire [$_{NP}$ la vérité]*, *dire [$_{S2}$ que . . .]*). In fact, this flexibility isn't unique to verbs. Prepositions, too, can sometimes take either an NP (4: 2.4) or a clausal complement. However, the subordinate clause needs to be introduced by *ce que*:

(267) a. Je m'attends À CE QU'elle me retéléphone.
     b. Vous doutez DE CE QU'elle arrive ce soir.
     c. Ils sont tous contents DE CE QUE vous soyez venus.
     d. Elle est hostile À CE QUE tu fasses cela.

Verbs which commonly take these kinds of PP complements are *se réjouir de ce que*, *s'apercevoir de ce que*, *se plaindre de ce que*, *consentir à ce que*, *tenir à ce que*, *travailler à ce que*, *voir à ce que*, *contribuer à ce que* and *s'opposer à ce que*. Adjectives which select this kind of PP complement are *jaloux de ce que*, *satisfait de ce que*, *favorable à ce que* and *opposé à ce que*. Note the appearance of this form after the word *jusque* to form *jusqu'à ce que*. Note also that, where *ce que* is introduced by *de*, the sequence is often reduced to *que*, as in *Ils sont tous contents que vous soyez venus*.

11   Adverbials

The highlighted phrases in (268b–d) have a similar function. They've been added to the **minimal sentence** (4: 1.2) in (268a) as optional extras, giving information about where, when and how the children are picking the flowers:

(268)   a. Les enfants cueillent les fleurs.
       b. Les enfants cueillent les fleurs CET APRÈS-MIDI.
       c. Les enfants cueillent les fleurs TRÈS RAPIDEMENT.
       d. Les enfants cueillent les fleurs DANS LE JARDIN.

Phrases with this function are called **adverbials**. (We came across adverbials in 4: 1.2 and 4: 7.5.) In 4: 11.1–2 we consider the form and distribution of adverbials. In 4: 11.3 we deal with adverbial clauses.

11.1   *Adverbials are phrasal categories*

Despite their common *function*, adverbials have widely differing *forms*. For example, *cet après-midi* in (268b) looks very much like an NP (it comprises a demonstrative determiner (4: 2.2) and a common (compound) noun (3: 5.3)), while *dans le jardin* in (268d) is quite definitely a PP (it comprises a preposition and an NP; 4: 2.4). Further examples of NP and PP adverbials are given in (269) and (270). Note that none of these highlighted phrases is actually necessary for the sentence to be grammatical; they've all been added as optional extras.

(269)   a. Pierre est arrivé LE 23 JUIN.
       b. Marie travaillait LE LENDEMAIN.
       c. On se verra LA SEMAINE PROCHAINE.

(270)   a. Il est passé À TOUTE VITESSE.
       b. Il arrivera AVANT LA FIN DE LA SÉANCE.
       c. Il s'est exprimé AVEC BEAUCOUP D'HABILETÉ.

The adverbial *très rapidement* in (268c) is headed by a word which has the characteristic derivational morphology – the *-ment* suffix (3: 5.2.1) – of an **adverb**, and we shall call it an adverb phrase, or AdvP. (Not all adverbs take the suffix *-ment*; adverbs which don't, include *mal, bien, trop, beaucoup, tant* and *peu*, as well as *peut-être, tard* and *tôt*.) Evidence that this adverbial is indeed a phrase (rather than just a word) comes from the fact that, like adjectives (4: 3.1), it can co-occur with modifiers like *très*, as in

(268c). Further evidence that adverbs head phrasal categories comes from the fact that they can often be replaced by PPs like *de (une) façon* + adjective or *de (une) manière* + adjective:

(271) a. Il mange ses pâtes DE FAÇON RAPIDE / RAPIDEMENT.
    b. Elle s'est exprimée IMPRÉCISÉMENT / DE MANIÈRE IMPRÉCISE.

We conclude, therefore, that, like the term complement, the term adverbial relates to the function of a phrase rather than its form/category. The function of an adverbial is to add optional extra information to a minimal sentence. Recall that complements are phrases whose *function* is to 'complement' the verb/noun/adjective, and that they can take the *form* of an NP, PP or subordinate clause, for example. The only generalisation which can be made about the *form* of a complement is that it's a phrase. In this section we've seen that the same is true of adverbials.

11.2 The distribution of adverbials

In 4: 11.1 we compared adverbials with arguments, and saw that both were phrasal constituents. Nevertheless, there's a difference between adverbials and arguments; adverbials have three characteristics which distinguish them from arguments. First, adverbials are optional. While arguments express essential information and are compulsory, adverbials express non-essential details and can be omitted. This is clear from the fact that (268a) gets along just fine without the adverbials in (268b–d). In contrast, if the subject or object is missing, the sentence is ungrammatical:

(272) a. *Cueillent les fleurs. (missing subject)
    b. *Les enfants cueillent. (missing object)

Second, adverbials are mobile. While arguments occupy specific positions (at least in sentences with unmarked word order; 4: 1.6; 4: 8.2–3), adverbials aren't associated with particular positions and can usually appear in a number of positions:

(273) a. Jean, HIER SOIR, a mangé du canard à l'orange.
    b. HIER SOIR Jean a mangé du canard à l'orange.
    c. Jean a mangé du canard à l'orange HIER SOIR.

Third, adverbials can stack up. While a clause can contain at most one subject, one direct object and one indirect object, there's no principled limit to the number of adverbials a clause can contain:

(274) a. Pierre arrivera [demain] [par le train de 10 heures].
    b. [Sans doute] Pierre arrive [lundi matin] [par le TGV].
    c. Marie a [rapidement] cueilli les fleurs [avec les sécateurs].

In summary, then, despite being phrasal constituents, adverbials differ from arguments in their flexibility; they are optional and mobile, and can stack up.

11.3   *Adverbial clauses*

We end this section with a look at the type of adverbial highlighted in (275):

(275) a. Je suis fatigué PARCE QUE J'AI COURU.   (**causal clause**)
    b. SI J'AVAIS DES SOUS, j'irais au marché. (**condition clause**)
    c. AVANT DE PARTIR, je lui parlerai.   (**temporal clause**)
    d. Je lis des livres POUR COMPRENDRE LE MONDE.

               (**purpose clause**)

All these adverbials have the properties discussed in 4: 11.1–2 (they are phrasal, optional and mobile, and they can stack up), but differ from the adverbials considered so far in that they contain a subordinate clause (4: 6). They are collectively called **adverbial clauses**. The different types of adverbial clause are set out below:

TEMPORAL CLAUSES

These adverbials give information about the time at which an event or action took place:

(276) a. QUAND JE L'AI VU, il ne portait plus son chapeau.
    b. J'irai prendre un bain PENDANT QUE VOUS PRÉPAREZ LE REPAS.

Other expressions – which might be thought of as complex complementisers (4: 6.1) – which can introduce temporal clauses are *tandis que*, *alors que*, *tant que*, *comme*, *dès que*, *aussitôt que*, *avant que* and *après que*. Note that *après* and *avant de* can also introduce non-finite adverbial clauses:

(277) a. APRÈS L'AVOIR VU, nous avons décidé de manger.
    b. Il faut voir un spécialiste AVANT DE VENDRE LA MAISON.

CAUSAL CLAUSES

The most common expression which introduces causal clauses is *parce que*, as in (275a).

CONDITION CLAUSES

Condition clauses express a situation where one circumstance or set of circumstances depends on another. The word which most frequently introduces condition clauses is *si*. There are very strict patterns governing the tense (4: 15) of the verbs in a matrix clause and a condition clause introduced by *si*. A present tense verb in the condition clause generally requires a future tense verb in the matrix clause, an imperfect in the condition clause requires a conditional in the matrix clause, and a pluperfect in the condition clause requires a conditional perfect in the matrix clause:

(278) a. S'il VIENT, je SERAI très content.
 b. S'il VENAIT, je SERAIS très content.
 c. S'il ÉTAIT VENU, j'AURAIS ÉTÉ très content.

Care must be taken not to confuse condition clauses introduced by *si* (like the ones we've seen here) with indirect questions (= subordinate interrogatives), also introduced by *si* (4: 6.2.2). The subordinate clause in (279) is an indirect question (the complement of the matrix verb *demander*), and therefore not an exception to the pattern of tenses in condition clauses:

(279) Il se DEMANDAIT [$_{S2}$ si Marie VIENDRAIT en voiture ou par avion].

Other expressions which can introduce (non-)finite condition clauses are *à condition que/de* and *à moins que/de*.

CONCESSIVE CLAUSES

Concessive clauses differ from condition clauses in that they imply a contrast between two (sets of) circumstances, in the sense that what is expressed in the matrix clause is exceptional considering the content of the adverbial clause. They contain subjunctive verbs, and are introduced by such complex complementisers as *bien que, quoique* and *malgré (le fait) que*. The complex complementiser *malgré que* exists, but is considered informal and frowned upon by traditional grammarians.

(280) a. BIEN QUE JE NE T'AIME PLUS, je ne veux pas divorcer.
 b. ?Il est parti en vacances, MALGRÉ QU'IL N'AIT PAS D'ARGENT.

PURPOSE CLAUSES

These adverbial clauses express what it was hoped to achieve by carrying out an act. Purpose clauses are introduced by *pour que, afin que/de* and *pour*:

(281) a. AFIN QUE TOUT SE RÈGLE RAPIDEMENT, passez me voir cet après-midi.
 b. Je viendrai en auto POUR QUE TU NE SOIS PAS DÉRANGÉ.

    c. Il a repris le travail AFIN D'AVOIR DE QUOI PAYER LE
    VOYAGE.
    d. J'ai téléphoné POUR TE FAIRE PLAISIR.

12   Negation

Recall from (20) in 4: 1.5 that sentences can vary with respect to a feature
called **polarity**. Sentences can be **positive** or **negative**. Negation is a grammatical phenomenon allowing the contradiction or rejection of all or part
of the meaning of a sentence. **Sentential negation** is considered in 4: 12.1–2.
Constituent negation is examined in 4: 12.3. Some peripheral aspects of
the behaviour of *ne* are considered in 4: 12.4.

12.1   Negative sentences

In written and formal spoken French, sentential negation is expressed by
two elements, namely preverbal *ne* and some other element, such as *pas,
plus, jamais, aucun(e)* and *personne*:

  (282) a. Je NE te vois PAS.   b. Je N'ai mangé AUCUNE tarte.
          c. Jean N'a JAMAIS fumé.   d. Elle N'aime PERSONNE.

There are reasons to believe that – like the unstressed non-subject proforms
(4: 4.1–2) such as *le, leur* and *en* – *ne* is a **clitic**. Like the proforms, *ne* is dependent on a verb and excluded from non-verbal contexts. Like the proforms, *ne*
is always preverbal and moves with the verb in inversion contexts (4: 7.2):

  (283) a. Ils N'Y SONT pas encore arrivés.
          b. N'Y SONT-ils pas encore arrivés?

Note, also, that *ne* is one of the few elements which can intervene between
a subject clitic, on the one hand, and non-subject clitics and/or the verb,
on the other, as in (282a), and, finally, that the single verbal context in
which non-subject clitics cannot appear, namely positive imperatives (4:
1.5; 4: 4.2), is also the single verbal context in which *ne* cannot appear.
The most sensible way of dealing with these facts is to conclude that, like
the proforms, *ne* is a clitic. The identical behaviour is then expected.
    Another dimension to the weakness of *ne* is the fact that it's omitted in
less formal spoken styles, a phenomenon called *ne*-deletion:

  (284) a. Je te vois pas.   b. J'ai mangé aucune tarte.
          c. Jean a jamais fumé.   d. Elle aime personne.

Ne-deletion is less common (but not impossible) in sentences with a negative subject like *personne* and *rien*, but this may be a strictly phonological

liaison/resyllabification phenomenon (2: 15.4), attributable to the fact that these words end in [n]:

(285) a. Personne (ne) veut me parler. b. Rien (n')a été fait.
c. Personne (n')est venu. d. Rien (ne) sera fait.

Further, native speakers find *ne*-deletion more acceptable when word-final [n] doesn't immediately precede the verb:

(286) a. Personne d'intéressant est venu.
b. Rien de grave a été fait.

Despite the clitic status of *ne* and the tendency in informal spoken French for it to be omitted, there's a small subcategory of verbs which have retained a feature of earlier stages in the development of the language, namely the ability to be negated using *ne* alone, for example *pouvoir*, *savoir*, *cesser* and *oser*, verbs which might be thought of as having something of a modal interpretation (4: 15.3).

(287) a. Je ne PEUX vous le dire. b. Jean ne CESSE d'y penser.
c. Je n'OSE le dire. d. Il ne SAVAIT quoi dire.

Here, *ne* cannot be deleted since there would otherwise be no overt marker of negation whatsoever, and the sentences would be indistinguishable from positive ones.

The second element in the expression of sentential negation has a different grammatical status altogether. *Pas*, *jamais*, *plus*, *guère* and the rather literary and archaic *point* are negative adverb(ial)s which give additional (negative) information to a minimal sentence. *Personne* and *rien* are negative pro-NPs. *Aucun(e)* is a negative determiner, as is *nul(le)* in (288a); in (288b) *nul(le)* is a negative pro-NP:

(288) a. Je n'en ai NUL BESOIN. b. NUL n'est censé ignorer la loi.

Nul(le) is literary in flavour and rare in modern spoken French, except in such expressions as *nulle part* or *nul doute*. The negative conjunctions *ni . . . ni . . .* are discussed in 4: 13.

12.2 The position of the negative markers

In 4: 12.1 we attributed the preverbal position of *ne* to its clitic status. The position of the other negative element in a negative sentence is dependent on a number of factors. The most straightforward situation involves *personne*, *aucun(e)* N and *nul(le)* (N). These occupy regular argument positions:

(289) a. AUCUN ÉLÈVE n'a rendu ses devoirs.   (subject)
        b. Je n'ai fait de bisous à PERSONNE.   (indirect object)
        c. Michel n'a NUL BESOIN de partir.   (direct object)

The situation with *rien* is slightly more complicated; it can occupy regular subject and indirect object positions, but mirrors the behaviour of bare *tout(e)(s)* when it's a direct object. Recall from 4: 8.1 and the examples in (200a, b) that the direct object *tout(e)(s)* usually floats leftward when it's 'bare' (*J'ai TOUT vu*, *Nous allons TOUT acheter*). This can be seen clearly with compound tenses (4: 15.2) and infinitives. Interestingly, *rien* patterns in exactly the same way:

(290) a. Je n'ai RIEN vu.   b. Nous n'allons RIEN acheter.

When we see parallel patterns like this, our first reaction is to look for an explanation. Here, we can attribute the parallel behaviour to the fact that *tout* and *rien* are both **universal quantifiers**; that is, they mean something like 'for all things'. So (200a) means '*For all things*, it's the case that I've seen them', while (290a) means '*For all things*, it's the case that I've *not* seen them'. In identifying a semantic link between *rien* and *tout(e)(s)*, we seem to have found the key to explaining their common syntactic behaviour.

Turning now to the position of the negative adverb(ial)s *pas*, *plus*, *guère* and *jamais*, we need to distinguish between finite and non-finite clauses in order to make any general statements. In finite clauses these elements follow the verb, as in (282a, b). With compound tenses (4: 15.2), they intervene between the auxiliary and the past participle, as in (282b). In non-finite clauses, in contrast, the negative adverbs are generally preverbal, like *ne*:

(291) a. J'ai décidé de NE PAS LE VOIR.
        b. Il m'a demandé de NE JAMAIS PARTIR.
        c. Nous espérons NE PLUS DEVOIR lui parler.

With a non-finite auxiliary (*être* or *avoir*) these adverb(ial)s can be either preverbal or postverbal (although the preverbal position in (292a, c) is more common):

(292) a. Il dit NE PAS AVOIR cassé la vitre.
        b. Il dit N'AVOIR PAS cassé la vitre.
        c. Elle aurait préféré NE JAMAIS ÊTRE venue.
        d. Elle aurait préféré N'ÊTRE JAMAIS venue.

12.3   Constituent negation

In 4: 12.1–2 we saw negative markers in negative sentences. However, negative markers don't always produce negative sentences. Rather than negating the whole sentence, a negative marker can negate single words or phrases in an otherwise positive sentence, as in (293):

(293) Le train est arrivé NON sans un retard d'une heure.

The negative marker in (293) doesn't negate the idea that the train arrived, just the idea that it was on time. Negatives used in this way are said to negate part of the sentence rather than the entire sentence. We therefore need to distinguish sentential negation (discussed in 4: 12.1–2) from **constituent negation**. The negated constituent in (293) is the PP *sans un retard d'une heure*. The lexical items used for constituent negation are the negative adverb(ial)s *pas*, *point* and so on, and *non*. Negative markers used in elliptical contexts are examples of constituent negation, too:

(294) a. 'Qui a fait cela?' 'PAS moi!'   b. PAS idiot, ce garçon!

Pas is also a constituent negator with APs/AdvPs like PAS *si vite!*, PAS *si fort!*, PAS *vrai!*, as well as with quantifiers like *tout(e)(s)* (4: 2.2):

(295) Pas tous les invités sont venus.

However, this example isn't judged acceptable by all speakers, some of whom prefer (296), in which *pas* occupies its regular postverbal position, with or without rightward quantifier floating (4: 8.1):

(296) a. Tous les invités ne sont pas venus.
       b. Les invités ne sont pas tous venus.

Non can be used to negate individual words as a prefix, as in *la non-existence*, *le non-alignement*, *la non-agression* and *le non-conformisme*. However, these creations are probably more morphological than syntactic in nature (3: 5.2.2). The use of *non* to negate words or whole phrases is most natural in explicitly contrastive contexts:

(297) a. [$_{NP}$ un livre, NON beau, mais, quand même, intéressant]
       b. [$_{NP}$ une personne, NON très instruite, mais intelligente tout de même]
       c. [$_{VP}$ mourir de ses remèdes et NON de leurs maladies]

In this use, *non* also appears in conjunction with other negative adverb(ial)s (*pas*, *plus*) as the following examples from Le Petit Robert show:

(298) a. Une voix NON PAS servile mais soumise.
       b. Compter NON PLUS par syllabes mais par pieds.
       c. Je veux une dissertation et NON (PAS) des notes.

　　　　d. Je voudrais NON (PAS) des stylos bille mais des crayons de
　　　　couleur.

12.4　Further uses of ne

At a couple of points in the chapter we've seen a non-negative use of *ne*.
(See (68a, b) in 4: 4.1 and (126b) and (132) in 4: 6.3.) This use is illustrated in (299):

　　(299)　a. Je crains qu'elle NE soit très malade.
　　　　　　b. Il est plus petit que je N'aurais pensé.

Note that (299a) means that I fear she *is* very ill, and that (299b) means
that he's smaller than I *would* have thought. That is, *ne* isn't negating the
subordinate clause in which it occurs. Rather than marking negation, *ne*
here is probably best thought of as a modal (4: 15.3). In these uses, *ne* is
called **pleonastic/expletive *ne***. In (299a) *ne* seems to function as an extra
marker of doubt or uncertainty, which is in part also reflected in the subjunctive verbal morphology (4: 6.3–4). In (299b) *ne* could be analysed as another
marker of a non-factual state of affairs ('I *didn't* think he was this small').
In both cases, *ne* is optional, and its appearance is as much a marker of
register as anything else.

13　Coordination

Coordination is a grammatical phenomenon which links together words or
phrases. In (300) two NPs have been conjoined in the subject and direct
object using the **coordinating conjunction** *et*:

　　(300)　[Le garçon ET la fille] ont vu [(ET) le chat ET le chien].

In (301) phrases other than NPs have been coordinated:

　　(301)　a. Marie est [vraiment mignonne ET très sympa].
　　　　　　　　　　　　　　　　　　　　　　(coordinated APs)
　　　　　　b. Je parle [à maman ET à papa].
　　　　　　　　　　　　　　　　　(coordinated indirect object PPs)
　　　　　　c. [Jean lave la vaisselle ET Marie fait les lits].
　　　　　　　　　　　　　　　　　　　　(coordinated clauses)

　Where more than two phrases are conjoined, the coordinating conjunction is optional, but usually placed between the final two:

　　(302)　[Le garçon, la jeune fille, (ET) mon oncle] ont vu [le chat, le
　　　　　　chien, (ET) le serpent].

Alternatives to *et* are *de même que* and *ainsi que*:

(303) a. [Marie AINSI QUE Paul] sont venus me voir.
b. J'ai acheté [une tarte, deux gâteaux DE MÊME QU'une baguette].

Ou behaves like *et* in coordinating phrases of the same category:

(304) a. Les pommes sont (OU) rouges OU vertes. (coordinated APs)
b. Pierre OU Marie va venir.   (coordinated NPs)
c. Ferai-je mes devoirs OU irai-je au cinéma?
(coordinated clauses)

A more formal alternative to *(ou)* . . . *ou* . . . is *soit* . . . *soit* . . .:

(305) a. SOIT tu restes SOIT tu pars.
b. Je viendrai SOIT lundi SOIT mercredi.

The negative equivalent to *et* is *ni* . . . *ni* . . . :

(306) a. Les pommes NE sont NI rouges NI vertes. (coordinated APs)
b. NI Pierre NI Marie NE vont venir.   (coordinated NPs)

Mais can coordinate phrasal constituents, as in (297a, b) and (307), but most commonly coordinates clauses, as in (308):

(307) a. Je n'ai pas vu un docteur MAIS une infirmière.
b. Les examens n'étaient pas trop difficiles MAIS trop fatigants.
c. Cette année nous n'allons pas en France MAIS en Espagne.

(308) On a loué une villa à Cannes MAIS je ne sais pas si on pourra y aller.

Linguistically significant about coordination is that usually only constituents of the same category can be coordinated.

14 Impersonal sentences

Consider the sentences in (309) and think in particular about the meaning of their subject *il*:

(309) a. IL pleut (tout le temps).   b. IL va neiger (demain).
c. IL a gelé (hier soir).   d. IL fera beau (la semaine prochaine).

These sentences contain weather verbs, and their subject is **impersonal/non-referential** *il* (4: 4.3; 4: 6.3). What's unusual about impersonal *il* is that it doesn't refer to anything. In fact, strictly speaking, impersonal *il* is meaningless, and its presence in these sentences is for purely grammatical reasons; it functions as the 'dummy' subject of the sentence, and is the source of the person (third) and number (singular) features that the verb agrees with. (Recall from 4: 1.1 that all sentences need a subject.) Impersonal *il* is used as the subject in these sentences because weather verbs aren't semantically related to any argument which might function as the subject. Impersonal *il* functions like English impersonal *it* in *It'll rain tomorrow*. (The phrases in brackets in (309) are time adverbials rather than arguments (4: 11.1). Note their optionality, one of the central properties of adverbials (4: 11.2).)

The subject of the sentences in (310) and (311) is also impersonal *il*. Unlike the weather verbs in the sentences in (309), however, the verbs in the sentences in (310) and (311) *are* associated with (highlighted) arguments.

(310)　a. Il y aura DU COURRIER.
　　　　b. Il s'agissait DE MON BONHEUR.

(311)　a. Il faut S'EN ALLER.
　　　　b. Il faudra QUE TU SOIS LÀ.
　　　　c. Il me fallait DE L'ARGENT.

Furthermore, the postverbal position of these phrases suggests that they are complements of the verbs, a conclusion which is supported by the fact that these phrases cannot replace impersonal *il* as the subject of the sentence:

(312)　a. *DU COURRIER y aura.
　　　　b. *DE MON BONHEUR s'agissait.

(313)　a. *S'EN ALLER faut.
　　　　b. *QUE TU SOIS LÀ faudra.
　　　　c. *DE L'ARGENT me fallait.

Because the verbs in (309)–(311) *always and only ever* appear with impersonal *il*, they are sometimes called intrinsic impersonal verbs. Other intrinsic impersonal expressions include *il est temps que* and *il n'en est/demeure pas moins que*. Slightly less straightforward are *il vaut mieux que* . . . and *il importe peu que* . . . which have the alternatives *mieux vaut que* . . . and *peu importe que* . . . , in which the adverbs *mieux* and *peu* seem to 'count' as the subject. However, a much more complex picture is painted by those verbs and verb-plus-adjective combinations which appear either with impersonal *il* or with a referential subject. These are discussed in 4: 14.1.

14.1 Verbs and related expressions with il

In (309)–(311) we saw verbs and verbal expressions which always and only ever appear with impersonal *il*. In these contexts, impersonal *il* is the subject that the verb needs, but can't get any other way. However, impersonal *il* also appears with verbs and verb-plus-adjective combinations where an alternative subject is available. Consider (314)–(315), in which the complement is a (finite or non-finite) clause, and (316), in which the complement is an NP:

(314) a. Il me plaît QUE TU SOIS VENU.
   b. Il m'importe peu QUE TOUT SOIT PRÊT.
   c. Il est possible QUE PIERRE MENTE.

(315) a. Il me plaît DE CHANTER.
   b. Il m'importe peu D'ENTENDRE TES HISTOIRES.
   c. Il est possible DE LE VOIR.

(316) a. Il est arrivé UNE CATASTROPHE.
   b. Il est mort QUATRE PERSONNES dans un accident d'automobile.

Unlike verbs like *falloir* (which can also take a (non-)finite complement clause but which are *intrinsically* impersonal), the sentences in (314)–(316) have alternative forms in which the postverbal phrase (the complement) replaces impersonal *il* as the subject:

(317) a. QUE TU SOIS VENU me plaît.
   b. QUE TOUT SOIT PRÊT m'importe peu.
   c. QUE PIERRE MENTE est possible.

(318) a. (DE) CHANTER me plaît.
   b. (D')ENTENDRE TES HISTOIRES m'importe peu.
   c. (DE) LE VOIR est possible.

(319) a. UNE CATASTROPHE est arrivée.
   b. QUATRE PERSONNES sont mortes dans un accident d'automobile.

Note, though, that the alternatives in (318) are very literary in flavour, and most speakers prefer to omit *de*. Also, in (319) note that, where the NP is preverbal, subject–verb agreement (4: 1.1) and past participle agreement (4: 7.5) are triggered.

Other verbs which behave like *falloir* are *paraître*, *sembler* and *s'avérer*. Verbs behaving like *plaire* and the expression *être possible* include *convenir*, *répugner*, *être essentiel/nécessaire/plausible*.

Note that with expressions like *être essentiel/(im)possible*, it's very common, in less formal spoken registers, to find *ce* instead of impersonal *il* (4: 6.3):

(320) a. C'est impossible de prévoir les difficultés.
     b. C'est essentiel d'arriver à l'heure.
     c. C'est possible qu'elle soit déjà partie.

14.2   More on impersonal structures

Recall from 4: 14.1 that verbs like *arriver* can alternate between two kinds of sentence; compare (319a) with (316a). Other verbs which behave this way are *exister, manquer, venir* and *tomber*:

(321) a. DES PROBLÈMES existent / IL existe des problèmes.
     b. BEAUCOUP DE PAGES manquaient / IL manquait beaucoup de pages.
     c. PLUSIEURS ÉTUDIANTS viendront / IL viendra plusieurs étudiants.
     d. DEUX ARBRES sont tombés / IL est tombé deux arbres.

Two restrictions apply to these alternations. First, the verb has to be intransitive (usually one which selects the auxiliary *être* in compound tenses (4: 15.2), but *manquer* and *exister* are exceptions). Transitive verbs don't allow this alternation; neither (322a) nor (323a) has an impersonal equivalent:

(322) a. TROIS GARÇONS regardent la télé.
     b. *IL regarde la télé trois garçons.
     c. *IL regarde trois garçons la télé.

(323) a. BEAUCOUP DE RÉFUGIÉS ont gagné la frontière.
     b. *IL a gagné la frontière beaucoup de réfugiés.
     c. *IL a gagné beaucoup de réfugiés la frontière.

Second, the postverbal NP in the impersonal sentence has to have an indefinite interpretation. Compare the grammatical examples in (321) with the ungrammatical ones in (324):

(324) a. *Il est arrivé LES DEUX HOMMES.
     b. *Il est venu MES ÉTUDIANTS.
     c. *Il est tombé CES ARBRES-LÀ.

14.3   Impersonal structures and the passive

The contrast between **active** and **passive sentences** was discussed in 4: 5.3 and is illustrated in (325):

(325) a. Le bûcheron a abattu des arbres.   (active voice)
       b. Des arbres ont été abattus (par le bûcheron).   (passive voice)

We also saw that reflexives can be used as an alternative to the passive:

(326) Des arbres se sont abattus.

Interestingly, a further possibility is provided by an impersonal structure:

(327) Il a été abattu des arbres (par le bûcheron).

Once again, in the impersonal sentence, the postverbal NP has to be interpreted as an indefinite, hence the ungrammaticality of (328c):

(328) a. Le bûcheron a abattu LES ARBRES.   (active voice)
       b. LES ARBRES ont été abattus (par le bûcheron). (passive voice)
       c. *Il a été abattu LES ARBRES (par le bûcheron).   (impersonal)

A further example of the impersonal passive is given in (329):

(329) Il a été vendu plusieurs disques cette semaine.

Though exceptional, it's also possible to find the impersonal structure with
certain intransitive verbs:

(330) a. Il dort un chien dans ce chenil.
       b. Dans ce restaurant il mange beaucoup d'étudiants.

The impersonal structure is also found in certain idiomatic expressions:

(331) a. Il a été procédé au dépouillement des urnes.
       b. Il prend forme dans ce laboratoire une théorie tout à fait
          nouvelle.
       c. Il a été mis fin à ces pratiques illégales.

Note also that reflexive passives (4: 5.3), which, as with true passives,
involve the promotion of the direct object to subject position, can also
appear in impersonal configurations (on condition that the postverbal NP
is indefinite in interpretation):

(332) a. Beaucoup de cierges se brûlent par an dans cette cathédrale.
       b. Il se brûle beaucoup de cierges par an dans cette cathédrale.

(333) a. Plusieurs portes s'ouvrent quand vous êtes riche.
       b. Il s'ouvre plusieurs portes quand vous êtes riche.

Summing up, a significant feature of impersonal sentences is their uncomfortable position within the context of the discussion of subjects in 4: 1.1, where the compulsory nature of subjects was understood as a consequence of the fact that the subject is what the sentence is 'about'. The problem with impersonal sentences is that their subject, impersonal *il* or *ce*, doesn't refer to anything, and can't, therefore, be what the sentence is 'about'.

15 Use of verb forms

A verb contributes more to the meaning of a sentence than its dictionary meaning. The sentences in (334) all contain the same verb, namely *travailler*, and, although the dictionary meaning of *travailler* is present in all these sentences, the form of the verb – *travaille, travaillera, a travaillé* – conveys additional information:

> (334) a. Jean travaille à Paris.
>   b. Jean travaillera à Paris.
>   c. Jean a travaillé à Paris.

The word *travaille* in (334a) is a present tense verb form which situates the action in 'the here and now'. The sentence expresses something along the lines of 'John's current place of work is in Paris'. In (334b) the word *travaillera* is a future tense verb form which situates the action at some time in the future with respect to utterance time. The compound form *a travaillé* in (334c), finally, is a perfect tense verb form which situates the action prior to utterance time. The semantic difference between these verb forms is, then, temporal in nature. In 4: 15.1 we consider the exact temporal value of French tenses, concentrating on the specific properties of compound tenses in 4: 15.2. Then we move on to non-temporal values of verb forms, namely modal meanings and aspectual meanings in 4: 15.3–4.

15.1 Tense and temporal reference

The word **tense** has two meanings in grammar. The first is semantic in nature. Here, tense is that part of the meaning of a sentence which indicates where the action is located within time. (The word 'tense' is etymologically related both to the French word *temps* and the English *time*.) For example, the difference in the meaning of the two sentences in (335) relates to temporal properties and is therefore a tense difference (in this first sense of the word).

> (335) a. Je travaille à la maison aujourd'hui.
>   b. Je travaille à l'université demain.

The second meaning of the word 'tense' is morphological in nature. Here, tense refers to sets – or **paradigms** – of verb forms like the ones we saw in 3: 3. For example, the set of six verb forms *suis/es/est/sommes/êtes/sont* is the present indicative 'tense' of the verb *être*. In this section we are interested in how temporal reference (tense in the first sense) is established by the use of a particular verb form (tense in the second sense).

When dealing with temporal reference, it's useful to distinguish between two kinds of tense. There are tenses which situate temporal reference with respect to utterance time. These are called **deictic tenses**. The present, future and perfect tenses in (334) are all deictic tenses. The temporal location of Jean's working in Paris is determined with respect to when the utterances are produced. In contrast, there are other tenses, which situate temporal reference, not with respect to utterance time, but with respect to some other reference time. These are called **anaphoric tenses**.

In (336a), in which an imperfect (*travaillais*) is used, the temporal reference of my working in Marseilles is established with respect to utterance time. The sentence expresses the idea that my working in Marseilles precedes utterance time; that is, that at some relevant point prior to the utterance of this sentence I worked or was working there (but that I'm not now). The imperfect tense is being used deictically here because the temporal properties of the sentence are established with respect to utterance time.

> (336) a. Je TRAVAILLAIS à Marseille.
> b. J'ÉTAIS déjà PARTI quand tu as téléphoné.

In (336b), in contrast, in which a pluperfect (*étais parti*) is used, the relevant temporal location of my departure isn't determined with respect to utterance time. Rather, my departure is situated in time with respect to your phone call (*quand tu as téléphoné*). The message in (336b) isn't so much that I left at some point in the past (i.e. before utterance time), but that I left before you called. The pluperfect, then, is anaphoric because the temporal properties of the sentence are established on the basis of something other than utterance time. We might represent this state of affairs using the following diagram:

> (337)   tu as téléphoné   NOW
> ————————✕————————————✕——→ TIME LINE
>   ✕
>   j'étais parti

The line represents the flow (from left to right) of time. One point on the line represents utterance time (NOW). The other point on the line represents your phone call. While the meaning of the sentence doesn't give the *exact* time of your call, it does indicate the *relative* time of the call; it's clear that you phoned *before* I uttered the sentence. Consequently, the

Table 4.3

Tense label	Tense form
present	nous donnons
past-historic	nous donnâmes
compound-past	nous avons donné
synthetic future	nous donnerons
analytical future	nous allons donner
recent-past	nous venons de donner

point on the line which represents your call is to the left of (= earlier than) the point representing utterance time. The fact, then, that the position of your phone call is determined with respect to utterance time means that the tense of *tu as téléphoné* is deictic.

What about the final point in the diagram? The point below the time line represents my departure. As was the case with your phone call, the meaning of the sentence gives the *relative* time of my departure rather than its *exact* time. However, rather than being determined relative to utterance time (NOW), the position of the point which represents my departure is determined relative to your phone call, and is therefore anaphoric. In summary, then, the tense of *as téléphoné* is deictic because (past) temporal reference is determined relative to utterance time, while the tense of *étais parti* is anaphoric because temporal reference is determined relative to a reference point other than utterance time.

A non-exhaustive list of the deictic tenses of French includes those shown in Table 4.3. All these forms of the verb *donner* can locate an action with respect to utterance time. Notice that although these verb forms all express semantic tense, that is they indicate temporal location, not all of them are morphological tenses (sets of verbal paradigms). Grammatical terminology refers to the tense paradigms in French, such as the present, past-historic and synthetic future, as **simple tenses**; forms (such as the compound-past) consisting of an auxiliary (*avoir* or *être*) and a past participle are called **compound tenses** (4: 15.2); and forms such as the analytical future and the recent-past – which strictly speaking are neither simple nor compound – are often called **periphrastic tenses**.

The anaphoric tenses include those listed in Table 4.4. Leaving aside the imperfect and the past anterior for the moment, it can easily be illustrated that, when used with a temporal value (see 4: 15.3 for other possible uses), the temporal reference of the anaphoric tenses is always determined relative to a reference point other than utterance time. Let's consider each of the remaining tenses in turn. (We've already discussed the pluperfect.)

(338)   Conditional: Le gouvernement a décidé que les prix
        AUGMENTERAIENT avant la fin octobre.

Table 4.4

Tense label	Tense form
imperfect	nous donnions
past anterior	nous eûmes donné
pluperfect	nous avions donné
conditional	nous donnerions
future-in-the-past	nous allions donner
flashback-past	nous venions de donner
future-perfect	nous aurons donné
conditional-perfect	nous aurions donné

(339) le gouvernement a décidé   la fin octobre

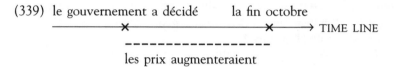

les prix augmenteraient

As the diagram shows, the event described by *augmenteraient* is temporally located between a point fixed by the deictic tense *a décidé* and the end of October. The utterance time could be before or after the end of October – further evidence that the temporal reference of the conditional is anaphoric (*not* determined by utterance time). (To show that no precise relative time point can be fixed we use a dotted line to indicate the time span in which the event is situated.)

(340) Future-in-the-past: Quand je suis arrivée, ma mère avait déjà décidé que nous ALLIONS PARTIR en ville.

(341)

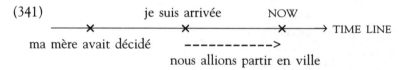

(342) Flashback-past: Ils ont remarqué que Marie VENAIT DE PARTIR.

(343)

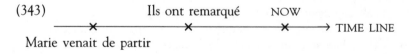

(344) Future-perfect: Quand tu arriveras, ces bruits bizarres AURONT CESSÉ.

(345)

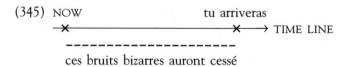

(346) Conditional-perfect: Pierre disait que les bruits bizarres
AURAIENT CESSÉ avant l'arrivée de ses parents.

(347) Pierre disait   l'arrivée de ses parents

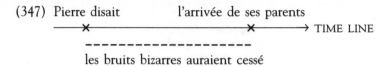

les bruits bizarres auraient cessé

Note that what have been termed anaphoric tenses can only be used anaphorically (they depend on something other than utterance time for their temporal reference). In contrast, the deictic tenses *can* also be used anaphorically. That is, their temporal reference can be determined *either* relative to utterance time (deictic use) *or* relative to some other time in the discourse (anaphoric use).

So far our discussion of the temporal properties (tense in the first sense of the word) of French verbal paradigms (tense in the second sense) has avoided direct reference to the imperfect. This is because the imperfect presents difficulties which need to be examined separately (see the discussion of **aspect** in 4: 15.4). However, it's clear that the temporal reference of the imperfect is one of past time. In its most common uses the temporal reference of an imperfect verb form is anaphorically dependent on a point in past time, usually expressed by a past-historic verb form (written French only) or a compound-past verb form (written and spoken French). Consider the typical example in (348).

(348) Le soleil brillait quand je suis arrivée/j'arrivai à Paris.

(349)

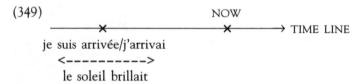

The double-arrowed dotted line in (349) represents the idea that the period during which the sun was shining extended for an unknown length of time both before and after my arrival. The period can be conceived of as a backdrop against which my arrival takes place (4: 15.4).

There is, however, a more literary use of the imperfect (sometimes referred to as the 'dramatic' imperfect) which marks a precise point in the past rather like a deictic tense. This use of the imperfect is generally accompanied by some indication of the precise time at which the action or event referred to took place. Consider the following examples from Grevisse:

(350) a. A vingt-cinq ans il entrait dans la renommée.
       b. Une demi-heure plus tard ... il se déshabillait pour se
          mettre au lit.

The past anterior, finally, is, from the point of view of temporal reference, similar to the pluperfect in that it's anaphorically dependent on a (past) verb form and expresses a state, action or event which is temporally located prior to the (past tense) reference point. Characteristic of the past anterior is that it only appears in clauses introduced by one of very few temporal expressions (*lorsque, quand, dès que, aussitôt que, à peine* and *après que*):

> (351) a. Lorsqu'il EUT VU sa mère, il comprit tout.
> b. Aussitôt qu'elles FURENT ARRIVÉES, la visite commença.

15.2 Compound tenses

Compound tenses are the combination of an auxiliary verb (*avoir* or *être*) and a past participle. Compound tenses using *être* can be divided into two classes. The first involves passive compound verb tenses (4: 5.3):

> (352) a. Pierre A ÉTÉ ÉCRASÉ (par l'autobus).
> b. La voiture ÉTAIT RÉPARÉE (par le mécanicien).
> c. Les arbres ONT ÉTÉ ABATTUS (par la tempête).

(Note that in (352a, c) the auxiliary *être* is itself a compound tense, comprising the auxiliary *avoir* and the past participle *été*.)

Second, there's a small set of intransitive verbs which, as a lexical property, have compound tenses which use the auxiliary *être*, namely *aller, partir, venir, rester, retourner, descendre, arriver, entrer, sortir, monter, mourir, naître, passer* and *tomber* (as well as morphologically derived verbs, such as *devenir, revenir* and *repartir*). Note that in the compound tenses shown in Table 4.5 the past participle agrees in number and gender with the subject (4: 7.5). In the case of all other verbs, the auxiliary *avoir* rather than *être* is used together with a past participle in compound tenses, as shown in Table 4.6.

We conclude this section with a brief discussion of the **double compound-past** (a combination of a compound-past and a past participle), which has two uses. The first is triggered by the syntactic environment. In 4: 15.1 we observed that in clauses introduced by *quand, lorsque, dès que, aussitôt que*, etc., a past anterior is used when the verb of the matrix clause is a past-historic. If a compound-past is used instead of the past-historic, then a

Table 4.5 Compound tenses with *être*

compound-past	Marie est arrivée
past anterior	Marie fut arrivée
pluperfect	Marie était arrivée
future-perfect	Marie sera arrivée
conditional-perfect	Marie serait arrivée

Table 4.6   Compound tenses with *avoir*

compound-past	Marie a vu la voiture
past anterior	Marie eut vu la voiture
pluperfect	Marie avait vu la voiture
future-perfect	Marie aura vu la voiture
conditional-perfect	Marie aurait vu la voiture

double compound-past is used instead of the past anterior, as in the following examples taken from Grevisse (1994):

(353) a. Quand elle [ma barbe] a été venue je l'ai rasée.
b. Aussitôt qu'elle a eu connu notre projet, Sa Sainteté a voulu l'encourager.

This first use of a double compound-past in a subordinate clause is generally acceptable to all native speakers of French. For some speakers (see 5: 3.4), however, the use of these verb forms isn't confined to these syntactic environments. Such speakers allow these forms to be used to stress the completed nature of an action:

(354) a. Roland avait eu vite percé à jour tout le truquage des démonstrations.
b. Ce petit vin nouveau . . . a eu vite grisé tous ces buveurs de bière.

15.3   Modality and the French verb

The term **modality** refers to aspects of meaning which, like tense (in the first sense of the word), are additional to the dictionary meaning of a verb. In contrast to tense, whose function is to temporally locate the action or event expressed by the sentence, the function of modality is to express the speaker's attitude, for example, to the truth of the statements being made. Modalities can be conveyed in French in a number of ways, for example, using distinctive **intonation** patterns (2: 16.3–4), or using certain 'modal' words, or certain tense forms in a 'special', non-temporal, way.

Let's start by examining the use of certain words to express modality. Consider the force of the statements expressed by the following sentences:

(355) a. C'est le facteur.   b. Il vient aujourd'hui.

There's no reason to doubt the speaker's commitment to the truth of these statements. Yet, if the speaker *weren't* so sure, a degree of doubt could be shown, for example by the use of expressions like *probablement* and *peut-être*:

(356) a. C'est probablement le facteur.
     b. Peut-être qu'il vient aujourd'hui.

Of greater interest here is how modal meaning can be expressed using verb forms. First, note the small set of verbs, for example *pouvoir* and *devoir*, which can give a modal interpretation to a sentence. The verb *devoir* can be used to express 'obligation' or 'necessity' (on the change from *ce* to *ça* see 4: 4.3):

(357) a. Ça doit/devrait être le facteur.
     b. Il doit/devrait venir aujourd'hui.

The verb *pouvoir* can express 'doubt' or 'uncertainty' about the truth of the statement:

(358) a. Ça peut/pourrait être le facteur.
     b. Il peut/pourrait venir aujourd'hui.

The use of conditional forms of *pouvoir* and *devoir* attenuates the statements even further. In (357b) the use of *devrait* weakens the sense of 'obligation', and in (358b) the use of *pourrait* makes the statement even more doubtful.

What we see, then, is that modality can be expressed by more than one feature of the sentence. The modality of 'doubt' can be expressed by the use of the verb *pouvoir* and reinforced by the use of a conditional verb form. As for the 'doubt' inherent in the adverb *probablement* in (356a), this, too, can be reinforced by a change in verb form:

(359) Ce sera probablement le facteur.

In summary, in particular contexts, the use of certain tense forms has a crucial effect on the modal interpretation of a sentence. This is especially the case when the usual temporal interpretation of the verb form seems inappropriate:

(360) Pierre aura toutes ses dents maintenant.

The use of the adverb *maintenant* here shows that the temporal setting is in the present, and yet a future tense verb form is used. The usual temporal interpretation of this verb form is clearly not appropriate; rather, the future has a modal interpretation. (The speaker doesn't know for sure whether Pierre has all his teeth, but reckons that he probably does.)

It's not only the future that can be used in this way. Note also that the imperfect in (361) is to be interpreted modally in that it attenuates the strength of the request:

(361) Je voulais vous voir maintenant.

The conditional and future are commonly found with modal interpretations. The conditional is associated with alleged or unproven claims, the truth of which the speaker wishes to distance him or herself from:

(362) a. Elle aurait tué son mari.
　　　 b. Le professeur serait malade.
　　　 c. Il se serait produit quelque incident à la frontière yougoslave.

The conditional can also be used to attenuate statements by making the speaker's commitment to what is being said less emphatic, as in (363), or to 'soften' direct requests, making them more polite (compare the direct (364) with the more polite (365)):

(363) a. Je dirais que tu n'es pas satisfait de ce que j'ai fait.
　　　 b. On penserait qu'ils ne veulent pas y aller.

(364) a. Je veux du chocolat.
　　　 b. Pouvez-vous m'aider?

(365) a. Je voudrais du chocolat.
　　　 b. Pourriez-vous m'aider?

Indeed, the modal uses of the conditional are so common that some grammarians prefer to treat it as primarily a mood rather than a tense. A mood is a set of paradigms which primarily marks a modal rather than a temporal value. It's a hotly debated question whether any moods can truly be identified in the French verbal system today. Traditionally the subjunctive is referred to as a mood, but whether the subjunctive can be viewed as a meaningful verbal category or simply as an extra marker of subordination is a difficult question to answer (4: 6.3–4).

15.4　Aspectual distinctions

The concept of **aspect** is related to that of tense discussed in 4: 15.1 in that aspect expresses a time-related property of actions, states and events. However, while tense distinctions are primarily concerned with the *position* of an action, event or state on the time line, aspectual distinctions relate to the *shape* of an action, event or state along the time line. Aspectual properties relate to whether an event is punctual or durative, whether it happens just once or is repeated regularly, whether it's beginning or ending. Of interest to us here is how information about the distribution of an action, event or state along the time line is encoded in the verb form.

The only real aspectual distinction which is encoded in French verbal morphology is the one illustrated in the following examples:

(366) a. Pendant que je LISAIS le journal, le téléphone A SONNÉ.
    b. Le ciel ETAIT sans nuages, le torrent SEMBLAIT une masse d'écume, et tout d'un coup un oiseau SE MIT à chanter.

In (366a) two events/actions are described. My reading the newspaper is presented as a durative, ongoing backdrop (with no clear start or end point), during which a punctual event occurs (the phone rang). Note that both occurred prior to utterance time, so the difference between the two isn't one of tense. Rather, the difference relates to the shape of the events/actions, that is, how they are distributed along the time line. My reading the newspaper is presented as an activity which extends in time; the phone ringing is presented as punctual. This contrast relates to aspect; *je lisais le journal* has durative or imperfective aspect (realised by an imperfect), while *le téléphone a sonné* has punctual or perfective aspect (realised by a compound-past). An imperfect is also used to express durative aspect in (366b), but the punctual aspect of *un oiseau se mit à chanter* is expressed by a past-historic.

Contrast the aspectual meanings expressed in the examples in (366) with those in (367):

(367) a. J'AI LU le journal, puis le téléphone A SONNÉ.
    b. Pour un bref moment le ciel FUT sans nuages, le torrent SEMBLA une masse d'écume et un oiseau SE MIT à chanter, mais tout d'un coup les bombardements ONT RECOMMENCÉ.

Whereas in (366) durative actions/events are presented as a backdrop for punctual actions/events, in (367) we are presented with a sequence of punctual actions/events.

Another type of past time context where the imperfect is found is shown here:

(368) Quand j'étais petit nous ALLIONS chez mes grands-parents.

Here the imperfect is said to have habitual aspect, but this label shouldn't be taken as radically different from the previous uses. The habitual interpretation of the events or actions described are due to the basic aspectual value of the imperfect tense, which specifies no precise beginning or end point. Instead, the events or actions are spread over an unspecified period of time in the past, and the habitual interpretation given to the imperfect is a consequence of our knowledge of how human beings act (that is, 'over an unspecified period when I was young we went to see my grand-parents' takes an interpretation, not of one single event taking place over an unspecified period, but of a series of repetitions of that event). The habitual reading of the imperfect in this sentence could be underlined by the addition of an adverbial, such as *souvent*:

(369) Quand j'étais petit nous allions SOUVENT chez mes
       grands-parents.

The imperfect is distinguished from the past-historic and the compound-past by its aspectual and not by its temporal value.

Compared with some languages, French verbal morphology isn't especially rich in the aspectual distinctions it encodes. However, this isn't to say that aspectual distinctions cannot be made in French. It's just that devices other than verb morphology are used, for example specific lexical items or periphrastic tenses. Thus, iterative aspect (doing something again and again) is expressed by the periphrastic *continuer à faire quelque chose*. The progressive aspect (being in the process of doing something) is expressed by *être en train de faire quelque chose*, inchoative aspect (beginning to do something) by *commencer à faire quelque chose*.

16   Final remarks

In this chapter we've explored how individual words are combined into longer sequences. Most importantly we've seen that sequences of words aren't random linear arrangements. Rather, individual words combine into structured phrases, and these initial phrases then combine into larger phrases, and ultimately into clauses and sentences. We've seen that sentences are in fact nothing more than phrases with some particular properties, namely a subject and a finite verb. While there are clear patterns to the way words combine into phrases, these patterns are actually very flexible. For example, all the following sequences of words are NPs: [$_{NP}$ l'homme à qui tu parlais hier], [$_{NP}$ nous], [$_{NP}$ quoi] and [$_{NP}$ celui-ci]. As we've explored phrase structure, we've seen time and time again that the structure of a particular phrase is determined by its head.

This exploration of French syntax rounds off our journey through the linguistic structure of French. In Chapter 5 we return to some of the themes of Chapter 1. In Chapter 1 we charted how what was once nothing more than one variety of Gallo-Romance among many rose in status to become the national standard language of one of the largest nation-states of Europe. In Chapter 5 we consider the extent to which French is a unified language. What we find is that there's actually considerable variation in the way 'French' is spoken, and that this variation is as much geographical and social as it is stylistic. Now that we have an idea of the linguistic structure of one important variety of French, we are in a position to understand the nature of the differences between the ways French is spoken by different people in different places and in different situations.

Further reading

For an introduction to the basic notions of syntax, see Palmer (1994) and Tallerman (1998). For overviews of French syntax, see Jones (1996), Lodge *et al.* (1997: ch. 8), Tellier (1995), Spence (1996: part IV), Kayne (1975), Ruwet (1972), Soutet (1989). For an overview from a historical and comparative perspective, see Harris (1978) and Posner (1997). For a reference grammar of French for native English speakers, see Hawkins and Towell (1996). The standard French reference grammar is Grevisse (1994). On verbal subcategories, see Jones (1996: ch. 2), Tellier (1995: secs 3.3.2, 5.1.1), Spence (1996: ch. 17). On copulas, see Jones (1996: sec. 2.5). On exclamatives, see Gérard (1980), Radford (1989). On constituent structure, see Tellier (1995: sec. 3.6). On NP structure, see Jones (1996: ch. 5), Tellier (1995: sec. 3.3.1); Harris (1978: secs 3.1–7). On proper nouns, see Gary-Prieur (1994), Kleiber (1992). On determiners, see Harris (1978: ch. 4), Picabia (1986), Spence (1996: ch. 14). On PP structure, see Tellier (1995: sec. 3.3.3). On the article *de*, see Englebert (1993). On AP structure, see Jones (1996: secs 7.2–4), Tellier (1995: sec. 3.3.4), Harris (1978: sec. 3.8), Spence (1996: ch. 16). On adjective position, see Bouchard (1998). On proforms, see Jones (1996: ch. 6), Harris (1978: ch. 5), Spence (1996: ch. 15), Couquaux (1986). On clitics, see Tellier (1995: ch. 12), Watson (1997), Cornish (1991), Herschensohn (1980), Morin (1975, 1979, 1981). On *en*, see Pollock (1986). On *on*, see Ashby (1992), Oukada (1982). On passives, see Jones (1996: sec. 3.2), Dobrovie-Sorin (1986), Gross (1993), Tellier (1995: secs 5.5, 10.3), Péry-Woodley (1991), Spence (1996: ch. 17). On pronominal verbs, see Jones (1996: secs 2.4.4, 3.3). On complement clauses, see Jones (1996: sec. 1.3.1), Tellier (1995: sec. 3.3.6, ch. 7). On complementisers, see Tellier (1995: sec. 6.4). On infinitival clauses, see Jones (1996: ch. 9), Huot (1981). On mood, see Jones (1996: sec. 4.9), Huot (1986). On indirect questions, see Harris (1978: sec. 11.2). On interrogatives, see Jones (1996: sec. 10.4), Tellier (1995: secs 8.1–2, 8.4), Harris (1978: sec. 2.4, ch. 10), Obenauer (1976). On inversion, see Jones (1996: secs 10.2–3), Atkinson (1973), Dupuis and Valois (1992), Kayne (1972). On relative clauses, see Jones (1996: sec. 10.5), Blanche-Benveniste (1997: sec. 4.5.1), Tellier (1995: sec. 8.3), Harris (1978: ch. 10), Bouchard (1982). On *qui* in subject relatives, see Blanche-Benveniste (1997: sec. 4.3.2), Kayne (1976), Léard (1990), Moreau (1971). On interrogative and relative movement, see Tellier (1995: secs 9.2, 9.4), Lefebvre (1982a). On past participle agreement, see Jones (1996: sec. 2.8.4). On remote quantification, see Battye (1995), Azoulay-Vicente (1989), Obenauer (1983, 1983/4). On dislocation, see Ashby (1988), Barnes (1985), Heilenman and McDonald (1993), Lambrecht (1980). On cleft constructions, see Jones (1996: sec. 10.7.2), Blanche-Benveniste (1997: secs 4.4.1–2). On the subject of infinitives, see Tellier (1995: sec. 7.2.1). On noun complements, see Jones (1996: sec. 7.5). On comparatives and superlatives, see Jones (1996: sec. 7.7). On adverb(ial)s, see Tellier (1995: secs 3.3.5, 3.3.7), Spence (1996: ch. 18), Leeman (1990), Nølke (1990). On adverbial clauses, see Harris (1978: ch. 12). On negation, see Callebaut (1992), Gaatone (1971), Muller (1991), Rowlett (1998), Jones (1996: sec. 7.6), Harris (1978: sec. 2.3). On the loss of *ne*, see Ashby (1976, 1981b), Coveney (1990b). On impersonal constructions, see Jones (1996: secs 2.4.5–6, 3.4). On *il y a*, see Blanche-Benveniste (1997: sec. 4.3.1). On verb forms, see Harris (1978: chs 6–9), Spence (1996: ch. 17). On aspect, see Comrie (1976), Wilmet (1991), Jones (1996: ch. 4). On tense, see Comrie (1987), Jones (1996: ch. 4), Lo Cascio (1982). On the (double) compound-past, see Carruthers (1994), Waugh (1987). On auxiliary selection, see Jones (1996: sec. 2.8.1).

5 Varieties of French

So far, we have seen French as a predominantly homogeneous entity, an approach supported by the particular social and political history of France which, as we saw in 1: 6, led to the dogma of French as a unitary standard, to be held up as the symbol of national unity. Clearly, within the French-speaking world, the written standard, assiduously promoted through education, is invested with considerable prestige – not to say awe – and one of the means by which it achieves identification (and, some might say, universality) lies in its very fixity, and the rejection of alternative linguistic usage.

Yet, while Francophones, from France to Quebec or Tahiti, are united in their consciousness of sharing the same language, even the most casual observer will notice more or less subtle differences in pronunciation, vocabulary, even syntax. Like all living languages, French exhibits considerable variability in the way it's used by individual speakers, who constantly adapt and modify it according to their needs. We might say, then, that, like any world language, French is in reality the sum of its varieties, of which the highly codified 'standard' is but one.

Where linguistic features associated with external factors, such as geographical area, the social characteristics of the speakers (age and sex, for instance), or the situation of language use, regularly occur in the speech of individuals or groups, we can speak of 'a variety of the language', that is, 'a set of linguistic items with a similar social distribution' (Hudson 1996: 22). As we examine varieties of French in this chapter, we'll be focusing on the notion of variation, or linguistic diversity, seen from two main angles, namely the geographical and the social, and on the choices that speakers make within the system of the language. With respect to geographical (or regional) varieties, we'll consider, first, the linguistic diversity that prevails within France itself (5: 1–3) and, then, turn to varieties elsewhere in the world (5: 4–5). Finally, we'll examine social and stylistic variation (5: 6–8).

1 Linguistic diversity within France

While the processes of linguistic standardisation and unification are now far advanced in France, it would be hasty to conclude that the country is monolingual. Admittedly, French is the only official language (1: 7), yet an initial sense of linguistic diversity in France comes from the observation that, side by side with French, other languages coexist to a greater or lesser extent. Indeed, seven non-French languages enjoy (an albeit limited) recognition in the educational system, and play a small part in the media. These have the status of *langues régionales*, although it's useful and less contentious to distinguish between non-Romance and Romance languages (1: 3.1). Note, first, that these aren't recent imports, but languages spoken by long-established communities in certain areas, and, second, that the linguistic boundaries don't always coincide with present-day political borders.

1.1   Non-Romance languages

The five non-Romance languages are spoken essentially on parts of the periphery of France. Basque is the most ancient, spoken by a community which probably predates the arrival of the Celts in Gaul. Within France it's confined to the extreme south-west (Pyrénées-Atlantiques), where it's thought to have about 40,000 speakers. (In northern Spain, where it's the official language of the Basque province, it may have as many as half a million speakers (Nelde *et al.* 1996).)

In the extreme western *départements* of Finistère, Côtes du Nord and Morbihan lies *la Bretagne bretonnante* or *la Bretagne celtique*. As with other languages, the precise number of speakers of Breton (a Celtic language closely related to Welsh, Irish and Gaelic) is difficult to evaluate, but at a conservative estimate (Ternes 1992: 376) around half a million people speak Breton and use it occasionally, while approximately 250,000 speakers (mostly farmers, fishermen and older members of the community) use it daily. Attempts to reverse the decline in the use of Breton, which occurred during the twentieth century, are today actively supported by some younger speakers and intellectuals, and reinforced by the existence of university research centres in Brest and Rennes (see Jones 1995).

To the north, in a small enclave at the northern tip of the *département* of Nord, around Dunkerque and the town of Hazebrouck, are 20–40,000 speakers of Flemish, a Germanic language related to Dutch. Given the small number of mostly elderly speakers, Nelde *et al.* (1996) suggest Flemish is the *langue régionale* whose survival in France is most under threat from a shift towards French.

On the eastern border, two other Germanic dialects are spoken: Lorrain in the north and east of the *département* of Moselle, and Alsatian in the Haut-Rhin and Bas-Rhin, with a total number of speakers estimated at 1,800,000. Of the two, Lorrain is perhaps the most vulnerable to extinction, since economic recession has struck the traditional mining and industrial activities where the language was formerly widely used. However, Alsatian seems to be holding its own in rural areas and as a means of daily communication within social village networks (see Tabouret-Keller 1981: 51–66, Vassberg 1993).

1.2 Romance languages

Besides French, there are four Romance languages spoken in France today. The major branch of Romance represented is Occitan, a cover term for all those varieties spoken south of a line which roughly goes from the Gironde (Bordeaux) in the west to the Hautes-Alpes near Grenoble in the east, and covers a third of France (see Appendix I). In reality, the term Occitan covers several distinct varieties: Provençal (strictly speaking, the local variety of Provence), Languedocien, Auvergnat, Limousin and Gascon. Estimations of the number of speakers are in the range 2–12 million, depending on whether we include only those two million or so people who use the language daily, those who occasionally use one form or another, or indeed those who merely understand them. Once again, it appears that these languages are more readily spoken by older speakers in rural areas, although efforts are being made towards a cultural revival of Occitan (of which one component is the development of a standard orthography), promoted since 1945 by the Institut d'Etudes Occitanes, based in Toulouse (see Ager 1990: 37–49).

A second Romance language, straddling the Franco-Spanish border, is Catalan, with about 200,000 speakers in France, in an area which roughly corresponds to the *département* of Pyrénées-Orientales. As with Basque, most Catalan speakers (over four million) live in Spain.

Corsican, third, is closely related to Tuscan and Sardinian. Despite the widespread use of French for official acts and communication with the 'continent', the 125,000 or so speakers of Corsican remain strongly attached to their language and eager to perpetuate it. Corsica is a *collectivité territoriale* and enjoys a special administrative status which involves recognition of Corsican as *la langue corse* (rather than being classed as a *langue régionale*) and powers devolved to the regional assembly to determine policy in educational and cultural affairs. Finally in this survey of the historical varieties spoken in France, on the Mediterranean between Nice and Menton, and also in Savoie, there are small enclaves of speakers of Piedmontese, a northern Italian dialect.

1.3 The languages of immigration

In the context of linguistic diversity within France, we shouldn't forget the speakers of so-called 'immigrant languages', for many of whom, in particular recent immigrants, the first or home language is Portuguese, Arabic, Italian or Spanish, to name but the largest groups. (See Vermes 1988 and Laroussi and Marcellesi 1993.)

Thus, a total of at least nine indigenous languages – including French – and (at a conservative estimate) over fifteen exogenous languages are spoken in France, and an estimated fifteen million inhabitants of France are either active bilinguals (regularly using French and another language) or passive bilinguals (able to understand a language other than French). Clearly, the overwhelming presence of Standard French in official life and in education conceals a situation of far greater linguistic diversity than is usually admitted and, indeed, than exists in many other European countries, including Belgium or Switzerland which are generally perceived as being plurilingual (1: 2.1).

2 Regional varieties of French

Geographical (or regional) variation in the way a language is spoken is one of the most noticeable ways we observe diversity in language. Anyone travelling across France will notice that spoken French isn't the homogeneous entity presented in the textbooks or classroom. As we'll see in 5: 3–4, there may be quite noticeable differences in pronunciation, vocabulary, even syntax. How can we account for such differences?

One obvious explanation can be sought by taking into consideration geographical and historical factors. We have seen (1: 5.1) that it wasn't until the nineteenth century that French, in the form of the national language, started to make serious inroads into the newly industrialised urban centres and far-flung provinces, gradually bringing about a shift away from the regional languages, whereby speakers of languages unrelated to French, such as Breton or Basque, adopted the dominant language. However, as we've seen, the process is as yet incomplete, and in many areas of France substantial numbers of speakers who have received their formal education through the medium of French also have access to some other language, usually used in the home or local community. We might also wonder to what extent the dialects of Old French have survived.

2.1 Language, dialects and patois

Before attempting to answer this question, the terms **dialect** and *patois* deserve attention, since they can be used in a number of sometimes confusing ways. In France, the terms *dialecte* and *patois* are often used by non-linguists to describe local varieties of French – typically spoken by the rural inhabitants of remote provinces – with the implication that these are corrupt, debased forms of the standard language. The term *dialecte* has more positive connotations than *patois*, for the former can be associated with a variety which has (or had) its own linguistic norm and an associated literary tradition, while the latter is disparagingly associated with oral vernaculars surviving in small, isolated communities. For lay people, then, the distinction between language and dialect (or *patois*) isn't linguistic, but has to do with social attitudes and the perceived superiority of the written standard, which alone deserves to be called a language. One consequence of this is that since, say, Standard French comes to be regarded as the language itself, all other varieties, whatever the historical or linguistic facts, are perceived in relation to the standard, and are viewed as dialects of, or deviations from, the standard. For instance, a prestigious medieval language with a rich cultural and literary heritage like Occitan is frequently referred to as a dialect.

Linguists, however, take a more egalitarian perspective, and more neutrally prefer to think in terms of 'varieties of a language' (see Hudson's definition at the beginning of the chapter). Hawkins defines 'dialect' as 'a shared set of speech habits' (1993: 57). From this perspective, Standard French is a dialect like all the others. As we pointed out in Chapter 1, it was initially the dialect of a region of northern France which, through historical accident, acquired prestige by being associated with the seat of power (1: 3.1). It's called a language merely because it's the official dialect and has been standardised. Conversely, non-standard dialects aren't linguistically inferior forms of communication, but merely varieties which haven't obtained social status. Thus, the descendants of the dialects of medieval France aren't substandard forms of French, for they predate the very notion of a standard. They were merely the unsuccessful rivals of Francien in the moves to establish a standard.

2.2 The dialects of French

Strictly speaking, the term 'dialects of French' covers only those varieties which emerged historically in the northern part of medieval France (the Langue d'Oïl area; 1: 3.1) and bear the names of the ancient provinces of that area. This is because Occitan, in all its varieties, is a separate language with its own dialects. As the map in Appendix I shows, the generally recognised dialectal entities are:

- the dialects of Oïl: in the north, Picard and Wallon (which extends into present-day Belgium); in the east, Champenois, and in the south-east, Bourguignon; in south-central areas, Orléanais and Tourangeau; in the south-west, Poitevin; in the west and north-west, Angevin, Gallo (in the non-Breton-speaking area of Brittany), and Normand. Closely related to the latter is Anglo-Normand which still survives in the Channel Islands of Jersey, Guernsey and Sark.
- Franco-Provençal: as mentioned in 1: 3.1, a further distinct group of dialects, known collectively as Franco-Provençal, was identified in 1870 by the Italian linguist Ascoli in the area between Grenoble, Lyons and Geneva, and extending into the Suisse Romande part of Switzerland and the Aosta Valley in Italy. This formerly unified language, based on the variety of Lyons, is today extremely fragmented. However, the

term Franco-Provençal indicates the underlying unity of the varieties of this dialect which can be characterised as a zone of linguistic transition between the dialects of Oïl and those of Oc.

With the map in Appendix I, remember that linguistic boundaries aren't clear-cut and precise. Lines on maps represent a consensus about a grouping of distinctive features, which separate one language variety from another along geographical lines. The dialects which, today, remain the most clearly defined are those which are furthest from the central area occupied by the standard, not just in geographical terms, but also politically, economically, culturally and linguistically – especially those of the north (Picard and Wallon), the east (Bourguignon and Franco-Provençal) and, to some extent, the north-west (notably Normand).

By way of illustration of the way Latin evolved differently in one area of northern France, consider the following transcription of a short extract of a modern rendition in Picard dialect of La Fontaine's fable *La Cigale et la fourmi* (by the poet and storyteller Leopold Simons):

[ʃœl sigal e ʃœl fuʀmi ʃe ʃœl pɔf bjɛt et əl kono
cette cigale et cette fourmi c'est cette pauvre bête et tu la connais

ʃe ʃœl sigal kə ʃtə dizo ɛl kɑ̃to kɑ̃ti fəzo ko
c'est cette cigale dont je te parlais elle chantait quand il faisait chaud

astœʀ al bʀe paski fe fʀo]
maintenant elle pleure parce qu'il fait froid

Note the following phonological characteristics:

- a velar articulation in [ko] and [kɑ̃to], instead of standard [ʃ], for *chaud* and *chantait*;
- diphthongisation of the blocked vowel (from Latin *bestia* or **besta*) in *bête* [bjɛt];
- the mid-high vowel [e] in the open final syllable of *fait* [fe] and [bʀe], for *brait*, glossed here as *pleure* (see below);
- the form of the second person singular subject clitic in [təlkono], as opposed to *tu*;
- the pronunciation of the adjective *froid* as [fʀo].

There are three lexical items of interest:

- the adverb [astœʀ] (*à cette heure*), used in the sense of *maintenant*;
- the verbs *braire* for *pleurer* (which in the standard is restricted to the meaning of braying like a donkey) and *dire* for *parler*.

Finally, in morphology and syntax:

- the feminine demonstrative proform [ʃœl], corresponding to standard *celle*, which has initial [ʃ] and is used as a determiner (as was possible in Old French);
- *disait* [dizo] and *chantait* [kãto] show the retention and generalisation of imperfect endings derived from the imperfect indicative of Latin first conjugation verbs.

2.3 The dialect situation today

Characteristic of the dialect situation today is, first, that, while heard occasionally in village markets, cafés and in the home, dialects are usually maintained within small, fairly isolated, rural communities and among elderly speakers. Just as, nowadays, there are probably no speakers of regional languages in France who cannot also speak French, there are no monolingual dialect speakers either. Studies such as Maurand (1981) show how, within a small rural community near Toulouse, the relationship between French and Occitan is maintained: French is associated with education, prestige, youth and women, whereas Occitan is associated with old age, lack of education, men and the rural world. A similar situation is documented by Hadjadj (1981) relating to two rural communities in the Provençal and Franco-Provençal area in 1975.

Second, many dialect speakers have both a negative image of their dialect (usually termed a *patois*), and a sense of insecurity with regard to their command of French. Gueunier *et al.* (1978) and Chaveau (1977: 105) report that dialect speakers use expressions such as *français écorché* and *français abrégé* to refer to their own linguistic usage. Rather than being aware of using a non-standard system, these speakers themselves conform to the commonly received (and, to the linguist, erroneous) opinion that dialects are substandard approximations of French. In the rare instances when dialects are written (occasionally in the local newspapers, in the transcription of traditional stories or poems or in the work of more deliberately 'regional writers'), the uneasy and sometimes erratic adaptation of the orthography of French only seems to blur the individuality of different varieties and make them appear 'inferior'. Thus, not only are the dialects subject to the increasing pressure of Standard French, but, in comparison, they enjoy little prestige. However, as reported by Coveney (1986: 19) and in Lafont (1982) there is evidence of a renewed interest in dialects and some reversal of negative attitudes towards them, notably, as symbols of distinct regional identities (see Bouvier and Martel 1991, Hawkins 1993, Auzanneau 1998, Pooley 1998). Yet this is still a very limited phenomenon, led by small numbers of highly literate and linguistically sophisticated urban enthusiasts, who themselves aren't native speakers of these dialects, and it isn't likely to alter significantly the course of the steady decline of the dialects.

Table 5.1

Provençal	Normand	Picard/Wallon	Catalan	Lyonnais	Alsacien	Lorrain	Franco-Provençal
anchois	câble	cabaret	aubergine	frangin	gamin	beurre	avalanche
bagarre	falaise	estaminet	abricot	gnole	choucroute	chope	chalet
boutique	harpon	frisquet	espadrille	moutard	quiche	poêle	crétin
casserole	mare	tricoter	galère	jacasser	frichti		mêlèze
escargot	crevette	houille					
langouste	flâner	boulanger					
magasin	masure	coron					
truc	potin	rescapé					

2.4 The future of the dialects

Given that non-standard dialects today exist as alternatives to French in very limited functions only (in the home or community or, for instance, to discuss local agricultural practices or tools, flora and fauna) and/or in a more or less artificial written form, the dialects of French, as 'pure dialects', may be said to be moribund. Yet it might be truer to say that the dialects aren't so much exterminated as eroded, infiltrated by the standard, particularly with respect to syntax and vocabulary. In other words, a process of linguistic convergence has occurred. Given the similarities in linguistic structure that exist between the central standard and the other dialects of the Langue d'Oïl particularly, and pressure to conform to the norm, speakers of these varieties have gradually altered their linguistic behaviour to bring it closer to the standard. Nevertheless, this is a two-way relationship, since the standard itself has, over the centuries, absorbed many lexical items borrowed from the dialects, a few of which are shown in Table 5.1.

Guiraud (1978: 114–27) provides a far more comprehensive list, giving attributions of provenance for over 1,200 items, which reveals that the majority of these borrowings stem from Occitan, Normand and Picard (see also Walter 1997, Wise 1997: 59–62). Those items which have secured a place in the lexicon of Standard French are often technical terms relating to certain professions and agricultural and industrial activities, as well as terms relating to culinary specialities or local products.

3 Les français régionaux in France

The language of the majority of French speakers often has a characteristic local flavour. It's by what's termed (in the non-specialised sense of the word) their 'accent' that we recognise a speaker as originating from Lille, Marseilles or Bordeaux. These regional differences in pronunciation are perhaps the most noticeable way in which we observe variation in the language. However, on closer scrutiny, some differences in the choice and form of words, and even syntax, may also be apparent.

3.1 What are les français régionaux?

The term *français régional* describes those varieties of French which, although closely related to the standard, especially with regard to syntax, morphology and lexis, contain some distinctive features of pronunciation and non-standard usages, which can be related, among other things, to their geographic provenance. One well-known definition of *les français régionaux* was formulated by the linguist and dialectologist Gaston Tuaillon (1974: 576), namely 'ce qui reste du dialecte quand le dialecte a disparu'.

In this view, *les français régionaux* are dialect-influenced French, insofar as they include dialectal features which have survived in the French spoken in a particular geographical area, and which aren't felt to be part of the common stock of Standard French, either because they are archaisms or have limited currency. The dialects therefore constitute the substrate (or base) of the regional variety. We shouldn't forget, however, that regionalisms may also stem from the independent evolution of the variety itself, and, in particular, from borrowings, either from French or from other contact languages (Taverdet and Straka 1977: 238). In short, varieties labelled *français régionaux* could be described as forming an intermediate level in a spectrum of variation which goes from the original, semi-moribund dialect to the standard language. However, note that, as with all instances of language use, there are no hard and fast boundaries between these three levels, but rather a continuum of variation, which may range from a usage which is only marginally different from the variety presented as the norm, to a variety in which the deviations from the standard are numerous and substantial. Furthermore, as previously implied, for the majority of speakers of French, notably urban speakers in the Langue d'Oïl area, the spectrum of variation won't include the dialectal level.

Les français régionaux do, however, differ from the dialects insofar as they are perfectly intelligible to speakers from other areas, whereas with dialects intelligibility isn't always guaranteed, either from dialect to dialect, or between a dialect and either regional or Standard French. Further, since there is mutual comprehension, the speakers of a particular variety of *français régional* may not even be aware of the regional features of their speech. They are secure in their feeling that the language they use is French and assume it conforms to the norm.

3.2   Some generally conservative features of le français régional

3.2.1   Phonology

Some conservative features of pronunciation cut across several *français régionaux*:

- the trilled [r], which prevailed until the seventeenth century when it began to be replaced by the uvular [ʀ] of today's Standard French, is still heard in many rural areas, namely Burgundy, Jura, Vosges, the Midi (as well as outside France, for example in Quebec);
- similarly, an aspirated [h], introduced in words of Germanic origin and present in Old and Middle French, can still be heard in parts of Normandy: *dehors* [dəhɔʀ], Lorraine: *haut* [ho], Alsace: *hache* [haʃ] and Wallonia;
- in the south, the *e-muet* of Standard French is generally pronounced word-finally after a single consonant and in interconsonantal position, and is therefore syllabic, hence *Toulouse, la ville rose* is pronounced with five syllables in the north [tu.luz.la.vil.ʀoz] and eight in the south

[tu.lu.zə.la.vi.lə.ʀɔ.zə], and *je me le demande* is pronounced in the south as [ʒə.mə.lə.də.mɑ̃.də] and in the north as [ʒə.mlə.dmɑ̃d];

- the distinction between the nasal vowels [ɛ̃] and [œ̃], which is no longer generally upheld in the standard and in large parts of Northern France from Normandy to Burgundy, is maintained in the south-east and south-west, albeit differently, in the form of a partially nasalised and higher vowel followed by an audible nasal consonant, for example *un matin* [ɛ̃matɛ̃ŋ].

3.2.2   Vocabulary

Regional varieties also maintain some lexical items which have either disappeared from Standard French or changed meaning. Examples of now archaic words in French are the Picard *toudis*, *œuvrer*, *bailler* and *quérir*, which have been replaced by *toujours*, *travailler*, *donner* and *chercher*, respectively, and *un besson* (*jumeau*) and *la prée* (*prairie*), which are still used in western areas to the south-west of Normandy. Similarly, *septante*, *octante*, *huitante* and *nonante* are still common in eastern dialects, in the varieties spoken in Belgium and Switzerland and the Channel Islands, although the standard abandoned them in favour of *soixante-dix*, *quatre-vingts* and *quatre-vingt-dix* before the eighteenth century.

Potential sources of misunderstanding are words used in regional varieties with slightly different meanings. For instance, in most rural regions of France, just as in Belgium, Switzerland and Canada, an invitation to *dîner* will mean lunch (*déjeuner* in the central area since the mid-nineteenth century) and not the evening meal, which is *le souper*. A Parisian would probably relax in his *pantoufles*, while a Québécois would put on his *chaussettes*, and a Lillois, his *chaussons*. While both the Parisian and Lillois would agree that their socks are *chaussettes*, the Québécois will wear *des bas* 'stockings', causing perhaps the same sort of surprise as the person from Lille, understood to be wearing baby bootees when donning his *chaussons*. Similarly, a Lyonnais who is *fatigué* isn't so much tired as ill; a Marseillais uses *espérer* in the sense of 'to wait'; for a Wallon *attendre* means 'to expect a baby', a state described by a Québécois as *être en famille*, which a metropolitan French speaker merely assumes to mean 'being with one's family'. In France, *avoir le bras long* suggests being influential, while in Canada it means being a thief or light-fingered.

Regionalisms may also be apparent in local words which either aren't part of the standard language or have entered the standard but may be used only with local reference, for example *le pochon* ('paper bag' in Brittany), *la marienne* ('afternoon nap' in Poitou), *un gone* ('brat' in Lyons), *le buron* ('shepherd's hut' in Auvergne), *la calanque* ('rocky inlet' in Provence), *le gave* ('mountain torrent' in the Pyrénées), *la ducasse* or *la kermesse* ('village fête' in Belgium or Flanders), *la drache* ('heavy rain' in Flanders), *le crachin* ('misty rain' in Brittany) and *la grésine* ('light rain' in Lorraine).

Lexical items such as these are both a way of identifying which part of France a speaker originates from and, occasionally, of enriching the vocabulary of the standard, for instance in integrating both a local culinary speciality or product and its name (*quiche, cassoulet, aïoli, bouill-abaisse, fondue* and so on). Note, though, that since many of these words of local provenance correspond to a bygone way of life or now defunct agricultural techniques or occupations, relatively few of them ever become fully assimilated.

3.3   Regional pronunciations

In addition to the conservative features of pronunciation (5: 3.2.1) found in many varieties of regional French, other distinctive features can define the 'accent' of a particular locality. By considering a few of the most salient characteristics for some broadly defined major areas, it will be seen that, when it comes to regional accents, the major differences with respect to the standard can be assigned essentially to features of vowel length, the distribution of mid-low and mid-high vowels, the opposition between [a] and [ɑ], the behaviour of *e-muet*, nasalised vowels and realisations of /ʀ/.

3.3.1   The north: Nord and Pas de Calais

With vowels, in the most extreme cases, the distinction between final [e] and [ɛ] has been lost in favour of mid-high [e], that between final [a] and [ɑ] in favour of [ɑ], hence no distinction between *les* and *lait* [le] or *la* and *las* [lɑ]. In final position [ɑ] is very general, for example in *papa* [pɑpɑ].

The system of nasal vowels is reduced to three with the loss of [œ̃], and even the distinction between [ɑ̃] and [ɔ̃] is unstable. A feature which is shared with the south is that [e, ø, o] lower in a closed syllable, as in *feutre* [fœtʀ], *côte* [kɔt], *espace* [ɛspas], and raise in an open non-final syllable, as in *chocolat* [ʃokolɑ]. However, [e] is always present before [ʀ], as in *bière* [bjeʀ].

The consonant [ʀ] often has a voiceless and more pharyngeal articulation, for example, *alors* [alɔʁ̥]. Final voiced consonants are frequently devoiced, as in *chômage* [ʃomaʃ] and *période* [peʀiɔt], and final consonant clusters reduced, as in *juste* [ʒys]. Words such as *travail* and *bouteille*, which in Standard French end in [j], are realised with final [l], as in [tʀaval] and [butɛl].

3.3.2   The east: Alsace and Lorraine

The vowels [œ, ɔ] raise before [ʀ], as in *peur* [pøːʀ], *alors* [aloːʀ] and *voyageur* [vwajaʒøːʀ]. Under stress, [a] is replaced by [ɑ], as in *camarade* [kamaʀɑt] (note also the devoiced final consonant) and *coupage* [kupɑːʒ]. In polysyllabic words stress is often shifted to the first syllable: *qualité* ['kɑlite]. Initial voiceless stops are frequently aspirated, as in *caractère* [kʰaʀaktɛːʀ] and *tête* [tʰɛt].

In Lorraine final voiced fricatives [v, z, ʒ] are frequently devoiced, as in *vive* [vif], *village* [vilaʃ], *neige* [nɛʃ] and *gas* [gas]. In Alsace, particularly, initial voiceless stops are voiced, as in *parapluie* [baʀaplɥi], as can be voiceless fricatives, as in *français* [vʀɑ̃ze].

3.3.3 The south-east: Jura, Vosges, Burgundy, Lyons

The contrast between [a] and [ɑ] is maintained. A noticeable lengthening of the vowel before final orthographic -*e* is widespread, distinguishing *ami* [ami] from *amie* [ami:]. The distinction between the short and long vowels [ɛ] and [ɛ:] is also well preserved, especially in Burgundy.

In Burgundy and Lyons [œ] raises to [ø] before a consonant, as in *fleuve* [fløːv], *jeune* [ʒøn], but *jeûne* [ʒøːn].

In the Vosges [ɛ] raises to [e] before a consonant, as in *père* [peːʀ]. In the Jura [ɛ, œ, ɔ] raise and lengthen in a closed syllable, as in *encore* [ɑ̃koːʀ] and *neige* [neːʒ].

With regard to consonants, [ʀ] is often trilled to give [r], although it may weaken or disappear before a consonant, as in *alors que* [aloːrkə] and *parce que* [paskə]. There is also a tendency to palatalise [t] before [j], hence *métier* [metʃe].

3.3.4 The south

In southern varieties the most noticeable features concern the distribution of mid vowels, which operates on a very simple basis, namely mid-high vowels in open syllables and mid-low in closed syllables, as in *rose* [ʀɔːz], *herbe* [ɛʀb] and *creuse* [kʀœːz] versus *laisser* [lese], *peu* [pø], *pot* [po] and *paix* [pe]. There is no contrast between [a] and [ɑ], [a] having generalised in all positions.

We noted earlier (5: 3.2.1) how Standard French *e-muet* is pronounced (although it can be realised as [œ, ə, ɛ, o]), and the frequent use of the trilled [r] in these varieties. Note, also, the very distinctive, partial nasalisation of nasal vowels which can be heard with an accompanying nasal consonant ([n] before [t, d], [m] before [p, b], [ŋ] word-finally), as in *pain* [pɛ̃ŋ], *tombe* [tɔ̃mbə] and *chante* [ʃɑ̃ntə].

3.3.5 The west and north-west

We also noted earlier the aspirated pronunciation of *h-aspiré* in words of Germanic origin such as *haie* ['hɛ]. This example also shows the tendency of final [ɛ] in open syllables not to raise to [e]. However, in a closed syllable Standard French mid-low [ɛ] and [ɔ] are lengthened and raised, as in *bête* [beːt] and *alors* [aloːʀ].

The distinction between [a] and [ɑ] is not well maintained, except through a distinction in length, in pairs such as *malle* and *mâle*. Elsewhere there is a tendency to the generalisation of [ɑ], as in *garage* [gɑʁɑːʒ] and *cave* [kɑːv]. The nasal vowels [œ̃] and [ɛ̃] have generally coalesced.

In Normandy in particular, final orthographic *-e* leads to the lengthening of the previous vowel, as in *amie* [amiː] (as in the east). Standard [wa] is realised as [e] or [we], as in *droit* [dʁwɛ] or [dʁe] and *pourquoi* [puʁkwɛ].

Final consonants, particularly [ʁ], are often not pronounced, as in *avec* [ave], *sur* [sy] and *pour* [pu].

3.3.6   Regional accents

Although there has undoubtedly been considerable levelling of regional accents over the last half century, due to greater mobility of the population and the influence of the media, there are few speakers who won't, occasionally, give a clue as to their geographical origins, either by a feature of their pronunciation or the use of a regional term, grafted onto otherwise standard syntax or morphology. Indeed, as Martinet and Walter convincingly demonstrate in their 1973 study, based on a corpus of highly educated, long-term residents of Paris, there is considerably less homogeneity in pronunciation than might be assumed for a group which, on the face of it, ought to represent the standard. Of course, this raises the interesting question of how real the concept of 'the standard' truly is.

3.4   Morpho-syntactic variation

The diversity and variation in regional pronunciations are matched by diversity in morphology and syntax, although speakers vary considerably in how much they use non-standard forms. Detailed studies, such as Brun (1931) on the French of Marseilles, or Séguy (1978) on that of Toulouse, give fascinating insights into the specific features of these varieties of regional French.

In the use of tenses for instance, the past-historic, seldom heard in speech in the standard, is still used quite frequently in the regional varieties of the south. Similarly, the double compound-past (4: 15.2) of the type *Quand J'AI EU MANGÉ, je suis sortie* or, more striking still to northern ears, *J'EN AI EU GOÛTÉ mais je n'en ai jamais acheté*, whose existence speakers in the north, north-west and east barely acknowledge and seldom use, is widespread in southern varieties. (See Walter 1988: 171 for a map showing the distribution of this feature; see also Taverdet and Straka 1977: 40.) Verb forms may also differ from those of the standard. For instance, the endings of the conditional and imperfect are realised as [o] in the north, as in *j'avos* and *j'auros*, and [a] in the west, as in *je pouvas*, as opposed to the standard *-ais* [ɛ]. Similarly, in the west, *-i* endings are used for the conjugation of the past-historic, for instance *il tapi* instead of *il tapa*, *elle se renversi* rather than *elle se renversa*. In the same area, the first person singular present tense of *aller* may be realised as [va] or [alɔ̃], as in *je vas faire* and *j'allons dire*.

A construction typical of the south-west is the so-called ethic dative, as in *Je ME LA MANGE, cette pomme*. In Provence *être* is frequently used as the auxiliary for compound tenses of intransitive verbs, as in *Je SUIS ÉTÉ malade*. In the north *avoir* predominates, as in *Il A tombé* and *elle A marié son cousin*, as does the infinitival construction replacing a subordinate clause, as in *quelque chose POUR MOI FAIRE*. This is similar to the western *POUR VOUS RENTRER les bêtes*. In Poitou *Il est APRÈS manger* means *Il est en train de manger*. Typical Wallon non-standard constructions involving prepositions include *aller AU docteur*, instead of *chez*, *chercher APRÈS mon crayon*, instead of simply *chercher* plus direct object, and *jouer SUR la rue*, instead of *dans*. In the south *un* and *une* can be used as indefinite proforms (*quelqu'un*), as in *UN QUI est pharmacien*. In Orléanais the form *d'aucun(s)* is used frequently in the sense of *quelque(s)*, as in *D'AUCUNS Parisiens*.

Other constructions frequently mirror constructions which are considered to belong to the less formal registers of the standard (4: 11.3; 5: 8.3.2), for instance the use of *que* as universal complementiser, as in *cette fille QUE je t'ai parlé*, or the conditional after *si*, as in *Si j'AURAIS su, j'AURAIS pas venu*, instead of *Si j'AVAIS su, je ne SERAIS pas venue* (note also the different auxiliary verb).

Finally, some of these non-standard constructions may involve loan translations from the substrate regional languages. These are particularly evident in the eastern frontier regional varieties. For instance, in Alsace you might hear *gréver* for *faire grève*, in Switzerland la *chambre de bain*, instead of *salle de bains*, in the north *prendre avec* for *prendre* and *emporter*.

4 Regional French outside France

The term *français régional* is also appropriate for varieties which have emerged in other Francophone parts of the world (1: 1–3). The individuality of these varieties is more or less marked depending on the distance, the extent to which close contacts are maintained with France or not, and the intensity of contact with other languages spoken in the area.

These varieties – from Belgium, Louisiana or Réunion – exhibit the same types of variation with regard to the standard as the varieties within France do: a characteristic local 'accent', the use of lexical items peculiar to the variety and minimal differences in syntax and morphology.

4.1 Canada

In order to illustrate some of these points, the example of Canadian French springs to mind, since it's the variety spoken by the most numerous and prestigious group of Francophones outside France. However, note that in the context of Quebec particularly, the regional variety has achieved the status of a regional norm (for use in schools and the media, for instance), independent of, though closely associated with, the metropolitan standard.

Witness the publication of Shiaty's (1988) *Dictionnaire du français Plus à l'usage des francophones d'Amérique* or Ostiguy and Tousignant's (1993) *Le Français québécois: normes et usages*, whose purpose is to describe spoken usage and define a pedagogic norm. At the risk of considerable oversimplification, and allowing as before for the fact that, within this variety as with all others, there is in reality a spectrum of variation, both geographical and social, some distinctive regionalisms are illustrated below. (See also Gagné 1979: 43, Walker 1984, Blanc 1993, Ball 1997.)

4.1.1   Phonology

The distinctions between the vowel pairs [a]/[ɑ] and [ɛ]/[ɛː] are more widespread and stable than in Standard French. The vowels [i, y, u] are laxed (weakened) under stress in closed final syllables, as in *pipe* [pɪp], *coupe* [kʊp] and *jupe* [ʒʏp], but not before the consonants [v, ʀ, ʒ, z], which cause lengthening. ([ɪ, ʊ, ʏ] are the lax counterparts of [i, u, y].) Conversely, stressed long vowels are strengthened by diphthongisation, that is, adding a glide which corresponds in fronting and rounding, namely [j, w, ɥ], hence *chaude* [ʃowd], *neige* [nɛjʒ] and *pur* [pyɥʀ].

Canadian French has retained four phonemic nasal vowels, although their phonetic realisation is a little different from Standard French. The distinction between the two front vowels /ɛ̃/ and /œ̃/ is stable, as is that between /ɑ̃/ and /ɔ̃/, although their articulation is more fronted than in the standard, for instance in *pain* [pɛ̃] (rather than [pɛ̃]), *gant* [gæ̃] (rather than [gɑ̃]). In parallel with the four short nasalised vowels of *bain* [ɛ̃], *un* [œ̃], *bon* [ɔ̃] and *banc* [æ̃], for instance, there are four diphthongised long vowels, which behave like their oral counterparts in terms of the glides which they take, as in *lundi* [lœ̃ɥdi], *banque* [bæ̃wk], *quinze* [kɛ̃jz] and *ombre* [ɔ̃wbʀ].

The principal consonantal characteristic is the palatalisation of stops, notably [t, d], which become the affricates [tˢ] and [dᶻ] before high front vowels and glides, as in *petit* [pətˢi], *du* [dᶻy], *tien* [tˢjɛ̃] and *duel* [dᶻɥɛl]. Final consonant deletion is frequent in consonant clusters, as in *communiste* [kɔmynis], but similarly widespread is the retention of final consonants, especially [t] word-finally, as in *bout* [but] and *capot* [kapot]. Lastly, the trilled [r], though prevalent in Montreal, especially among older speakers, is now rivalled by the standard uvular [ʀ] amongst younger speakers.

4.1.2   Morphology

Many subject clitic proforms have reduced variants, for example *tu* [t], *il* and *ils* [i], *elle* [al] or [a]. Plural *elles* is replaced by *ils*, *lui* reduced to [i], as in *je lui parle* [ʒipaʀl].

The indefinite *on* has almost completely replaced *nous* as a subject proform, as in ON *dit pas ça nous-autres, eux-autres, oui.* On, however, is frequently replaced by *ça*, as in ÇA *sait pas faire*. Note, also, in the first example how *autres* is added to disjunctive proforms.

Verb stems are frequently regularised, for example *je vas*, *vous disez* and *ils vontaient* (cf. *vais*, *dites* and *allaient*, respectively), as are infinitives and past participles, for example *tiendre* instead of *tenir*, *reviendre* for *revenir*, *taisé* instead of *tu* (from *taire*), *mouru* instead of *mort*.

4.1.3 Vocabulary

The lexicon comprises some items which are obsolete in Standard French, although they may be present in regional varieties (the versions in brackets are the Standard French equivalents), for example *icitte* (*ici*), *espérer* (*attendre*), *conter* (*raconter*), *les hardes* (*vêtements*), *catin* (*poupée*), *acceptance* (*acceptation*), *besson* (*jumeau*), *mitaine* (*mouffle*), *capot* (*manteau*), *ouvrage* (*travail*), *devant que* (*avant de*), *mouiller* (*pleuvoir*), *tirer* (*traire*) and *jaser* (*parler*).

Neologisms abound, also, for local flora, fauna and realia, for instance *épinette* 'spruce', *poudrerie* 'windblown snow', *beigne* 'doughnut', *avant-midi* (*matinée*) and *cacasser* (*bavarder*). Some terms represent what might be termed 'anti-anglicisms', for example *fin de semaine* (*week-end*), *traversier* (*ferry-boat*) and *magasiner* (*faire du shopping*). Canadian French has also exploited possibilities offered by derivation, as in *jardinERIE* 'garden centre', *circulETTE* 'handout' and *inlogeABLE* (*inhabitable*), to create new scientific or technical terms, or avoid sexism in language, as in the feminines *auteurE* and *écrivainE* 'woman writer'.

A further source is provided by English words, either borrowed or transposed, for instance *anticiper* (*prévoir*), *disconnecter* (*couper*), *centre d'achat* (*centre commercial*), *expecter* (*attendre*), *checker* (*vérifier*), *mouver* (*déménager*), *truster* (*avoir confiance*), *dissatisfait* (*mécontent*), *dépendre* (*compter sur*) and *jouer les second violons* (*passer au second plan*).

4.1.4 Syntax

Here, too, there are similiarities with other forms of regional French or the more informal registers of spoken French. *Ne* is absent from sentential negation (4: 12) in spoken Canadian French, as in *J'ai pas vu*. In the following sentence, note the use of the conditional in the condition clause (4: 11.3) introduced by *si*: *Ça serait meilleur* SI ÇA SERAIT CHAUD. Conjunctions such as *avant que* and *bien que* are followed by an indicative and not a subjunctive. In interrogative sentences (4: 1.5) *quand*, *où*, *comment* and *pourquoi* are frequently reinforced by *que*, as in QUAND QUE *vous viendrez?* and OÙ QUE *tu vas?* Similarly, a temporal clause introduced by *quand* may take the form QUAND C'EST QUE *vous viendrez?* For interrogative constructions, inversion (or movement; 4: 7) is seldom used, being replaced by intonation or the use of compound interrogatives, as in *qui c'est qui, de quoi, quoi que* and *où c'est que*, hence, QUOI QUE *tu fais?* and DE QUOI QUE *tu parles?* Note, also, the position of the non-subject proform in negative imperative structures *Fâchez-VOUS pas, Parlez-MOI plus.*

By way of illustration, note how this brief extract from Antonine Maillet's *La Sagouine* (1974) attempts to signal in its adaptation of the orthography of Standard French several of the features listed above:

> Nous autres, parsoune s'en vient frotter chus nous. Parsoune s'en vient non plus laver nos hardes. Ni coudre, ni raccommoder. Ils pouvont ben nous trouver guenilloux: je portons les capots usés qu'ils nous avont baillés pour l'amour de Jésus-Christ. Par chance qu'ils avont de la religion: ils pensont des fois à nous douner par charité leux vieilles affaires. Leux vieilles affaires et leux vieilles hardes qu'étiont neuves un jour que ça nous faisait rêver d'en aouère des pareilles. Je finissons par les receouère pour nous payer de nos journées d'ouvrage, mais quand c'est que j'en avons pus envie.
>
> (Maillet 1974: 17)

4.2   Regional varieties in the Indian Ocean: Réunion

In the Indian Ocean the existence of a regional variety of French has also been attested. The situation of Réunion is particularly interesting since this is the only territory to come under French colonial rule in the seventeenth and eighteenth centuries (1: 2.5) which has remained continuously in French hands since the first settlements. Although the early linguistic and social histories of the Mascarene islands are fairly similar, their paths diverge after 1814 when Mauritius, the Seychelles and Rodrigues passed into British hands. While English became the official language of these territories, no strong policy of 'anglicisation' was pursued, a factor which was decisive in the maintenance of both French and the French-lexicon creole (5: 5), spoken by the majority of the population. As for Réunion, one further important contributing factor to its present linguistic situation is that the number of ethnic whites, whether direct settlers from France or Creoles (that is, Europeans born on the island), has always been substantial, and indeed even today represents approximately 25 per cent of the population (Chaudenson 1979a: 176). Réunion's status as a *département d'outre-mer* (1: 2.2) has also involved the presence of a number of metropolitan French civil servants, and has provided some opportunities for education or work in France for native-born Réunionnais.

Thus, on a linguistic level, several varieties are in contact, forming a continuum of varieties, namely Standard French (the official language), a regional French (spoken by the prosperous middle classes, not solely of white ethnic origin) and a French-lexicon creole (see Gueunier 1985: 161–74). The regional variety has been characterised by Chaudenson (1979a: 79) as the variety which developed independently of the standard out of the dialects of French spoken by the original colonists. Note also that, with the exception of the Zoreils (the metropolitan French), all Réunionnais speak creole, 25 per cent being bilingual French–creole speakers.

Although there are special factors which, to some extent, set Réunion apart from the other islands in its settlement history and linguistic evolution, the characteristics of the forms of regional French spoken in Réunion and Mauritius, according to Chaudenson (1979b: 528–43), differ in degree rather than kind. As we'll see, many of the features of pronunciation or morpho-syntax find parallels in contemporary or older metropolitan regional varieties.

4.2.1   Phonology

Some of the most salient features of the pronunciation of the regional variety of French found on Réunion concern the weak rounding of front rounded vowels, the absence of the distinction between mid-low and mid-high vowels, and of the contrast between [a] and [ɑ], although the nasal [œ̃] is maintained.

With consonants, the most noticeable feature is the weakly articulated [ʀ], which may disappear entirely, especially after the back vowels [o] and [u], as in *porte* [poːt] and *C'est pour parler* [sepuːpale]. A weakened articulation of the voiceless stops [t] and [d] results in the affricates [tˢ] and [dᶻ] before high front vowels (note that the same feature is present in Canadian French; 5: 4.1.1), the glide [j] and the consonant [ʒ], as in *il a dit* [iladᶻi]. Also noteworthy is a tendency to merge [ʃ] and [ʒ] with [s] and [z] respectively, as in *chat* [sa] and *bouge* [buːz].

Voiced stops tend to nasalise after a nasal vowel, and are realised as the corresponding weak nasal consonant, as in *la jambe* [laʒãᵐ]. Consonant clusters are reduced, as in *capable* [kapab], a feature shared with informal registers of French, and, just as in dialects or regional French varieties of the west and north-west (see also Canada), final [t] is pronounced, as in *canot* [kanɔt] and *bout* [but].

4.2.2   Morpho-syntax

With periphrastic temporal and aspectual verb forms (4: 15), many features are common to seventeenth-century varieties of French or regional varieties, for instance *être à* and *être après* (*être en train de*). Similarly, *finir de* is used for a completed action and the future is expressed by *aller* + infinitive.

Avoir, and not *être*, is the usual auxiliary for intransitive verbs, as in J'AI *monté*. The indicative is preferred to the subjunctive in contexts such as *Il faut que tu* VIENS, *Je veux que tu* PRENDS and *pour que tu* FAIS.

There is some levelling in the distinction between the use of direct and indirect proforms, as in *Vous pouvez* LA *téléphoner* (*lui téléphoner*) and *Je* LES donne un livre (leur donne) (4: 4.1–2). Also noticeable is the absence of à, de and que as functional morphemes (words with a purely grammatical function), as in un CHAUFFEUR TAXI (de taxi) and On peut penser C'EST VRAI (que c'est vrai).

4.2.3   Vocabulary

The regional variety found on Réunion contains specific terms, often borrowed from other indigenous languages, to refer to local features such as flora, fauna, food and technical or agricultural terms, as in [tat] 'woven basket' and [kari] 'curry'. Other items may share with one or other dialect of French a meaning which differs from the standard, for example tirer instead of prendre, gagner for obtenir and chemin in place of rue or route, or may be neutral in connotation while having low-register or vulgar connotations in the standard, such as bougre (homme), marmaille (enfant) and baiser (tromper).

Lexical creativity also manifests itself by derivation, for example the noun arrosement is derived from arroser (arrosage) and jurage comes from jurer (jurement). Adjectives may be derived from verbs with the suffix -eur (3: 1.3; 3: 5), for example assassineur (assassin) or baiseur 'of poor quality', 'unreliable', and adverbs from adjectives with the suffix -ment, as in droitement (droit), or from another adverb, as in moindrement (moindre).

Although Canadian French and the regional variety found in Réunion obviously have some specific features, many of these can also be found in continental varieties, in other dialects or styles. Thus, these varieties remain close relatives of Standard French, as well as being distinctive varieties with their own norms, through the unique combination of these features.

4.3   Regional varieties in Africa

The notion that there exist varieties of French in Africa, which owe their existence to the particular conditions prevailing in one country or another, and don't merely reflect an imperfect mastery of the (written) standard, is a fairly recent one (see Makouta-Mboukou 1973). Although French may, as a result of colonisation, enjoy a special status by virtue of being the official language of several countries of sub-Saharan Africa, it's the mother tongue of only a minute proportion of the population. For most people, French (which is used to conduct public affairs and international business, and in the media, tourism, science and technology and literature) is a second language acquired at school. In other words, diglossia is a characteristic feature of these societies. It should also be remembered that, as an official and second language, French coexists with many other local languages. Societal bilingualism or multilingualism is therefore very frequent. As Manessy and Wald (1984) point out, this gives rise to considerable feelings of insecurity on the part of speakers for whom Standard French represents the desirable norm, and the non-recognition of variation within the French spoken in Africa.

Recently, however, the varieties of French spoken in sub-Saharan Africa have drawn the attention of researchers who have concluded that they present so many common features that it's possible to identify an African French which might serve as a regional norm, notably in education (see Manessy 1994). Bodies such as the Observatoire du français contemporain en Afrique Noire monitor and record regionalisms in both written and spoken usage. The study of the lexis has attracted particular attention centred on the IFA project (*Inventaire des particularités lexicales du français en Afrique Noire*) covering twelve African countries, namely Benin, Burkina Faso, Cameroon, Central African Republic (CAF), Chad, Ivory Coast, Mali, Niger, Rwanda, Senegal, Togo and Zaire. The project team published, in 1983 and 1988, a compilation of over 10,000 lexical items specific to the regions concerned in three main categories: borrowings, neologisms and terms which have undergone semantic shift. Borrowings stem unsurprisingly from African languages, such as *néos* (a type of fruit) and *toubab* 'white man', or European languages other than French, for instance from English *boy*, *coconotte*, *man* and *bill*. These borrowings, once integrated, may give rise to new derivatives either by compounding or using French suffixes, such as *boy-magasin*, *boy-chauffeur*, *boy de table*, and the female counterpart *boyesse*, *toubabesse* 'white woman' and *toubabiser* 'to behave like a white person'. Many neologisms relate to local flora and fauna, for example, *baobab*, *oiseau-palmiste*, *capitaine* (types of tree, bird and fish respectively) material objects, for instance *essencerie* (*pompe à essence*), or cultural practices and idiomatic expressions, such as *avoir bouffé un nid de guêpes* 'to be overexcited'. Similarly, a Standard French item may lead by derivation to the creation of verbs, such as *arriérer* (*reculer*), *cigaretter* (*fumer*), *doigter* (*montrer du doigt*), *confiturer* (*mettre de la confiture sur son pain*), *enceinter* 'to make pregnant' and *gréver* (*faire grève*). Some verbs are used reflexively, such as *se déambuler*, or intransitively, while in Standard French they are transitive, as in *préparer* (*faire la cuisine*), *accorder* (*donner son accord*). For further examples, see Lafage (1993) and Dumont and Maurer (1995).

As this very schematic and incomplete survey of *les français régionaux* has illustrated, the greater part of linguistic variation in this geographical perspective concerns phonology and vocabulary. Within France, morpho-syntactic variation is particularly vulnerable to normative pressures exerted by the promotion of the standard in education. Similarly, regional accents are also in the process of undergoing levelling, albeit more slowly. For their part, lexical items will either disappear with the way of life and realities they describe, or become part of the common stock of the standard. Outside France, a different problem is posed, namely that of the relationship between the French of France and that of other countries which use it; that is, how to achieve the delicate balance between geographical variation, local norms and preserving mutual understanding within the wider Francophone world.

5   French-lexicon creoles

When presenting the diffusion of French world-wide it has frequently been noted that, in many parts of the world, French is in contact with other languages, especially with French-lexicon creoles. Before tackling the fundamental and highly controversial question of the relationship between French and these creoles, especially in the context of varieties of French, let's consider the term creole and the origins of creoles.

5.1   The origins of creoles

The term *créole* originally referred to whites of European descent, born and raised in the tropics. It was later extended to include indigenous and other peoples of non-European origin and, finally, to refer to the languages spoken in and around the Caribbean, West Africa, the Indian Ocean and other parts of the world, where new languages had arisen out of the particular social conditions that prevailed after colonisation of these territories.

In social and historical terms, the label creole refers to a language which, it's thought (Hall 1966, Hudson 1996), developed from an earlier pidgin, that is a trade or vehicular language devised, for the purposes of basic communication, by adults who didn't share a language. The need for these pidgins arose in the period of colonisation by Europeans of newly discovered territories (from the sixteenth to eighteenth centuries), mostly situated in the equatorial areas, and the organisation of plantation economies dependent on large populations of slave labour imported from Africa. The pidgin would thus provide a means of communication between slaves and their owners, and among slaves from different ethnic and linguistic groups. Creoles are usually defined as pidgins which have stabilised and expanded their linguistic resources after 'acquiring' native speakers (the children of the pidgin speakers). In other words, after becoming mother tongues and having to fulfil a wide variety of communicative functions (particularly for children for whom the creole was a first language), emergent creoles needed to acquire a more extensive vocabulary and develop a more explicit system of grammatical relations. In the social conditions prevailing in the areas concerned, it's hardly surprising that, at the very least, the expansion of the lexicon should have drawn widely on the dominant European language (or **lexifier language**), hence the term French-lexicon creole. (Note that once a creole has established itself, it will be subject to the normal processes of language change, while exhibiting the same range of variation as any other natural language.)

The view that creoles were merely corrupt or degenerate versions of European languages, used in the plantations of the tropics as a marginal mode of communication between slaves and their masters, and were therefore unworthy of interest, is one that linguists themselves shared until late into the nineteenth century. Widespread recognition of creoles as languages in their own right is more recent still. Controversy still rages as to the exact processes at work in the genesis of creoles, but on one thing most are agreed: namely, these languages developed surprisingly quickly, in a matter of decades rather than centuries. (For an exposé of the various hypotheses concerning the genesis of creoles see Romaine 1988, Sebba 1997.)

5.2 The distribution of French-lexicon creoles

According to Hancock (1977), there are 127 pidgin and creole languages in the world, fifteen of which are classified as French creoles and concentrated in two main equatorial areas. In the Caribbean, French-lexicon creoles can be subdivided into Greater Antillean creoles (Haitian and Louisiana French Creole) and Lesser Antillean creoles (Guadaloupean, Dominican, Martiniquan, St Lucian, Trinidadian, Grenadian and Guyanais). In the Indian Ocean the major concentrations are in the Seychelles, Rodrigues, Mauritius, Réunion and New Caledonia. Although French-lexicon creoles survive only precariously on islands with a mixed or English-dominated colonial history, such as Dominica, St Lucia, Trinidad and Grenada, it's thought that approximately ten million people in the world now speak a variety of French-lexicon creole, over half of whom are in Haiti (Green 1986, Prudent 1990).

5.3 The French connection

There are a number of reasons to discuss creoles in a book about French. First, the history of the places where French creoles are found makes clear the link between French colonisation (and the development of the slave trade) and the emergence of distinct societies, cultures and languages. Second, a large portion of creole vocabulary is etymologically related to Standard or dialectal French, just as many correspondences can be established between the sound systems. Indeed, as Posner argues (1986), these factors alone justify considering French creoles part of the same language family as French. More down-to-earth arguments would include the fact that there is a degree of mutual comprehensibility, not only among different French creoles (a fact with intriguing implications), but also between creole and French. Native speakers of French may experience some difficulties understanding creole but then, as remarked by Green (1986: 175), they would also experience considerable difficulty understanding many metropolitan dialects and *patois*. Above all, French and creole coexist in many creole-speaking communities (typically in a relationship of diglossia) and in many bilinguals. Many monolingual creole speakers even believe themselves to be speaking a form of French, although this perceived relationship to French often gives rise to feelings of linguistic insecurity (Gueunier *et al.* 1978: 184–9, Baker 1986: 87).

5.4   Some features of French creoles

Although each French-lexicon creole forms a distinctive linguistic system, there are striking similarities between creoles, even when the length and continuity of contact with French differ greatly, and when contact between one regional variety and another can never have been great. At one end of the scale we might place Réunionnais, where, as we saw in 5: 4.2, contacts between creole and French have been constant and extensive, making Réunionnais both different from other Indian Ocean creoles and more similar to French. At the other end of the scale, there's Haitian (Haiti has been independent for two centuries), where only a small proportion of the population come into contact with French. For further details on these and many other points, see Green (1988: 420–75) and Chaudenson (1979a, 1979b, 1995). In order to exemplify some of the features of creoles we discuss in the rest of the section, here is an extract from the story of Little Red Riding Hood in Mauritian Creole:

[ɛn fwa dãɛn pei ɛn tˢi fi ki tˢapɛl ʃapeɣɔ̃ ɣuːʒ
Il y avait une fois dans un pays une petite fille qui s'appelait Chaperon Rouge.

li tˢabi tultã avɛk ɣuː li pɔ ɛn ɣɔb ɣuːʒ ɛn bɔne ɣuːʒ
Elle s'habillait toujours de rouge. Elle portait une robe rouge, un bonnet rouge

avɛk ɛn tʀiko ɣuːʒᵊ ɛn ʒu so mãmã dˢĩ ãlɛ̃ kɔ̃sa
et un tricot rouge. Un jour sa maman lui dit:

al ɡet to ɡɣãmɛ ki ɣeziᵈ dãɛn bwa
'Va voir ta grand-mère qui habite dans le bois

li malad li pɛna mãʒe dɔn li de ɡalɛt
Elle est malade, elle n'a rien à manger. Donne-lui deux galettes

sɛtadi de dˢipɛ̃ avɛk ɛn po dˢibɛ avɛk ɛn po lakɣɛm]
c'est-à-dire deux pains avec un pot de beurre et un pot de crème.'

5.4.1   Phonology

The vowel systems operate either with seven oral vowels (Haitian) or five (Mauritian), two high [i, u], two mid [e, o] and [a] (Haitian also has [ɛ, ɔ]). There are no front rounded vowels; corresponding to the French front rounded vowels [y, ø, œ] we find the unrounded [i, e, ɛ], as in *du* [di], *deux* [de], *du beurre* [dᶻibɛʀ]. With nasal vowels, the absence of rounding has also led to the coalescence of [ɛ̃] and [œ̃], although Haitian is exceptional here. In the text in 5: 5.4, note how *un* and *une* are realised as [ɛn].

Characteristic of consonants is the reduction of consonant clusters and of post-vocalic [ʀ], especially in Caribbean varieties, as in *partir* [pati] and *sortir* [soti], whereas in Indian Ocean varieties [ʀ] is usually realised with a weakened articulation, for example [paᵛti]. Prevocalically, Indian Ocean varieties use a velar or uvular fricative [ʀ, ᵛ], so, in Mauritian, we hear [ᵛeziᵈ] and [gᵛãmɛᵛ], as in Haitian and Louisianais, but in Martinique, Guyana and the Seychelles this tends to labialise to [w], as in *terrible* [tewib]. Another characteristic is the palatalisation of stops [t, d, k, g] before [i, j] – for instance, Mauritian *dit* is pronounced [dᶻi], while a more limited development concerns the depalatalisation of [ʃ, ʒ] in Indian Ocean creoles, leading to merger with [s, z], as in *chat* [sa] *joli* [zoli] and *manger* [mãze] (Mauritian).

5.4.2 Morpho-syntax

Nouns are marked neither for gender nor, in most instances, for number. Many nouns have restructured, incorporating determiners, hence 'water' [dilo]/[dlo] < *de l'eau*, 'bird(s)' [zwazo] < *les oiseaux*, 'elephant(s)' [nelefã] < *un éléphant*, 'loaf/loaves' (Mauritian) [dᶻipɛ̃] < *du pain*. The determiners have been reanalysed as part of the noun, and their presence is unrelated to whether the noun is singular or plural in the particular context. Unlike nouns in French, nouns can be determiner-less (4: 2.1): (Louisianais) *des plis gros bêtes que yena dans moune* (*des plus grosses bêtes qu'il y a dans* LE *monde*). The postnominal particle [la] is used as a determiner, with definite reference, as in [famla] *la femme*; [sa] is used as the sole demonstrative, before the noun (Guyana, Indian Ocean) or after it (Louisiana and Caribbean), for example [ʃatsa] *ce chat*.

One of the most conspicuous differences from French lies in the use of preverbal particles to mark tense and aspect, while the verb itself remains essentially invariable. These particles take many forms, such as:

- progressive: [ape], [ap], [pe]; [mo ape travaj] 'I am working' (Louisianais), [u pe ale] 'Where are you going?' (Mauritian);
- past: [te], [ti]; [mwɛ te malad] 'I was ill' (Dominican), [li ti fin malad] 'He had been ill' (Mauritian);
- perfective: [fin]; [lulu fin degize] 'The wolf has disguised himself' (Mauritian).

Note, in (Mauritian) [li malad], a much-debated point, namely whether creoles possess copulas or not. Whereas in French (but not in Russian!) the verb *être* would be necessary in this context, as in *Je suis malade* (4: 1.4), many creoles have a more complex, tripartite system using *se* with a noun phrase [se to liv] *c'est ton livre*, *ye* in an interrogative sentence [kote li ye] *où est-il?* and the zero copula, as illustrated above, before an adjective.

Negatives are formed using [pa], which precedes the verb, except in Réunionnais, for example (Mauritian) [li pa vini] and (Réunionnais) [li mãz pa].

The word order of sentences is generally subject–verb–object, although, contrary to French, non-subject proforms don't cliticise onto the verb, as in (Seychelles) *il nous a dit* [i ti dir nu]. In Haitian, and most other Caribbean varieties, there is no overt marker for relative clauses, whereas Indian Ocean creoles mark subordination by [ki], as in (Mauritian) *qui réside* [kiɣeziᵈ].

5.4.3   Vocabulary

The core vocabulary of French-lexicon creoles can, with few exceptions, be traced back to French in a more or less standard form, especially if one allows for restructured forms such as [dilo] or [dlo] (5: 5.4.2). However, some lexical items show a change of grammatical category, as in the adjectives *capable* [kapa/kapav] and *content* [kɔ̃tã] which function as the verbs 'to be able to' and 'to like', respectively, or nouns reanalysed as adverbs, such as [lɛ], which can be traced to *l'heure*, but means 'when'.

Lexical creativity manifests itself in the process of reduplication, which serves for intensification or emphasis, for instance (Haitian) [litebɛlbɛl] 'she was extremely beautiful' or (Mauritian) [vitvit] 'at the double'.

5.5   The French/creole continuum

Although various lexical and phonological correspondences can be established between French and French creoles, there are nevertheless significant morpho-syntactic differences between the two. These parallels and differences not only offer fascinating grounds for speculation on the genesis of languages in general (see Bickerton 1975, 1981, 1984a, b), but are also a rich source for the exploration of language evolution, variation and matters of language contact, in addition to the intrinsic linguistic interest of these languages.

In many of the countries we have mentioned, where French and creole coexist, the relationship between the two has been described as a continuum. The presence of a standard language such as French, and the prestige it exerts by virtue of its role in society, may bring creole speakers to shift towards it, producing a spectrum of varieties (Bickerton 1975: 24) and leading to eventual decreolisation. Such situations bring to mind comparisons with the evolution of the dialects in France. But, as Posner (1986: 127) points out, speakers' attitudes towards the languages they speak are crucial. If there is a feeling of identity and continuity with French, we might speculate that, in some contexts, the creoles might evolve towards convergence with their original lexifier language (French), whereas in contexts where, for reasons of national and cultural identity, autonomy is sought, the evolution might take the path of divergence, through the standardisation of the creole itself as a means of increasing literacy, education and economic development (Aub-Buscher 1993).

6 Social variation

Taking account of geography enables us to observe and catalogue different varieties of French, but this is just one of the factors which undermine what Lyons (1981: 24) calls 'the fiction of homogeneity', that is, the belief that all members of a speech community speak exactly the same language. In the context of varieties of French, geographical variation is the most significant aspect of the social dimension of variation, but other, personal, extra-linguistic, factors may influence a speaker's linguistic system. Indeed, the choices that speakers make are determined, first, by their own social characteristics (where they come from, their age, sex, ethnic or social background, for instance) giving rise to what is termed **inter-speaker variation**, or variation according to user, and, second, as we'll discuss more fully later (5: 7), by the situation of language use (also known as **intra-speaker variation**). Note, finally, that these factors affecting language use, whether social or stylistic, don't operate independently of each other, but constantly interact.

Returning to social variation determined by speaker characteristics, age is clearly one factor influencing language use. This is a phenomenon that sociolinguists refer to as age-grading. For instance, French-speaking children may use vocabulary that an adult would not, for instance *nounours* or *faire dodo*. Similarly, they might use *tu* as a general form of address until, through education and more extensive contacts outside the family circle, they become aware of the social conventions regulating the use of *tu* and *vous* and gradually adopt the adult norms. In adulthood, a clear correlation can be established between linguistic usage and occupation. The higher up the professional scale individuals are, the more their speech is likely to conform to the prestigious variety, and, conversely, the less likely they are to use regional or dialectal forms. Coveney (1996) gives an instance of how age-grading affects linguistic behaviour, when he reports, in a study of the variable use of *ne* in spoken French, that, although young speakers in the 17–23 age range use *ne* very infrequently in negative sentences, their use of *ne* increases as they reach their mid-twenties and enter the world of work. On the other hand, there is evidence that people who move out of work and into retirement also alter their linguistic behaviour and make less use of the more formal varieties.

Age, linked in some instances to ethnic origin, also appears to be a determining factor in the linguistic behaviour of adolescents and young adults, who are the most resistant to pressure from the prestige standard. Their

speech, dubbed *la langue des jeunes* by the media and some linguists, is characterised, above all, by intense lexical creativity (5: 8.3.3). *La langue des
jeunes* acts as a powerful badge of identity, too, a means of distancing the
group from both children and adults, or even an expression of revolt against
authority (linguistic and otherwise) and social conditions.

A second factor in language use is gender. In France, as in most western
societies, speech habits for males and females are influenced by cultural
stereotypes and conventions. These account, for instance, for the fact that
women are allegedly more cooperative in conversational exchanges, use less
slang and fewer swear words. The most characteristic difference between
male and female behaviour, however, is what Fasold (1990: 92) terms 'the
sociolinguistic gender pattern', according to which women have a tendency
to adhere more closely to the prestigious standard forms, while men use
more vernacular forms. While it has been suggested that these differences
might be explained in terms of social roles, or even by the innate conservatism of women, a more satisfactory explanation might again lie in the
power of language to act as a badge of identity or solidarity. In other words,
women identify with other women, while men identify with other men,
through their use of linguistic patterns that contrast with those used by the
opposite sex.

As implied above, a final factor which closely interrelates with age and
sex to produce social variation in language use is related to socio-economic
status, as correlated with education, occupation, income and lifestyle.

7   Stylistic variation

Aside from the variation induced by the social characteristics of the speakers,
to account more fully for variation within French we also need to consider
variation according to use, or intra-speaker variation (5: 6). In this section
we'll consider the dimension of style, or the way in which speakers, according
to circumstances, draw upon their own linguistic repertoire to manipulate
and adapt the resources and alternatives that the language has to offer.
After defining the terms stylistic varieties and register (5: 7.1), we'll consider
the areas where variation occurs in the language system, together with the
factors that determine the selection of stylistic varieties in French (5: 7.2–6).
Finally, we'll examine the characteristic features of the registers of French,
and the status of these varieties in relation to the standard (5: 8).

7.1   *Stylistic varieties and registers*

When speaking, or even writing, native speakers of any language can, to
a greater or lesser extent, depending on the individual, control a range of
stylistic varieties and say more or less the same thing in different ways
appropriate to the context. Intra-speaker variation lies within the users
themselves and forms an integral part of their linguistic competence.

Drawing upon their own linguistic repertoire, speakers adopt certain structures and lexical items, and even modify their pronunciation, depending on the medium of communication (writing or speech), or what Halliday (1968) calls the mode of discourse. Manner of discourse, that is, the context in which communication takes place, also affects the (in)formality of the language used. Style (or register, as it's sometimes called) will be influenced by subject matter (whether discussing theoretical syntax or the World Cup), by the speaker's intentions (to inform, amuse, persuade), but, above all, by the relationship between the various participants in a particular setting. So variation manifests itself in the speakers' response to their perception of the level of (in)formality of a communicative situation, by selecting the appropriate variety or style, and altering their linguistic behaviour accordingly.

As a rather simple illustration, consider the behaviour of a particular individual (for reasons we'll point out later, the speaker has to be male), alternatively using the following forms of address:

(1) Je vous prie d'agréer, Madame, mes hommages respectueux.
(2) Mes hommages, Madame.
(3) Enchanté, Mademoiselle.
(4) Mon général.
(5) Bonjour Madame, deux croissants, s'il vous plaît.
(6) Comment allez-vous, Lambert?
(7) Ça va, Jean?
(8) Comment va ma petite chérie?

In these examples we observe Monsieur X adapting his style to the medium (writing in (1) versus speech in (2)–(8)), the sex of the addressee (female in (1), (2), (3), (5) and (8), but male in (4), (6) and (7)), his status in relation to the addressee (inferiority in the case of (1), (2), (3) and (4), equality in (5) and (6)), and the relationships of deference ((1), (2), (3) and (4)), friendship (7) or affection (8), which Monsieur X wishes to convey. Finally, we see him altering his linguistic behaviour according to his perception of the (in)formality of the communicative situation.

We conclude that the user is male and fully aware of the niceties of usage concerning the forms of address appropriate to a man greeting members of his own or of the opposite sex (only a man would use the title *Mon général*; a woman would merely use *Général* or *Monsieur*). In addition, this insight into his linguistic repertoire (the set of linguistic varieties he has at his command) enables us to hazard an estimation of the speaker's age, level of education and socio-economic status.

Our positive responses to Monsieur X's utterances (our approval that they are contextually appropriate) therefore rest, not only upon recognition of the existence of variation within French, but also on our appreciation that this variation occurs between certain boundaries, both social and linguistic.

Should Monsieur X have produced (9) instead of (2), his lapse into stylistic incongruity, through not respecting the context (a man addressing a married woman) in which it's considered appropriate for the phrase *mes hommages* to occur, would provoke instant revision of our judgement of Monsieur X, leading us to conclude that he is perhaps not as well educated as we originally thought, or as he'd have us believe.

(9) Mes hommages, Mademoiselle.

Such examples also illustrate, on the one hand, the links between linguistic and social behaviour in an individual, and, on the other, the social significance superimposed on language in terms of the value judgements that members of the speech community place on the utterances of others.

Similarly, (10) isn't acceptable, for it obviously contravenes the structural rules of question formation in French (4: 7.1–2). So, while variation along a scale of (in)formality is a normal feature of language use, it remains subject to the constraints imposed by the grammar itself.

(10) *Allez-vous comment Lambert?

7.2   Variation within the language system

Where does variation occur? If French manifests the normal range of variation on both an individual and a social level, and if a view of French as a homogeneous and fixed construct cannot realistically be maintained, we should nevertheless not conclude that variation is random and anarchic. It has been suggested, notably by Martinet and Walter (Martinet 1945, 1955, Martinet and Walter 1973, Walter 1976, 1988, Gadet 1989), that variation in French (most notably in the sound system) is due to internal readjustments and governed by the principle of least effort. In this view, a language is a self-regulating system, and the principle of least effort works towards reducing the number of distinctions existing in the language and maximising the work that each performs. However, this is held in check by the need to maintain sufficient distinctions to ensure communicative clarity and effectiveness. Therefore, the language system can be seen as consisting of an assembly of stable, non-variable elements, together with a number of 'weak points', subject to variation.

7.3   Areas of instability in the sound system

We saw earlier (2: 11.3) that the contrast between the nasal vowels [ɛ̃] and [œ̃] distinguishes the meanings of very few words, and that even when the distinction isn't maintained, communication isn't seriously impeded. Thus, the contrast may be considered by speakers not to be cost-effective;

that is, given the effort required, the rewards may be so insignificant that the less frequent vowel [œ̃] appears redundant. The maximal system of French vowels includes other vowel pairs showing a low functional yield, that is, where the meaningful contrasts they offer with their counterparts in the system are fewest, for example the distinctions between [a] and [ɑ], and [ɛː] and [ɛ] (2: 8.7.3; 2: 12).

A further area of possible variation is suggested by the vigorous pronouncements of pedagogues and grammarians since the seventeenth century in favour of the maintenance of [ɛ] in final open syllables (2: 10.3), enabling, for example, contrasts between *piquet* [pikɛ] and *piquait* [pikɛ], and the differentiation in speech of verb tenses of the type *je parlai* [paʀle] and *je parlais* [paʀlɛ]. Vowel harmony (2: 10.4) and the behaviour of *e-muet* also provide scope for variation in usage, with optional deletion of *e-muet* (2: 9.2) or the possibility of adding an epenthetic *e-muet*, unmotivated by orthography, to serve as a lubricant in complex consonant clusters, for example *best seller* [bɛstəsele:ʀ], rather than [bɛstsele:ʀ]. Finally, while the vowels of French are described normatively as requiring firm and constant muscular tension, and not being subject to reduction, whatever their position in the word or utterance, we noted the possible elision of the vowel [y], as in *Tu as vu?* [tavy], or [e] in *C'est un imbécile* [stɛ̃ɛ̃besil] versus [setɛ̃ɛ̃besil] or [setœ̃ɛ̃besil] (2: 8.7.2; 2: 15.2).

The consonant most subject to variation is [ʀ], as we saw in the survey of geographical varieties. Complex consonant clusters can also undergo reduction, particularly in the context of consonant + liquid before a word starting with a consonant, as in *une autre fois* [ynotfwa], as opposed to [ynotʀəfwa]. This, as we saw, is linked to the behaviour of *e-muet* which, in turn, can bear on some aspects of assimilation (2: 6). A further area of choice, which is highly salient sociolinguistically, is the 'optional' category of liaisons in connected speech. In this respect, additional difficulties can arise for speakers since, in many cases, the liaison consonant has to be retrieved from the written form, and cannot be predicted from the spoken form of the words taken in isolation, for example *aspects* [aspe] but *des aspects incongrus* [dezaspezɛ̃kɔ̃gʀy], *quand* [kɑ̃], but *quand il viendra* [kɑ̃tilvjɛ̃dʀa].

7.4 Variation in morpho-syntax

In syntax we could argue, as we did for vowel contrasts, that preverbal *ne* is redundant, and that postverbal *pas* or *rien* are sufficient to express sentential negation. In speech, as in *Je pense pas, C'est pas évident* or *Il a rien fait, ne* is frequently omitted. Sentence structure also offers scope for variation, for instance with regard to inversion in interrogatives, as in *Irez-vous?, Est-ce que vous irez?, Vous irez?*, or in subordinate clauses, as in *l'homme dont Jean parle, l'homme dont parle Jean*, or on purely stylistic grounds, *peut-être faudra-t-il, peut-être qu'il faudra* (4: 7.1–3). In writing particularly, there is choice within the tense system between the past-historic and the compound-past, as in *Le 1er août, la radio annonça/a annoncé une nouvelle baisse de l'euro*, the synthetic future or the analytical future, as in *Elle viendra/va venir*, not to mention the sequence of tenses, for instance *Je n'accepterais pas que l'on me donnât/me donne*, or indeed the knottier points of agreement *la décision que j'ai pris/prise*. The use of subject proforms (4: 4.3) *on* versus *nous*, or *tu* versus *vous*, are also related to questions of style and formality.

7.5   Lexical variation

The lexicon is an area where variation is particularly noticeable and, consequently, much more elusive to capture, since, of all aspects of language, vocabulary is most subject to change (3: 5.1; Wise 1997). It's estimated that some 25–30,000 new words enter the language every year (Pierre Encrevé, *Le Nouvel Observateur*, 27 September 1990) in response to the changing needs of the community. Social, cultural and technological change in particular imply a constant change in vocabulary, through either the creation or borrowing of new words, the extension, restriction or shifting of the meanings and function of old words, and the loss of some lexical items. This is reflected in dictionaries notably in the use of style labels, such as *littéraire, vulgaire, grossier, technique, familier, populaire* and *vieilli*. These would appear to present us with a bewildering array of what Sauvageot (1972: 115) terms *lexiques parallèles*, comprising numerous terms presented as synonyms. Here are a few examples, but note that the list is far from exhaustive for each of the terms illustrated:

manger	se nourrir	se sustanter	s'alimenter	se restaurer
	bouffer	bâfrer	grailler	picorer
voler	dérober	subtiliser	faucher	chiper
	chaparder	chiner	barboter	piquer
enfant	bambin	gamin	garçon	gosse
	marmot	mioche	môme	lardon
sale	malpropre	crasseux	crotté	souillé
	immonde	infâme	infect	dégueulasse

The publication in recent years of dictionaries bearing titles such as *Dictionnaire du français branché* (Merle 1989), *Dictionnaire de l'argot* (Colin and Mével 1992), *Dictionnaire du français non conventionnel* (Cellard and Rey 1991) and *Comment tu tchatches! Dictionnaire du français contemporain des cités* (Goudaillér 1997) seems, however, to present a more polarised situation through the distinction they make between items felt to be worthy of official recognition and those which hover on the fringes of polite society.

7.6   Stylistic variation within the social context

Insofar as styles are tied to the (in)formality of the relationship between the participants in a conversation and the context in which communica-

tion is taking place, they are themselves norms for particular communicative situations. For instance, while we would accept as an appropriate
response to a misunderstood question *Quoi?*, *Tu dis?* or even *Hein?* in the
family circle or among close friends, we might judge it more fitting to resort
to *Comment?*, *Pardon?* or even *Plaît-il?* between strangers, or in a formal
social situation such as a job interview. Again, the social context dictates
when it's appropriate to describe our mood as *J'en ai ras le bol*, *Je déprime*,
J'ai le cafard, *J'en ai plein les bottes* or *C'est pas la joie*, rather than *Je suis
déprimé(e)/découragé(e)/démoralisé(e)*.

Conversely, an impeccably formed statement, such as *J'EUSSE préféré des
pommes qui FUSSENT plus mûres*, is equally inappropriate when purchasing
fruit from a market stall, as its identification with a very formal and elevated
style makes it sound totally pretentious or ridiculous. Examples such as
these demonstrate how stylistic variation (and style shifting by speakers) is
closely associated with context and notions of appropriateness and acceptability.

Note, further, that, in the context of a complete utterance, speakers do
not, in most instances, switch wholesale between sets of distinct alternatives as they move from one communicative situation to another. What
we observe in reality, just as we did with geographical varieties, is a range
of available alternatives, forming a continuum or scale, ranging from extreme
formality at one end to extreme informality at the other. From a social
point of view, when native speakers assess the level of (in)formality of the
style being used (by themselves or by others), their judgements rest on an
assessment of the ratio of formal to informal features within an utterance,
rather than on single utterances containing a gamut of features that others
don't. For example, consider the remark in (11a) overheard on France-Inter
in 1990, and pronounced as (11b):

(11) a. Eh bien, dans ce cas, il me semble que ses chances soient
       inexistantes
     b. [e.bjɛ̃.dɑ̃.sə.ka.il.mə.sɑ̃bl.kə.se.ʃɑ̃s.swa.ti.nɛg.zis.tɑ̃t]

The remark could also have been rendered as (11c):

     c. [bɛ̃.dɑ̃.ska.im.sɑ̃b.kə.se.ʃɑ̃s.swa.i.nɛg.zis.tɑ̃t]

The pronunciation in (11b), with the carefully articulated *e-muet*, the use
of the subjunctive and the liaison in *soient inexistantes* provides several clues
to a more formal style; (11c) would be perceived as more informal, because
of the absence of liaison, the deletion of *e-muet*, the reduction of *eh bien*
to [bɛ̃], and of *il* to [i] before the consonant. The speaker nevertheless
followed the above remark with:

(12) a. Oui, y a pas d'espoir.

pronounced as:

> b. [wi.ja.pa.dɛs.pwaːʀ]

The absence of the negative particle *ne* and the reduction of *il y a* to [ja] would probably not make most listeners revise dramatically their judgement of his style, whereas if (12) were added to (11c), the impression of informality would only be reinforced.

Any attempt, therefore, to define the major stylistic levels of French on a scale of (in)formality will rest on identifying the most salient features of each, and their frequency. As we've seen, these features variously relate to pronunciation, intonation, syntax and lexis.

Summarising, when we consider from a social perspective how stylistic variants are used, three factors are relevant: stylistic appropriateness in a given situation, the status or value placed on a particular variety by society and, finally, the range of stylistic varieties an individual commands (the linguistic repertoire).

8   The stylistic continuum

For the purposes of the description here, we'll divide the continuum of stylistic variation into three levels, namely *le français soigné*, *le français familier* and *le français non standard*. (For a somewhat different approach, see Guiraud 1978, Müller 1975/1985, Gadet 1989.) It should be borne in mind, though, that these are artificial and rather simplistic divisions imposed by considerations of space, and that the reality behind them consists of subtle, imperceptible shifts, rather than rigidly defined, discrete categories.

After defining these styles in terms of the (in)formality of the communicative situation, we'll describe each one, first in terms of its functions, and, second in terms of the relevant linguistic markers (linguistic markers being, in Labov's (1972a) terms, the linguistic variables that carry social significance).

8.1   Le français soigné

Although authorities like dictionaries refer to this *niveau de langue* as *le français soutenu, littéraire, recherché* or *cultivé*, these terms clearly share with the label *soigné* positive connotations of elegance, refinement, sophistication and so on. *Le français soigné* is the style adopted in more formal and guarded situations, those demanding an awareness of the need 'to rise to the occasion'. In writing, this is the vehicle for the formal presentation of argument, information or requests, and might be found in essays, articles, academic papers, administrative or legal communications and job applications, as well as some imaginative and literary works. In speech, it might

occur in situations which don't correspond to true dialogue, the distance
– physical or social – between the speaker (who may even be speaking from
a prepared text) and his audience being such as to preclude reciprocal interaction. This would apply, for instance, to political speeches, lectures,
sermons, news broadcasts or poetry recitals. We might therefore charac-
terise this register as one which is used when the content or message takes
precedence over personal interaction (Brown 1982: 77).

While only a minority of native speakers would claim to command
this register fully (since a number of the contexts in which it's appropriate
are beyond the scope of everyday communicative experience), there is
nevertheless a general consensus that this register is the finest manifesta-
tion of *le bon français*, an attitude due in no small part to the perceived
socio-economic and cultural status of those who practise it. Nevertheless,
stylistic appropriateness remains essential. While (13), taken from a review
article (Domenac'h, in *L'Express*, 28 September 1990), would be positively
viewed:

(13) . . . il n'intéressa guère, bien qu'il éclairât magistralement la
condition féminine . . .

a parallel utterance, such as (14), might be viewed, in casual conversation,
as unnecessarily precious and pretentious, or be interpreted as seeking deliberate comic effect:

(14) Elle insista pour qu'on lui apportât un œuf à la coque.

The label *soigné* stresses the element of care or even conscious effort required
to attain and maintain this register. In the rest of this section, we'll see some
of its salient features in pronunciation, morpho-syntax and vocabulary.

8.1.1   Phonology

The contexts in which the formal style of *le français soigné* is used in speech,
and the conscious desire on the speaker's part to communicate effectively,
typically call for particular attention to be paid to a pronunciation which
will, as closely as possible, aim to reflect a textbook, standard type of pronunciation, including the avoidance of 'regional' features. This pronunciation
may therefore be generally described as conservative in nature. The careful
delivery demanded by public speaking or reading aloud usually brings about
a fairly monotonous intonation, with careful syllable timing and a slow
tempo. Similarly, the muscular tension characteristic of vowels is scrupu-
lously respected, hence the maintenance of vowel contrasts like [a] and [ɑ],
[œ̃] and [ɛ̃], and even the length contrast in such pairs as *mettre* [mɛtʀ]
and *maître* [mɛːtʀ]. Similarly, the contrast between mid-low and mid-high
vowels, in pairs like *jeune* [ʒœn] and *jeûne* [ʒøn], or *hôte* [ot] and *hotte* [ɔt],

is more likely to be maintained, despite the small number of pairs for which the contrast is distinctive.

Speakers may also take care to distinguish between future and conditional endings, realised as [e] and [ε] respectively, as in *je partirai* [e] and *je partirais* [ε], against the modern tendency to generalise the high vowel in final open position in casual speech. Indeed, the perception of this realisation of [ε] in final open syllables as the more elevated may lead to overgeneralisation and the extension of this pronunciation to contexts such as *les*, *mes* or *des*, and even to all *-ai* verb endings.

Careful articulation also leads to an avoidance of assimilation and vowel harmony, hence [obskyʀ], and not [opskyʀ], for *obscur*, or [mɛ̃tənã] for *maintenant*, and not [mɛ̃nã], [efemɛːʀ], and not [ɛfɛmɛːʀ], for *éphémère*.

When identifying a formal style, native speakers are also aware of behaviour with regard to *e-muet*, which tends to be realised more often in contexts where it can optionally be deleted, as in *Il marche vite* [il.maʀ.ʃə.vit], where *e-muet* is preceded by two consonants belonging to different syllables, or in the initial syllable of a word, as in *revenir* [ʀə.və.niːʀ] or [ʀə.vniːʀ]. (Remember that the full stop is a convention to indicate syllable boundaries.) In consecutive syllables, where alternate *e-muet* can be deleted, the second pronunciation above is more positively viewed than the equally possible [ʀvə.niʀ], which is associated with a less formal style. Note, also, that in poetic diction the pronunciation of *e-muet* may be essential to rhythm, as in (15):

(15) Comme le soir tombait l'homme sombre arriva
    [kɔ.mə.lə.swaʀ.tɔ̃.bɛ.lɔ.mə.sɔ̃.bʀa.ʀi.va]
    1 2 3 4   5 6 7 8 9 10 11 12

    Au bas d'une montagne en une grande plaine
    [o.ba.dy.nə.mɔ̃.taɲ.ã.ny.nə.gʀã.də.plɛn]
    1 2 3 4 5   6   7 8 9 10   11 12

                           (V. Hugo, 'La Conscience', 1964)

Since *e-muet* occurs more frequently, the consonant clusters which might have resulted from its deletion aren't simplified, for instance *autre chose* [otʀəʃoz], and not [otʃoz]. Similarly, complex consonant clusters are fully articulated, as in *expliquer* [eksplike] or *capable* [kapabl].

A further feature which is perceived as a strong marker of formality in connected speech is the realisation of optional liaisons (2: 15.5.3); the more a liaison is realised, the higher the style. It's interesting to note the increasing occurrence of what Encrevé (1983, 1988) terms *liaisons sans enchaînement* in the speech of politicians, broadcasters and public speakers. In *liaisons sans enchaînement*, the liaison consonant is pronounced, but without subsequent resyllabification onto the following vowel. In other words, the liaison consonant is pronounced, despite being followed by a pause, as in *(ceci) est intolérable* [ɛt | ɛ̃.to.le.ʀabl], as opposed to [ɛ.tɛ̃.to.le.ʀabl] with no pause, or [ɛ | ɛ̃.to.le.ʀabl] with no liaison. This practice may be interpreted as a desire to conform to the stereotype of 'good pronunciation', while maintaining clarity and expressiveness. But, while liaisons, when used correctly, are very positively viewed, misuse of liaisons (*liaisons mal-t-à-propos*) are equally strongly negatively viewed, and are seen as indicating either ignorance or hypercorrection, as in *cent enfants* [sɑ̃.zɑ̃.fɑ̃], or *les plus hardies*, overheard on France-Inter in 1999 as [plyzaʀdi].

8.1.2 Morpho-syntax

The most salient morpho-syntactic features relate to tense and mood, namely the past-historic, the past anterior and the subjunctive, especially in the imperfect and pluperfect, all of which feature far less prominently, if at all, in more informal contexts. Given the context, it's perhaps not surprising to find such an example in Marguerite Yourcenar's inaugural speech to the Académie française, reproduced in *Le Monde*, 22 January 1981:

> (16) Madame de Staël EÛT ÉTÉ sans doute inéligible par son
> ascendance suisse et son mariage suédois . . .

or, from the pen of a member of the Académie, in an open letter to the prime minister:

> (17) La guerre de l'accent circonflexe occupait presque autant de
> place que la guerre du Golfe. Pour empêcher qu'on SUPPRIMÂT
> quelques inutilités ou aberrations purement graphiques, on
> brandissait l'arme absolue de *l'usage*. . . . (M. Druon, *Le Figaro*,
> 29 September 1998).

Similarly, inversion may be used, and oral discourse may be punctuated by set phrases, such as *dirais-je* and *puis-je*. Characteristic of written texts is complex inversion for stylistic purposes (4: 7.2), as in *Sans doute faudra-t-il que le gouvernement agisse* and *Peut-être l'auteur de ces lignes avait-il espéré choquer*. Similarly, changes in word order, for example, the position of adjectives, may be induced by the search for stylistic effect, or considerations of rhythm and euphony:

> (18) IMPRESSIONNANT, son livre l'est par son architecture . . .
> CLANDESTINS, les personnages le sont par leur image sociale.
> (B. de Cassole, *L'Express*, 21 September 1990)

We noted earlier (4: 12) that, in formal spoken styles and in written French, preverbal *ne* isn't deleted. Generally, it marks sentential negation together with a second negative marker; additionally, with verbs like *oser*, *savoir* and *pouvoir*, it may be the sole marker of sentential negation, reflecting archaic usage:

> (19) C'est que, dans le monde de Hitchcock, aucune victime NE SAURAIT plaider l'innocence.

> (20) Qui NE COMMET chaque jour des fautes de français?

Further evidence of the conservative nature of this register at all levels is to be found in the maintenance of the first person plural subject proform *nous*, with *on* being restricted to its impersonal use, and in the use of certain impersonal constructions without the subject clitic proform *il*, as in *point n'est besoin de*, *mieux vaudrait* and *reste à déterminer*.

One syntactic feature, which is particularly salient in the quality press and in scientific and technical literature, is the use of nominal constructions (nouns, or nouns and adjectives) replacing relative clauses or an NP preceded by a preposition:

> (21) A long terme, on peut envisager LA MISE AU POINT de CIRCUITS MOLÉCULAIRES, sortes de transistors ou de mémoires chimiques. (G. Charles, *L'Express*, 21 September 1990)

The highlighted expressions correspond, respectively, to *envisager que l'on mettrait au point* and *des circuits de molécules*. The synthetic nature of these constructions contrasts fairly sharply with those found in less formal styles.

The tendency towards concision and economy has an impact on the creation of nouns or new adjectives derived from nouns (3: 5.2), with the most favoured suffixes being *-ique*, *-al*, *-el*, *-if* and *-isme*, hence:

> (22) Ce qui vient d'éclater, c'est cette bizarrerie IDÉOLOGIQUE qui avait fait du socialisme français l'héritier et le défenseur de deux idées-forces du reste rigoureusement contradictoires, qui n'avaient en commun que de s'être affirmées en France à la même époque, à la fin du XIXème siècle: le LUTTISME de classe et le PARLEMENTARISME. (Pierre Encrevé, *Le Nouvel Observateur*, 27 September 1990)

Other examples include *revendicatif*, *attractif*, *conjoncturel*, *consensuel*, *événementiel*, *relationnel*, *médiatique*, *capitalistique*, *jospinisme*, *lepénisme* and *convivial*.

8.1.3 *Vocabulary*

With respect to vocabulary, the major characteristic is again a measure of conservatism, manifesting itself in the avoidance of Anglo–American borrowings and the retention of many items that have become obsolete in spoken usage, although still found in poetic or literary works, for example set phrases originating in bygone modes of life or activities, as in *être aux abois, redorer son blason, faire litière de, une veillée d'armes, la réponse du berger à la bergère, sonner le glas de* and *à cor et à cri*. Archaisms occur in every lexical category. For example, there are verbs such as *musarder, bafouer, se gausser de, se tenir coi* and *rendre l'âme*, including impersonals such as *il sied*. Some archaic adjectives are *affable, amène, accorte* and *fugace*. Archaic adverbs and conjunctions include *maintes et maintes fois, de surcroît, en outre, dès lors*, or and *certes*. Nouns belonging to *le français soigné* are derived from Latin or Greek roots, such as *théorie* meaning 'a large number of people walking in procession', *pléthore, physionomie, conjoint(e)*, or are items more typical nowadays of literary or poetic usage, such as *noces, les écueils, l'aube, la fange, le décès* and *le trépas*. Not only is this vocabulary conservative, but, at the same time, it can be characterised as generally neutral or objective, as evidenced by the number of abstract or learned terms it contains, such as *irrésolution, claudication, floraison, hépatique, somnolence, obésité, cécité, irascibilité, revendicatif, problématique, édifier, élucider* and *affabuler*. Though polysyllabic, learned words are seldom abbreviated, hence *masochiste*, rather than *maso*. Note the use of a wide range of adverbs formed with the suffix *-ment*, where less formal styles may prefer *d'une façon . . ., d'une manière . . .*, such as *inconsciemment, péremptoirement, exclusivement, inopportunément* and *imperturbablement*. In negative constructions (4: 12), not only are *pas, pas du tout* and *pas beaucoup de* rivalled by *ne* alone in certain fixed contexts (5: 8.1.2), but they may even be supplemented by *nullement, point, guère* and *aucunement*. For the expression of causality or concession (4: 11.3), the more frequently used *parce que* or *bien que* may be replaced by *comme, car, puisque, pour ce que, attendu que, d'autant que, alors même que, lors même que, quoique, alors que, non que, non pas que*.

In short, *le français soigné* is characterised, first, by the closeness of its spoken form to the standard pronunciation, and, second, by its closeness to the written standard in terms of vocabulary and syntax. Thus, speakers tend to draw upon all of the resources, past and present, of the written norm to achieve their aims. It may even be said that the rarity value of a particular feature of pronunciation, lexical item or structure with regard to other stylistic varieties is what gives *le français soigné* the greatest prestige.

8.2 Le français familier

Whereas *le français soigné* is a written or spoken style where it could be claimed that the written language, and the influence of the normative tradition transmitted via education, take precedence, *le français familier* and *le français non standard* are varieties primarily – but not exclusively – realised in speech. It's this principal difference in function that goes some way to explaining what are sometimes felt to be striking divergences between French as it's taught and French as it's spoken by native speakers.

We'll deal first with *le français familier*. Whereas *le français soigné* corresponds to formal or guarded situations, those in which the user is to some extent constrained, socially and linguistically, a useful definition of *le français familier* is provided by Le Petit Robert (1991: 756):

> ... 4. (1680) qu'on emploie naturellement en tous milieux dans la conversation courante, et même par écrit, mais qu'on évite dans les relations avec des supérieurs, les relations officielles et les ouvrages qui se veulent sérieux.

This definition raises several important points. First, *le français familier* isn't the prerogative of any particular group or class within society, and isn't necessarily colloquial (in the pejorative sense of the word). Rather, it's the French that's used in unguarded and informal situations, with our peers and those we feel at ease with. Thus, it's primarily used in dialogue, for instance in conversations in the home, with close colleagues or friends, although it may find some expression in writing (personal correspondence, informal memos), and may be reproduced, for deliberate effect, in newspapers, *bandes dessinées*, novels or plays where the effect of dialogue is desired. The situations in which *le français familier* is used, therefore, imply an absence of social barriers, giving the speakers licence to express themselves spontaneously, with a minimum of self-consciousness and restraint, and in a personal way, to convey feelings of warmth, solidarity, kinship and so on.

Despite mass education, we should be wary of seeing *le français familier* merely as the spoken form of written French. Within the stylistic continuum there is scope for individual choice; the extent to which speakers adopt the salient features of this variety are, in part, determined by what they perceive the norm for the particular communicative situation to be. For instance, a student may express him or herself somewhat differently when speaking to his or her parents rather than to fellow students; a teacher will probably not use the same style with close colleagues as with his or her students, children or friends. Speakers may feel it appropriate to be more or less casual within this register, but the differences will be of degree rather than kind.

Since *le français familier* is primarily a spoken register, it can make use of devices and modes of expression which are specific to the medium of speech and are, to a large extent, 'untranslatable' into writing. The use of emphatic stress, changes in intonation, delivery, hesitation markers and even gestures can clarify an otherwise obscure or excessively elliptical utterance. Similarly, and this may be especially true in the case of French, where the prestige of the written word and the weight of the purist tradition have for so long equated *bien parler* with *parler comme un livre*, certain lexical items or grammatical structures may be excluded from writing as too colloquial or taboo.

The essential characteristics of *le français familier* are therefore linked to the fact that, unlike *le français soigné*, this style is listener-oriented rather than message-oriented, in other words the province of dialogue and reciprocal interaction. Rather than wishing to convey information in abstract and impersonal terms, speakers are more concerned with expressiveness and engaging with the person(s) they are communicating with in a personal way. This explains why a greater emphasis is placed on expressive devices at all levels, including a willingness, particularly in the domain of vocabulary, to innovate or adopt neologisms more readily.

8.2.1 Phonology

Some of the features typical of *le français familier* are a natural consequence of a more rapid and spontaneous delivery than the more careful diction typical of *le français soigné*, and are therefore common to most speakers. For example, assimilation (2: 6) has very high visibility in this register, and is therefore frequently reproduced in strip cartoons, as in *chuis* instead of *je suis*, *manman* for *maman*. The simplification of consonant clusters of the type [esplike] for [eksplike], and the deletion of liquids in clusters, as in *j'en veux plus* [ʒɑ̃vøpy] and *il a quatre cinq ans* [katsɛ̃kɑ̃], once held to be restricted to the ill-educated, are also widespread, and can be explained as an attempt to restore a consonant + vowel syllable pattern. The same may be said of the reduction of hiatus, that is, the deletion of a pre-vocalic vowel, as in *qui était* [kete] (4: 7.4). Not only is the subject clitic *il* regularly reduced to [i] before consonants, as in *il m'a dit* [imadi], but the frequently occurring impersonal *il y a* is realised as [ja]. In rapid delivery, [y] is frequently deleted prevocalically in the clitic *tu*, as in *tu as vu* [tavy], as are other vowels, for instance, the vowel [ɛ] in *mais enfin* [mɑ̃fɛ̃], *c'est-à-dire* [stadiʀ], [e] in *déjà* [dʒa], the glide plus vowel sequence [wa] in *voilà* [vla], and [u] in *tout à l'heure* [t:alœːʀ]. Indeed, whole syllables may disappear when unstressed, as in *enfin* [fɛ̃], *encore heureux* [kɔʀøʀø], *il (ne) faut pas exagérer* [fopa], and the clitic *vous* can be reduced to its liaison consonant, as in *vous (n') avez pas vu ma sœur?* [zavepavy] or *vous avez fini?* [zavefini].

Similarly, unstressed *e-muet* is prone to deletion, particularly in *ce que* [skə] and *parce que* [paʀskə] or [paskə], and fewer optional liaisons are realised (2: 15.5.3), in particular those involving polysyllabic prepositions or adverbs, as in *extrêmement intéressant* [ɛkstʀɛmːɑ̃ɛ̃teʀesɑ̃], the auxiliaries *être* and *avoir* with a following past participle, adjective or adverb; hence, *ils sont allés* [ilsɔ̃ale], *nous avons étudié* [nuzavɔ̃etydje], *cet enfant est infernal* [sɛtɑ̃fɑ̃ɛɛ̃fɛʀnal] and *c'est un idiot* [sɛɛ̃idjo].

A noticeable feature of spoken utterances is the frequent use of emphatic stress on non-final syllables, underlining either one aspect of the content of the message, or subjective reactions such as impatience or exasperation, as in *J'en ai assez* and *Ça fait QUINZE jours que j'attends* ['kɛ̃zʒuʀ] (rather than [kɛ̃zʒuʀ]), or admiration, as in *C'est LE look de l'hiver* ['lœluk].

While some of these features may be considered the norm for *le français familier*, notably the deletion of [l] in the proform *il* before a consonant, as in [idi], the reduction of *il y a* [ja], assimilations, the use of reduced forms, [bɛ̃] for *bien*, [fɛ̃] for *enfin*, which aren't felt to be particularly salient, others are more stigmatised and define a 'sub-norm'. In other words, the presence of one or more of these features will be assessed as colloquial, careless, 'sloppy' speech. This applies, for instance, to the generalisation of [e] in final open syllables, as in *mais* [me] and *chantais* [ʃɑ̃te], the deletion of pre-vocalic [a], as in *ça a été* [saete], the reduction of *je lui* to [ʒɥi], the reduction of [ks] and [gz] to [s] and [z] respectively, as in *expliquer* [esplike] and *exagérer* [ezaʒeʀe], and, especially, non-standard realisations of [ʀ] and dialectal features of pronunciation, for instance the northern or Midi French use of [ɔ] in a final syllable closed by [z], as in *rose* [ʀɔːz].

8.2.2   Morpho-syntax

The definition of *le français familier* depends as much on its characteristic syntactic and lexical features as it does on pronunciation. Although in a highly literate society like that of France, spontaneous spoken utterances don't exclude features of the written language totally, there are tendencies which differentiate the spoken from the written language, and structures which are favoured for the specific purposes of spoken language. For instance, frequent use is made of paratactic constructions, that is, the simple juxtaposition of clauses without overt subordination or coordination. In conversation this is perfectly transparent, given the context, the interpretation of gestures and intonation. We might therefore hear statements, such as:

(23)   Il m'a insultée, je m'en vais.

(24)   Vous nous accompagnerez, je pense.

(25)   Tu es prête, allons-y.

instead of:

(26)   a. Je m'en vais PARCE QU'il m'a insultée.
        b. Il m'a insultée, DONC je m'en vais.

(27)   Je pense QUE vous nous accompagnerez.

(28)   PUISQUE tu es prête, allons-y.

Similarly, yes–no questions (4: 1.5) more frequently take the form of declarative sentences (with subject–verb–object word order) together with rising intonation, as in *Tu viens?* and *Vous avez mangé?* A more strongly rising intonation could indicate incredulity, as in *Vous n'avez pas faim!*; a falling intonation, impatience, as in *Tu viens!* An alternative device for interrogation, which also preserves declarative word order, is the use of *est-ce que*, which, although itself an inversion, is so stereotyped as no longer to be perceived as such: *Est-ce que le chat est dehors?* Inversions are fairly infrequent, hence *Peut-être faudra-t-il appeler le médecin* is less likely than *Peut-être qu'il faudra* . . . , once again preserving canonical subject–verb–object word order.

In the use of subject proforms, *nous* is frequently replaced by impersonal *on*, although *nous* may be prefixed to *on* for emphasis, as in:

(29) a. ON a mangé à deux heures.
     b. NOUS, ON a mangé à midi comme d'habitude.

Emphasis and the expression of contrast may result in a high incidence of constructions involving the stressed proform used in conjunction with the subject clitic, as in MOI, JE *n'ai jamais dit ça*. As noted in 4: 4.3, *ça* itself is frequently used as a generic subject proform, as in the film title *Un éléphant, ÇA trompe énormément* or *Les hommes, ÇA se mène par le bout du nez.*

Equally characteristic of speech are the dislocated constructions mentioned in 4: 8.2, where the nominal subject is taken up by the corresponding clitic (these are particularly stigmatised in written French as being pleonastic or tautological), as in ILS *sont fous, ces Romains* and *Jacqueline et Pierre,* ILS *sont encore arrivés en retard.* However, these aren't restricted to speech, as shown by the following: *L'Eglise ivoirienne n'en demandait pas tant. Cette basilique,* ELLE *ne l'avait pas réclamée* (*L'Express,* 21 September 1990).

In fact, the use of these dislocated constructions gives speakers considerable freedom in selecting the order of constituents:

(30) a. En fait, Timothée, il est content, de sa nouvelle école?
     b. En fait, il est content, Timothée, de sa nouvelle école?
     c. En fait, sa nouvelle école, Timothée, il en est content?

Cleft sentences (4: 8.3), which allow a constituent of the sentence to be emphasised, are introduced by means of a variety of presentative forms, such as:

(31) a. VOILÀ dix ans qu'elles ne se parlent plus.
     b. CE QUI me plaît, C'EST les romans policiers.
     c. C'EST Shell QUE j'aime.
     d. ENCORE UNE de finie.
     e. C'EST eux QUI ont téléphoné.

(Note that in (31b, e) the verb agrees with *ce*, rather than the logical subject.)

In negative constructions, omission of the negative particle *ne* is one of the best-known and most frequently observed features of contemporary spoken French (4: 12.1). As shown by Coveney (1996) and Gadet (1989: 130–3), a variety of factors come into play in the retention or deletion of *ne*. For instance, *ne* is more likely to be retained in contexts where the subject clitic is *vous*, or where the second particle isn't *pas*, whereas in frequent collocations, such as *faut pas*, *il y a pas* and *c'est pas*, or with the clitic *tu*, there is a high incidence of loss of *ne*, across all categories of speakers. The requirement of normative grammar to make the past participle of transitive verbs agree in gender and number with a preceding direct object (4: 7.5) isn't always observed in speech, as in *les propositions qu'il a FAIT au ministre*. In the use of tenses, the past-historic and past anterior feature very seldom (if at all), and the use of the synthetic future is rivalled by the analytical future, particularly with reference to an event which will occur shortly; for example, *On va aller au cinéma ce soir* is rather more likely than *Nous irons au cinéma ce soir* or *On ira au cinéma ce soir*. The subjunctive is well preserved in frequently used constructions, such as *il faut que*, *vouloir que*, *avant que* and *pour que* (and indeed, is quite often extended to *après que*), but is restricted to the present or the perfect tense, as in:

> (32) a. Il voulait que je le SACHE (*SUSSE).
>   b. Elle m'a consulté avant que ce projet (ne) SOIT PRÉSENTÉ (*FÛT PRÉSENTÉ).

The more subtle and less common uses of the subjunctive are frequently disregarded, as in *S'il arrive le premier et s'il VEUT commencer la réunion*, rather than *S'il arrive le premier et QU'il VEUILLE . . .*, or *Le fait qu'il n'EST pas venu m'inquiète*, instead of *ne SOIT pas venu*. These examples underline the conventional and non-semantic nature of the subjunctive in the majority of its uses. Since there are few contexts where the use of the subjunctive marks a difference in meaning (4: 6.3), and since for many verbs the present subjunctive and indicative forms are identical, the principle of economy can again be seen to be at work. In matters of morpho-syntax, the above features, which typify the informal spoken French of *le français familier*, aren't seen as particularly 'deviant' with regard to the norm, and are therefore shared by many speakers, although the majority of them are absent from writing.

8.2.3 Vocabulary

In contrast to *le français soigné*, which has a predilection for abstract, learned and expressively neutral terms, the vocabulary of *le français familier* is more colourful, expressive, innovative and receptive to borrowings and neologisms. We noted earlier the coexistence of one, or several, apparently synonymous terms for such everyday actions as eating, drinking (*boire* and *siroter*), sleeping (*dormir* and *roupiller*), or for everyday objects (*livre* and *bouquin, voiture* and *bagnole, argent* and *fric*, and so on). As Lodge (1989) points out, the various members of these series are clearly perceived by users in terms of their appropriateness to writing or speech, or, more exactly, in terms of their neutrality/objectivity versus subjectivity/affectivity. It's more appropriate to ask a friend *Qu'est-ce que tu penses de ma bagnole?*, rather than the more formal and, here, stilted *Que penses-tu de mon automobile?* The demand for expressiveness and vividness is one of the major traits of *le français familier*, and is one factor motivating both lexical change and innovation. For example, adverbs, as intensifiers, are particularly prone to becoming outmoded through being overworked; thus *extrêmement* and *complètement* were once replaced by *vachement, carrément* or, more recently, the prefixes *super-* and *hyper-*, as in:

(33) a. Il est très sympathique. b. Il est vachement sympa(thique).
     c. Il est super-sympa. d. Il est hyper-sympa.

Another possibility is reduplication, for emphasis:

(34) a. Il est très très sympa. b. C'est pas facile facile.

A further device is to use one part of speech for another, for instance an adjective as an adverb, as in *Elle a eu son bac* FACILE (instead of *facilement*) and *Il assure* GRAVE (instead of *totalement* or *absolument*).

Similarly, nouns take on the role of prepositions, as in QUESTION *travail, il est obsédé* (instead of *en ce qui concerne/pour/quant au*) or *Elle a filé* DIREC-TION *la sortie* (instead of *vers/en direction de*).

Le français familier also features and creates new compounds by non-affixal derivation, for instance using nouns like attributive adjectives, as in *une ville* FANTÔME (*fantomatique*), *un travail* MONSTRE (*monstrueux*) and *un remède* MIRACLE (*miraculeux*). In some cases, the head noun may be deleted, as in *des (camions) poids lourd, un (costume) deux pièces* and *deux (sandwichs) jambon-beurre*. Lexical creativity also makes use of suffixal derivation favouring, in particular, diminutive and augmentative suffixes such as *-et, -ette, -ot -otte*, for instance *boulotte* 'small and plump', *gentillet* 'quite pleasant', *croquignolet* (*mignon*), *lingette* 'baby wipe' and *turbulette* 'baby sleeping bag'. The pejorative suffix *-ard* is also productive, as in *ringard* 'old fashioned and ridiculous', *braillard* 'raucously noisy', *vachard* 'mean' and *revanchard* 'spitefully vengeful'. Prefixes include *hyper-*, as well as *anti-, hypo-, ultra-* and *méga-*, as in *hyper-sophistiqué, ultra-confidentiel* and *une loi anti-casseurs*. In the spoken language, polysyllabic words are frequently abbreviated, as in *déca(féiné), sympa(thique), porno(graphique), télé(vision), nœud pap(illon), clim(atisation)* and *maso(chiste)*.

Expressiveness may also be achieved by an abundant use of adjectives with strong affective meanings, as in *atroce, génial, dément, affolant, désastreux, monstrueux, géant,* and the use of metaphors, in particular those drawing unflattering parallels between various members of the animal kingdom and human beings, for instance, *un(e) vrai(e) chameau* 'mean and bad-tempered', *une bourrique* 'stubborn', *un cochon* 'dirty' and *une pie* 'talkative'.

Finally, *le français familier* appears to be much more permeable to foreign borrowings (1: 7.1), particularly from English. Anglicisms are very frequent in the domains of fashion, advertising or business and the media, for instance, *le look, le know-how, le management, le challenge, le scoop* and *le press-book.* Readers of women's fashion magazines may be informed that *Chez Givenchy le look évolue* and exhorted to wear *des jodphurs british en whipcord, des poignets zippés* or *motifs western,* to add to the already well-integrated *sweat(shirt)s, teeshirts* and *cardigans,* not to mention *les joggings* 'track-suits'. Naturally, some of these innovations enjoy but a brief popularity, and eventually disappear without trace, while others, in time, find their way into the common stock.

To conclude, then, although *le français soigné,* particularly the written style, does exert an influence on *le français familier* in allowing variation within fairly narrow morpho-syntactic and phonological limits only, vocabulary is one domain where far more creativity is possible, and which, in the long term, can have a profound influence on the written language itself.

8.3   Le français non standard

Descriptions of *le français non standard,* the most informal style of French, traditionally use style-labels such as *français populaire, vulgaire, argotique* and *très familier,* which are unsatisfactory on several counts. The label *populaire,* in particular, defines the register in purely sociological terms, as this definition given in Le Petit Robert brings out: . . . *qui est créé, employé par le peuple, et n'est guère en usage dans la bourgeoisie et parmi les gens cultivés* (1991: 1483).

But, as Bourdieu (1983), Gadet (1992) and Lodge (1989, 1993) have wondered, who is, or are, *le peuple?* How can we, today, identify this homogeneous 'working-class' group whose linguistic usage sets it apart from the rest of French society? Is style shifting on the scale of (in)formality the prerogative of the higher social groups? Are slang or non-standard linguistic forms the exclusive province of the lower social groups? There is, as Gadet (1992) points out, a historical basis for *le français populaire,* which originally designated the speech of the lower socio-economic groups in Paris in the nineteenth century. But increased social mobility, access to education and the influence of the media now make class-based distinctions in speech much less straightforward. As for the labels *vulgaire* and *argotique,* these define the register solely in terms of a vocabulary to which only the 'ill-educated' or 'deviant' members of society would resort. Yet, it's well attested – as speakers of French themselves will frequently concede – that speakers of whatever socio-economic group will, in certain circumstances, make use of stylistic features, both lexical and, to a lesser extent, morpho-syntactic, which are said to be exclusive to this nebulous and less prestigious group of society. What all these labels have in common, though, is their negative connotations, and the lack of status or value placed on the typical features of the register by society as a whole. These negative reactions are due to a purist attitude, which sees these forms both as an attack on the idealised perception of the standard (notably where grammar is concerned) and as an infringement of the aim of achieving maximum intercomprehension and acceptability (notably in socially acceptable vocabulary).

We have chosen the label *le français non standard* to reflect the fact that the characteristic features of this style are part and parcel of French, and form part of the linguistic competence of all speakers, even though traditional grammar, and the prescriptive tradition of education with its emphasis on the written standard (Chapter 1), either refuse to acknowledge them, or seek actively to eliminate them.

When we examine *le français non standard*, we're dealing essentially with a spoken register, since this is the domain of the most casual and informal communication. It may, however, find some expression in writing, for the purposes of linguistic and social realism, in *série noire* novels (detective stories), *bandes dessinées* or satirical columns in some newspapers. See, for instance, the works of Frédéric Dard (better known as San Antonio) or Alphonse Boudard.

8.3.1 Phonology

In terms of pronunciation, the feature to which most importance is given, as noted by Gueunier *et al.* (1978: 151) and Léon (1988), is the presence of an identifiable urban or rural 'accent', even if this identification is made on the basis of one or two non-standard features only, for example the northern and south-western pronunciation of mid-low [ɔ] in a closed syllable, as in *côte* [kɔt] as opposed to [kot] and alveolar, rather than uvular, realisations of [ʀ] (see 5: 3.3 for some further typical features of regional pronunciations). Utterances might also be classified as non-standard on the grounds that they contain a high proportion of the features described earlier (5: 8.2.1) as belonging to the most informal end of the scale of *le français familier*. Comments such as 'sloppy', 'inelegant' and 'careless' pronunciation would rest on the observation of a high proportion of assimilations, as in *je (ne) sais pas* [ʃepa] and *maintenant* [mɛ̃nɑ̃], and the frequent reduction of consonant clusters, as in *exprès* [espʀe], *il se dégonfle* [isdegɔ̃f], *capable* [kapab], *parce que* [paskə] and *plus* [py]. Also stigmatised are non-deletions of *e-muet* prevocalically, as in *parce qu'on* [paskəɔ̃], or, on the other hand, orthographically unmotivated insertions of *e-muet*, as in *lorsque* [lɔʀsəkə] and *exprès* [eksəpʀe]. A low incidence of liaisons, generally restricted to the obligatory context of determiner followed by noun, as in *les amis* [lezami], or clitic plus verb, as in *nous avons* [nuzavɔ̃], is also seen as a marker of informality. However, extending the use of liaisons to *h-aspiré* initial words, as in *des Hollandais* [dezolɑ̃de] or *des haricots* [dezaʀiko], or prescriptively unmotivated contexts, such as *cinq amis* [sɛ̃kzami], is seen as particularly deviant. The loss of unstressed vowels, and even entire unstressed syllables or words, as in *encore heureux* [kɔʀøʀø], *(il) faudrait savoir* [fodʀɛsavwaːʀ] or *(vou)s (n') allez pas me faire croire* [zalepamfɛʀkʀwaːʀ], also contribute to judgements of carelessness and laxity in pronunciation.

As remarked earlier, these aren't features that will be found only in the most informal speech style, nor indeed features used only by the members of a particular social group. The difference, once again, is one of degree.

8.3.2 Morpho-syntax

In the area of morpho-syntax, the features that are most stereotyped (by members of higher social groups) as characterising *le français non standard* relate, in particular, to the various uses of *que*. First, *que* is widely used to introduce the adverbial clauses described in 4: 11.3.

(35) a. Viens ici QUE je te donne de mes nouvelles. (= POUR QUE)
   b. Ma cousine, elle est venue QUE j'étais pas là.   (= QUAND)
   c. Il peut plus marcher QU'il est si gros.   (= PARCE QUE)
   d. Il range jamais rien, QUE son garage c'est un vrai bordel.
         (= AU POINT QUE, PAR CONSÉQUENT)

(Note also the dislocated structure in (35b)). *Que*, as complementiser, can also introduce all manner of subordinate clauses, as in:

(36) a. Le garçon QU'elle lui plaît.   (À QUI elle plaît)
   b. La boutique QU'elle est au coin de la rue
      du Port, elle ferme jamais avant huit heures.   (QUI)
   c. Ce QUE tu te rends pas compte . . .   (DONT)
   d. C'est pas un type QUE tu peux compter dessus.
         (SUR LEQUEL tu peux compter)

Additionally, *que* may be used to reinforce other complementisers, such as *quand, comme* and *si*:

(37) a. Il m'a dit le nom du bled d'OÙ QU'il vient.
   b. COMME QUE je l'ai dit à Jules . . .
   c. SI QUE tu crois que je vais me laisser faire . . .

Example (38) illustrates the use of *que* as a marker of coordination:

(38) Elle a trouvé une robe QUE si je trouvais la même je
   l'achèterais.   (ET)

Interrogative constructions usually retain the subject–verb–object word order of standard declarative sentences. Questions are usually formed using intonation patterns or the introducer *est-ce que*, as in *Est-ce que tu en veux?*, *Où est-ce que tu as mis ça?* Side by side with these constructions, in more emphatic contexts *est-ce que* can be reinforced by the introducer *c'est*, giving rise to question patterns, such as *Qui est-ce que c'est que tu as vu?*, *Qui c'est que tu as vu?* or *C'est qui que tu as vu?* In the first sentence, *c'est* is judged to be merely redundant. In the other two examples, in contrast, either the interrogative *est-ce que* would be used in higher registers, or interrogative movement of *qui* would be accompanied by subject–clitic inversion, as in *Qui as-tu vu?* (4: 7.2). Constructions which will be judged as even more deviant with respect to the norm are those which can be interpreted either as resulting from the addition of *que* as a reinforcement of the interrogative phrase word (in the same way as we saw *que* earlier reinforcing other elements), or as resulting from the contraction of *est-ce que*, as in *Où que tu vas?* corresponding to *Où (Où + que) tu vas?* or *Où (est-ce) que tu vas?* Emphasised with the introducer *que* we then find sequences such as:

(39) a. C'est OÙ QU'il va ce soir?
      b. C'est QUI QUI vient avec moi?
      c. QUI C'EST QUI vient avec moi?
      d. QUAND C'EST QUE tu pars faire tes courses?

This last example is perhaps worth considering in the light of Vaugelas's comments on seventeenth-century usage (1: 4.4).

In the domain of verbal morphology, past participle agreement is often omitted, as in *Elle s'y est encore mal pris pour expliquer son cas*. There is also some tendency to realign irregular verb forms, as in *il mourira* instead of *il mourra*, or *vous faisez* instead of *vous faites*. (See Gadet 1992 for further examples.)

Speakers also sometimes have recourse to the preposition *à* followed by an NP to indicate possession (4: 2.1), as in *C'est le jules à Monique* 'Monique's boyfriend' and *C'est la voiture à mon gendre* 'my son-in-law's car'. A final feature we'll mention is the apparent blurring of the traditional grammatical categories of adverbs and prepositions. Thus, adverbs are used as prepositions, as in *Il lui a tapé DESSUS (sur elle)* and *Le bistrot qui est EN FACE la gare (en face de)*, and, conversely, prepositions as adverbs, as in *Sa robe neuve, elle est sortie AVEC?*

As the above comments show, the point of reference by which utterances such as these are judged is very much the standard, as represented by prescriptive grammar, which inescapably leads to assessments of such forms as being not merely non-standard but substandard. Consequently, these tend to be dismissively characterised as the performance of the poorly educated or unsuccessful. Yet, as the following examples show, such stylistically marked constructions aren't, by any means, exempt from the speech of members of the most prestigious or well-educated groups of French society, for example, overheard on France-Inter in 1990, from a cabinet minister, *Quand on voit* COMME QUE *vous avez gouverné* . . ., *les électeurs, i(ls) cherchent aut(re) chose* [iʃɛʀʃotʃoz], and, from a reporter, *Le grand trou qu'(il) y a* [kija] AUTOUR. . . .

8.3.3   Vocabulary

With vocabulary, we'll concentrate on those areas of the lexicon which are, on the whole, exclusive to this register. In fact, there is a general consensus on the part of French speakers about some items which are felt to be so very strongly marked stylistically that they are only to be used sparingly, under circumstances of great emotional stress, to make a point controversially or expressively and/or in very casual circumstances among kindred spirits. We shall examine, in particular, two categories of items which fall under the headings of *vulgaire* and *argot*. We make this distinction for convenience, although it should be said that these categories aren't mutually exclusive, for an expletive such as *merde* might be assessed as *vulgaire* but not as *argot*, a word like *bouquin* 'book' might be labelled *argot* but not *vulgaire* whereas *chiant* 'boring' would be both.

LE VOCABULAIRE VULGAIRE

Characteristic of items in this category is that they name directly, and without camouflage, realities that, in polite society, are usually referred to indirectly or euphemistically. Although many of the items have been part of the lexical stock of French for centuries, their use in formal situations is restricted by social and moral taboos. However, in *le français non standard*, many exclamations draw upon these items, for instance *Merde!*, *Crotte!*, *Quel bordel!*, as well as insults like *putain, cocu, couillon* and *con*. The domains which are best represented are those which describe parts of the body, bodily functions, work, the realities of daily life and personal characteristics.

Greater expressiveness may be sought in metaphorical extensions of items usually referring to the animal world, which are insulting or offensive when applied to human beings, for instance *gueule* 'mouth of a dog', as in *Ferme ta gueule!*, *pattes* 'legs', *poulet* 'policeman', *souris* 'woman', *cochon* or *porc* 'uncouth, coarse person', *pondre* 'to give birth' and *crever* 'to die'.

A high proportion of lexical items belonging to *le vocabulaire vulgaire* have negative or pejorative connotations, whether they apply to descriptions of states of mind, expressed in concrete rather than abstract terms, as in *il s'est dégonflé* 'he lost his nerve', *je m'emmerde, ça me fait chier* 'I am very bored' and *je suis foutu(e)* 'I'm exhausted/done for', or to everyday activities or realia, as in *bosser* 'to work hard', *bouffer* 'to eat inelegantly', *pinard* 'bad wine' and *bidoche* 'poor-quality meat'. The description of the physical world is also rich in terms with negative connotations which are linked to the most favoured suffixes, namely, *-asse*, *-ard* and *-aud*, as in *dégueulasse* 'dirty', *salaud*, *salopard* 'contemptible/disgusting person', *costard* 'suit', *connard* 'idiot' or *paillasse* 'prostitute'.

While many of these terms are unlikely to find their way into the written language, at least for formal communication, this vocabulary isn't beyond the reach of most speakers, who might resort to it in times of stress, or for particular expressive purposes, while, in more guarded situations, they'll opt for more stylistically neutral versions. Consider, however, the interesting stylistic range in the following, taken from an article by Alain Schifrès in *Le Nouvel Observateur* (23–29 January 1990): *La grammaire fut inventée pour servir l'humanité en général et faire chier les mômes en France.*

L'ARGOT

This, again, is a term which can be used with several (and sometimes overlapping) meanings. *Argot* isn't a modern phenomenon; its origins can be traced back to the fourteenth century (Calvet 1994). Historically, first of all, the word *argot* referred to the jargon, or code, used by the criminal urban classes to escape the attentions of the police or of outsiders. In this sense it was, and still is, a marker of exclusion and identification, whose purpose is to unite the members of a certain group while excluding others. Using *argot*, therefore, is essentially a matter of using a particular vocabulary for the purposes of concealment; hence, also, the need to renew this vocabulary should any part of it become common knowledge. Second, *argot* is also an appropriate label for the specialised vocabulary used by members of a trade or professional group, when discussing their own field of specialism. (Note that some linguists prefer the term 'occupational style'; Wise 1997.) We may therefore speak of the *argot* of linguists, doctors or pigeon-fanciers or, indeed, the *argot* of the army or *lycée*. Third, many French speakers occasionally apologise for using *un mot d'argot*, or express a value judgement on the speech of a third party in terms of *Il/Elle parle argot*, which is generally equated with speaking badly. Why should this be? A first reason lies in the recognition of the excluding function of *argot*, since it doesn't seek to achieve maximum intercomprehension – quite the reverse. Second, *argot*, in its historical sense, still survives in the usage of a subgroup of society whose criminal activities are frowned upon. But *argot* isn't a separate language. It's essentially a vocabulary grafted onto the syntax of (standard or non-standard) French. It's mostly spoken, and can be very ephemeral; indeed, the very fact that different terms are adopted from professional or occupational *argots* (school, the army, the media, advertising) or, especially, by older speakers, from youth slang, motivates their replacement or renewal.

It's often claimed that *argot* is particularly creative or inventive in the formation of neologisms, yet *argot*, like any other area of the lexicon, renews itself by drawing upon the resources that are available to the language system as a whole. The similarity of the processes involved is simply obscured by the fact that some of the domains of *argot* may be a closed book to the man in the street when they concern activities which are beyond the respectable citizen's experience, such as drug trafficking, prison and prostitution. *Argot* isn't very rich in abstract concepts, the areas of concern being everyday life and activities, sleeping, eating, drinking, money, sex, work and so forth. But where the domain of *le français vulgaire* can be characterised by its bluntness, *argot* frequently resorts to euphemism, metaphor or other processes of concealment, such as *le verlan* (see below). Commonly used metaphors are *un rond* 'money', *pattes* 'legs', *la lourde* 'door', *faucher* 'to steal' and *le ruban* 'the pavement'. A second process which is favoured is metonymy (naming the whole by one of its parts or salient characteristics), as in *le plumard* 'bed' and *le bavard* 'barrister'. Humorous, ironic or grotesque periphrases abound also, as in *se rincer la dalle* 'to drink', *casser la croûte* 'to eat', *faire la manche* 'to beg', *se mettre à table* 'to confess', *être bourré* and *être rond (comme une barrique)* 'to be drunk'. In many cases, a word taken from the standard vocabulary will be given a metaphorical meaning, for instance *la neige* 'cocaine', *le bahut* (usually 'sideboard', here 'place of work' or *lycée*), *le cageot* (usually 'packing case for fruit', here 'a girl'), *une tuile* (usually 'roof tile', in *argot* 'bad luck'), *potable* (usually 'safe to drink', in *argot* 'acceptable') and *la galère/galérer* (usually 'galley', here a difficult situation/to try very hard but in vain). *Argot* may also borrow from other languages, for instance, from Arabic, as in *barca* 'enough' and *toubib* 'doctor', or English, as in the following, all related to drugs, *se shooter, speed, dealer, joint* and *crack*.

Increasingly, since the early part of the twentieth century and, in particular, through films, television and popular songs, and increased social mobility, the barriers between *argot* and general vocabulary have been breaking down. This is a two-way process. At times, *argot* brings back into fashion archaic words, such as the recently reintroduced *la maille* 'money' (as in Old French), and, in other instances, sees its creations become socially acceptable.

LA LANGUE DES JEUNES

Lexical creativity is also a characteristic feature of what, in the last few years, has come to be known as *la langue des jeunes*. The term *langue* should be interpreted with some caution, as it consists (like *argot*) of a distinctive lexis, grafted onto the syntax of French, to which speakers resort for particular purposes. As noted earlier (5: 6), there is evidence that teenagers and young adults actively use language as a badge of group identity and, to some extent, to exclude non-members, notably members of older generations or representatives of authority and tradition. To quote *Le Nouvel Observateur* (15–21 October 1998) *Tchatcher Molièreman, c'est la loserie grave.*

While some lexical items have broad currency across the age-group, for instance *cool, kiffer* 'to like', *tchatcher* 'to talk/speak', there are also distinctive *argots* connected with different regions or urban areas or ethnic subgroups. In the constant creation of lexical items, borrowing and derivation play a large part. For instance, Arabic 'kiff' gives rise to the verb *kiffer* and English 'lose' gives *loserie* 'dead loss'. Also associated with *la langue des jeunes* is *le verlan*, a type of word game which aims to disguise words, essentially by inverting the syllables, as in the word *verlan* itself (< *l'envers*), hence, *céfran* (< *français*), *quebla* (< black) and *beur* (< *arabe*). To preserve the cryptic nature of this vocabulary, a word may undergo several metamorphoses, as one form becomes too well known or hackneyed, as in *asmeuk* (< *comme ça*) via the intermediate forms *kommas* and *sakome*. Any word in the language may be subject to *verlanisation*, even a *verlan* form. This 'second-generation' *verlan* is known as *veul* and (re)generates forms such as *feume* (< *meuf* < *femme*). Whether *verlan* is a passing fashion or will continue to flourish is a moot point, but the widespread acceptance of terms such as *beur/beurette* may suggest that it will leave some permanent traces in the lexicon of French.

9 Final remarks

What conclusions can we draw at the close of this volume and, in particular, of this survey of geographical and social variation in French? Francophones may adhere to the long-established myth of an idealised standard, the variety to which they grant the highest aesthetic status and prestige, yet French cannot be seen as a homogeneous and static entity. What we hope to have shown is the interplay of internal pressures which define the language system as a whole and, at the same time, seek to adapt it to the communicative needs of its users through variation within the system. The grammatical and prescriptive tradition may seek to conceal or even counteract what are perceived as excessive deviations, but the fact remains that French, as a living natural language, only exists as the sum of its varieties, and that its survival can only be achieved through taking into account the needs and practices of all Francophones as they evolve over time and space.

Further reading

Nelde *et al.* (1996) provides information on the vitality of minority languages across Europe and numbers of speakers. See also Walter (1988), Rossillon (1995). For a comprehensive and detailed survey of French in the world, see Robillard and Benianimo (1993). See Hawkins (1993) on regional variation in France, Laroussi and Marcellesi (1993) for information on the situation of regional languages in France today and official attitudes towards them, and Calvet (1993) for details on the languages spoken by immigrant groups in Paris; see also Carton (1987) on regional accents and Vermes (1988) for surveys of the languages spoken in France. On the themes of French linguistic policy and speaker attitudes towards regional languages in France and the French-speaking world, see Marley *et al.* (1998).

On French in Canada, see Blanc (1993); Walker (1984) provides a description of the pronunciation of Canadian French; see also Ostiguy and Tousignant (1993) on the spoken norm. For a discussion of the present state and the future of French in Africa, see Lafage (1993). On creoles, see Aub-Buscher (1993) for the Caribbean creoles, Chaudenson (1979a, 1979b, 1995) for a more general presentation and discussion of the origins of French-lexicon creoles. An interesting description of the linguistic situation of Mauritius is provided by Baggioni and Robillard (1990). Depecker (1988) provides a guide to non-metropolitan words and expressions.

Sanders (1993) provides examples of phonological and syntactic features which typify social varieties; a fuller description and discussion of stylistic variation can be found in Gadet (1989). Calvet (1994) gives an account of *argot*, Gadet (1992) of popular and familiar usage. See also Lodge (1993) for a discussion of the relationship between formal and informal French. For a modern bilingual dictionary of slang, see Marks and Johnson (1993). Monolingual dictionaries of slang, such as Cellard and Rey (1991) and Colin and Mével (1992), provide etymologies and numerous illustrative examples. For the lexis of urban youth culture, see Goudailler (1997).

Appendix I Dialects and regional languages

Appendix II   French in the world

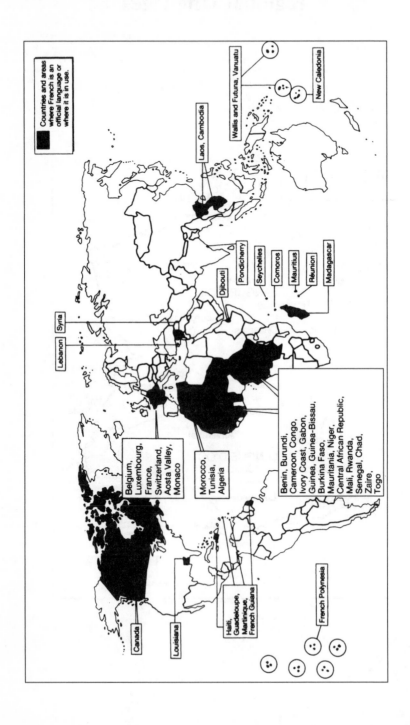

Countries and areas where French is an official language or where it is in use.

Wallis and Futuna, Vanuatu

New Caledonia

Laos, Cambodia

Pondicherry

Seychelles

Comoros

Mauritius

Réunion

Madagascar

Djibouti

Syria

Lebanon

Belgium, Luxembourg, France, Switzerland, Aosta Valley, Monaco

Morocco, Tunisia, Algeria

Benin, Burundi, Cameroon, Congo, Ivory Coast, Gabon, Guinea, Guinea-Bissau, Burkina Faso, Mauritania, Niger, Central African Republic, Mali, Rwanda, Senegal, Chad, Zaire, Togo

Canada

Louisiana

Haiti, Guadeloupe, Martinique, French Guiana

French Polynesia

Glossary

See also Crystal (1992, 1997), Hurford (1994) and Trask (1993, 1996a, 1997, 1998).

active sentence (*phrase active*). A **sentence** containing a **transitive verb**, in which the **agent** is the **subject** and the **patient** is the **direct object** (*Jean lit un livre*). See **passive sentence**. The feature distinguishing passive from active sentences is called voice.

adjective (*adjectif*). Words like *beau*, which describe **nouns** and head **phrases**. Attributive APs occur within NPs (*le TRÈS BEAU chat*); predicative APs occur outside NPs (*Le chat est TRÈS BEAU, Je trouve le chat TRÈS BEAU*). Comparative adjectives compare entities (*Ce livre est PLUS/ AUSSI/MOINS INTÉRESSANT (que ce magazine)*); superlative adjectives indicate that an entity has a feature to a greater extent than any other (*C'est le livre LE PLUS/MOINS INTÉRESSANT que j'aie lu*).

adverb (*adverbe*). Words like *bien*, *tôt* and *facilement*, which head **phrases** and function as **adverbials** (*Tu l'as TRÈS BIEN fait*).

adverbial (*circonstant/complément circonstanciel*). **Phrases** optionally added to **minimal sentences** to detail the circumstances (e.g. time, place, manner) of an action etc. Adverbials are of various **categories** ($[_{NP}$ ce matin], $[_{PP}$ après l'avoir vu], $[_{AdvP}$ assez gentiment]), including **clauses** ($[_{S2}$ quand je suis en France]).

adverbial clause (*proposition adverbiale*). A **subordinate clause** which functions as an **adverbial**.

affixation (*affixation*). Attachment of an affix to a **root**, either as a prefix (*PRÉvoir*), or as a suffix (*faisABLE*).

agent (*agent*). The entity responsible for an action (*JEAN a cassé la vitre, La vitre a été cassée par JEAN*). See **patient**.

agent phrase (*complément d'agent*). An optional PP headed by *par* (in **passive/causative sentences**) indicating the **agent** (*La vitre a été cassée (PAR JEAN), Elle a fait réparer la vitre (PAR JEAN)*).

agreement (*accord*). Morphological dependency, e.g. between an **adjective** and the **noun** it describes (*les grandES filles*), a **finite verb** and its **subject** (*Nous partONS*).

allomorph (*allomorphe*). The phonetic form of an abstract **morpheme**, which varies according to the morphological context in which it appears: [in] in *inoffensif*, [ɛ̃] in *impensable* and [il] in *illégal* are all allomorphs of the same morpheme.

allophone (*allophone*). The phonetic form of an abstract **phoneme**, which varies according to the phonological context in which it appears: the **voiceless** [l̥] and the **voiced** [l] (in *plat* [pl̥a] and *las* [la]) are allophones of /l/.

alveolar ridge (*alvéoles*). The hard ridge behind the top teeth, used in the **articulation** of [t, d, n, s, z].

analytical future (*futur périphrastique*). **Paradigms** like *vais rire/vas rire/va rire/allons rire/allez rire/vont rire*.

anaphoric tense (*anaphore verbale/temporelle*). Temporal location established with respect to a time other than **utterance** time. See **deictic tense**.

anticipatory assimilation (*assimilation régressive*). See **assimilation**.

antonym (*antonyme*). The linguistic term for opposites; *grand* is the antonym of *petit*.

apex (*pointe*). The tip of the tongue.

argument (*argument*). **Phrases** (usually NPs or **proforms**) bearing the grammatical relation of **subject**, **direct object** or **indirect object** to the **verb**. The subject of the **sentence** is what the VP says something about (but see **impersonal il**), is usually preverbal (but see **inversion**) and determines subject–verb **agreement** (JEAN *dort*/IL *dort*). A direct object is the other argument of a **transitive verb** (*Marie a vu* LES FILLES, *Marie* LES *a vues*). An indirect object is either a PP or a clitic proform (*J'ai donné le livre* À MARIE, *Je* LUI *ai donné le livre*).

article (*article*). See **determiner**.

articulation (*articulation*). Modification of the airstream to produce speech.

articulator (*articulateur*). A **speech organ** involved in **articulation**. We distinguish those speech organs which move (active articulators) from those which don't (passive articulators).

aspect (*aspect*). The distribution over time of the event etc. denoted by the VP, e.g. habitual (*Je me lave tous les jours*), inchoative (*Je commence à travailler*), progressive (*Je suis en train de travailler*) and iterative (*Je continue à faire des fautes*).

assimilation (*assimilation*). A phonological phenomenon whereby an **allophone** adopts features from a following **segment** (regressive/anticipatory assimilation; /absɔly/ → [apsɔly]) or a preceding segment (progressive assimilation; /ʃəval/ → [ʃv̥al]).

attributive adjective (*adjectif épithète*). See **adjective**.

auxiliary (*auxiliaire*). See **verb**.

back vowel (*voyelle postérieure*). See **vowel fronting**.

bilabial consonant (*consonne bilabiale*). A **segment** articulated using both lips: [p, b, m].

blade (*lame*). The upper surface of the tongue immediately behind the **apex**.

category (*catégorie*). Words which behave the same way (e.g. verbs, nouns). A subcategory is a finer-tuned classification and distinguishes, for example, **transitive** from **intransitive verbs, common** from **proper nouns.**

causal clause (*proposition adverbiale de cause*). An **adverbial clause** indicating why something is the case (*On rentre PARCE QU'IL PLEUT*).

causative (*causatif*). A sentence structure indicating that someone/something was made to do something (*Je ris → Tu me fais rire*).

central vowel (*voyelle centrale*). See **vowel fronting.**

clause (*proposition*). A **phrase** expressing an entire idea and comprising a single VP. **Sentences** may contain a single clause [$_{S1}$ Je t'aime] or more than one clause [$_{S1}$ J'ai dit [$_{S2}$ que je t'aime]].

cleft sentence (*phrase clivée*). A pragmatically determined sentence pattern with the structure *C'est* A *qui/que* B (*C'EST toi QUI m'embêtes, C'EST à Paris QUE je veux habiter*) which is used to focus on A.

clitic proform (*pronom clitique*). A **proform** which cannot be separated from a **verb** (*JE TE LE dis*). See **disjunctive proform.**

close vowel (*voyelle fermée*). See **vowel height.**

common noun (*nom commun*). See **noun.**

comparative (*comparatif*). See **adjective.**

complement (*complément*). A **phrase** which combines with a **head**, e.g. (*à*) *Robert* in [$_{VP}$ voir ROBERT], [$_{PP}$ avec ROBERT], [$_{VP}$ penser À ROBERT].

complementiser (*complémenteur*). A grammatical word introducing a **subordinate clause** (*Tu sais QUE je t'aime, Demande-lui DE partir, C'est facile À faire, Je ne sais pas SI elle sera là*).

complex inversion (*inversion complexe*). See **inversion.**

compound-past (*passé composé*). **Paradigms** like *ai ri/as ri/a ri/avons ri/avez ri/ont ri.*

compound tense (*temps composé*). See **tense.**

compounding (*composition*). Creating a new word from two existing ones (*gratte-ciel*).

concessive clause (*proposition adverbiale de concession*). An **adverbial clause** providing a context within which the content of the **matrix clause** is unexpected (*BIEN QU'IL PLEUVE, on va faire un pique-nique*).

condition clause (*proposition adverbiale de condition*). An **adverbial clause** indicating the conditions to be met for the content of the **matrix clause** to be realised (*Je t'épouserai SI TU M'AIMES*).

conditional (*conditionnel*). **Paradigms** like *irais/irais/irait/irions/iriez/iraient.*

conditional-perfect (*conditionnel passé*). **Paradigms** like *aurais fait/aurais fait/aurait fait/aurions fait/auriez fait/auraient fait.*

conjugation (*conjugaison*). A morphological **subcategory** of **verb** (*-er, -ir* and *-re* verbs).

consonant (*consonne*). A **segment** involving significant obstruction of the airstream: [p, n, l].

constituent negation (*négation partielle*). See **negation.**

constituent question (*interrogation partielle*). See **interrogation**.

coordinating conjunction (*conjonction de coordination*). See **coordination**.

coordination (*coordination*). A syntactic phenomenon allowing words or phrases of the same type to be linked by a **coordinating conjunction**, e.g. *et* and *ou* (*Jean* ET *Marie, à Toulouse* OU *à Paris*).

copula (*copule*). See **verb**.

declarative sentence (*phrase énonciative/déclarative/affirmative*). See **sentence**.

definite article (*article défini*). See **determiner**.

deictic tense (*temps déictique*). Temporal location established with respect to **utterance** time. See **anaphoric tense**.

demonstrative determiner (*déterminant démonstratif*). See **determiner**.

demonstrative proform (*pronom démonstratif*). See **proform**.

derivational morphology (*morphologie dérivationnelle*). See **morphology**.

determiner (*déterminant*). A **category** occurring with **nouns** within an NP: definite articles (*le, la, les*), indefinite articles (*un, une, des*), partitive articles (*du, de la, des*), demonstratives (*ce, cette, ces*), possessives (e.g. *mon, ta, vos*), quantifiers (*plusieurs, beaucoup de*) and interrogatives (*quel(le)(s), combien de*).

deverbal noun (*nom déverbal*). **Nouns** derived from **verbs**: *décider* → *décision*.

devoicing (*assourdissement*). Realisation of a **voiced phoneme** as a **voiceless allophone**: /b/ → [p] in *absolu*.

diacritic (*signe diacritique*). A mark added to a character: ´, `, ^ on *é, è, ê*.

dialect (*dialecte*). A variety of a language used by groups smaller than the total community of speakers.

diglossia (*diglossie*). A sociolinguistic situation in which two languages or varieties are used within a speech community with complementary or distinct functions.

direct object ((*complément d'*) *object direct*). See **argument**.

direct question (*interrogation directe*). See **interrogation**.

disjunctive proform (*pronom disjoint*). **Proforms** morpho-syntactically independent of **verbs**: *eux, moi*. See **clitic proform**.

ditransitive verb (*verbe bitransitif*). See **verb**.

dorsum (*dos*). The back of the tongue.

double compound-past (*temps surcomposé*). **Verbs** of the form *avoir eu/été* + **past participle** (*J'ai eu fini, Elle a été revenue*). See **tense**.

elision (*élision*). Omission of the final **vowel** of a vowel-final word, when followed by a vowel-initial word (/laɔʀɑ̃ʒ/ → [lɔʀɑ̃ʒ], /ʒəaʀiv/ → [ʒaʀiv]). (NB: words starting with *h-aspiré* don't trigger elision, *la haine* [laɛn], *[lɛn]). Omission of a **consonant** in a consonant cluster (/akatʀpat/ → [akatpat]).

enchaînement. See **resyllabification**.

exclamative sentence (*phrase exclamative*). See **sentence**.

expletive *ne* (*ne explétif*). The non-negative use of *ne* (*Je crains qu'il* NE *vienne, C'est pire que je* NE *croyais*).

feminine (*féminin*). See **gender**.

finite verb (*verbe conjugué/tensé/fini*). A **verb form** marked for subject **agreement**, **tense** and **mood** (*étions, fassiez*). See **non-finite verb**.

flashback-past (*passé récent du passé*). **Paradigms** like *venais de faire/venais de faire/venait de faire/venions de faire/veniez de faire/venaient de faire*.

fricative (*fricative/constrictive*). **Segments** produced by forcing the airstream through a narrow constriction in the **vocal tract**, causing audible friction: [v, s, ʒ].

front vowel (*voyelle antérieure*). See **vowel fronting**.

fusion (*fusion*). The combination of two or more affixal **morphemes** into a single, unanalysable affix (the **tense** and **agreement** suffixes in *sortAIENT* [sɔʀtɛ]).

future-in-the-past (*futur proche du passé*). **Paradigms** like *allais faire/allais faire/allait faire/allions faire/alliez faire/allaient faire*.

future-perfect (*futur antérieur*). **Paradigms** like *aurai fait/auras fait/aura fait/aurons fait/aurez fait/auront fait*.

geminate (*consonne géminée*). A 'long' **consonant**; a sequence of two identical **plosives**, the first of which is unreleased (*là-dedans* /ladədɑ̃/ → [ladːɑ̃]).

gender (*genre*). The distinction between masculine and feminine **nouns** and **proforms** (*LE stylo, LA feuille, ils, elles*).

generic proform (*pronom neutre*). A **proform** denoting a class (*ça, on*).

glide (*glissante/semi-consonne*). A **segment** which is phonetically a **vowel**, but phonologically a **consonant** ([j, w, ɥ]).

glottal stop (*coup de glotte*). A **consonant** [ʔ] produced by a total closure of the **glottis**.

glottis (*glotte*). The space between the **vocal cords**.

grapheme (*graphème*). An orthographic symbol.

h-aspiré. See **elision**; **liaison**.

head (*tête*). 1. The word which determines the syntactic **(sub)category** of a **phrase** (*partir* in the VP *partir en Espagne, fier* in the AP *très fier de moi*). 2. The sequence of words within a relativised NP with which the **relative proform** is coreferential (*le livre* is the head of *LE LIVRE dans LEQUEL je lisais* because the relative proform *lequel* is coreferential with it).

high vowel (*voyelle fermée*). See **vowel height**.

imperative sentence (*phrase injonctive/impérative*). See **sentence**.

imperfect (*imparfait*). **Paradigms** like *allais/allais/allait/allions/alliez/allaient*.

impersonal il (*il impersonnel*). The **clitic proform** *il* which functions as **subject** in some **sentences**, but doesn't refer to anything.

impersonal sentence (*phrase impersonnelle*). A **sentence** whose syntactic **subject** is **impersonal il**/*ce* (*IL faut partir, C'est dommage que tu partes*).

inchoative aspect (*aspect inchoatif*). See **aspect**.

indefinite article (*article indéfini*). See **determiner**.

indicative (*indicatif*). See **mood**.

indirect object (*(complément d')objet indirect*). See **argument**.

indirect question (*interrogation indirecte*). See **interrogation**.

indirect transitive verb (*verbe transitif indirect*). See **verb**.

infinitive (*infinitif*). The **verb form** listed in dictionaries (*naître, parler, sortir, voir*).

inflectional morphology (*morphologie flexionnelle*). See **morphology**.

inter-speaker variation (*variation inter-locuteur*). The way language varies depending on the social characteristics of the speakers. See **style/register**.

interrogation (*interrogation*). Using language to ask questions. Yes–no questions invite a 'yes' or 'no' answer (*Est-ce qu'il pleut?*); constituent questions contain **interrogative phrases** (*dans quelle chambre, quels hommes, comment, qui*) and invite specific information (*Comment t'appelles-tu?*). Questions are either direct (*A-t-elle fini?, Qui a-t-elle dit qu'elle a vu?*) or indirect (*Je sais QUI ELLE A VU, Je me demande SI JE RÊVE*).

interrogative determiner (*déterminant interrogatif*). See **interrogative phrase**.

interrogative movement (*mouvement interrogatif*). See **movement**.

interrogative phrase (*syntagme interrogatif*). A **phrase** containing an interrogative determiner (*QUEL homme, COMBIEN D'hommes*) or proform (*qui, quoi, que*).

interrogative proform (*pronom interrogatif*). See **proform**; **interrogative phrase**.

interrogative sentence (*phrase interrogative*). Alternative term for **direct question**.

intonation (*intonation*). The pitch pattern of an **utterance**, which can be used, e.g. to turn a statement into a question.

intra-speaker variation (*variation intra-locuteur*). The way language varies depending on what a speaker is using it for. See **style/register**.

intransitive verb (*verbe intransitif*). See **verb**.

inversion (*inversion*). A **marked word order** in which the **subject** of the sentence follows the **finite verb**. In subject–clitic inversion, a **subject clitic** immediately follows the finite verb (*Il est parti → Est-il parti?*). In stylistic inversion, a subject NP follows both the finite verb and, in the case of **compound tenses**, the **past participle** (*L'enfant est parti hier → Quand est parti l'enfant?*). Complex inversion involves an inverted subject clitic and non-inverted subject NP (*Quand l'enfant est-il parti?*). Inversion can be triggered by **interrogation** and sentence-initial **adverbials** (*Peut-être (Jean) est-il parti*).

iterative aspect (*aspect itératif*). See **aspect**.

larynx (*larynx*). The part of the throat which contains the **vocal cords**.

left dislocation (*dislocation à gauche*). A pragmatically determined **sentence** pattern in which a **phrase** appears sentence-initially, and then reappears as a **resumptive clitic proform** in its 'usual' place (*CE LIVRE, je L'ai acheté hier*).

leftward quantifier floating (*déplacement de* tout(e)(s) *vers la gauche*). **Movement** of *tout(e)(s)* to the left of a **past participle/infinitive** (*Ils les ont tous vus, Je veux tout faire*).

lexicon (*lexique*). A speaker's mental dictionary.

lexifier language (*langue lexificatrice*). The language which is the source of the majority of the vocabulary of a pidgin or creole.

liaison (*liaison*). A phonological phenomenon in which a word which is vowel-final when pronounced in isolation (*petit* [pəti]) is consonant-final when followed by a vowel-initial word (*petit ami* [pətitami]). (NB: words starting with *h-aspiré* don't trigger liaison, *les hibous* [leibu], *[lezibu].)

lip rounding (*arrondissement des lèvres*). A feature of **vowels**. Round vowels [ɥ, u] are distinguished from unrounded/spread vowels [i].

liquid (*liquide*). [l] and [ʀ].

logical subject (*sujet logique*). The NP interpreted as the **subject** of a **subordinate infinitive** (*J'ai vu* JEAN *partir, Elle a fait réparer la voiture à* JEAN).

low vowel (*voyelle ouverte*). See **vowel height**.

manner of articulation (*mode d'articulation*). The way a **consonant** is produced in the **vocal tract**: **plosive, fricative, nasal, liquid**.

marked word order (*ordre non canonique*). Deviation from the usual, unmarked word order (subject–verb–direct object–indirect object) for syntactic or pragmatic reasons: **interrogation** (*AVEC QUI es-tu parti?*) and dislocation (*À MARIE on a donné un gros cadeau*).

masculine (*masculin*). See **gender**.

masquerade (*alternance que/qui*). Alternative term for ***que/qui* alternation**.

matrix clause (*proposition principale/matrice*). See **sentence**.

mid-high/close/low/open vowel (*voyelle semi-fermée/ouverte*). See **vowel height**.

minimal sentence. See **sentence, minimal**.

modality (*modalité*). The expression of the speaker's attitude towards the truth/necessity/likelihood of the content of the **sentence**.

mood (*mode*). The morphological (and possibly semantic) contrast between **indicative** and **subjunctive** verb forms.

morpheme (*morphème/monème*). Morphologically indivisible unit of meaning.

morphology (*morphologie*). Patterns of word formation and structure, both derivational (creating different words) and inflectional (creating different forms of the same word).

movement (*déplacement*). A change in the position of **interrogative/relative phrases** (*Tu as vu* QUI? → QUI *tu as vu?*, *L'homme [je danse* AVEC *L'HOMME] est vieux* → *L'homme [*AVEC QUI *je danse] est vieux*). See also **remote quantification; leftward/rightward quantifier floating; left/right dislocation**.

mute e (*e-muet/caduc*). An unstressed central mid vowel [ə], often omitted: /ʒə.mə.lə.də.mãd/ → [ʒəm.ləd.mãd].

nasal (*nasale*). **Segments** produced with the **velum** lowered, allowing the airstream to escape though the **nasal cavity**.

nasal cavity (*fosses nasales*). The **vocal tract** from the nostrils to the top of the **pharynx**. Escape of the airstream through the nasal cavity is blocked by raising the **velum**.

negation (*négation*). A grammatical phenomenon which allows the contents of all (sentential negation: *Je ne fume pas*) or part (constituent negation: *une explication pas tout à fait crédible*) of a **sentence** to be rejected or denied.

negative polarity (*polarité négative*). See **polarity**.

non-finite verb (*verb non fini*). **Verb** forms unmarked for **tense**, **mood** and subject **agreement**: **infinitives**, **present/past participles**.

non-referential *il* (*il impersonnel*). An alternative term for **impersonal** *il*.

noun (*nom/substantif*). Words denoting things, people, places, concepts, etc., and heading an NP. Common nouns usually co-occur with a **determiner** [$_{NP}$ la maison]; proper nouns usually don't [$_{NP}$ Paris].

null morpheme (*morphème zéro/vide*). See **zero realisation**.

number (*nombre*). The distinction between singular and plural **nouns** and **proforms** (*le visage, les visages, il, ils*).

official language (*langue officielle*). The language (or one of the languages) of government, administration and public services, at national, regional or local level.

open vowel (*voyelle ouverte*). See **vowel height**.

oral (*son oral*). **Segments** produced with the **velum** raised, preventing the airstream from passing though the **nasal cavity**.

oral cavity (*cavité orale/buccale*). The **vocal tract** from the lips to the top of the **pharynx**.

palate (*palais*). The roof of the mouth.

paradigm (*paradigme*). A set of morphologically related forms: *faisais/faisais/faisait/faisions/faisiez/faisaient*.

partitive article (*article partitif*). See **determiner**.

passive morphology (*morphologie du passif*). See **passive sentence**.

passive sentence (*phrase passive*). A **sentence** containing a **transitive verb** with **passive morphology** (a combination of the **auxiliary** *être* and a **past participle**), in which the **patient** is the syntactic **subject**, and the **agent** is contained optionally within an **agent phrase** (*Le livre a été écrit (par mon prof)*). See **active sentence**.

past anterior (*passé antérieur*). **Paradigms** like *eus fait/eus fait/eut fait/eûmes fait/eûtes fait/eurent fait*.

past-historic (*passé simple*). **Paradigms** like *allai/allas/alla/allâmes/allâtes/allèrent*.

past participle (*participe passé*). A **non-finite verb form** used in **compound tenses** and **passive sentences** (*Il a ACHETÉ un livre, Le livre a été ACHETÉ*).

patient (*patient*). The entity which undergoes the effects of an action (*Elle a mangé LA TARTE*). See **agent**.

periphrastic tense (*temps périphrastique*). See **tense**.

person (*personne*). A grammatical feature of **nouns** and **proforms** functioning as **arguments** of a **verb**; first person includes the speaker (*je, nous, Jean et moi*); second person includes the addressee but not the speaker (*tu, vous et les autres*); third person includes neither speaker nor addressee (*elle, Marie et lui*).

personal proform (*pronom personnel*). An **unstressed** (**clitic**) **proform** (*je/tu/il/elle/nous/vous/ils/elles*) encoding the **person**, **number** (and **gender**) of the **subject**.

pharynx (*pharynx*). The **vocal tract** between the **glottis** (**larynx**) and the back of the mouth.

phoneme (*phonème*). The abstract representation of a **segment**.

phonetics (*phonétique*). The study of speech.

phonology (*phonologie*). The study of speech sound systems.

phrase (*groupe/syntagme*). A sequence of words which, taken together, form a syntactic and semantic unit.

place of articulation (*point d'articulation*). The position of the active **articulator**.

pleonastic *ne* (*ne explétif*). An alternative term for **expletive** *ne*.

plosive (*plosive*). A **manner of articulation** involving total blockage and sudden release of the airstream: [p, d, k].

pluperfect (*plus-que-parfait*). **Paradigms** like *avais fait/avais fait/avait fait/ avions fait/aviez fait/avaient fait*.

plural (*pluriel*). See **number**.

polarity (*polarité*). The distinction between **negative** and **positive** clauses (*Elle est partie, Il n'est pas là*).

positive (*positif/affirmatif*). See **polarity**.

possessive determiner (*déterminant possessif*). See **determiner**.

predeterminer (*prédéterminant/quantifieur* tout). The word *tout(e)(s)* in NP-initial position (*TOUS mes espoirs, TOUTE l'année*).

predicative adjective (*adjectif attribut*). See **adjective**.

prefix (*préfixe*). See **affixation**.

preposition (*préposition*). Words like *sur, avec* and *dans* which head PPs (*sur la liste, avec son frère, dans un instant*).

present (*présent*). **Paradigms** like *vais/vas/va/allons/allez/vont*.

proform (*pronom*). A grammatical word used to stand for a **phrase**: demonstrative (*celui*) and relative/interrogative (*lequel*). See **clitic proform; disjunctive proform; personal proform**.

progressive aspect (*aspect progressif*). See **aspect**.

progressive assimilation (*assimilation progressive*). See **assimilation**.

pronominal verb (*verbe pronominal*). **Verbs** whose (in)direct object is co-referential with their **subject** (*se tromper*).

pronominalisation (*pronominalisation*). Replacement of a **phrase** by a **proform**.

pronoun (*pronom*). An alternative term for **proform**.

proper noun (*nom propre*). See **noun**.

purpose clause (*proposition adverbiale de but*). An **adverbial clause** indicating rationale (*J'ai téléphoné POUR TE FAIRE PLAISIR*).

quantifier (*quantifieur*). A **determiner** whose function is to express quantity within NP (*plusieurs, trop de, tout(e)(s)*). See **remote quantification**.

que/qui alternation (*alternance* que/qui). The finite declarative **complementiser**'s sensitivity to whether or not it's followed by an empty **subject** position (*Qui veux-tu QUE je tue* – ?, *Qui veux-tu QUI* – *soit tué?*).

recent-past (*passé récent*). **Paradigms** like *viens de rire/viens de rire/vient de rire/venons de rire/venez de rire/viennent de rire*.

reciprocal clitic proform (*pronom clitique réciproque*). A **clitic proform** coreferential with the **subject**, e.g. *Marie et Pierre SE sont vus* (where Marie saw Pierre and Pierre saw Marie). See **reflexive clitic proform**.

reflexive clitic proform (*pronom clitique réfléchi*). A **clitic proform** coreferential with the **subject**, e.g. *Marie et Pierre SE sont brossé les dents* (where each one brushed his/her own teeth, rather than Marie brushing Pierre's teeth and Pierre brushing Marie's teeth). See **reciprocal clitic proform**.

reflexive verb (*verbe pronominal*). An alternative term for **pronominal verb**.

regressive assimilation (*assimilation régressive*). See **assimilation**.

relative clause (*proposition relative*). See **relativisation**.

relative proform (*pronom relatif*). See **proform; relativisation**.

relativisation (*relativisation*). Modification of a (pro)nominal by a **clause** (*la ville DANS LAQUELLE JE VIS*). Here, *la ville* is the head of the relative, *laquelle* is the relative proform, and *dans laquelle je vis* is the relative clause.

remote quantification (*quantification à distance*). **Movement** of a **quantifier** from within a **direct object** to the left of the **infinitive/past participle** (*Nous avons lu TROP de romans* → *Nous avons TROP lu de romans, Il veut voir BEAUCOUP d'églises* → *Il veut BEAUCOUP voir d'églises*).

resumptive proform (*pronom de rappel/pronom résomptif/pronom de reprise*). See **left dislocation**.

resyllabification (*enchaînement*). A phonological phenomenon whereby the final consonant(s) of one syllable become(s) the initial consonant(s) of the next syllable (*une école* /yn.e.kɔl/ → [y.ne.kɔl]).

right dislocation (*dislocation à droite*). A pragmatically determined sentence pattern in which a **phrase** appears sentence-finally, but appears as a resumptive **clitic proform** in its 'usual' place (*Je L'ai acheté hier, CE LIVRE*).

rightward quantifier floating (*déplacement de* tout(e)(s) *vers la droite*). **Movement** of *tout(e)(s)* to the right of the **finite verb** (*TOUS les garçons sont partis* → *Les garçons sont TOUS partis*).

root (*racine*). See **affixation**.

rounded vowel (*voyelle arrondie*). See **lip rounding**.

rounding (*arrondissement des lèvres*). An alternative term for **lip rounding**.

schwa (*schwa*). An alternative term for **mute e**.

segment (*segment*). The idealised units into which an **utterance** can be divided.

semi-consonant (*semi-consonne*). An alternative term for **glide**.

semi-vowel (*semi-voyelle*). An alternative term for **glide**.

sentence (*phrase*). The largest unit of syntactic analysis. Simple sentences contain a single **clause** [$_S$ Donc je suis parti]; complex sentences, more than one clause: a subordinate clause contained within a matrix clause [$_{S1}$ Elle sait [$_{S2}$ que tu mens]] or two coordinated clauses [[$_{S1}$ J'ai faim] et [$_{S2}$ je veux manger]]. Declarative sentences usually make statements (*Tu es mignon*); interrogative sentences usually ask questions (*Est-ce que tu es mignon?*); imperative sentences usually give orders (*Sois mignon!*); exclamative sentences usually express surprise, etc. (*Comme tu es mignon!*).

sentence, minimal (*phrase minimale*). A **sentence** whose VP contains no more than a **verb form** and its **complements**, i.e. no **adverbials**.

sentential negation (*négation de phrase*). See **negation**.

simple tense (*temps simple*). See **tense**.

singular (*singulier*). See **number**.

speech organs (*organes de la parole/appareil phonatoire*). Parts of the **vocal tract**, from the **glottis** to the lips/nostrils, used in **articulation**.

spread vowel (*voyelle non arrondie*). See **lip rounding**.

standard language (*langue standard*). An abstract set of norms prescribing correct usage in terms of pronunciation, grammar, vocabulary and spelling. Usually has the status of **official language**.

stem alternation (*alternance vocalique*). A morphological phenomenon whereby a root morpheme has more than one form: [apəl-]/[apɛl-].

stop (*occlusive*). A consonant produced with a total blockage of the airstream in the mouth: [m, t, g].

stress (*accent*). Syllabic prominence marked by loudness, pitch and/or length.

stressed proform (*pronom accentué/fort*). An alternative term for **disjunctive proform**.

style/register (*style/registre*). Language variation related to the (in)formality of the situation in which speakers find themselves.

stylistic inversion (*inversion stylistique*). See **inversion**.

subcategory (*sous-catégorie*). See **category**.

subject (*sujet*). See **argument**.

subject–clitic inversion (*inversion du clitique sujet, inversion pronominale*). See **inversion**.

subjunctive (*subjonctif*). See **mood**.

subordinate clause (*proposition conjonctive/enchâssée*). See **sentence**.

suffix (*suffixe*). See **affixation**.

superlative (*superlatif*). See **adjective**.

syllable (*syllabe*). A phonological unit centred on a **vowel** or vowel-like sound, optionally preceded and/or followed by one or more **consonant(s)**.

syntax (*syntaxe*). The study of phrase and sentence structure.

synthetic future (*futur simple*). **Paradigms** like *irai/iras/ira/irons/irez/iront*.

temporal clause (*proposition adverbiale de temps*). An **adverbial clause** indicating when something was the case.

tense (*temps*). 1. The temporal location of the action etc. described by the VP. 2. The paradigm to which a **verb form** belongs. Tenses are either simple (*pars*), compound (*suis parti*) or periphrastic (*viens de partir*).

tonic proform (*pronom accentué/fort*). An alternative term for **disjunctive proform**.

transitive verb (*verbe transitif*). See **verb**.

universal quantifier (*quantifieur universel*). The words *tout* and *rien*.

unmarked word order (*ordre direct*). See **marked word order**.

unrounded vowel (*voyelle non arrondie*). See **lip rounding**.

unstressed proform (*pronom faible/clitique/conjoint/non accentué*). An alternative term for **clitic proform**.

utterance (*énoncé*). A self-contained stretch of speech.

uvula (*luette*). The extreme end of the **velum**.

vehicular language (*langue véhiculaire*). A language used for non-official communication between groups or individuals speaking different vernacular languages.

velum (*palais mou/voile du palais*). The soft back part of the **palate**.

verb (*verbe*). A **category** whose members can be **finite** (marked for subject **agreement**, **tense** and **mood**: *parlerais*) or **non-finite** (*parler, parlant, parlé*). Verbs belong to morphological subcategories (*-er, -ir, -re* verbs) and syntactic subcategories: **intransitive verbs** (*rire*), **transitive verbs** (*dévorer*), **indirect transitive verbs** (*plaire*), **ditransitive verbs** (*donner*), **copulas** (*être*), **auxiliaries** (*être, avoir*).

vernacular language (*langue vernaculaire*). The mother tongue of all or most of the members of a particular speech community.

vocal cords (*cordes vocales*). Two muscular membranes in the **larynx** which can be made to vibrate to produce certain **segments**.

vocal tract (*appareil vocal*). The passage above the **glottis** used to produce speech.

voice (*voix*). 1. See **active sentence**. 2. An alternative term for **voicing**.

voiced (*voisé/sonore*). See **voicing**.

voiceless (*sourd*). See **voicing**.

voicing (*sonorité*). Whether the **vocal cords** are apart (voiceless), together (glottal stop) or vibrating (voiced). **Vowels** are usually voiced; **consonants** can be voiced or voiceless.

vowel (*voyelle*). A **segment** produced with very little constriction within the **vocal tract** above the **glottis**.

vowel fronting (*antériorité*). The position of the tongue, on the horizontal axis, during the production of **vowels**. Front vowels [i, y, e, ø, ɛ, a, œ] are distinguished from back vowels [u, o, ɔ, ɑ]. Mute e [ə] is a central vowel.

vowel harmony (*harmonie vocalique*). A phonological phenomenon whereby the phonetic features of one vowel are influenced by those of a neighbouring vowel.

vowel height (*aperture*). The vertical position of the tongue during the production of **vowels**. Four levels are distinguished: high/close [i, y, u], mid-high/close [e, ø, o], mid-low/open [ɛ, œ, ɔ] and low/open [ɑ, a].

vowel quality (*timbre*). The properties of a **vowel** determined by the position of the tongue, the **velum** and the lips.

vowel quantity (*durée/longueur des voyelles*). Whether a vowel is short (*mettre* [mɛtʀ]) or long (*maître* [mɛːtʀ]).

yes–no interrogative/question (*interrogation totale*). See **interrogation**.

zero realisation (*réalisation zéro*). A morphological term indicating that a **morpheme** has no overt phonetic form, in other words, is null, e.g. the plural markers in *tous leurs pains* [tulœʀpɛ̃].

Bibliography

Abercrombie, D. (1967) *Elements of general phonetics*, Edinburgh: Edinburgh University Press.

Ager, D. E. (1990) *Sociolinguistics and contemporary French*, Cambridge: Cambridge University Press.

—— (1996) *'Francophonie' in the 1990s*, Clevedon: Multilingual Matters.

Ager, D. E and French, J. F. (eds) (1986) *La Francophonie*, Portsmouth: AFLS/Portsmouth Polytechnic.

Aitchison, J. (1987) *Words in the mind*, Oxford: Blackwell.

Amiot, D. (1995) 'De la construction du sens des adjectifs préfixés par *pré*: *prétuberculeux* vs. *précolombien'*, *Journal of French Language Studies* 5: 1–16.

Anderson, S. R. (1988) 'Morphological theory', in F. J. Newmeyer (ed.) *Linguistics: the Cambridge survey*, vol. 1: *Linguistic theory: foundations*, 146–91, Cambridge: Cambridge University Press.

Antoine, G. and Martin, R. (eds) (1985) *Histoire de la langue française 1880–1914*, Paris: CNRS.

Armstrong, L. (1982) *The phonetics of French*, London: Hall and Hyman.

Ashby, W. J. (1976) 'The loss of the negative morpheme *ne* in Parisian French', *Lingua* 39: 119–37.

—— (1981a) 'French liaison as a sociolinguistic phenomenon', in W. Cressey and D. J. Napoli (eds) *Linguistic symposium of the Romance languages*, 46–57, Washington, DC: Georgetown University Press.

—— (1981b) 'The loss of the negative particle *ne* in French: a syntactic change in progress', *Language* 57: 674–87.

—— (1988) 'The syntax, pragmatics and sociolinguistics of left- and right-dislocations in French', *Lingua* 75: 203–29.

—— (1991) 'When does linguistic change indicate change in progress?', *Journal of French Language Studies* 1: 1–19.

—— (1992) 'The variable use of *on* versus *tu/vous* for indefinite reference in spoken French', *Journal of French Language Studies* 2: 135–57.

Atkinson, J. C. (1973) *Two forms of subject inversion in Modern French*, Paris: Mouton.

Aub-Buscher, G. (1993) 'French and French-based creoles: the case of the French Caribbean', in Sanders (ed.), 199–214.

Auzanneau, M. (1998) 'Identités poitevines: une réalité mouvante', in Marley et al. (eds), 27–41.

Ayres-Bennett, W. (1987) *Vaugelas and the development of the French language*, London: MHRA.

—— (1990) 'Women and grammar in seventeenth century France', *Seventeenth Century French Studies* 12: 5–25.

—— (1996) *A history of the French language through texts*, London: Routledge.

Azoulay-Vicente, A. (1989) 'Cas partitif et quantification à distance', *Recherches Linguistiques de Vincennes* 18: 81–100.

Baggioni, D. and Robillard, D. de (1990) *Ile Maurice: une francophonie paradoxale*, Paris: L'Harmattan.

Baker, P. (1972) *Kreol*, London: Hurst.

—— (1986) 'Mauritian Creole', *Proceedings of the workshop of the international group for the study of language standardization and the vernacularization of literacy*, 86–8, University of York.

Balibar, R. and Laporte, D. (1974) *Le Français national*, Paris: Hachette.

Ball, R. V. (1990) 'Lexical innovation in present-day French: "*le français branché*"', *French Cultural Studies* 1: 21–35.

—— (1997) *The French-speaking world*, London: Routledge.

Balzac, H. de (1974) *Le Cousin Pons*, Garnier Classique, ed. Meininger, Paris: Garnier-Flammarion.

Barnes, B. (1985) *The pragmatics of left detachment in spoken French*, Amsterdam: Benjamins.

Battye, A. C. (1995) 'Aspects of quantification in French in its regional and diachronic varieties', in J.-C. Smith and M. Maiden (eds) *Linguistic theory and the Romance languages*, 1–35, Amsterdam: Benjamins.

Bauche, H. (1951) *Le Français populaire*, Paris: Payot.

Bauer, L. (1988) *Introducing linguistic morphology*, Edinburgh: Edinburgh University Press.

Bazylko, S. (1981) 'Le statut de [ə]', *La Linguistique* 17: 91–101.

Beaucé, T. de (1988) *Nouveau discours sur l'universalité de la langue française*, Paris: Gallimard.

Bec, P. (1967) *La Langue occitane*, Paris: Presses Universitaires de France.

Becherel, D. (1981) 'A propos des solutions de remplacement des anglicismes', *La Linguistique* 17: 119–31.

Bescherelle, Le Nouveau (1990) *L'Art de conjuguer*, Paris: Hatier.

Bickerton, D. (1975) *Dynamics of a creole system*, Cambridge: Cambridge University Press.

—— (1981) *Roots of language*, Ann Arbor, Mich.: Karoma.

—— (1984a) 'The language bioprogram hypothesis', *The Behavioral and Brain Sciences* 7: 173–221.

—— (1984b) 'The language bioprogram hypothesis and second language acquisition', in W. E. Rutherford (ed.) *Language universals and second language acquisition*, 141–61, Amsterdam: Benjamins.

Blanc, M. (1993) 'French in Canada', in Sanders (ed.), 239–56.

Blanche-Benveniste, C. (1997) *Approches de la langue parlée française*, Paris: Ophrys.

Blanche-Benveniste, C. and Jeanjean, C. (1987) *Le Français parlé*, Paris: CNRS/Didier Erudition.

Bloomfield, L. (1933) *Language*, Chicago, Ill.: Chicago University Press. (Rev. edn 1935.)

Blyth, C. (1997) 'The sociolinguistic situation of Cajun French', in Valdman (ed.), 25–46.

Borrell, A. (1986) 'Le vocabulaire "jeune", le parler "branché"', *Cahiers de Lexicologie* 48: 69–87.

Bostock, W. W. (1986) *Francophonie*, Melbourne: River Seine.

Boswell, C. (1992) *The French language*, 2nd edn, Egham: Runnymede.

Bouchard, D. (1982) 'Les constructions relatives en français vernaculaire et en français standard: étude d'un paramètre', in Lefebvre (ed.), vol. 1, 103–33.

—— (1998) 'The distribution and interpretation of adjectives in French: a consequence of Bare Phrase Structure', *Probus* 10: 139–83.

Bourdieu, P. (1982) *Ce que parler veut dire*, Paris: Fayard.

—— (1983) 'Vous avez dit "populaire"?', *Actes de la Recherche en Sciences Sociales* 46: 98–105.

Bourhis, R. Y. (ed.) (1984) *Language conflict and language planning in Quebec*, Clevedon: Multilingual Matters.

Bouvier, J.-C. and Martel, C. (eds) (1991) *Les Français et leurs langues*, Aix-en-Provence: Publications de l'Université de Provence.

Brick, N. and Wilks, C. (1994) '*Et Dieu nomma la femme*: observations sur la question de la féminisation des noms d'agent et sur les désignations d'Edith Cresson dans la presse', *Journal of French Language Studies* 4: 235–9.

Broglie, G. de (1986) *Le Français, pour qu'il vive*, Paris: Gallimard.

Brown, G. (1982) 'The spoken language', in R. Carter (ed.) *Linguistics and the teacher*, 75–87, London: Routledge.

Brulard, I. (1997) 'Linguistic policies', in S. Perry (ed.) *Aspects of contemporary France*, 191–207, London: Routledge.

Brun, A. (1931) *Le Français de Marseille*, Paris: Champion.

Brunot, F. (1905–67) *Histoire de la langue française des origines à nos jours*, 13 vols, Paris: Armand Colin.

Callebaut, B. (ed.) (1992) *Les Négations*, special issue of *Langue Française* 94.

Calvet, L.-J. (1993) 'The migrant languages of Paris', in Sanders (ed.), 105–19.

—— (1994) *L'Argot*, Paris: Presses Universitaires de France.

Canada Yearbook (1999) *Statistics Canada*, Ottawa.

Caput, J.-P. (1972, 1975) *La Langue française*, 2 vols, Paris: Larousse.

—— (1986) *L'Académie française*, Paris: Presses Universitaires de France.

Carayol, M. and Chaudenson, R. (1978) 'Diglossie et continuum linguistique à la Réunion', in Gueunier *et al.* (eds), 175–90.

Carr, P. (1993) *Phonology*, Basingstoke: Macmillan.

Carrington, L. D. (1988) 'Creole discourse and social development', Manuscript Report 212, Ottawa: International Development Research Centre.

Carruthers, J. (1994) 'The *passé surcomposé régional*: towards a definition of its function in contemporary spoken French', *Journal of French Language Studies* 4: 171–90.

Carton, F. (1974) *Introduction à la phonétique du français*, Paris: Bordas.

—— (1981) 'Les parlers ruraux de la région Nord-Picardie: situation sociolinguistique', in Tabouret-Keller (ed.), 15–28.

—— (1987) 'Les accents régionaux', in Vermes and Boutet (eds), vol. 2, 29–49.

Carton, F., Rossi, M., Autesserre, D. and Léon, P. (1983) *Les Accents des Français*, Paris: Hachette.

Catach, N. (1987) 'Entrecôte vert pré ou l'expansion déterminative libre en français', *Cahiers de Lexicologie* 51: 73–93.

—— (1993) 'The reform of the writing system', in Sanders (ed.), 139–54.

—— (1995) *L'Orthographe*, 6th edn, Paris: Presses Universitaires de France.

Cellard, J. and Rey, A. (1991) *Dictionnaire du français non conventionnel*, 2nd edn, Paris: Hachette.

Certeau, M. de, Julia, D. and Revel, J. (1975) *Une Politique de la langue: la révolution française et les patois: l'enquête de Grégoire*, Paris: Gallimard.

Charpantier, J. (1987) 'La Louisiane controversée: subsidence créole, efflorescence zydéco, mouvement français, Cajun Power', *Etudes Créoles* 9: 121–40.

Chaudenson, R. (1979a) *Les Créoles français*, Paris: Nathan.

—— (1979b) 'Le français dans les îles de l'Océan Indien (Mascareignes et Seychelles)', in Valdman (ed.), 542–617.

—— (1989) *Créoles et enseignement du français*, Paris: L'Harmattan.

—— (1992) *Des Îles, des hommes, des langues: langues créoles, cultures créoles*, Paris: L'Harmattan.

—— (1995) *Les Créoles*, Paris: Presses Universitaires de France.

Chaurand, J. (1972) *Introduction à la dialectologie française*, Paris: Bordas.

—— (1977) *Introduction à l'histoire du vocabulaire français*, Paris: Bordas.

—— (1985) 'Les français régionaux', in Antoine and Martin (eds).

Chaveau, J.-P. (1977) 'Mots dialectaux qualifiés de "vrais mots"', *Travaux de Linguistique et de Littérature* 15: 105–18.

Colin, J.-P. and Mével, J.-P. (1992) *Dictionnaire de l'argot*, Paris: Larousse.

Comrie, B. (1976) *Aspect*, Cambridge: Cambridge University Press.

—— (1987) *Tense*, Cambridge: Cambridge University Press.

Corbett, G. (1991) *Gender*, Cambridge: Cambridge University Press.

Corbin, D. (1987) *Morphologie dérivationnelle et structuration du lexique*, 2 vols, Tübingen: Niemeyer.

Cornish, F. (1991) 'Non-discrete reference, discourse construction, and the French neuter clitic pronouns', *Journal of French Language Studies* 1: 123–38.

Cornulier, B. de (1981) 'H-aspirée et la syllabation', in D. Goyvaerts (ed.) *Phonology in the 80s*, 183–230, Ghent: Story Scientia.

Couquaux, D. (1986) 'Les pronoms faibles sujet comme groupes nominaux', in Ronat and Couquaux (eds), 25–46.

Coveney, A. (1986) 'Standardization of modern French', *Proceedings of the workshop of the international group for the study of language standardization and the vernacularization of literacy*, 19–21, University of York.

—— (1990a) 'Variation in interrogatives in spoken French: a preliminary report', in Green and Ayres-Bennett (eds), 116–34.

—— (1990b) 'The omission of *ne* in spoken French', *Francophonie* 1: 38–43.

—— (1996) *Variability in spoken French*, Exeter: Elm Bank.

Crombettes, B., Denarolle, P., Copeaux, J. and Fresson, J. (1980) *L'Analyse de la phrase*, 2nd edn, Nancy II.

Crystal, D. (1992) *An encyclopedic dictionary of language and languages*, Oxford: Blackwell.

—— (1997) *A dictionary of phonetics and linguistics*, 4th edn, Oxford: Blackwell.

Dauzat, A. (1922) *La Géographie linguistique*, Paris: Flammarion.

—— (1946) *Les Patois*, Paris: Delagrave.

Delattre, P. (1940) 'Le mot est-il une entité phonétique en français?', *Le Français Moderne* 8: 47–56.

—— (1947) 'La liaison en français, tendances et classification', *The French Review* 21: 148–57.

—— (1966) *Studies in French and comparative phonetics*, Paris: Mouton.

Deniau, X. (1992) *La Francophonie*, 2nd edn, Paris: Presses Universitaires de France.

Depecker, L. (1988) *Les Mots de la francophonie*, Paris: Belin.

Depecker, L. and Pages, A. (1985) *Guide des mots nouveaux*, Paris: Nathan.

Désirat, C. and Hordé, T. (1988) *La Langue française au 20ᵉ siècle*, 2nd edn, Paris: Bordas.

Diderot, D. and d'Alembert, J. (eds) (1751–72) *Encyclopédie, ou dictionnaire raisonné des sciences, des arts et des métiers*, 17 vols, Paris, Facsimile: Stuttgart-Bad Cannstatt: Froman-Holzbog (from 1966).

Di Cristo, A. (1998) 'Intonation in French', in D. Hirst and A. Di Cristo (eds) *Intonation systems*, 195–218, Cambridge: Cambridge University Press.

Dobrovie-Sorin, C. (1986) 'A propos du contraste entre le passif morphologique et *se* moyen dans les tours impersonnels', *Lingvisticæ Investigationes* 10: 289–312.

Dubois, J. (1965) *Grammaire structurale du français: nom et pronom*, Paris: Larousse.

Dubois, J. and Lagane, R. (1988) *La Nouvelle Grammaire du français*, 2nd edn, Paris: Larousse.

Dumont, P. and Maurer, B. (1995) *Sociolinguistique du français en Afrique francophone*, Vanves: EDICEF.

Dupuis, F. and Valois, D. (1992) 'The status of (verbal) traces: the case of French stylistic inversion', in P. Hirschbühler and K. Koerner (eds) *Romance languages and modern linguistic theory*, 325–38, Amsterdam: Benjamins.

Durand, J. (1990) *Generative and nonlinear phonology*, London: Longman.

—— (1993) 'Sociolinguistic variation and the linguist', in Sanders (ed.), 257–85.

—— (1996) 'Linguistic purification, the French Nation-State and the linguist', in C. Hoffmann (ed.) *Language, culture and communication in contemporary Europe*, 75–92, Clevedon: Multilingual Matters.

Edwards, J. (1985) *Language, society and identity*, Oxford: Blackwell.

Encrevé, P. (1983) 'La liaison sans enchaînement', *Actes de la Recherche en Sciences Sociales* 46: 39–66.

—— (1988) *La liaison avec et sans enchaînement*, Paris: Seuil.

Englebert, A. (1993) 'Le status grammatical de *de*', *Journal of French Language Studies* 3: 127–44.

Etiemble, R. (1964) *Parlez-vous franglais?*, Paris: Gallimard. (Rev. edn 1973.)

Ewert, A. (1954) *The French language*, London: Faber and Faber.

Fasold, R. W. (1984) *The sociolinguistics of society*, Oxford: Blackwell.

—— (1990) *The sociolinguistics of language*, Oxford: Blackwell.

Ferguson, C. A. (1959) 'Diglossia', *Word* 15: 325–40. (Reprinted in P. P. Giglioli (ed.) (1972) *Language and social context*, Harmondsworth: Penguin.)

Flaitz, J. (1988) *The ideology of English: French perceptions of English as a world language*, Paris: Mouton.

Flikied, K. (1997) 'Structural aspects and current sociolinguistic situation of Acadian French', in Valdman (ed.), 255–86.

Foley, J. (1979) *Theoretical morphology of the French verb*, Amsterdam: Benjamins.

Fónagy, I. (1989) 'Le français change de visage?', *Revue Romane* 24: 225–54.

Fouché, P. (1959) *Traité de prononciation française*, 2nd edn, Paris: Klincksieck.

Foulet, L. (1921) 'Comment ont évolué les formes de l'interrogation', *Romania* 47: 243– 348.

François, A. (1959) *Histoire de la langue française cultivée des origines à nos jours*, 2 vols, Geneva: Jullien.

François-Geiger, D. and Goudailler, J.-P. (eds) (1991) *Parlures argotiques*, special issue of *Langue Française* 20.

Frémy, D. and Frémy, M. (annual) *Quid*, Paris: Laffont.

Gaatone, D. (1971) *Etude descriptive du système de la négation en français contemporain*, Geneva: Droz.

Gadet, F. (1989) *Le Français ordinaire*, Paris: Armand Colin.

—— (1992) *Le Français populaire*, Paris: Presses Universitaires de France.

Gagné, G. (1979) 'Quelques aspects "socio-linguistiques" du français au Canada et au Québec', in Valdman (ed.), 33–59.

Gardner-Chloros, P. (1991) *Language selection and switching in Strasbourg*, Oxford: Berg.

Gary-Prieur, M.-N. (1994) *Grammaire du nom propre*, Paris: Presses Universitaires de France.

George, K. (1993) 'Alternative French', in Sanders (ed.), 155–70.

Gérard, J. (1980) *L'Exclamation en français*, Tübingen: Niemeyer.

Gertner, M. H. (1973) *The morphology of the Modern French verb*, Paris: Mouton.

Gervais, M.-M. (1993) 'Gender and language in French', in Sanders (ed.), 121–38.

Gordon, D. C. (1978) *The French language and national identity: 1930–1975*, Paris: Mouton.

Goudailler, J.-P. (1997) *Comment tu tchatches! Dictionnaire du français contemporain des cités*, Paris: Maisonneuve and Larose.

Grammont, M. (1894) 'La loi des trois consonnes', *Mémoires de la Société de Linguistique de Paris* 8: 53–90.

Green, J. N. (1986) 'Creole registers and popular French', in Ager and French (eds), 159–85.

—— (1988) 'Romance creoles', in Harris and Vincent (eds), 420–75.

Green, J. N. and Ayres-Bennett, W. (eds) (1990) *Variation and change in French*, London: Routledge.

Green, J. N. and Hintze, M.-A. (1990) 'Variation and change in French linking phenomena', in Green and Ayres-Bennett (eds), 61–88.

Grevisse, M. (1994) *Le Bon Usage*, 13th edn, rev. A. Goosse, Louvain-la-Neuve: Duculot.

Griolet, P. (1986a) *Cadjins et créoles en Louisiane*, Paris: Payot.

—— (1986b) *Mots de Louisiane*, Paris: L'Harmattan and France-Louisiane.

Gross, G. (ed.) (1993) *Sur le passif*, special issue of *Langages* 109.

Gueunier, N. (1985) 'Variation individuelle chez des locuteurs du sudréunionnais', *Etudes Créoles*, 8: 161–74.

—— (1992) 'Le français langue d'Afrique', *Présence Francophone* 40: 99–120.

Gueunier, N., Genouvrier, E. and Khomsi, A. (eds) (1978) *Les Français devant la norme*, Paris: Champion.

Guiraud, P (1965) *Le Français populaire*, Paris: Presses Universitaires de France.

—— (1978) *Patois et dialectes français*, 3rd edn, Paris: Presses Universitaires de France.

Hadjadj, D. (1981) 'Etude sociolinguistique des rapports entre patois et français dans deux communautés rurales du centre de la France en 1975', in Tabouret-Keller (ed.), 71–99.

Hagège, C. (1987) *Le Français et les siècles*, Paris: Odile Jacob.

—— (1998) 'Paroles d'homme', *Le Monde de l'Education*, February, 26–7.

Hall, R. A. Jr (1966) *Pidgin and creole languages*, Ithaca, NY: Cornell University Press.

Halliday, M. A. K. (1968) 'The users and uses of language', in J. Fishman (ed.) *Readings in the sociology of language*, Paris: Mouton.

Hancock, I. F. (1977) 'Repertory of pidgin and creole languages', in A. Valdman (ed.) *Pidgin and Creole Linguistics*, 362–91, Bloomington: Indiana University Press.

Harris, M. B. (1978) *The evolution of French syntax*, London: Longman.

—— (1988) 'French', in Harris and Vincent (eds), 209–45.

Harris, M. B. and Vincent, N. B. (eds) (1988) *The Romance languages*, London: Routledge.

Haugen, E. (1966) 'Dialect, language, nation', *American Anthropologist* 68: 922–35. (Reprinted in J. B. Pride and J. Holmes (eds) (1972) *Sociolinguistics*, Harmondsworth: Penguin.)

Haut Conseil de la Francophonie (1999) *Etat de la francophonie dans le monde*, Paris: La Documentation Française.

Hawkins, R. D. (1993) 'Regional variation in France', in Sanders (ed.), 55–84.

Hawkins, R. D. and Towell, R. J. (1996) *French grammar and usage*, London: Arnold.

Heilenman, L. K. and McDonald, J. L. (1993) 'Dislocated sequences and word order in French: a processing approach', *Journal of French Language Studies* 3: 165–90.

Herschensohn, J. (1980) 'On clitic placement in French', *Linguistic Analysis* 6: 187–219.

Hope, T. E. (1971) *Lexical borrowing in the Romance languages*, Oxford: Blackwell.

Houdebine, A.-M. (1977) 'Français régional ou français standard?: à propos du système des voyelles orales en français contemporain', *Studia Phonetica* 13.

Hudson, R. A. (1996) *Sociolinguistics*, 2nd edn, Cambridge: Cambridge University Press.

Hugo, V. (1964) *La Légende des siècles*, Paris: Garnier.

—— (1972) *Les Contemplations*, Paris: Livre de Poche.

Huot, H. (1981) *Constructions infinitives du français*, Geneva: Droz.

—— (1986) 'Le subjonctif dans les complétives: subjectivité et modélisation', in Ronat and Couquaux (eds), 81–111.

Hurford, J. R. (1994) *Grammar: a student's guide*, Cambridge: Cambridge University Press.

International Phonetic Association (1989) *The principles of the International Phonetic Association*, rev. edn, London: IPA.

Inventaire du Français d'Afrique (1988) *Inventaire des particularités lexicales du français en Afrique noire*, 2nd edn, Paris: EDICEF/AUPELF.

Jones, M. A. (1996) *Foundations of French syntax*, Cambridge: Cambridge University Press.

Jones, M. C. (1995) 'At what price language maintenance?: standardization in Modern Breton', *French Studies* 49: 424–38.

Judge, A. (1993) 'French: a planned language', in Sanders (ed.), 7–26.

Katamba, F. (1993) *Morphology*, Basingstoke: Macmillan.

Kayne, R. S. (1972) 'Subject inversion in French interrogatives', in J. Casagrande and B. Saciuk (eds) *Generative studies in Romance languages*, 70–126, Rowley: Newbury House.

—— (1975) *French syntax*, London: MIT Press. (French trans. P. Attal (1977) *Syntaxe du français*, Paris: Seuil.)

—— (1976) 'French relative *que*', in F. Hensey and M. Luján (eds) *Current studies in Romance linguistics*, 255–99, Washington, DC: Georgetown University Press.

Klausenburger, J. (1984) *French liaison and linguistic theory*, Stuttgart: Steiner.

Kleiber, G. (1992) 'Quand le nom propre prend l'article: le cas des noms propres métonymiques', *Journal of French Language Studies* 2: 185–205.

Labov, W. (1972a) *Sociolinguistic patterns*, Philadelphia: University of Pennsylvania Press.

—— (1972b) *Language in the inner city*, Philadelphia: University of Pennsylvania Press.

Lafage, S. (1993) 'French in Africa', in Sanders (ed.), 215–38.

Lafont, R. (ed.) (1982) *Langue dominante, langues dominées*, Paris: Edilig.

Lambrecht, K. (1980) 'Topic, French style, remarks about a basic sentence type of modern nonstandard French', *Berkeley Linguistics Society* 6: 337–60.

Lanly, A. (1977) *Morphologie historique des verbes français*, Paris: Bordas.

Laroussi, F. and Marcellesi, J.-B. (1993) 'The other languages of France', in Sanders (ed.), 85–104.

Lass, R. (1984) *Phonology*, Cambridge: Cambridge University Press.

Lathuillère, R. (1966) *La Préciosité*, Geneva: Droz.

Léard, J.-M. (1990) 'L'hypothèse que je crois qui est négligée: le status de *que*, *qui* et *dont* dans les imbriquées', *Travaux de Linguistique* 20: 43–72.

Leeman, D. (ed.) (1990) *Sur les compléments circonstanciels*, special issue of *Langue Française* 86.

Lefebvre, A. (1988) 'Les langues du domaine d'oïl', in Vermes (ed.), vol. 1, 261–90.

Lefebvre, C. (1982a) 'Qui qui vient? ou Qui vient?', in Lefebvre (ed.), vol. 1, 45–101.

—— (ed.) (1982b) *La Syntaxe comparée du français standard et populaire*, 2 vols, Quebec: Office de la Langue Française.

Léon, P. (1966) *Prononciation du français standard*, Montreal/Paris: Didier.

—— (1988) 'Variation situationnelle et indexation sociale', in Slater *et al.* (eds).

Le Page, R. B. and Tabouret-Keller, A. (1985) *Acts of identity*, Cambridge: Cambridge University Press.

Lepelley, R. (1989) *Dictionnaire du français régional de Basse-Normandie*, Paris: Bonneton.

Lo Cascio, V. (1982) 'Temporal deixis and anaphor in sentence and text: finding a reference time', *Journal of Italian Linguistics* 7: 31–70.

Lodge, R. A. (1989) 'Speakers' perceptions of non-standard vocabulary in French', *Zeitschrift für Romanische Philologie* 105: 427–44.

—— (1993) *French: from dialect to standard*, London: Routledge.

—— (1998) 'French is a logical language', in L. Bauer and P. Trudgill (eds) *Language myths*, Harmondsworth: Penguin, 23–31.

Lodge, R. A., Armstrong, N., Ellis, Y. M. L. and Shelton, J. F. (1997) *Exploring the French language*, London: Arnold.

Lyons, J. (1968) *An introduction to theoretical linguistics*, Cambridge: Cambridge University Press.

—— (1981) *Language and linguistics*, 2nd edn, Cambridge: Cambridge University Press.

Maillet, A. (1974) *La Sagouine*, Paris: Grasset.

Makouta-Mboukou, J. P. (1973) *Le Français en Afrique noire*, Paris: Bordas.

Manessy, G. (1994) *Le Français en Afrique noire*, Paris: L'Harmattan.

Manessy, G. and Wald, P. (1984) *Le Français en Afrique noire tel qu'on le parle, tel qu'on le dit*, Paris: L'Harmattan/IDERIC.

Marks, G. A. and Johnson, C. B. (1993) *Harrap's slang dictionary*, London: Harrap.

Marley, D., Hintze, M.-A. and Parker, G. (eds) (1998) *Linguistic identities in France and the French-speaking world*, London: AFLS/CILT.

Martinet, A. (1945) *La Prononciation du français contemporain*, Geneva: Droz.

—— (1955) *Economie des changements phonétiques*, Berne: Francke.

—— (1969) *Le Français sans fard*, Paris: Presses Universitaires de France.

—— (1990) 'Remarques sur la variété des usages dans la phonie du français', in Green and Ayres-Bennett (eds), 13–26.

Martinet, A. and Walter H. (1973) *Dictionnaire de la prononciation française dan son usage réel*, Paris: France-Expansion.

Matthews, P. (1974) *Morphology*, Cambridge: Cambridge University Press.

Maurand, G. (1981) 'Situation sociolinguistique d'une communauté rurale en domaine occitan', in Tabouret-Keller (ed.), 99–120.

McMahon, A. M. S. (1994) *Understanding language change*, Cambridge: Cambridge University Press.

Merle, P. (1989) *Dictionnaire du français branché suivi du guide du français tic et toc*, Paris: Seuil.

Milner, J.-C. (1978) *De La Syntaxe à l'interprétation*, Paris: Seuil.

—— (1982) *Ordres et raisons de langue*, Paris: Seuil.

Milroy, J. and Milroy, L. (1991) *Authority in language*, 2nd edn, London: Routledge.

Mitterand, H. (1968) *Les Mots français*, 3rd edn, Paris: Presses Universitaires de France.

Molière, J.-B. P. de (1959) *Œuvres complètes*, Oxford: Oxford University Press.

Moreau, M.-L. (1971) 'L'homme que je crois qui est venu: *qui, que*, relatifs et conjonctions', *Langue Française* 11: 77–90.

Morin, Y.-C. (1975) 'Remarques sur le placement des clitiques', *Recherches Linguistiques de Montréal* 4: 175–81.

—— (1979) 'More remarks on French clitic order', *Linguistic Analysis* 5: 293–312.

—— (1981) 'Some myths about pronominal clitics in French', *Linguistic Analysis* 8: 95–109.

Müller, B. (1975) *Das Französische der Gegenwart*, Heidelberg: Winter. (French trans. (1985) *Le Français d'aujourd'hui*, Paris: Klincksieck.)

Muller, C. (1991) *La Négation en français*, Geneva: Droz.

—— (1994) 'Du féminisme lexical', *Cahiers de Lexicologie* 65: 103–9.

Nelde, P., Strubell, M. and Williams, G. (1996) *Euromosaic*, Luxembourg: European Commission.

Nølke, H. (ed.) (1990) *Classification des adverbes*, special issue of *Langue Française* 88.

Noreiko, S. (1993) 'New words for new technologies', in Sanders (ed.), 171–84.

Nouguier, E. (1987) *Dictionnaire d'argot*, Paris: Even.

Nurse, P. (ed.) (1978) *Le Cid: Pierre Corneille*, Oxford: Blackwell.

Nyrop, K. (1899–1930) *Grammaire historique de la langue française*, 6 vols, Copenhagen: Gyldendals. (Repr. 1936–68 Paris: Picard.)

Obenauer, H.-G. (1976) *Etudes de syntaxe interrogative du français*, Tübingen: Niemeyer.

—— (1983) 'Une quantification non canonique: la "quantification à distance"', *Langue Française* 58: 66–88.

—— (1983/4) 'On the identification of empty categories', *The Linguistic Review* 4: 153–202.

Offord, M. (1990) *Varieties of contemporary French*, London: Macmillan.

Ostiguy, L. and Tousignant, C. (1993) *Le Français québécois*, Montreal: Guérin.

Oukada, L. (1982) 'On *on*', *The French Review* 56: 93–105.

Palmer, F. R. (1994) *Grammatical roles and relations*, Cambridge: Cambridge University Press.

Palsgrave, J. (1530) *L'esclarcissement de la langue françoyse*, London: Hawkin.

Péry-Woodley, M.-P. (1991) 'French and English passives in the construction of text', *Journal of French Language Studies* 1: 55–70.

Petit Robert, Le (1991) *Dictionnaire alphabétique et analogique de la langue française*, Paris: Robert.

Peytard, J. (1975) *Recherches sur la préfixation en français contemporain*, 2 vols, Paris: Champion.

Picabia, L. (ed.) (1986) *Déterminants et détermination*, special issue of *Langue Française* 72.

Picoche, J. (1979) *Précis de morphologie historique du français*, Paris: Nathan.

Picoche, J. and Marchello-Nizia, C. (1989) *Histoire de la langue française*, Paris: Nathan.

Pollock, J.-Y. (1986) 'Sur la syntaxe de *en* et le paramètre du sujet nul', in Ronat and Couquaux (eds), 211–46.

Pooley, T. (1998) 'Picard and regional French as symbols of identity', in Marley *et al.* (eds), 43–58.

Pope, M. K. (1952) *From Latin to Modern French*, 2nd edn, Manchester: Manchester University Press.

Posner, R. R. (1986) 'La créolisation: altération typologique', *Etudes Créoles* 9: 127–34.

—— (1996) *The Romance languages*, Cambridge: Cambridge University Press.

—— (1997) *Linguistic change in French*, Oxford: Oxford University Press.

Price, G. (1984) *The French language*, 2nd edn, London: Arnold.

—— (1991) *An introduction to French pronunciation*, Oxford: Blackwell.

Prudent, L. F. (1990) 'La difficile construction de la linguistique créole aux Antilles', *Nouvelle Revue des Antilles* 3: 3–12.

Radford, A. (1989) 'The status of exclamative particles in modern spoken French', in D. Arnold, M. Atkinson, J. Durand, C. Grover and L. Sadler (eds) *Essays on grammatical theory and Universal Grammar*, Oxford: Oxford University Press, 223–84.

Radford, A., Atkinson, M., Britain, D., Clahsen, H. and Spencer, A. (1999) *Linguistics*, Cambridge: Cambridge University Press.

Rickard, P. (1989) *A history of the French language*, 2nd edn, London: Routledge.

Rivarol, A. de (1991) *De l'universalité de la langue française*, Paris: Obsidiane.

Roach, P. (1986) 'Rethinking phonetic taxonomy', in T. Akamatsu and D. Barber (eds) *Working Papers in Linguistics and Phonetics* 4: 61–78, University of Leeds.

Robillard, D. de and Benianimo, M. (eds) (1993, 1996) *Le Français dans l'espace francophone*, 2 vols, Paris: Champion.

Romaine, S. (1988) *Pidgin and creole languages*, London: Longman.

Ronat, M. and Couquaux, D. (eds) (1986) *La Grammaire modulaire*, Paris: Minuit.

Rossillon, P. (ed.) (1995) *Atlas de la langue française*, Paris: Bordas.

Rowlett, P. (1998) *Sentential negation in French*, Oxford: Oxford University Press.

Rudder, O. de (1986) *Le Français qui se cause*, Paris: Balland.

Ruwet, N. (1972) *Théorie syntaxique et syntaxe du français*, Paris: Seuil.

Rychner, J. (ed.) (1967) *Les XV joies de mariage*, Geneva: Droz.

Sanders, C. (1993) 'Sociosituational variation', in Sanders (ed.), 27–54.

—— (ed.) (1993) *French today*, Cambridge: Cambridge University Press.

Saussure, F. de (1955) *Cours de linguistique générale*, 5th edn, Paris: Payot.

Sauvageot, A. (1962) *Français écrit, français parlé*, Paris: Larousse.

—— (1972) *Analyse du français parlé*, Paris: Hachette.

Schane, S. A. (1968) *French morphology and phonology*, London: MIT Press.

Sebba, M. (1997) *Contact languages*, London: Macmillan.

Séguin, J.-P. (1972) *La Langue française au XVIIIᵉ siècle*, Paris: Bordas.

Séguy, J. (1978) *Le Français parlé à Toulouse*, 3rd edn, Toulouse: Privat.

Shiaty, A. E. (ed.) (1988) *Dictionnaire du français Plus à l'usage des francophones d'Amérique*, Montreal: Centre éducatif et culturel.

Slater, C., Durand, J. and Bate, M. (eds) (1988) *French sound patterns*, AFLS Occasional Papers 2, Colchester: AFLS and University of Essex.

Smith, J. C. (1990) 'A pragmatic view of French deixis', *York Papers in Linguistics* 14: 263–78.

Soutet, O. (1989) *La Syntaxe du français*, Paris: Presses Universitaires de France.

Spence, N. C. W. (1982) 'Another look at the "loi des trois consonnes"', *French Studies* 1: 1–11.

—— (1996) *The structure(s) of French*, Egham: Runnymede.

Stephens, J. (1993) 'Breton', in M. Ball (ed.) *The Celtic languages*, London: Routledge, 349–409.

Tabouret-Keller, A. (ed.) (1981) *Regional languages in France*, special issue of *International Journal of the Sociology of Language*, 29.

Tallerman, M. O. (1998) *Understanding syntax*, London: Arnold.

Taverdet, G. and Straka, G. (eds) (1977) *Les Français régionaux*, Paris: Klincksieck.

Tellier, C. (1995) *Eléments de syntaxe du français*, Montreal: Presses de l'Université de Montréal.

Ternes, E. (1992) 'The Breton language', in D. Macaulay (ed.) *The Celtic languages*, Cambridge: Cambridge University Press, 370–452.

Thiele, J. (1987) *La Formation des mots en français moderne*, trad. et adapt. A. Clas, Montreal: Presses de l'Université de Montréal.

Tranel, B. (1987) *The sounds of French*, Cambridge: Cambridge University Press.

Trask, R. L. (1993) *A dictionary of grammatical terms in linguistics*, London: Routledge.

—— (1994) *Language change*, London: Routledge.

—— (1996a) *A dictionary of phonetics and phonology*, London: Routledge.

—— (1996b) *Historical linguistics*, London: Arnold.

—— (1997) *A student's dictionary of language and linguistics*, London: Arnold.

—— (1998) *Key concepts in language and linguistics*, London: Routledge.

—— (1999) *Language: the basics*, 2nd edn, London: Routledge.

Tuaillon, G. (1974) 'Compte rendu de l'ALIFO', *Revue de Linguistique Romane* 38: 576.

—— (1988) 'Le français régional', in Vermes (ed.), vol. 1, 291–300.

Tucker, G. R., Lambert, W. E. and Rigault, A. A. (1977) *The French speaker's skill with grammatical gender*, Paris: Mouton.

Valdman, A. (1976) *Introduction to French phonology and morphology*, Rowley: Newbury House.

—— (1993) *Bien entendu! Introduction à la phonétique française*, New York: Prentice Hall.

—— (ed.) (1979) *Le Français hors de France*, Paris: Champion.

—— (ed.) (1997) *French and creole in Louisiana*, New York: Plenum.

Vassberg, L. (1993) *Alsatian acts of identity*, Clevedon: Multilingual Matters.

Vaugelas, C. F. de [1647] (1970) *Remarques sur la langue française*, ed. J. Streicher, Geneva: Slatkine.

Vermes, G. (ed.) (1988) *Parler sa langue*, 2 vols, Paris: L'Harmattan.

Vermes, G. and Boutet, J. (eds) (1987) *France pays multilingue*, 2 vols, Paris: L'Harmattan.

Vetters, C. (1989) 'Grammaire générative et textuelle des temps verbaux', *Recherches Linguistiques de Vincennes* 18: 101–45.

Wagner, R. L. (ed.) (1964) *Textes d'étude: ancien et moyen français*, Geneva: Droz.

Walker, D. C. (1984) *The pronunciation of Canadian French*, Ottawa: Ottawa University Press.

—— (1995) 'Patterns of analogy in the Canadian French verb system', *Journal of French Language Studies* 5: 85–107.

Walter, H. (1976) *La Dynamique des phonèmes dans le lexique du français contemporain*, Geneva: Droz.

—— (1982) *Enquête phonologique et variétés régionales du français*, Paris: Presses Universitaires de France.

—— (1988) *Le Français dans tous les sens*, Paris: Laffont. (English trans. P. Fawcett (1994) *French inside out*, London: Routledge.)

—— (1990) 'Une voyelle qui ne veut pas mourir', in Green and Ayres-Bennett (eds), 27–36.

—— (1994) *L'Aventure des langues en occident*, Paris: Laffont.

—— (1997) *L'Aventure des mots venus d'ailleurs*, Paris: Laffont.

—— (1998) *Le Français d'ici, de là, de là-bas*, Paris: Lattès.

—— (ed.) (1977) *Phonologie et société*, Paris: Didier.

Warnant, L. (1973) 'Dialectes du français et français régionaux', *Langue Française* 18: 100–26.

Wartburg, W. von (1967) *Evolution et structure de la langue française*, 8th edn, Berne: Francke.

Watson, K. (1997) 'French complement clitic sequences: a template approach', *Journal of French Language Studies* 7: 69–89.

Waugh, L. (1987) 'Marking time with the "passé composé": towards a theory of the perfect', *Lingvisticæ Investigationes*, 9: 1–48.

Wenger, B. (1988) *Die vier Literaturen der Schweiz*, 4th edn, Zurich: Pro Helvetia. (French trans. M. Secretan (1988) *Les Quatre Littératures de la Suisse*, 3rd edn, Zurich: Pro Helvetia.)

Wilmet, M. (1991) 'L'aspect en français: essai de synthèse', *Journal of French Language Studies* 1: 209–22.

Wilson-Green, A. (ed.) (1937) *Voltaire: lettres sur les Anglais*, Cambridge: Cambridge University Press.

Wioland, F. (1991) *Prononcer les mots du français*, Paris: Hachette.

Wise, H. (1997) *The vocabulary of Modern French*, London: Routledge.

Wright, R. (1982) *Late Latin and early Romance*, London: Cairns.

—— (1991) *Latin and the Romance languages in the early middle ages*, London: Routledge.

Yaguello, M. (1981) *Alice au pays du langage*, Paris: Seuil. (English trans. M. Yaguello and T. A. le V. Harris (1998) *Language through the looking glass*, Oxford: Oxford University Press.)

—— (1987) *Les Mots et les femmes*, Paris: Payot.

—— (1988) *Catalogue des idées reçues sur la langue*, Paris: Seuil.

Index